S84

In 1879, Chile initiated a conflict with her neighbors Peru and Bolivia that continued for five years and became known as the War of the Pacific. This revisionist work, based on a wide array of primary sources, is the first to focus on how that war affected Chilean society, the nation's political and financial institutions, and its economy.

Opening with a consideration of the events that led to the declaration of war, which he argues was the consequence of political pressures, William F. Sater then examines the state of preparedness of the Chilean armed forces. Ensuing chapters discuss relations between the military and civilians, noting that mutual hostility hampered the war effort, threatened traditional civil liberties, and complicated the government's efforts to create institutions to enable Chile to carry on a long and costly struggle. Sater also considers the effect of the war on Chile's agricultural, mining, and industrial sectors, concluding that contrary to traditional views, the war's impact was limited. He also explores how the conflict affected the nation's fiscal systems, civilian life, and political institutions. A prolonged guerrilla war exhausted Chile's patience and resources, Sater demonstrates. Only in later years was its importance inflated in the Chilean psyche so that today it is commemorated in statues, paintings, and songs as the nation's coming of age.

William F. Sater is a professor of history at California State University, Long Beach. His publications include *The Heroic Image in Chile* (1973) and many articles.

Chile and the War of the Pacific

William F. Sater

University of Nebraska Press • Lincoln and London

Copyright 1986 by
the University of Nebraska Press
All rights reserved
Manufactured in the United States
of America

The paper in this book
meets the guidelines for permanence
and durability of the Committee
on Production Guidelines for Book
Longevity of the Council
on Library Resources.

Library of Congress
Cataloguing in Publication Data

Sater, William F.
Chile and the War of the Pacific

Bibliography: p.
Includes index.
1. War of the Pacific, 1879-1884 - Chile.
2. Chile - History - 1824-1920.
I. Title.
F3097.S26   1986
983'.061   85-24584
ISBN 0-8032-4155-0 (alk. paper)

In the interest of timeliness and economy
this book was printed from camera-ready
copy supplied by the author.

For Rachel M. Sater
My Dearly Beloved Daughter

Contents

	Acknowledgments	ix
	Introduction	1
1	Prelude	5
2	The Active War	17
3	Cucalones versus Militares	35
4	The Pen and the Sword	62
5	El Pago de Chile	75
6	The Economic Consequences of the War	97
7	Greenbacks and Nitrates	131
8	Life on the Home Front	155
9	The Politics of War	179
10	The Quest for Peace	197
	Epilogue	223
	Appendix: Tables	231
	Notes	279
	Bibliography	323
	Index	337

Acknowledgments

This book owes much to the efforts and kindness of many people. In Chile, the staff of the Sección de Diarios, headed by Francisco Benimeli, not only tirelessly carted newspapers from one end of the Biblioteca Nacional to another, they also shared their workspace, allowing a poor gringo to escape Santiago's piercing summer heat and the winter's bitter touch. The late Patricio Estelle and don Javier González gave me free rein of the National Library's holdings as well as those of the Archivo Nacional while the remainder of the staff of the Sección Chilena provided equally hospitable service. Of particular note is Rodolfo Bustamante who always found time to microfilm whatever documents I discovered. For close to twenty years, the men and the women of the Biblioteca Nacional have been gracious, generous, and hospitable to me, and I cheerfully, albeit somewhat inadequately, praise their contributions. I would be terribly remiss, moreover, if I did not thank formally Mario and Nana Bronfmann for their hospitality and for their friendship. The Organization of American States awarded me a post doctoral fellowship which financed my research in Chile. Dean Simeon Crowther and the Foundation of the California State University, Long Beach, provided additional funding and the time necessary for the publishing of this book. The staff of the university library, particularly Roman Kochan, went to great lengths to obtain needed materials and, Juanita Knox conscientiously contacted numerous American libraries in search of obscure books. Paul Drake, of the University of California, San Diego, copied countless documents in the Library of Congress and while he may have forgotten his generosity, I have not.

Various individuals generously used their precious time to read this manuscript, offering valuable insights and corrections: Frederick M. Nunn of Portland State University; Keith Ian Polakoff of California State University, Long Beach; Jaime Rodríguez of the University of California, Irvine; and Linda Alexander Rodríguez of the University of California, Los Angeles. I am deeply grateful to them for their candor, tact and generous assistance. Finally, Maryilyn Speigel contributed an interest in history and an eagle's eye for errors. I also wish to mention Barbara Burden. She devoted countless hours always with good cheer, to help ready this volume for publication. For this, as well as her friendship, I am extremely grateful.

This volume could not have been completed without the support of many people who helped me surmount not only professional but also some personal difficulties: Joseph Natterson; my brother, James C. Sater —whose kindness has gone beyond fraternal affection; Joshua Hoffs; Christon Archer; and especially my close friends Daniel P. Greenson, Barbara McSwain, and Jaime and Linda Rodríguez. These people have significantly enriched my life: I owe them a debt of gratitude which I can only recognize but never adequately repay.

On a lighter note, I hereby absolve all the various institutions, organizations, foundations, and individuals mentioned in the acknowledgment section of any errors to be found in this book. It is enough that they helped: they do not to bear the blame.

Chile and the War of the Pacific

Introduction

Until the early nineteenth century, Spain controlled the Pacific Coast of South America. The region was divided into two administrative entities: the Viceroyalty of Nueva Granada and the Viceroyalty of Peru. Independence not only ended Madrid's domination, it also shattered its former colonies' boundaries. Nueva Granada splintered into Venezuela, Colombia, and Ecuador while Peru, Chile, and Bolivia emerged phoenix like from the ashes of the old Viceroyalty of Peru.

Following independence, the nations of Latin America's west coast managed to coexist if not in harmony then with at least grudging respect. While often willing to engage in fratricidal, internecine struggles, neighbor generally did not make war on neighbor. This state of international grace compared very favorably with the situation on the continent's eastern seaboard where Argentina and Brazil had fruitlessly battled to possess Uruguay and then, in a moment of rare accord, united to cannibalize hapless Paraguay. The western nations did not live in the best of all possible worlds. Occassionally, as in 1835 to 1838, they too warred on each other, but the boundary markers remained in place and nations did not swallow up their neighbor's lands or populations. This arcadian state lasted until 1879, when Bolivia, Chile, and Peru became involved in a conflict, paradoxically named the War of the Pacific, that lasted until 1884.

When the guns finally fell silent, Santiago had seized La Paz's seacoast, converting the latter into the hemisphere's only landlocked republic, and had occupied Lima's provinces of Tarapacá, Tacna, and Arica. Although the Moneda—the Chilean equivalent to the White House—would subsequently return Tacna, Chile had, as a consequence of this war, increased its territory by a third and acquired a monopoly of the world's supply of nitrates.

The War of the Pacific constituted one of the more significant military and naval encounters of the late nineteenth century. Like the other epic conflicts of the post 1850s—the struggle between the Union and the Confederacy or the clash between France and Prussia—the War of the Pacific utilized the latest military and naval weapons. The American and European encounters, however, lacked one dimension of the War of the Pacific. The Franco-Prussian conflict was fought exclusively on land and although the North American struggle included some naval engagements, these could not match the extent or the variety of the maritime battles which occurred during the South American conflagration.

The onset of the War of the Pacific surprised Chile, which, unlike the newly created German empire or even the United States, lacked a long military tradition. Although Santiago had triumphantly fought against the Peruvian Bolivian Confederation during the 1830s, that conflict had demonstrated Chile's incapacity for engaging in a prolonged military conflict. Following that 1838 confrontation, the Moneda's military adventures consisted of pacifying the Indians on its southern frontier, an endeavor which did not prepare the professional military for fighting a more conventional conflict. Then in 1879, Chile, an underdeveloped nation whose economy rested upon mining and agriculture, suddenly became involved in a war demanding technical and administrative skills that the country did not possess. The burden of directing the War of the Pacific proved particularly onerous for the Moneda which, unlike the United States or Prussia, had to fight far from its centers of population and without the benefit of any internal lines of communications.

Because Chile defeated its enemies, a series of myths developed. Various historians, particularly those of Bolivia and Peru, have alleged that Santiago confidently embarked upon the War of the Pacific possessing a vast arsenal of military and naval stores, a well trained officer corps, and the unanimous support of its highly nationalistic citizenry. Chile, in short, was described as a racially homogeneous, well governed, and cohesive nation-state which deliberately unleashed a highly motivated citizen army on its hapless and ill prepared neighbors. Indeed, some scholars argue that Santiago's armed forces easily invaded the North where they seized their opponents' land, looted their cities, and then returned home to the applause of a grateful nation.

These statements are like desert mirages that disappear when closely inspected. As this book will clearly demonstrate, Chile was anything but the Prussia of the Pacific. The Moneda's naval and military establishments, ill-equipped and commanded by men of limited experience and

Introduction

less aptitude, responded sluggishly during the first months of the war. Instead of being a unified state, Chile suffered from severe political divisions which threatened to erupt into rebellion. Although some Chileans enlisted in order to defend their nation, most served unwillingly and without understanding the nature of the conflict. The Chilean state, moreover, lacked the administrative infrastructure, the financial resources, and the technical skills required to wage a struggle of such epic proportions while fulfilling its peacetime obligations. In addition, the prosecution of the war was complicated by the fact that the president was often harassed by a legislature many of whose members resembled *franc-tireurs* rather than the loyal opposition. In short, instead of unleashing a juggernaut, Santiago fought the war in gasps: each offensive quickly exhausted the nation's fiscal and human resources, followed by months of rearming, which in turn resulted in yet another spasm of martial energy.

In addition to demonstrating the precarious nature of Santiago's victory, this book will show how a newly independent nation like Chile responded to a crisis which threatened its political sovereignty and territorial integrity. As the first chapter indicates, Chile's leaders entered the 1879 conflict hesitantly, driven more by political pressure than by personal conviction. The Moneda's reluctance proved well founded. The military and naval campaigns tested and found seriously wanting both the leadership and the technical institutions of the armed forces. In part this problem resulted from a clash over who should direct the war: the civilian government or the professional military. Only with great difficulty could the president assert his authority over his officers. Civilians became more deeply involved in the war effort as the Moneda had to assume the responsibility not only for funding the war but also for satisfying the military's manpower and logistical needs. Both tasks proved difficult. Chile's economic resources were extremely limited and many of its population proved parsimonious both with their treasure and with their blood. Thus, the state had to resort to extraordinary measures to obtain revenues and recruits. Although the conflict did not alter drastically the nation's social life, the struggle with Peru and Bolivia became a political issue which certain interests used, often to the detriment of the nation, for their own partisan ends. In truth, the War of the Pacific exhausted Chile, and its citizens greeted the end to the five years of intermittent bloodshed with a sigh of relief not a shout of triumph.

Next to the movement for independence, the War of the Pacific has emerged as perhaps the most important event to engulf Chile in the nineteenth century. The conflict with Lima and La Paz seriously threatened Santiago's sovereignty and territorial integrity. Ironically, as subsequent regimes squandered the few real advantages gained during the hard fought struggle, the conflict grew increasingly vivid in the Chilean imagination; it became more treasured and revered by each succeeding generation. Thus Chileans faithfully celebrate the war's important battles, the conflict's heroic figures adorn the stamps and the money, the monuments to the great exploits and outstanding figures abound, and the street names—Tarapacá, Chorillos, Concepción, Santa Cruz, Prat, Condell—continually remind the Chileans of their victorious forefathers' sacrifice and their heritage of glory.

1

Prelude

> The imprudent policy observed by don Hilarión Daza... with respect to the question sustained by the Compañía de Salitres y Ferrocarril... caused... the forcible occupation of the Bolivian Littoral and the disastrous war of the Pacific.
> *Proceso político contra Daza*

One of the more enduring myths enshrouding the War of the Pacific is that the Moneda cleverly engineered the events which precipitated the 1879 conflict. This interpretation clearly brands Chile as the aggressor while depicting Bolivia and Peru as the victims. Although doubtless comforting to the allies' apologists, this description of the Moneda is far off the mark, for it is clear that the Chilean government declared war only after much agonizing and in response to a combination of Peruvian and Bolivian provocation as well as domestic pressure.

THE CAUSE

In February 1878, the Bolivian congress levied a ten cent surcharge on each quintal of nitrate exported by the Compañía de Salitres y Ferrocarril, a corporation controlled largely by Chilean and English investors. The company, which began operating in Bolivia under a license issued by La Paz in 1873, extracted nitrate (*salitre*) and iodine (*yodo*) from a portion of the Atacama Desert once claimed by both Chile and Bolivia. Normally, neither nation would have contested the ownership of such a wretched area; however, the discovery of guano and nitrates in the 1860s made the Atacama suddenly valuable to both countries. Bolivia claimed the territory down to the 25 south latitude while Chile demanded the area north to the 23 south latitude.

The dispute over the boundary line became so heated that the two countries contemplated declaring war when Spanish intervention in Peru momentarily suspended the argument. Thus, in 1866, Chile and Bolivia divided the contested territory at the 24th latitude south, granting the nationals of both nations the right to exploit all existing mineral deposits but specifying that Santiago and La Paz should share equally the tax revenues the area generated. The treaty remained in force until a rebellion in La Paz overthrew the government of General Mariano Melgarejo. The latter's successors repudiated most of the former dictator's acts, including his 1866 agreement with Chile, thus reopening the diplomatic controversy. The Moneda then sent an envoy to La Paz to negotiate a settlement to guarantee its nationals' interests, including the protection of Chilean investments in the newly discovered Caracoles silver mines, and, if possible, the extension of Santiago's sovereignty over the disputed area.

By 1873, diplomats on both sides had arranged a new settlement, the Lindsay-Corral treaty. This pact increased Chilean participation in the administration of the disputed area while forbidding unilateral changes in the rate of taxation. Bolivia's legislature, however, rejected the pact, and both nations were once again forced to the edge of war. Already embroiled in a boundary dispute with Argentina, that threatened its eastern border, Santiago preferred to accommodate Bolivia. Thus, in 1874, the Moneda arranged a settlement which, while affirming the 24th parallel as Chile's border, called for Santiago to abandon its claims to joint sovereignty. In return, La Paz agreed that for the next twenty-five years it would not increase the impost levied on products exported by Chilean corporations operating in the Atacama region.[1]

The increase of taxes on the Compañía de Salitres y Ferrocarril clearly violated the 1874 treaty. Initially, it appeared that the dispute would be resolved amicably when La Paz indicated that although it would not repudiate the tax legislation, it would not enforce it either. Yet in December 1878, the Bolivian dictator, General Hilarión Daza, apparently changed his mind and ordered the Compañía de Salitres y Ferrocarril either to pay the surcharge or forfeit its holdings. When the company rejected Daza's demand, the local Bolivian official confiscated the corporation's property on 11 January 1879 announcing that he would sell it at public auction on 14 February 1879. Chile's envoy to La Paz protested, citing the 1874 treaty, and demanded that Bolivia rescind this order. When Daza would not retreat, the Chilean departed for Santiago. Not content with diplomatic protests, on 14 February, the day of the proposed auction, Chilean troops occupied Antofagasta, the capital of the Bolivian province of Atacama. Santiago justified this act by arguing that Bolivia's imposition of the ten-cent surcharge nullified the 1874 treaty, thereby permitting Chile to reoccupy the territory it had previously claimed and which it had ceded to La Paz. This doctrine, called "revindication" by the Moneda, provided the rationale for the Chilean seizure of all the territory up to the 23rd parallel.

What motivated General Daza to increase taxes so arbitrarily still remains unclear. Bolivia, of course, desperately needed money and the Compañía de Salitres offered a tempting solution to its financial dilemma. And initially at least, the dictator did not regret his actions. "I bring good news for which you will thank me eternally . . . I have really stuck it to the gringos [the English shareholders]," he wrote a friend, "decreeing the revindication of the salitreras and they cannot get rid of us no matter how much they shake the entire world."[2] Whether greed or economic necessity inspired his edict, Daza had selected precisely that moment to act because Chile was already embroiled in a diplomatic dispute with its rival Argentina. Self-confident to the point of arrogance and armed with newly purchased naval vessels, Buenos Aires had become increasingly abrasive, challenging Santiago's control of Patagonia and the Strait of Magellan. While the Moneda might have been willing to surrender the former, which possessed scant economic importance, it desperately wanted to ensure its retention of the Strait which constituted Chile's lifeline to Europe.

Anxious to avoid conflict, Santiago sent the historian Diego Barros Arana to Argentina with instructions to cede Patagonia but to retain control over the waterway. A better scholar than negotiator, he not only granted Argentina the desert territory but also partial control over the vital Strait. An embarrassed Moneda repudiated Barros Arana's agreement and sought to reopen negotiations. Buenos Aires agreed, but unfortunately it sent Manuel Bilbao, a former Chilean, to represent its cause. Writing a series of articles in Santiago's prestigious *El Ferrocarril*, Bilbao alienated many by truculently espousing Argentina's claims and then by insulting most of Chile's statesmen, including the foreign minister, José Alfonso. Infuriated by his activities, a hostile crowd demonstrated in front of the Hotel Santiago where the Argentine envoy was staying. The gathering degenerated into a riot: a mob of approximately 4,000 attempted to destroy a statue located on Santiago's main avenue of Buenos Aires, which had been erected in honor of the Argentine capital. When the Chilean fleet seized two guano ships operating in the disputed territory with Argentine permission, Buenos Aires, furious at this violation of its waters, responded by mobilizing its fleet. Chile then dispatched its ironclads, the *Blanco Encalada* and *Almirante Cochrane*, to the south.[3]

Anxious to avoid a war, Chile's president, Aníbal Pinto, ordered his envoys to try to resolve the dispute as quickly as possible. Santiago was militarily vulnerable because an economic crisis had forced the government to reduce the size of the army and disarm a portion of the fleet. Chile, Pinto privately admitted, could ill afford to keep its fleet on a war footing, let alone engage in a protracted conflict. The domestic political situation appeared dangerous because the same economic crisis which forced the nation to disarm, had flooded the capital with the unemployed who, as the Bilbao riots demonstrated, could easily turn violent. Unfortunately, with a congressional electoral campaign already underway, opposition politicians used the diplomatic crisis to attack the government. Aware that a war would bankrupt the nation, Pinto ignored his critics in an attempt to find a peaceful solution to the Argentine crisis. Buenos Aires, economically beleaguered, apparently had second thoughts about war as well. Its consul in Chile, Mariano Sarratea, reached an agreement with the Chilean foreign minister on 6 December 1878 that called for both nations to control the Strait until Buenos Aires and Santiago could reach a comprehensive settlement.[4]

Most Chileans regarded the agreement as degrading, "a pact" according to a pamphlet, "arranged only by merchants."[5] Anti-Argentine feeling increased and demonstrations occurred throughout the nation, particularly in the capital where the military had to patrol a meeting called to protest the settlement. The press shared the public's anger labeling the Fierro Sarratea proposal "the result of the miserable policy and the moral decadence which has afflicted this nation for years."[6] Others predicted that the legislature would not approve a document which so shamelessly betrayed Chile.[7]

Fortunately for the government, not all shared this opinion. Benjamín Vicuña Mackenna, Pinto's rival in the 1876 presidential campaign, argued that Patagonia simply did not justify a war. While the senate agreed with Vicuña, the chamber of deputies proved more recalcitrant, debating the issue long after its colleagues in the upper house had ratified the treaty. Although the diehards professed only the highest motives, Pinto sourly observed that it was mainly his political opposition, particularly the Conservative Party, which used the treaty issue to denounce what it characterized as the government's craven capitulation to Buenos Aires. In addition to the politicians there were others, the president claimed, who wished to capitalize on the Argentine crisis in order "to make a business out of war."[8] Eventually the lower house accepted the Fierro Sarratea Treaty, but twelve members of the opposition stalked out of the chamber, denouncing Pinto's policy of appeasement.

With Chile's attention focused on its east, Daza, apparently convinced that Santiago possessed neither the inclination nor the resources to deal with two diplomatic disputes simultaneously, decided to push his nation's claims against the Compañía de Salitres y Ferrocarril. Indeed, the caudillo privately assured a friend that the Moneda's abject surrender to Buenos Aires proved that La Paz could act with impunity. Thus, when challenged by Bolivia, Chile "would strike its flag as it did with Argentina." If Pinto proved intractable, Daza had a trump card: a secret military alliance with Peru. Six years earlier, in 1873, the two nations promised to aid each other should a third party threaten their sovereignty or territorial integrity. This pact certainly reassured Daza who confidently boasted "we can count on the support of Peru." Thus, buttressed by the promise of military aid and convinced that Chile would passively accept the violation of the 1874 treaty, Daza recklessly imposed the tax on the Compañía de Salitres y Ferrocarril and, when it did not acquiesce, he confiscated its property. Diplomatic dispatches indicate that the La Paz government acted deliberately and that it was prepared, if necessary, to use force in order to defend Bolivia's right to levy the tax. Two weeks after Chile occupied the disputed territory, Daza declared war.[9]

THE CHILEAN REACTION

The conflict arrived at an unfortunate moment for Santiago. Numerous contemporaries reported that so many of the public had lost faith in the Moneda's economic and political policies that Chile seemed on the verge of a rebellion. Regrettably the legislature inspired even less confidence than Pinto and a worried *La Patria* warned that divisions within the congress "resemble those which led to the military uprisings in Spain." The fear of insurrection did not appear exaggerated: the Bilbao riots demonstrated the fragile state of Chile's internal situation; it was obvious to the Moneda that it had to mollify public opinion if it wished to survive.[10]

Unfortunately, the Bolivian situation did not lend itself to an easy solution. Many Chileans loathed La Paz which, according to the press, persecuted Chilean miners living in the littoral. This mistreatment particularly galled those who believed that the disputed territory belonged to Santiago legally, by virtue of previous land grants—which the Moneda had so shamefully ignored—and morally, because Chilean capital and labor had developed the region. Without Chile, the territory would have remained an undeveloped desert. Thus, while some Chileans would not fight for Patagonia, they considered the Atacama differently. The Moneda, they believed, had acted too generously toward La Paz; it negotiated a treaty in 1866 which Bolivia repudiated. Then in 1873, it arranged another pact, which the Bolivian congress refused to ratify. Finally, after four years, General Daza impudently violated the third agreement, claiming that the tax increase was a domestic issue. Coming on the heels of what many perceived as a humiliation at the hands of Buenos Aires, the Bolivian action offended the nation's sense of dignity. Santiago's sense of honor was at stake: the government felt forced to react decisively or foreit the respect of the entire continent, if not the world.[11]

Consequently, the press demanded some vigorous action. *El Taller* warned that unless the Moneda prevented Bolivia's illegal seizure of its nationals' property, Chile would appear to be a "nation of shameless imbeciles." The government's apparent indifference fanned fears that Santiago would capitulate to La Paz, leading another journalist to wonder if we will "have a second act of the Chilean-Argentine tragicomedy?"[12] Others denounced the Pinto administration, claiming it had deliberately repressed information about the status of the dispute, while angry crowds massed in Santiago's Plaza de Armas and Valparaíso's Plaza de Intendencia to hear the speakers denounce the Moneda's cowardly Bolivian policy.[13]

Lamentably, the occupation of Antofagasta brought Pinto little relief. As one ingrate noted, "The government has fulfilled a responsibility whose omission would have merited the most justified and energetic reprobation of the entire country."[14] Many objected, for example, to the Moneda invoking the doctrine of "revindication," which, the critics claimed, undermined Santiago's position.[15] Apparently, Pinto naively believed that La Paz would docilely accept the loss of the disputed territory. Bolivia's declaration of war, however, demonstrated that Chile could not unilaterally return to the status quo ante of 1874. Once confronted with La Paz's officially promulgated belligerence, the Chilean public demanded that the government order the army to cross the twenty-third parallel in order to improve the nation's defensive positions. The press also complained that the Moneda refused to call the congress into session so it could ratify the Moneda's occupation of Antofagasta.[16]

PERUVIAN INVOLVEMENT

A second threat loomed; the possibility of Peruvian intervention. Seemingly almost every government, including the Moneda, knew of Bolivia's secret military alliance within weeks of its signing, but the Chileans ignored the pact, perhaps because they never expected that it would be invoked. As long as Lima refused to honor the agreement, the dispute remained an issue between Chile and Bolivia. For a variety of reasons, some political, various Peruvians supported La Paz, demanding that Lima side with its traditional ally. Still, President Mariano Prado initially offered to mediate the issue, sending José Antonio de Lavalle south in hopes of resolving peacefully the dispute. Even before his arrival, however, the Chilean press reported the existence of a Peruvian-Bolivian alliance, noting with alarm Peru's frantic naval and military preparations. Thus, when Lavalle reached Valparaíso on 4 March 1879, the crowd greeting him appeared distinctly cool. Still, the Peruvian ignored the hostility, and proceeded immediately to Santiago where, on 5 March, he met Pinto.

Lavalle offered Santiago Lima's good offices but on the condition that Chile first return the territory it had taken from Bolivia. The Peruvian envoy expected that Pinto would refuse this precondition because Daza had not unequivocally promised that he would rescind the tax on the Compañía de Salitres if the Moneda retreated from Antofagasta. Lavalle admitted, moreover, that a unilateral Chilean withdrawal, given the state of public opinion, would have resulted in the overthrow of Pinto's government.[17]

The issue of the secret treaty eroded Lavalle's credibility, lending legitimacy to the Chilean press which described the mediation mission as a ploy to give Peru more time to rearm. In mid March, Lima wired Lavalle, warning that Santiago might raise the issue of the 1873 alliance. If questioned about the existence of a military pact, Peru's government instructed its envoy to state that Lima would not honor its treaty obligations as long as Chile withdrew from the littoral. The situation did arise and Lavalle dutifully parroted his government's position. Domingo Santa María, a close aide of Pinto, rejected mediation on these grounds, arguing that Chile could not abandon the lands its nationals had developed. Seizing the offensive, the Chilean questioned why, if Prado were simply a disinterested Good Samaritan, Lima was rearming. The envoy responded that the government reacted in this fashion in order to pacify Peruvian public opinion but that President Mariano Prado harbored no evil intentions toward Chile.

On 21 March, Pinto finally asked Lavalle whether a treaty with Bolivia existed and, if so, would his government honor it. The minister, while stating that he had no formal instructions on this issue, offered his personal opinion that he doubted that Peru would remain neutral. Pinto, still anxious to keep Lima out of the war, promised not to arm any Pacific port and even offered to negotiate a treaty limiting the export of nitrates from Chilean territory in order to protect Peru's *salitre* monopoly. Lavalle forwarded Pinto's suggestions although he did not expect Lima to accept them.

Santa María appeared particularly depressed because his discussions with Lavalle indicated that Chile could not prevent Peruvian involvement. Yet neither the economic crisis nor the possibility of Argentine involvement deterred Chile's war hawks. "Moral victories," he observed, "will satisfy no one. The war might truly be a calamity but war we will have to endure for a hundred reasons.... We began our war with Spain this way. History will tell us how we ended it."[18]

Days later, Pinto informed Lavalle that Lima's military preparations indicated that Peru might soon side with Bolivia. Observing that the Chilean public demanded action, the president informed Lavalle that Lima must state whether it would remain neutral. When Peru would not repudiate its Bolivian alliance, Pinto received permission from the Council of State to request the legislature to declare war on Peru and Bolivia. On 4 April, the congress authorized Pinto to sever diplomatic relations and ôn 5 April, it proclaimed that a state of belligerency existed between Chile, Peru, and Bolivia. The War of the Pacific had begun.[19]

CHILE'S MOTIVATIONS

Numerous scholars have debated why Pinto declared war. Although neither the president nor Santa María wanted a conflict, a few have argued that the Moneda initiated the struggle in order to divert the attention of the restless masses from a desperate economic situation.[20] If so, then the government certainly proceeded in an extremely dilatory manner. During the early stages of the Bolivian crisis, for example, Pinto did not put either his army or navy on a war footing. On the contrary, he continued to reduce the size of the military and sold off units from the fleet. Indeed, the telegraph traffic emanating from the Ministry of Interior, the most powerful branch of the executive government, indicates that Santiago was more involved in manipulating the 1879 congressional elections than in implementing any grand military strategy. The government, moreover, sent reinforcements north only after 19 February, and these troops did not cross the twenty-third parallel until the end of March. Thus, not only was Chile ill prepared for a struggle, but it continued to react indecisively as well. Clearly Pinto did not charge into conflict but lurched unsteadily into what he feared would be an Armaggedon. As Isidoro Errazuríz subsequently charged on the floor of the congress: "if the nation were disposed to level any charge against the present government, it would not be that of an excess of zeal or activity in its operations, but ... a lack of energy in the development of an appropriate plan."[21]

Prelude

Others have alleged that the Moneda went to war to protect the interests of the Compañía de Salitres y Ferrocarril. The conspiracy theory enjoys a certain appeal because Chile was an oligarchy in which a few individuals controlled the nation's destiny. Thus, it is quite easy to believe that a group of nitrate barons decided that the Chilean government should invade Antofagasta in order to protect their investments from Daza's money lust. Certainly the Compañía de Salitres possessed powerful allies. Depending on which stockholder's list is consulted, various members of congress, including government ministers, owned shares in the company.[22] Nor did the corporation hesitate to use its influence. As Guillermo Gibbs, one of the principal stockholders observed: "We have several very influential Chileans amongst our shareholders and should the government not carry out the promise made to take immediate action in the matter, strong pressure will be brought to bear on them in Congress and no doubt they will find themselves forced to act more energetically." The company apparently also subborned the newspaper *La Patria* and its editor, Isidoro Errazuríz, in order to promote the company's cause in the press while other members of the corporation tried to influence Pinto directly.[23]

The stockholders enjoyed only marginal success. Francisco Puelma, for example, put aside the cause of the Compañía de Salitres to work instead for the candidates of the Montt Varista Party in the 1879 congressional elections. Moreover, the shareholders of the Compañía did not receive good value for their subsidies. Although *La Patria* published some statements on the Bolivian situation, it certainly did not overwhelm its readers on this topic. During the critical first six weeks of 1879, only approximately a third of its editorials were devoted solely to the Bolivian crisis and most of these appeared after 11 January, when La Paz announced it would auction off the corporation's holdings. Indeed, an analysis of the nation's leading journals indicates that the press appeared more preoccupied with various religious, political, and economic issues than with the plight of the Compañía de Salitres. Not until after 10 February 1879, did the news media become interested in the dispute.[24]

The charge of economic pressure surfaced virtually from the onset of the war, an allegation which both the Chilean legislature and the press vehemently rejected. Chile did not, they insisted, go to war to save the Compañía de Salitres but to enforce its treaty rights, rights which the Moneda had already compromised once with Argentina and which the nation would not permit to be betrayed again. The Chilean press claimed that the Peruvians, anxious to preserve the integrity of their nitrate monopoly, had urged Bolivia to increase the taxes on the Compañía de Salitres y Ferrocarril, and that it was therefore Lima's *salitre* barons, not those of Santiago, who deserved the onus for precipitating the war.[25] Indeed, rather than defending the mining corporation, some journalists accused the government of contemplating the betrayal of both the nitrate company and the nation's international honor in order to avoid jeopardizing the holdings of those Chilean capitalists who possessed substantial investments in Bolivia. The press argued that Melchor Concha i Toro, the president of the chamber of deputies and a large stockholder of a Bolivian silver mine in Huanchaca, refused to call the congress into session in order to prevent it from declaring war on La Paz. *Las Novedades* even alleged that Concha i Toro had offered the Moneda $2,000,000 to settle the dispute with Daza and to return to the 1874 boundary lines. "Unfortunately," it noted, "the Chilean people do not receive dividends from the speculations of this señor and . . . instead are trying to defend its [the nation's] dignity and its name, a national dignity which no government would be sufficiently strong or audacious to compromise without being torn apart and thrown from the Moneda like one throws garbage into the street."[26] Others lamented that the government had subordinated the Bolivian question to "the convenience of some businessmen, to the shame of the nation and a new dishonor for Chile." These allegations, like those attributing the war to the machinations of the Compañía de Salitres, lack substance. It is known, however, that Lorenzo Claro, a prominent member of the National Party and the founder of various banks in Bolivia, tried to persuade Pinto not to protest Daza's imposition of the ten cent export tax which the financier considered quite legal and proper.[27]

It is extremely difficult to sort out the various charges and countercharges. In the midst of the crisis, for example, the directors of the nitrate company feared that Santiago would not protect it against La Paz, particularly when they learned that the government would not act, if at all, until after it had exhausted the diplomatic alternatives. The Moneda's refusal to react more resolutely tends to indicate that owners of the Compañía de Salitres enjoyed but limited influence in Santiago. Moreover, if the shareholders could so callously plunge Chile into war, why, six months later, could these same capitalists not stop its supposedly domesticated legislature from increasing the export tax on nitrates far in excess of that which Bolivia had originally proposed? Nor was the company able to prevent Santiago from levying taxes on the import and export of items needed to develop the railroad. (Ironically, the corporation had the temerity to claim that its concession from La Paz had exempted such items from taxation and to demand that Chile respect this dispensation.) These requests failed to achieve their purpose, again indicating that the company did not possess such enormous influence with the Congress. As Baron von Gülich, Germany's minister to Chile, noted, "seeking the origin of the present war in the *salitre*'s interests reminds one of my youth in which they joked about those who sought the origin of the revolt of the Belgians against Holland in the playing of 'The Deaf of Portici.' " If this is true, however, then why did Pinto eventually request his congress to declare war against La Paz and Lima?[28]

Domestic politics, not economic pressure, played a significant if not decisive role in precipitating the conflict. With congressional elections scheduled for the fall of 1879, the various parties desperately needed an issue to use against the Pinto regime. Earlier these elements had manipulated the Argentine crisis to discredit Pinto's Liberal Party and to galvanize public opinion against the government. Unfortunately for Pinto, the Bolivian crisis overlapped the Argentine situation and many Chileans feared that Santiago would humble itself as shamelessly before La Paz as it had groveled before Buenos Aires. Certainly, there was the emergence of the same coalition which had opposed the Fierro Sarratea treaty—the Conservatives, Liberal Democrats, and various dissident Liberals—criticizing what they regarded as the the government's traitorous Bolivian policy. These deputies denounced Pinto, claiming that his vacillating if not supine foreign policy had precipitated the Bolivian crisis, a crisis he could not resolve, the critics charged, because the administration was too involved in rigging the election. Consequently, they demanded convening the Congress into extraordinary session in order to force the government to act more aggressively toward La Paz.[29]

Pinto would not grant this request, perhaps fearing a repetition of the Argentine debates when foes of his government used the legislature as a forum to denounce his administration. The Moneda, however, miscalculated; denied access to congress, the opposition took to the streets where they invariably tied the Bolivian issue to the government's ineptitude, corruption, and electoral intervention. Despite this pressure, and much to the distress of the Compañía de Salitres, Pinto delayed seizing Antofagasta. Following the occupation of the littoral, Pinto again hesitated. It was Bolivia, not Chile, which first declared war and then, due to legal issues as well as the wretched condition of its fleet, the Moneda still did not react. Instead, Pinto ignored La Paz concentrating on conciliating Peru for which he was willing to restrict the nitrate production of his presumed favorite, the Compañía de Salitres y Ferrocarril.[30]

As Pinto temporized and hoped, the Peruvians armed and the president's political opposition harangued. Aware of Lima's activities, the war party so inflamed the public that Pinto had little choice. Various diplomats, including Lavalle, and the press concluded that the president faced two options: either enforce Chile's treaty obligations or be overthrown.[31] As one deputy commented: "Who knows what action the public would have taken if the government had delayed one day more in occupying the littoral."[32] *El Taller* warned: "Be careful señores, the blood is boiling in the veins of the people. You know that the first misfortune for our soldiers will be the last day of your power and who knows to what point will the anger and the justice of the people arrive."[33]

Advocates of a more aggressive policy deliberately held public meetings in front of the president's summer residence as well as at the homes of various political figures. Antonio Varas, a prominent legislator and the man who would subsequently serve as minister of the interior during the first months of the conflict, privately observed to Pinto: "I have seen the 'rotos' marching beneath my window with an enthusiasm which I have not witnessed in my life. Either we occupy all Antofagasta or they will kill you and me." The Minister of the Interior, Belisario Prats, felt equally intimidated. If Paris was worth a mass, Santiago certainly deserved a war. Aníbal Pinto, driven by an inflamed public, had no choice but to declare war if he wished to remain president.[34]

2

The Active War (1879-1881)

> In war you do not have to be nice, you only have to be right.
> Winston Churchill

> I do not want to be a soldier,
> the war drives me crazy,
> the salary that I earn is paltry,
> and the work is hard.
> "Quejas de un soldado." by Daniel Meneses

As has been noted, various scholars have described Chile as a warrior nation which entered the war as confidently as von Moltke's legions invaded France in 1870. A careful examination of the Moneda's army and navy reveals, however, the wretched condition of the nation's armed forces in 1879. Predictably, therefore, each battle, particularly early in the conflict, exposed the lack of training of Chile's officer corps and the country's primitive military organization. Instead of unleashing a blitzkrieg, the Moneda agonized at virtually each stage of its involvement in the War of the Pacific.

THE PRUSSIA OF THE PACIFIC

Committed perhaps in a moment of desperation, Santiago's declaration of war constituted a momentous act whose enormity became apparent only after its martial passions had cooled. Peru and Bolivia's combined population was at least twice that of Chile. The allied armies, excluding their territorial reserves, contained three times as many men as Santiago's regular forces. While La Paz possessed no navy, Lima did: two ironclads, two coastal defense monitors, a corvette, one gun boat, and various transports.

The onset of the war caught Chile unprepared. The economic depression of the mid-1870s had forced President Pinto to slash the size of his army by 20 percent. Theoretically, the army could draw upon the National Guard but the latter had suffered even more drastic budget cuts than the professionals. Its manpower levels reduced by 70 percent, equipped with weapons which generally endangered the life of the user more than his proposed target, inadequately clothed, and commanded by officers with more political connections than military skills; the *Guardia* offered little help and less hope.

Nor did the fleet escape the economic shearing. The navy sold some of its ships and disarmed others, beaching their officers and discharging their crews. The remaining vessels required extensive repairs: the ironclads *Almirante Cochrane* and *Blanco Encalada* needed careening and new armor plate; the wooden *O'Higgins, Chacabuco, Esmeralda*, and the *Covadonga* barely functioned. Only the corvette *Magallanes* and the lighter *Tolten* were seaworthy.[1]

Unaware that their nation was materially ill prepared, the Chilean public described their enemy as a horde of inferior Indians and blacks, men of impure heritage, unknown parentage, and questionable sexual orientation, who would collapse once confronted with a show of strength. Consequently, when the Moneda could not provide instant victory, the press became hostile, accusing the government of failing to act decisively.[3]

Professional soldiers—men like General Justo Arteaga Cuevas, who had earlier predicted a "decisive and easy" victory—recanted once they had seen the terrible state of the expeditionary army entrusted to their care. Before launching an offensive, the seventy-four-year-old general demanded that the Moneda supply additional ammunition, clothing, and medicine. To provide the needed logistical support, the Moneda assigned various civilians, including the former Minister of Finance, Rafael Sotomayor, to Arteaga's staff.[3]

Unfortunately, Arteaga's stamina and mental abilities proved inadequate to the tasks confronting him. Eventually the indecisive commander became aware of the government's growing dissatisfaction with him. Perhaps fearful for his reputation, in July 1879 he resigned his command. His successor, Erasmo Escala, was such a devout Catholic that his staff was required to devote a portion of their time to planning religious ceremonies which the general insisted his troops attend.[4] The general's religious zeal nothwithstanding, the army was unable to invade the north until the navy first secured the sealanes by destroying the Peruvian fleet, a possibility which seemed increasingly remote in mid-1879.

THE NAVAL CAMPAIGN

At the onset of the war, Pinto had urged Admiral Juan Williams Rebolledo to attack the Peruvian navy at its home base of Callao. Williams refused, claiming that Callao was too well protected and that his ships could not sustain a blockade so far from Antofagasta. Instead, the admiral proposed quarantining Iquique, an important nitrate port in the province of Tarapacá. Depriving Lima of its principal source of revenue, he argued, would force its fleet to leave the safety of Callao to attack Williams's squadron. The admiral's argument carried the day: on 5 April, the Chilean fleet blockaded Iquique.[5]

After weeks of inactivity, the Chilean public began carping about Williams's decision. As a result, the admiral, without informing the Moneda, sailed for Callao where he hoped to destroy the ironclads the *Huáscar* and the *Independencia*. When the admiral reached the port, he discovered that his quarry had already sailed. Thus the Chilean fleet withdrew without attacking the other vessels lying at anchor. The return voyage proved as farcical as the first part of the mission: some of the corvettes ran out of coal or suffered mechanical breakdowns, forcing them to slip into port either under sail or at the end of a tow rope.[6]

When Williams docked in Iguigue, he learned that while he had ventured north, the *Huáscar* and *Independencia* had attacked the ships blockading Iquique, sinking the *Esmeralda*. The *Covadonga*, however, had fled Iquique with the *Independencia* in hot pursuit. The Peruvian commander foolishly followed the shallow draft *Covadonga* over a reef, ripping the bottom out of his ship, thus reducing Lima's fleet by almost half.

Iquique outraged the Chilean public. Forgetting the destruction of the *Independencia*, the press flayed the government for entrusting the blockade to two weak wooden vessels. The Moneda was equally incensed: furious that Williams had abandoned Iquique without consulting Santiago and, worse yet, that his insubordination had accomplished nothing. Although various officials privately condemned the admiral, and some of the press publicly questioned his judgment, Williams's political allies managed to insulate the officer from any retribution.[7]

Williams's protectors, however, could not save him from himself. As Miguel Grau and the *Huáscar* harried Chile's sealanes and menaced its ports, Williams sulked in his cabin, the victim of an increasingly hostile press and acute hypocondria. The Moneda desperately wished to replace him but feared that this act would provoke a political crisis.[8] In July the *Huáscar* captured the *Rimac*, a transport carrying military supplies and troops to the north. The loss of the ship forced the fleet to assign many of its units to convoy coastal shipping and caused a public outcry which led to the government's resignation.[9] The new Minister of the Interior, Domingo Santa María, like his predecessor, feared that dismissing Williams would precipitate another political crisis. The admiral graciously solved Pinto's dilemma: in August, in a disagreement over strategy, Williams abandoned the blockade of Iquique without first obtaining permission from Santiago. Rather than confront an outraged Moneda, he simply resigned.[10]

Although freed of Williams, the Moneda had to find a successor, a task made more difficult because many observers described some of the navy's most senior officers as alcoholics, incompetents, or neurotics. The president finally selected a regular officer, Galvarino Riveros, as fleet commander, but only after he also purged the fleet of those commanders he considered too dangerous to retain in positions of authority.[11]

While Riveros reorganized his squadron, the *Huáscar* razed the Chilean coast and the *Unión* threatened Santiago's control of the Strait of Magellen. Santiago could not repel this naval onslaught because some of its vessels were in drydock, undergoing repairs to their engines and hulls, while the remaining serviceable ships were diverted to protect the supply lines to Europe. As Sotomayor sarcastically observed: Lima ruled the waves.[12]

In the spring, Santiago learned that Grau had sailed to Iquique with reinforcements. Sotomayor and Riveros divided the fleet into two flotillas: one would linger near Mejillones, while the other would patrol the high seas to the west. On 8 October, alerted by provincial officials, Riveros' squadron moved to intercept the *Huáscar* and the *Unión* off Mejilliones. When the Peruvians tried to outrun Riveros, a second squadron, under the command of Captain Juan Latorre, cut off their escape route. Within minutes the Chilean gunners had straddled the ironclad, slaughtering most of its officers, including Grau. The survivors tried to scuttle their ship but a Chilean boarding party closed the sea cocks in time to capture it as a prize.[13]

THE TARAPACÁ CAMAPAIGN

Having virtually gutted Peru's navy, the Moneda, after some debate, decided that invading the nitrate fields would permit Chile to exert economic leverage on Peru while providing Santiago with the revenue to finance its own war effort. Pinto, disheartened by the professional military's incompetence, ordered Sotomayor to select the landing place. The minister ultimately decided to land at two sites: the small bay of Junín and Pisagua which, although heavily defended, had access to a rail line that would allow the Chileans to penetrate the interior more easily.[14]

Tarapacá's coastal range does not slope gently into the ocean; instead it forms a high plateau which ends abruptly, virtually at the water's edge. Consequently, Pisagua's beach was an ungenerous trickle of sand divided in two by a rocky promentory: Playa Blanca, in the north, and Playa Huala. The allies supplemented these natural obstacles with two artillery batteries and stationed over 1,500 troops both on the shore as well as atop the 300-meter high bluffs which overlooked the beach.

Initially the invasion seemed in trouble because a navigational error put the Chilean invasion fleet twelve miles off course and the coastal fog, the infamous *camanchaca*, delayed the landing. In addition, the bumbling of the drunken Captain Enriqué Simpson delayed the landing of the first wave, allowing the allied troops to regroup. Consequently, when the Chileans stormed Playa Blanca, they encountered heavy resistance. Although the first wave contained only half as many men as Sotomayor had originally specified, they managed to hold on to their beachhead until reinforcements landed and scaled the bluffs. By early afternoon, they captured the garrison of Hospicio and linked up with the troops who had landed at Junín.

Although they were safely ashore, the expeditionary force remained at great risk because it depended upon the oasis of Dolores, located in the interior, for its drinking water. In order to assure access to this vital waterhole, Sotomayor ordered José Francisco Vergara, then commanding a cavalry unit, to seize the town. Vergara, by capturing Dolores, not only protected Escala's supply lines but severed Iquique logistical lifeline to the north, thus putting the Chilean army into a position to starve Iquique into submission.[15]

Unfortunately, the allies did not roll over and play dead. On 11 November, General Hilarión Daza left Tacna for the south to rendezvous with the army of General Juan Buendía who was defending Tarapacá. After a few days of marching, the Bolivian troops, weakened by *soroche*, exhaustion, and hunger, straggled into Camarones. Depressed by his men's wretched condition, Daza funked: without informing Buendía, the Bolivian simply returned to Arica.[16] Buendía, unaware of Daza's action, ordered his men north from Pozo Almonte in order to link up with the Bolivian army. Instead of meeting his ally, the Peruvian's troops literally ran into the Chilean advance party near Dolores.

This encounter caught Escala completely by surprise because the Chilean had expected an attack from the north. After sighting the Peruvian forces at Agua Santa, the threat became clear: if Buendía recaptured Dolores, he could cut off the Chilean expedition from its water supply and thus force Escala either to withdraw or surrender. As the Peruvians advanced, Sotomayor decided to dig in on Cerro San Francisco, a mountainous mesa jutting approximately 200 meters above the valley floor. The allied army hoped to envelop the Chilean position on both sides, thus surrounding Sotomayor's men on their mountain redoubt. Regrettably, the Chileans proved less cooperative, repelling the enemy advances and inflicting heavy casualties. Demoralized by their losses, the Bolivian expeditionary force disintegrated, the remnants fleeing into the pampa; the Peruvians, however, regrouped and retreated either to Tacna or Arica. Escala, who arrived at Dolores only after the battle's conclusion, failed to pursue the fleeing enemy, preferring instead to conduct a Mass of thanksgiving, a pious act which the Chilean army would subsequently rue.[17]

Some government officials who accompanied the Tarapacá expedition complained about the botched landing—which some attributed to Simpson's drunkenness—the failure of the supply system, and the breakdown in discipline which resulted in the looting of Pisagua. Eduardo de la Barra specifically castigated Simpson as well as Emilio Sotomayor, claiming that both men had collapsed when confronted with a crisis. Even a regular officer like General Manuel Baquedano described the Pisagua episode as "heroic but disordered."[18]

In truth, San Francisco resembled a surprise party more than a military battle. Colonel Sotomayor, for example, often acted indecisively as well as inefficiently. Had he been left to his own devices, Sotomayor would have made his stand at Santa Catalina, north of Dolores, which did not command the high ground. It took the combined efforts of Vergara and his two brother officers to convince the colonel to defend Cerro San Francisco thus gaining a substantial geographical advantage over the enemy. Escala however, emerged as the most maladroit. The general had committed a multitude of military sins: he had divided his army, dispersed his cavalry, and would not have sent his artillery to Dolores had Rafael Sotomayor not insisted. Without those guns, which arrived on the day of the battle, the Chileans could not have defeated the allied army. The failure to capture the remnants of Buendía's army, however, constituted Escala's cardinal error; the troops who escaped would later obtain sweet revenge for their defeat at Dolores. As one military historian subsequently observed: "The valiant Chilean army knew how to win; but its high command did not know how to take advantage of the victory."[19]

After capturing Iquique, the victorious Chileans rested on the wilted laurels of their victory at San Francisco. A few units still remained in Pisagua but the bulk of the army marked time around Dolores. Vergara, always the enthusiast, suggested that he reconnoiter the area around Tarapacá where he knew Buendía's men had taken refuge. Escala agreed, and on 24 November, Vergara captured Negrerios where he learned that Buendía's command consisted of but 1,500 ill-equipped, exhausted, and demoralized soldiers. This report was false; although the allies had suffered heavy losses, they were more numerous and in far better condition than the Chileans believed. This crucial failure to evaluate accurately the enemy's strength would soon have disastrous results for Escala's army.

Vergara, acting on incorrect intelligence and believing that he could easily mop up Buendía's army, requested both reinforcements and permission to advance on Tarapacá. Escala agreed, ordering approximately 2,000 men, under the command of Colonel Luis Arteaga, to rendezvous with Vergara. Thus the colonel blithely trudged into the desert although his men were poorly equipped and carried but one day's water ration. Meanwhile, the elusive Vergara, expecting that the reinforcements would carry additional supplies, had marched to Isluga, only fifteen kilometers from Tarapacá. By the time the two units met, on the afternoon of 26 November, Vergara's men had consumed almost all of their rations.

Unaware that most of the enemy garrison consisted of rested and relatively well equipped units, Vergara and Arteaga decided to attack although their men were exhausted, hungry, and nearly dehydrated. Arteaga planned an assault which required one Chilean unit to seize the high ground overlooking Tarapacá in order to seal the Peruvian garrison's escape route. When this objective had been captured, the remaining Chilean units would attack the city. The Peruvians, however, sighting the Chileans before they could take the heights, rushed in reinforcements and repulsed the attackers, inflicting heavy casualties on the outnumbered and exhausted men. Santiago had suffered a very costly defeat: over 750 perished, including Colonel Ricardo Ramírez, two female nurse-water bearers, plus sixty-seven other wounded who died when the Peruvians deliberately torched the building the Chileans were using as a hospital. Ironically, because the Peruvians retreated from Tarapacá to Tacna, the Chileans had achieved a strategic victory.[20]

Initially, Chile seemed pleased with the Peruvian withdrawal. This attitude quickly changed when the casualty lists appeared and the nation learned how Ramírez and his comrades had died. Vicuña Mackenna, for example, dubbed Tarapacá the army's battle of Iquique. Although incensed by the Peruvian atrocities, the nation generously saved some of its ire for the Moneda, calling Tarapacá a disasterous triumph, a battle devoid of tactics, where poorly equipped and exhausted troops perished heroically but needlessly. Some of the press severely criticized Escala—a man "whose initiative seems to have been lost in the pampa like the trace of his path which the desert wind erased"—particularly for his failure to pursue the enemy after San Francisco. Pinto, who was dismayed to have lost so many troops, became furious, blaming Escala for impetuously attacking without knowing the Peruvians' strength. "Because of our intemperance, we have given the enemy a victory, and we have lost the opportunity to capture a good enemy division." Sotomayor was equally despondent, claiming that his generals had vainly tried to imitate the Prussian army.[21]

THE DRIVE FOR TACNA AND ARICA

Perhaps to avenge the martyrs of Tarapacá, the public demanded that the government launch another offensive. Unfortunately, the Moneda could not respond. The recent campaign had decimated the expedition's ranks, consumed its supplies, equipment, and transport, while revealing the flaws in the newly created supply and medical services. Before the army could proceed, Sotomayor would not only have to find new recruits, amass additional provisions and transport, but he would also have to reorganize the army's technical branches, particularly its medical corps. This proved a herculean and time consuming task. Yet, as Tarapacá had demonstrated, supplies, particularly water, were essential for success in a desert war.[22]

Rather than permit the infantry, cavalry, and artillery to operate as they did traditionally, in a loose confederation, Sotomayor wished to integrate these combat arms into divisions under the leadership of one commander. As part of the effort to improve military administration, the Moneda created the post of chief of staff to act as the commanding general's deputy. Escala disliked Sotomayor's plans for reorganization as well as his candidates for deputy. Indeed, it required a direct order from the government before the general grudgingly accepted Colonel Pedro Lagos as his chief of staff.[23]

These efforts, which created the infrastructure essential for Chile's eventual victory, failed to impress the public which instead called for a war of "audacity, action, and energy."[24] Eventually some of the press became dissatisfied with Escala and faulted him for failing to reorganize the army and for lacking the will to pursue Buendía's men. It was a shame, they lamented, that Chile's soldiers had to pay a blood tax for their commander's blunder. While the more charitable tried to rationalize the army's poor performance, they also suggested that the nation could not always count on luck or allied error to save them. Others cynically doubted that the nation would see the military reformed or the war vigorously prosecuted in the near future. After all, summer had arrived: "The government is on vacation: the courts are closed; the Congress is not in session; the army is resting on its laurels; and the navy is wasting coal and patience in blockades and running around."[25]

This pessimism did not do justice either to the Moneda or its delegates. Sotomayor, anxious to pursue the war, suggested attacking Lima but Pinto demurred. The Moneda hoped to negotiate a peace treaty with Bolivia by offering it a strip of Peruvian seacost as compensation for the loss of the Atacama, a tactic that, if successful, would not only have ended La Paz's belligerence but would have neatly interposed it between Santiago and Lima. This so called Bolivian stratregy required, however, that Chile first capture Tacna.[26]

Although Escala initially argued that invading the south's harsh desert climate and lack of water would tax his troops endurance, he nonetheless accepted the Moneda's decision and began planning the invasion. Rather than assault the heavily defended port of Arica, a council of war instead suggested that the army land at Ilo. Control of this harbor would ensure an adequate supply of water and forage and also threaten the enemy's supply lines to its garrisons in Arequipa and Moquegua. Anxious to avoid another Tarapacá, Pinto ordered the army not to advance inland but to dig in after seizing the harbor and to wait for a Peruvian counterattack. In order to goad the enemy commander, Admiral Lizardo Montero, into reacting, the president instructed his cavalry units to ravage the area around the port. Pinto's plan failed to realize that Montero would not strain his supply lines and march his men across a burning desert simply to gratify the Chilean president: Mohammed would have to go to the mountain.[27]

As the Chileans prepared for the invasion, tensions mounted and tempers, fanned by the desert wind and personal animosities, frayed. Escala, believing that Tacna's defenders possessed a large army, refused to invade the north until he received reinforcements. When Sotomayor protested, Escala agreed to lead the expedition, but only on the condition that he be absolved of any responsibility should the campaign miscarry. The general's demand not only strained his already precarious alliance with Sotomayor, but if accepted, it would have virtually paralyzed the preparations for the invasion.

In an attempt to placate the general, Sotomayor requested that José Vergara resign his commmission to serve as Escala's secretary, hoping that the civilian's presence might improve the general's disposition.[28] Vergara agreed to Sotomayor's request and even succeeded in briefly smoothing the general's ruffled feelings.[29] Having overcome this crisis, Sotomayor returned to his administrative duties, but it was not until mid-February 1880 that the newly reorganized and reequipped army of the north was ready for action. Yet, despite his best efforts, the minister was depressed: "We will go to Lima," he bemoaned, "more disorganized perhaps than when we left for Antofagasta but we will go."[30]

Consistent with its earlier performances, the convoy that sailed from Pisagua on 25 February arrived at Ilo late. Happily for the Moneda, the city offered no resistance so by early afternoon, the troops of Colonel Lagos controlled Ilo where they used captured rolling stock to transport the convoy's supplies inland. The minister's plan called for the army to seize Conde, a strategic communications center whose fall, he hoped, would provoke Montero to retaliate. When it became clear that the Peruvians would not react, the army begged to move inland. Painfully aware of its earlier ineptitude, Pinto hesitated, fearing that the expedition's leaders did not have the necessary skills to lead their troops across the desert.

The Moneda's lack of confidence extended to the navy as well. While the fleet had demonstrated its bravery at Iquique and Angamos, at Pisagua and Ilo it showed that some of its officers had yet to master the art of navigation. Santa María despaired because of his sailors who "sail thirty or forty miles beyond the point where they should have gone." Officers of questionable skills or intemperate habits still retained their commands while others devoted more effort to advancing their careers than waging war. In February, 1880, Captain Manuel Thompson, jeopardized his ship and in the process lost his life foolishly dueling with Arica's shore batteries. In retaliation for the death of Thompson, an infuriated fleet bombarded Arica from 29 February to 3 March, much to the delight of Santiago. Moreover, not only did the fleet not obliterate Arica, it also failed to seal the port's harbor allowing the *Unión* to slip past the Chilean flotilla, bring needed war materiel to beleagured Arica, and then escape to Callao.[31]

Nor did the army provide the Moneda with great joy when a unit raiding Mollendo discovered liquor in a warehouse, became drunk, and then joined by a few officers, pillaged the port. According to a Peruvian claim, these men even desecrated a church and the Host. The looting lasted for more than a day and required the use of force before the rioting ceased and the men returned to Ilo on 11 March.[32]

Mollendo confirmed the Moneda's fears that its commanders could neither lead nor control the army. Yet, Montero's refusal to attack forced Pinto to abandon his passive strategy. With great trepidation, he ordered General Manuel Baquedano to leave the security of the coast to attack

Moquegua, located deep in the desert. Baquedano repeated many of the errors of his predecessors, permitting his men to leave, for example, without carrying adequate supplies. In one case, a riot erupted when thirsty troops arrived at a camp site only to discover that other units had already consumed their water ration. That incident made Sotomayor vow that henceforth he would participate more actively in directing the campaign. The cilivian's involvement, however, exacerbated the already poor relationship between Sotomayor and his general in chief.[33]

At the same time, the long simmering hostility between Lagos and Escala finally erupted. The commanding general had often feuded with his chief of staff, particularly because he resented having to share his authority. Tired of chaffing under Escala's rule, Lagos resigned, citing the general's sloopy conduct of the war. A furious Escala petulantly tendered his resignation which, much to his chagrin, the Moneda accepted.

Although the minister both distrusted and disliked Escala, Sotomayor would have preferred that he retain his command, fearing the consequences of his resignation. The civilian's judgment proved quite prescient because after the inept Escala quit, he quickly became a political martyr: one journalist even compared him to Christ. Still, the crisis passed, although the government debated for over a week to determine who should replace Escala. Basing their decision more on political than professional considerations, the Moneda finally selected Manuel Baquedano to command the expeditionary force while José Velásquez, former head of the artillery, would serve as his chief of staff.[34] The resolution of this organizational dispute did not pacify Vergara who remained despondent: "Our army has no administration and whatever strategy it tries produces confusion and disorder." His superiors, including Santa María and the president, also appeared despondent.[35]

Finally good news arrived from the north: Baquedano had captured Moquegua. Even this feat was anticlimatic because the Chileans had not destroyed the enemy; the Peruvian defenders had merely abandoned the town, taking refuge on a mesa overlooking the city. Rising fifty meters above the valley, Los Anjeles lay sandwiched between two rivers which had clawed deep gorges on either side of the plateau. Enveloping the Peruvians' flanks appeared impossible because the narrow ravines on either side of the mesa appeared insurmountable. However, a Chilean scouting party, which included some miners, discovered that troops could successfully scale the ravines and thus outflank the enemy's defensive line. Unfortunately for Baquedano, some of his men lost their way and could not locate the spot where they were to begin their ascent. Others, however, managed to scale one side of the mesa, and attack the Peruvian right, forcing them to retreat. Just as the enemy began to withdraw, other Chilean units reached the top of the plateau and joined the battle. Caught in the middle of a narrowing triangle, the Peruvians collapsed but, as at Dolores, a good portion of the enemy successfully escaped.[36]

The victory at Los Anjeles did not alter the strategic situation since Peru's garrisons at Tacna and Arica remained intact. Rather than attempt a costly assault on Arica, the Chileans planned to advance inland from Ilo to Tacna and then cut off the port from its supply lines. To accomplish this task, however, the Chileans would have had to cross a desert less generous and more unforgiving than that surrounding Tarapacá, a region seemingly devoid of resources and one about which they knew nothing.

This plan, while testing the endurance of the army, also required an enormous amount of logistical support. Sotomayor would have had to acquire and then distribute large quantitites of food, water, as well as horses and mules to permit Baquedano's troops to traverse the desert. The civilian labored strenuously to accomplish this mission. Perhaps he struggled too hard: he died of a stroke on 20 May, almost on the eve of the final drive on Tacna.

Although disheartened by his death, the army still launched its offensive leaving Ilo on 8 April. The crossing taxed the men: the poor roads delayed the supply trains; various fevers, a particularly virulent form of smallpox, and other diseases ravaged the soldiers; discipline deteriorated as the troops discarded their equipment. Yet by early May, the artillery, plus the fourth division, occupied Ite and then rendezvoused with the rest of the expedition at Buenavista and Yaras, thirty-eight kilometers from Tacna.

Thanks to the unpatriotic candor of the Chilean press, the Peruvians knew of Baquedano's movements and decided to make their stand at Campo de la Alianza, a promontory commanding the road to Tacna. Vergara, once again serving as an active officer, urged an attack on the enemy's right in order to cut off Tacna from its water supply and thus force the city to surrender. Baquedano overruled his cavalry commander's suggestion. Rather than outflank his enemy, Baquedano ordered a frontal assault under the cover of an artillery barrage directed at the enemy's batteries and his redoubts. Since the Chilean canons used shrapnel, which could not penetrate the Peruvian defenses, when Baquedano's assault began, his men suffered heavy casualties. Nevertheless, the Chilean's sledge hammer tactics succeeded in defeating the enemy but at great cost: three divisions endured high casualty rates; 30 percent either died or suffered wounds; and only the fourth division, which had served as a reserve, emerged only slightly less battered. Seizing the Peruvian city, moreover, did not end the campaign: Santiago still had to capture

Arica in order to control the province and because it needed the port's facilities to resupply its troops. Possessing Arica's habor would also allow Chile to cut Lima's supply lines to its cities in the south.

Precisely because it was so important, Lima reinforced the garrisons with additional equipment and troops, making Arica Peru's Gibraltar. This comparison is not exaggerated because, like the British base, the Peruvian defenses rested on a mountain, El Morro, which rose perpendicularly 206 meters from the ocean, and then sloped gradually toward the Andes. In addition to a series of strong points and gun emplacements, located along the side and atop the mountain, the defenders could call upon the guns of the monitor *Manco Capac*.

Baquedano, after unsuccessfully attempting to bombard the city into submission, ordered Colonel Pedro Lagos to lead an assault force to capture the fort atop the Morro. Advancing under darkness, the Chilean troops stormed the Peruvian positions and in a bloodly battle captured the high ground. Arica's vital port and most of Lima's southern provinces were finally in Chilean hands.[37]

Although successful, the ponderously slow pace of the Tacna campaign displeased the Chilean public. The country cavalierly ignored the logistical problems, the shortages of water and transport, to urge the government to abandon "the wearisome policy of inaction" which inspired "only impatience, disgust, and even a sense of insecurity."[38] Rather than recognize, as did Pinto, that Chile had to wage a war "more against the desert than the Peruvians," the nation sought instead those malefactors who, it believed, had prevented instant victory.[39] Predictably the Moneda, "which walks with feet of lead" and whose order of the day is "disembark and then go to sleep" emerged as the principal scapegoat.[40] Some attributed its failures to a preoccupation with partisan politics; others uncovered a conspiracy of bankers, usurers, and currency speculators who wished to prolong the war in order to maximize their profits.[41] Sotomayor, "that deaf martinet" was also pillored, chastized for living aboard the *Abtao*, for neglecting the needs of the troops, and for being more obsessed with destroying Escala than the Peruvians.[42] Eventually, this general hostility spilled over onto the military. One journalist sarcastically inquired if Escala were waging a war or conducting a novena while another colleague worried that he would not learn from his mistakes in the Tarapacá campaign. After all, "to be general in chief of the Chilean army requires, at least, that you not be an imbecile."[43] Even the triumphant Baquedano became a target of criticism when he became mired in Tacna's desert, requiring months, according to one critic, to accomplish what "our grandfathers" achieved in one day.[44]

Not even success could satisfy the jaded Chileans. Pisagua became "a miraculous victory" which but for the heroism of the troops would have been "the most horrible defeat"; Ilo was "an unpardonable blunder," while Los Angeles emerged as "a sad or fruitless skirmish" where the military high command squandered its advantages.[45] Tacna, with more reason, merited disdain.

News of that battle had reached Chile in a agonizingly slow fashion, encouraging some to believe that the Moneda had deliberately suppressed the casualty reports and tried to hide the fact that the allies had successfully retreated. When the public learned the details of the battle, it became outraged, leading one journalist to suggest that Santiago hold a "dance of death" rather than a ball to celebrate the victory.[46] Although the fault for the bungled and bloody victory lay clearly with Baquedano, his defenders tried to blame instead the Moneda, claiming that the general was merely following his orders. Santa María, however, demurred, describing the engagement as a "brutal frontal attack" in which Chile uselessly sacrificed its infantry while permitting the enemy units to escape. Baquedano's wasteful tactics particularly outraged the civilian official who urged that the Moneda find "a serious and energetic general" to lead the war.[47] The victory at Arica momentarily distracted the nation until a correspondent for *El Mercurio* published an extremely unflattering description of the encounter at Tacna. Baquedano dismissed this commentary, observing the "strategy of the pen very easy, very cheap, and very safe."[48]

Infuriated by Tacna's high casualties, the Chileans demanded a holocaust to punish the Peruvians and to convince them of Santiago's resolve. *El Ferrocarril*, which normally revered private property, urged the Moneda to destroy the assets of foreigners residing in Peru and to unleash a terror campaign against Lima's citizens. Vicuña Mackenna enthusiastically endorsed Vergara's policy of shooting franctireurs, arguing that if Santiago had earlier acted more savagely, Peru would have capitulated.[49]

This sense of frustration also applied to the war at sea. Even before Arica fell, the government ordered the navy to blockade Callao. The fleet, however, could do little more than harass the port whose powerful coastal fortifications easily repulsed the Chilean vessels. Twice, on 22 April and 10 May, the squadron fruitlessly dueled with these batteries. Thus, the blockade degenerated into a waiting war where the crews, according to a naval surgeon, diverted themselves with alcohol, masturbation, and unnatural sex.[50]

The Peruvian defenders refused to accept the blockade passively. On 3 July, the Chilean transport *Loa* was patrolling the harbor when it sighted a launch filled with fresh provisions. Doubtless tired of the ship's stale rations, the captain, Juan Peña, ordered the crew to unload their prize.

Just as the men had almost completed their task, they apparently triggered a bomb which sank the *Loa*, killing over 100 of its crew, including Peña.[51]

The Moneda's enemies tried to blame the government for the sinking of the *Loa*. Some described Peña as an incompetent officer whose friendship with Pinto had protected him from dismissal. One newspaper, citing a string of the dead officer's errors, concluded that Peña had taken the easy way out by going down with his ship; had he survived, he surely would have had to face a court martial.[52]

The question of Peña's culpability faded when the Chileans lost yet another vessel under identical circumstances. The *Covadonga* had taken up its station blockading Chancay when it too tried to take alongside a launch which exploded, sinking the warship and killing about half its crew, including Captain Pablo Ferrari. The destruction of this icon of Chile's naval glory, outraged the public and, according to one journalist, spoiled the nation's independence day celebrations. Rather than blame Ferrari, who should have known better, particularly after the *Loa* episode, anti-government journalists managed to indict the Moneda whose policies, they argued, had destroyed many ships, such as the *Esmeralda*, and whose strategy of blockading Callao each day became less defensible.[53]

The public demanded that the navy, rather than remain in Callao's harbor "consumed by torpedoes and tedium," should ravage Peru's coast until its citizens "spill tears of blood."[54] Riveros tried to slake the nation's thirst for vengeance by bombarding Chorillos, Ancón, and Chancay, but the largely ineffective shelling could not redeem the officer's reputation. Others demanded a land assault on Lima which had become a kind of a Jerusalem to the Chileans who yearned to liberate it even if they had to build "100 bridges of corpses [and] drink their own blood."[55] Some Chileans promised that the capture of the Peruvian capital would ensure the collapse of the enemy's war effort and dismissed as absurd the idea that Pierola would continue to fight from some altiplano redoubt. Thus, the nation rejected a proposal to attack Arequipa: it was the city on the Rimac, which the more educated likened to Carthage, that the Moneda had to destroy in order for Chile to triumph.[56]

THE FINAL PUSH

The collapse of the abortive Arica peace conference, which occurred in October 1880, removed the last rationale for not striking at the Peruvian capital. The press urged the Moneda to exterminate the enemy just as completely as Great Britain and Argentina had annihilated the Zulus and the Indians; if the government did not comply, journalists warned, it would lose popular support.[57] Pinto remained unconvinced, fearing that attacking Lima would strain Chile's financial resources and tax the administrative skills of its citizens as well as its officer corps. Consequently, he would have preferred to unleash a naval war which, he believed, would paralyze the Peruvian sugar economy, forcing Lima to the peace table. Still, when the Arica conference failed, he could not delay the campaign. Popular pressure, the fear of "exposing the nation to disturbances"[58]—the same force which pressured him to declare war in April 1879, impelled Pinto to order the attack on Lima in October 1880.

Mounting this campaign proved more difficult than preparing the earlier expeditions. Not only did the Moneda have to increase the army by 20,000, thus almost doubling its size, the new minister, José F. Vergara, had to provide the means to feed, clothe, and transport the men to the front. After having resolved some of the logistical problems, including finding additional ships and launches, Vergara began to plan the military phase of the war. In order to use his limited transport vessels efficiently, he suggested that General Villagrán establish a bridgehead at Pisco before the main part of the army departed Arica. A Council of War concurred and the general's division sailed on 14 November, reaching its destination in four days and securing the port virtually without bloodshed. When the fleet returned to Arica to pick up the remainder of the army, however, Vergara discovered that Baquedano had ordered some of the transports to other locations, thus disrupting the invasion schedule. There was another serious problem: the main force of the army did not possess enough mules to carry out the invasion. While the Moneda scoured Chile for 1,000 mules, harnesses, and drivers, Villagrán's troops remained exposed in the north. Aware of this situation, the public demanded that the government evacuate the Pisco area whose climate, they declared, menaced the expedition. It was not until early December that Pinto could gratify this wish and the council of war could plot its next step.[59]

Once the army secured Pisco, the high command met to plan the final assault on Lima. Vergara urged the council to invade Ancón, a resort town north of Lima and then drive south toward the capital. The Council of War rejected his suggestion, deciding instead that Villagrán's units would march overland from Pisco to the port of Chilca where, on 22 December, the main body of the army would land. After consolidating the two columns, the expeditionary force would advance on Lima. Thus, an invasion force of 22,000–23,000 Chilean troops embarked at Arica, arriving on 21 December at Chilca where the authorities discovered that they knew nothing about the possible landing sites. After a brief appraisal of the situation, the Chileans went ashore at Curayaco.

The army's progress halted when Villagran refused to proceed to Chilca, claiming that his men lacked the necessary supplies to complete the mission. The balky general stated that he would continue only if Baquedano absolved him from any responsibility should the expedition flounder. An unpopular and apparently self-serving officer, Villagrán may have hoped to disgrace Baquedano whom he loathed and considered a rival.[60] While not Villagrán's first act of insubordination, it was his last: an outraged Baquedano dismissed him. For once the commanding general enjoyed the complete support of his civilian advisors. Even Vergara approved, hoping that Baquedano's action would "correct the tendency of many of our high ranking military who do nothing but grumble and complain."[61] Patricio Lynch completed Villagrán's task so that as the new year of 1881 began, Chile was poised to capture Lima.

The capital's defenses consisted of two lines of trenches. The first extended from San Juan, near Chorillos, west to the sea. Vergara suggested that the Chileans outflank these positions and then wheel toward the ocean. If properly executed, this envelopment would have permitted the Chileans to capture both Lima and its defenders while minimizing their losses. Baquedano, however, demonstrating his usual disdain for subtlety, rejected Vergara's suggestion and again insisted on a frontal assault. Either overawed by the general's logic or rank, the rest of the Council of War acceded to Baquedano's wishes.

On 12 January 1881, the Chilean troops pushed off and, at dawn of the next day, assaulted the Peruvian defenses. Although some units encountered strong opposition, the troops under Colonel Sotomayor tore a piece out of the Peruvian center, thus shattering the enemy's defenses. While the victorious Chileans mopped up pockets of resistance, some of their comrades began to loot Chorillos, precipitating a riot which Baquedano had to suppress with force.[62]

At that point, all that separated the Chileans from Lima was a line of sandbagged strong points and artillery positions, dug in along the Surco River. When Baquedano suggested that Nicolás Piérola retreat from his fortified positions and surrender Callao, for a brief instant it seemed that the belligerents might forgo additional bloodletting. Had these requests been met, the capital would have been stripped of its defenses, an unpleasant prospect for the Limeños who feared that their city might suffer the same fate as Chorillos. While the two sides negotiated, however, fighting erupted again and any possibility of a peaceful surrender of the capital was shattered.

On 15 January 1881, the Chileans unleashed their final assault. Baquedano's men easily broke through the Peruvian line and by 6 PM had captured Miraflores. The inhabitants of Lima, perhaps anticipating the Chileans, began looting the Chinese quarter. As the smoke from the burning city sorched the sky, Piérola decamped for the altiplano while the advance guard of the Chilean army, confident that the war had ended, entered the former viceregal capital. This optimism proved ill founded however: only the active phase of the conflict had actually ceased; Santiago would remained mired in the north for months until it eventually arranged a peace treaty with its enemies.[63]

The first phase of the War of the Pacific had revealed serious flaws in the nation's officer corps and military bureaucracies. In part they were not completely responsible for all of the problems. Obviously a stringent budget had hamstrung the armed forces. On the other hand, outmoded military institutions under the direction of maladroit, if not completely incompetent officers, had jeopardized Chile's chances for success. Under the pressure from a public which demanded instant victory, Pinto had been forced to become more involved in the conduct of the war, sending his proxies—Rafael Sotomayor and then José Francisco Vergara—to assume not merely logistical but eventually also military functions. As subsequent chapters indicate, however, this civilian involvement upset the military who, in turn, tried to ensure their monopoly of the war by refusing to cooperate with the Moneda and, when that failed, by calling upon allies in the press and parliament for help.

3

Cucalones Versus Miltares

> I do not know whether our Generals will frighten the enemy, but I know that they frighten me whenever I think of them.
> Lord North

> Who is that officer
>   So dandyish and so bedecked
>   with plumes...
> He was not at Pisagua,
>   he has fought no war,
>   no battles
> But he cares for his braid
>   like a young girl her skirt.
>   "Payas sobre los falsos soldados."
>   H. Acuna.

Prior to 1879, the chain of command linking the government and the professional military appeared intact and the officer corps ostensibly followed the directives of the Moneda with grace if not good humor. The onset of hostilities quickly demonstrated the falsity of this impression. The military, believing that it alone possessed the necessary technical skills, tried to direct the war without consulting the Moneda. Conversely, President Pinto, seeing his officers wallowing in indecision, concluded that the government had to assume a more active role in directing the war effort. The armed forces resisted this civilian intrusion and, in so doing, precipitated a power struggle between the professional military and the executive branch, a struggle that not only severely strained the relations between the Moneda and its officers but also complicated, and perhaps prolonged, the War of the Pacific.

Chile's armed forces could not escape the decay which saps any peacetime military. The nation's army had not fought a foreign enemy since its 1838 confrontation with the Peruvian-Bolivian Confederation although twice, in 1851 and 1859, it had crushed abortive revolutions. But, until 1879, the army had abstained from participating in European-style war; instead it devoted its energies to pacifying the Indians in the south. Consequently most commanders, particularly those in the more technical services, lacked training. Many refused to remedy this lack of education, believing that "It was enough to be a Chilean soldier in order to conquer."[1] As Santa María subsequently noted, Chile triumphed in the War of the Pacific not because of its military leaders' expertise but "through Araucanian like assaults."[2]

Politics, in addition to inexperience, also complicated the conduct of the war. Many of the nation's senior officers had acquired their commands through favoritism or political connections, and, while perhaps astute in the *tertulia*, these men were unqualified for combat. Regrettably, the same political forces that had advanced some officers' careers insulated them from retaliation no matter how justified. Consequently, the government could not simply delegate its authority to the military; instead it had to become more intimately involved in the conduct of the war, first by creating new logistical infrastructures and then by formulating as well as implementing strategic policy. The Moneda's participation infuriated the professional officer corps who resisted the intrusion of civilians, causing a series of unseemly squabbles which not only tested Chile's institutions but also delayed the prosecution of the war. Thus, Pinto had to wage two struggles: one against the foreign enemy and the other against certain officers and their political allies in order to triumph.

This conflict between the generals and politicians over the direction of the war was epitomized by the term "Cucalon." Generally, when an individual's name emerges from the anonymity of history, it signifies an important event or perhaps the advent of a new intellectual movement. Antonio Cucalon, however, was a less than heroic figure: a Peruvian newspaper correspondent accompanying the *Huáscar* on one of its forays, he fell overboard during a high seas chase and drowned. Henceforth, the hapless journalist's name became synonymous with the amateur military strategists who filled Santiago's cafes, criticizing the direction of the various military or naval campaigns. Professional officers, as well as their devotees, applied the term to any civilian who dared either to meddle in the direction of the war or to censure the military's actions. Unfortunately, the clash between *cucalones* and *militares* began virtually from the onset of the war's first campaign.

THE GENERAL

Justo Arteaga Cuevas assumed command of Chile's expeditionary army when he had already passed his seventieth year. A professional soldier, he had also served numerous terms as a deputy in the legislature. Arteaga's star temporarily declined when he supported the losing side of the 1851 revolution. Fleeing Chile, he remained in exile until an 1857 amnesty permitted him to return. Four years later, the Pérez administration allowed him to resume his military career.

While he might have once been an active and aggressive officer, by the time Arteaga became general-in-chief, his mind had entered the antechamber to senility, senescence, where yesteryear is remembered more vividly than yesterday. Obsessed with minor details, he fell easily into the trap of false praise and suffered as well from a faulty memory. Predictably Arteaga had difficulty in deciding which objective—Ilo, Iquique, or Lima—he should attack.[3] Various civilian observers questioned if the officer possessed the commitment, "audacity, activity, or intelligence," to direct a long campaign: José Alfonso bluntly informed the president that his commanding general was insane.[4]

Normally, the Moneda would have dismissed Arteaga but the general's two sons, Domingo, a deputy, and Justo, the editor of the influential newspaper *Los Tiempos*, labored hard to protect their father from government retaliation. Privately, however, their parent's condition preoccupied them as well: Domingo, for example, suggested that the government assign only the best junior officers to Arteaga's staff, apparently believing that this tactic might protect the general from himself.[5]

Arteaga's associates and relatives also tried to shoulder some of his responsibilities. The family, for example, selected another son, Benjamín, as well as Pedro Nolasco Donoso, a friend, to accompany the general to Antofagasta. But these civilian aides proved inadequate to the task. Benjamín, for example, was described as "incompetent, lacking good judgment, [and] incapable of understanding the mission entrusted to his father, much less capable of implementing it" while Donoso proved equally maladroit.[6] Unfortunately for Pinto, Arteaga's sons demonstrated more skill in using information provided by their father to destabilize the Varas Ministry than in selecting the general's aides.[7]

Aware of Arteaga's limitations, but acutely sensitive to his political influence, the Moneda requested that José Francisco Vergara serve as Arteaga's aide. The civilian agreed but became disheartened when he discovered that his country's fate had been entrusted to "an old man whose intellectual faculties were in complete decay and whose presence of mind had never been famous anyway."[8]

Thus, for the first weeks of the war, Arteaga remained rooted in Antofagasta, employing his limited mental energies to invent reasons to excuse his inactivity. Observers attributed his sloth either to the general's anxiety or senescence. Regardless of its etiology, his failure to act threatened both Chile's security and the Varas ministry's stability.[9]

In June 1879, the Moneda sent Santa María north hoping that the civilian minister could convince Arteaga to carry the war to the enemy. After conferring with Rafael Sotomayor, Isidoro Errazuríz, and Vergara, Santa María requested that Arteaga convene a Council of War. The general demurred. He claimed that his officers refused to cooperate with civilians and, furthermore, stated that army regulations did not recognize the legitimacy of such a meeting. At Santa María's insistence, Arteaga agreed to confer with the Moneda's delegates although he lampooned the gathering. The conference, which began on 24 June, became a marathon event during which Arteaga characteristically seemed incapable of deciding what target the army should attack.

After a week, Santa María returned to Santiago with mixed news: although Arteaga had promised to attack Tarapacá, the minister no longer had any confidence in his capacity to direct such a campaign. The Moneda also doubted the general's ability but, succumbing to the pressure of Arteaga's sons, nevertheless allowed him to retain his command. The government, however, granted Rafael Sotomayor greater power in hopes that he could get the war moving. Santa María had planned to return to the north to explain the new situation to Arteaga when the general suddenly resigned his command. While some civilians urged Santa María to cajole the general into remaining, Vergara was delighted. The general, he claimed, had delayed the war and had threatened to divide the army into two warring camps. His resignation, therefore, solved the Moneda's political problems while ridding the army of deadwood. Accept the resignation, he urged, before the general relented. Santa María agreed, apparently believing that Arteaga, in a rare moment of lucidity, had recognized his own incompetence and wished to abandon his post before he harmed his *patria*.[10]

Not all Chileans rejoiced when the general departed. Roberto Souper, a National Guard officer, complained that the *cucalones* had hounded his beloved leader from office in order to replace him with someone more malleable. *Los Tiempos* argued that Santa María's meddling and the

Moneda's refusal to provide sufficient equipment, ammunition, and troops, not Arteaga's age, had prevented the general from attacking the north.[11] These complaints did not convince *La Patria*, which seemed delighted that Arteaga had resigned.[12] The general arrived in Santiago in mid-July where a few friends, including various high ranking members of the military, awaited him. Pinto sent an official delegate as well as a government coach which the general refused.[13] This act may have been Arteaga's last public gesture: he died almost three years to the day that he returned from his last campaign.

Arteaga personified Clemanceau's dictum that war was too serious to be left to the generals. On the other hand, the former field commander was physically as well as mentally incapable of overseeing such a massive undertaking; thus forcing the Moneda to intervene. Perhaps civilian involvement was inevitable: the war, after all, outstripped the nation's resources and administrative abilities to cope, but Arteaga's failures clearly opened the way for Santiago to assume the direction of the war. The Moneda's instrument was Rafael Sotomayor who represented more than the government's eyes and ears: he became the military's super ego. Unfortunately, the Arteaga episode would not be the last confrontation between civilian and military authorities during the War of the Pacific.

THE ADMIRAL

Pinto also had to contend with the navy in the person of its commander, the powerful Admiral Juan Williams Rebolledo. The son of a British naval officer who had participated in Chile's war for independence, Williams had served in the fleet since 1844. During the otherwise disastrous 1865 fiasco, he distinguished himself by breaking the Spanish blockade and capturing the *Covadonga*. But while Williams had successfully terrorized the enemy squadron in the 1860s, a decade and a half of peace had sapped his strength and eroded his judgment but not his ego.

Williams decided to blockade Iquique, arguing that he lacked adequate supplies and ships to attack Callao. Yet even after the Moneda remedied these deficiencies, the admiral discovered other causes for inaction: the crew's health had deteriorated; coal supplies still remained inadequate. Consequently, Williams's flotilla loitered in Iquique's harbor, a temporary haven for homeless barnacles. The admiral periodically unleashed his ships to attack unarmed loading facilities at Pica and Huanillos but these sorties generally failed to impress the Peruvians. One raid on Pisagua, for example, slaughtered three women, one infant, and an unidentified Asian while injuring only a few stray soldiers.[15]

Eventually the press began questioning Williams's abilities. Fearful of alienating the public and thus destroying his budding political career, the admiral launched his ill fated sortie on Callao. This expedition not only accomplished nothing positive, it jeopardized Chile's northern coastal cities; indeed, only Prat's heroism and Condell's luck prevented the Peruvian ironclads from ravaging the undefended littoral.[16]

Evidence indicates that Williams never intended to attack the *Huáscar* and *Independencia*. An English merchant marine officer had informed the admiral that Grau had already left Callao for Arica. This news must have delighted the Chilean officer because it offered him a painless way to resuscitate his faltering career.[17] In 1865, Williams had become a hero by his daring raids on the Spanish fleet and in 1879, he hoped to regain his popularity by appearing to assault Peru's naval bastion of Callao. The fates, however, did not prove cooperative. Prat's heroic death and the sinking of the *Independencia* accentuated the futility of Williams's foray. The press, moreover, questioned the issue of the admiral's competence, wondering how he could have left only two weak wooden shells to maintain the blockade of Iquique.[18] The government did not have to wonder about Williams's performance: it knew that the admiral had "attacked" Callao secure in the knowledge that his supposed targets had already sailed.[19]

The Moneda, however, dared not dismiss Williams. Many of the junior officers, perhaps remembering the officer's salad days, still revered the admiral. More significantly, the Conservative Party was considering nominating him as its candidate for president in 1881. Since any mistake would ruin Williams's potential political career, the Conservatives worked hard to protect their candidate's reputation. They feted him, for example, at a special banquet and Carlos Walker Martínez defended the admiral in a parliamentary debate, forcing Varas to state openly his confidence in Williams. Varas, of course, did not trust the admiral, but he could ill afford to cause a political crisis. So he affirmed his support of the fleet's commander although he refused to publish any statement in the official newspaper, claiming that it was absurd to use the press to squelch rumors. Consequently, although various government officials privately yearned to dismiss Williams for awhile, at least, the admiral's political connections buffered him from the Moneda's wrath.[20]

Williams's relations with his colleagues, however, began to deteriorate. The army, which depended upon the fleet for resupply and protection, became disgusted and frightened because of Williams' treatment of Arteaga as well as his indecisiveness. The civilian administrators appeared equally discontented. Sotomayor, who once supported Williams, realized that the admiral would not abandon his policies even after the campaign had proved them bankrupt. Not surprisingly, relations between Williams and his advisor degenerated, particularly after Sotomayor warned the Moneda that he could no longer protect the admiral against his own poor judgment. The naval officer's political connections and his continued popularity in the fleet, however, forced the government to tolerate him. Williams was aware of the situation and coyly threatened to resign. Ironically, the government could not accept his offer because Varas had no one to replace him. Simpson, despite his repeated promises to abstain, remained besotted with drink while the abstemious Luis Goñi lacked supporters in the fleet.[21] So the ministry remained wedded to Williams in an intensely unhappy but politically convenient marriage.

While Grau ravaged Chile's coastal shipping, Williams retired to his bed chamber where he dedicated his efforts, not to devising a strategy to defeat Peru but to gargling in hopes of healing an ulcerated throat. When the admiral did pursue the *Huáscar*, it was always to no avail, thus lowering the fleet's morale while outraging the public which correctly believed that Chile, not Peru, should control the sealanes.[22]

Williams the sea wolf had become toothless. A former comrade-in-arms from the 1865 war described the admiral as palsied, old in appearance, irrational, and reeking of drink. In order to explain his often bizarre behavior, some critics claimed that he suffered from syphilis. Williams, for example, developed a phobia about torpedoes and ordered his squadron to break off the blockade in order to ride out the dark hours on the high seas where he could avoid a possible enemy attack. Once, incorrectly believing that the enemy had dared to attack his ships—an act which he apparently considered in poor taste—he ordered the fleet to bombard Iquique.[23]

The public's hostility toward his inept policies eventually induced Williams to alter his strategy. The same officer, who earlier had insisted on maintaining the naval quarantine, now yearned to abandon the blockade of Iquique. And so, acting without government permission, he unilaterally ordered his ships to sail for the south. He reached Antofagasta on 4 August but this time the Conservatives could not save the admiral. Infuriated by his insubordination, the Moneda ordered Williams to Santiago to explain his conduct; however, even the impervious admiral could discern his fate. Rather than suffer public humiliation, he resigned his command on 12 August 1879.[24]

The antigovernment press made the fallen officer a martyr, blaming Williams's failures on the government's refusal to provide adequate supplies and sturdy ships. "Now one must not only die like a lion, he must also be able to overcome material disadvantages. Thus is the administration of the Moneda." Even *Los Tiempos*, which earlier had sided with Arteaga in his disputes with the navy, defended Williams, stating that "It is cruel, even odious, that today Admiral Williams . . . should be called to account and be subjected to the verdict of judges who have not exposed even a hair of providential heads."[25] Like Arteaga, he arrived at Santiago's train station where his crestfallen supporters awaited him. Carlos Walker Martínez, his parliamentary champion, even sent his carriage which carried the admiral into retirement but not obscurity.[26]

The admiral's resignation did not, as expected, convulse the fleet. Indeed, Eulojio Altamirano even reported that many Chileans believed that Williams's time had come. In order to avoid political problems within the fleet, the civilian attaché urged the government to replace Williams with another professional officer, nominating Captain Galvarino Riveros over the more senior Admiral Goñi because of the latter's poor health.[27]

THE MILITARY'S NEMESIS: RAFAEL SOTOMAYOR

The conflicts, first with Arteaga and then Williams, demonstrated to Pinto that his professional military lacked the skills to direct the war. Since the president could not personally assume command of the land and naval campaigns, he decided to entrust this awesome task to Rafael Sotomayor. A former intendant, Sotomayor was a financier, a Montt Varista deputy, and a minister in the administrations of Manuel Montt and Pinto. Originally sent north to convince Williams that he should attack Callao, Sotomayor remained in the war zone as the government's delegate to the army and the navy. As relations with the military soured, the Moneda increased its dependence on him. In July, the Council of Ministers elevated Sotomayor to the status of *Comisario General de Gobierno*, endowing his orders with the same authority as if "they emanated from the president." A month later, Sotomayor became Chile's first *Ministro de Guerra y Marina en Campaña*, apparently the equivalent of the minister of the war in the field. While legal purists complained that Pinto had overstepped his authority by creating a post not specifically authorized by the 1833 Constitution, the government's partisans claimed that Pinto possessed the implied power to delegate his executive authority to whomever he wished.[28]

Historically, and consistent with the prevailing laissez faire policy, the army had relied upon private contractors to provide it with food, equipment, and medical care. While perhaps adequate in peacetime, this system could not satisfy the needs of an army involved in a war, particularly a conflict located so far from the heartland of Chile. Thus the military had to establish its own logistical services. The newly created quartermaster and medical corps, however, intially functioned in an extremely inefficient manner. Consequently, Sotomayor assumed responsibility for feeding the armed forces, providing transportation and medical care, and distributing clothing, fuel, and equipment.[29]

Because of the ineptitude of the armed forces, Sotomayor's involvement in the war became less logistical and more military. He not only helped plan the strategy which permitted Chile to capture the *Huáscar*, he also organized and supplied the elements which invaded Pisagua as well as supervised the landing. It was largely at his behest that Escala ordered the artillery to Dolores where it arrived just in time to permit the Chileans to triumph. Sotomayor, moreover, established the provisional government which administered the newly captured Tarapacá. After a careful analysis Sotomayor concluded that the army's organizational structure did not function well in a desert setting. Thus, over the strenuous objections of Escala, he divided the expeditionary force into four divisions, each to contain units from all three combat arms, plus an army of reserve. Following the successful landing at Ilo, Sotomayor personally reconnoitered Moquegua's valley. In early April, he ordered the fleet to blockade Callao in anticipation of another invasion of the north.[30]

Sotomayor did not enjoy his role as strategist. The work exhausted him and his daughter Virginia, who lay dying in Chile, repeatedly begged him to return home so they could spend her last hours together. Sadly Sotomayor refused: he desperately wanted to go but "no one else will take any initiative in the indispensable tasks." So, Virginia died alone while her father mourned her passing in the arid north. Sotomayor also suffered financial problems: he owed substantial sums of money to his creditors who unpatriotically dunned him to pay up while the navy, still smarting over his intervention in its affairs, charged him two pesos a day for the rations he consumed while he remained on board a warship directing the campaign.[31]

Initially, the public reserved most of its ill will for Varas and Santa María, describing the latter as a lawyer who capriciously ruined the careers of professional officers. After Santa María became minister of the interior, however, Sotomayor emerged from the shadows to share the wrath of the opposition. Indeed, the minister became one of the major targets of the anti-government press which deliberately ignored the logistical problems confronting Sotomayor in order to pillory him for failing to press the war more vigorously.[32] These attacks became increasingly bitter and personal. It was alleged, for example, that Pinto retained Sotomayor in his post because the president owed money to the minister's bank or that he was grooming him to be his presidential successor. Predictably, the Conservative party became the most virulent, elevating Sotomayor to the rank of "Supreme Cucalon" and blaming him for "all the mishaps endured and the tears spilled." Not even the death of the minister's daughter provided a brief respite as Benjamín Vicuña Mackenna complained that Sotomayor spent too much time grieving and too little fighting.[33]

DEFENDER OF THE FAITH: ERASMO ESCALA

The ungracious remarks of the press did not vex Sotomayor as much as did General Erasmo Escala, Arteaga's replacement. A graduate and former director of the Escuela Militar, and a veteran of all of Chile's wars, the general nonetheless inspired little confidence. Santa María, for example, considered him oversensitive, violent, and irascible although, unlike his predecessor, Escala was at least combative. Although the minister recognized the danger of installing a man with such potent political connections at the head of the expeditionary forces, he hoped that the "clumsy" officer's aggression, if properly directed, would prove beneficial to the motherland. However, Escala's difficult personality and declining health quickly exhausted the government's goodwill. By early 1880, Santa María described his general-in-chief as "incapable of commanding an expedition," and urged the Moneda to accept Escala's resignation if he should ever offer it.[34]

A variety of other problems limited the general's efficiency. Escala became obsessed with minutiae, responding more swiftly to a private's complaint than a minister's entreaty. In March 1880, Colonel Francisco Barceló ordered one of his men lashed one hundred times for having discharged his weapon under dangerous circumstances. When the potential victim appealed to Escala, the general not only reduced the soldier's punishment but punished Barceló by temporarily relieving him of his command. This act both humiliated the colonel and caused administrative problems in Barceló's unit. Predictably, various military commanders objected to Escala's actions which, they claimed, undermined their authority.[35]

On a higher level, Sotomayor lamented the general's unfortunate habit of heeding the counsel of the last individual who spoke to him. Particularly vexing were Escala's confessor and a ubiquitous Colombian Lieutenant Colonel named Zubiría. The latter inflated the general's flaccid ego, manipulated his sense of inferiority, and played on his paranoia, thus encouraging him not to cooperate either with his military subordinates or Sotomayor. Escala, for example, communicated with his chief of staff only in writing although both men shared the same encampment. Obviously, these personality problems complicated the conduct of the war, leading one old soldier to note that "Whoever had served with Bulnes,

Aldunate, and Cruz cannot sit and wait for the present [situation] to end."[36]

Despite his defects, the Moneda had no viable alternative to Escala: José Villagrán had antagonized too many of his brother officers when he became involved in a squabble over a promotion; Basilio Urrutia, although willing to serve, if Escala resigned voluntarily, was too ill to assume command of the army. Thus, while Sotomayor despised Escala, he concluded, as did various members of the government, that replacing him might prove politically disastrous. Hence the Moneda remained tied to Escala and naively hoped that he might either still be restrained or that he would perhaps resign because of ill health.[37]

The government increasingly relied on José Francisco Vergara to act as Escala's military superego, particularly when relations between the general and Sotomayor degenerated.[38] "Do not leave the general's side," begged Santa María, "you have to be the soul of his soul." Unfortunately, Vergara was not Escala's nanny. Thus, he could not prevent the general's clumsy attack on Moquegua or his failure to equip properly Baquedano's troops.[39]

The Conservative party, eager to protect Escala so he could run as its presidential candidate in the 1881 elections, blamed the general's failures on the government's niggardliness and Sotomayor's meddling. Predictably, the liberal journals disagreed and described Escala as a religious fanatic whose outmoded tactics had squandered Chilean lives and dissipated the chances for victory. Noting Escala's tendency to be absent from each of the war's important battles, one newspaper remarked: "At Pisagua, his cloudy destiny took him to Junín; at Dolores, it kept him at Hospicio; at Tarapacá, it called him to Iquique, and today, where will it lead him?"[40]

Escala's inactivity, his reluctance, if not his open resistance to reorganizing the army, and his growing unpopularity within the army as well as his poor relations with Sotomayor alienated the Moneda. Not without reason did Sotomayor declare that keeping Escala under control required more skill than defeating the enemy. But, insulated by his political allies and enjoying some residue of popularity, Escala's position appeared impregnable.[41]

Ironically, Escala lost his command over an unrelated event. Colonel Pedro Lagos, a close friend of Barceló, had earlier denounced Escala for intervening when Barceló had disciplined his wayward soldier. This protest occurred just as Lagos and Escala had argued over former's responsibilities as chief of staff. Escala, infuriated by Lagos's earlier refusal to abase himself before the general, wished to humiliate his subordinate. The general petulantly ordered that Lagos should be denied the use of the telegraph unless he first received Escala's approval. This step, Escala reasoned, would prevent the colonel from communicating with his subordinates and would place him under the general's control. Lagos, furious at this petty act, resigned, citing a variety of Escala's errors including the looting of Mollendo.[42]

Escala refused to accept Lagos's resignation, preferring to use it as an excuse for trying him before a military court. Sotomayor, tired of seeing his commanding general occupied in such a sterile issue, ordered Lagos to Santiago, an act which enraged Escala who feared that Lagos would escape his jurisdiction and hence avoid any possible punishment. Furious, Escala then telegraphed his resignation to the Moneda. The general, however, quickly repented this act, retracting his resignation on the condition that he be permitted to sail south to discuss the war with Pinto. In the interim, Sotomayor had traveled to Iquique where, for the first time, he could use the telegraph system to inform the Moneda about the situation in the north without the general's knowledge. Acquainted with Sotomayor's view, Santiago granted Escala permission to depart for the capital for consultations. Once the officer was on the high seas, the Moneda accepted his resignation.[43] Escala arrived in Santiago stripped of his command and, despite the distribution of a handbill inviting people to meet the general at the train station, virtually unheralded.[44]

Escala's supporters predictably blamed the general's resignation on Sotomayor and on a government which deliberately dismissed all victorious generals "like a useless and forgotten piece of furniture," to ensure that no military leader would emerge to challenge the civilian politicians.[45] Others, however, rejoiced, delighted that the maladroit warrior, "whose ghastly service record . . . is a terrible rosary of blunders and folly," no longer commanded the nation's expeditionary force.[46]

THE SECOND SOTOMAYOR: JOSÉ FRANCISCO VERGARA

A few diehards hoped that the Moneda might permit the general to return to his command in the north but Escala passed onto the inactive list. He subsequently ventured into public life only to defend the Church from the religious reforms of the Santa María government. A month before the signing of the armistice with Bolivia, Escala died, "the victim," wrote the still loyal *El Independiente*, "of emotions and passions." Among his pallbearers was Colonel Barceló.[47]

Finding a replacement for Escala proved almost as complicated as prising the general from his command. Santa María favored Urrutia because he was willing to work with Vergara and Sotomayor and because he "was valiant and respected in the army."[48] Pinto and Sotomayor, on the other hand, supported Villagrán although they recognized that certain factions in the army opposed him as did Altamirano, who seriously doubted his loyalty and candor.[49]

Filling the vacancy for the chief of staff position also vexed the Moneda. Pinto had originally wished to select Vergara but, recognizing that the professional officers would not accept a *cucalon*, nominated Villagrán to head the general staff. Eventually the government chose Baquedano to command the expeditionary forces and Villagrán to act as his deputy.[50]

Within a month after Escala's fall from power, Sotomayor succumbed to a stroke. Even death, which generally makes the ungenerous relent, did not temper the hostility of the Conservative press which blamed Sotomayor for destroying two of their party's potential candidates. While gracelessly acknowledging Sotomayor's contributions to the war, *El Estandarte Católico* still steadfastly denied that he possessed the legal right to demand the military's obedience. *El Independiente* acted only slightly more graciously, when it agreed that finding another man with Sotomayor's skills would be difficult. Unlike its Conservative colleague, the newspaper advocated that a civilian, not an officer, succeed Sotomayor although it insisted that his powers be limited solely to advising the military.[51]

The death of Sotomayor did not end the rivalry between the *cucalones* and the *militares*. The struggle continued; only the protagonists changed. Another civilian, José Francisco Vergara, succeeded don Rafael. A former editor of *El Deber* as well as a deputy, Vergara first participated in the war as Arteaga's aide and later served as Escala's secretary. Although he liked Escala personally, he nevertheless described him as an affable fool, endowed with a "brain incapable of generating or even of receiving the most elementary idea." Generals, of course, do not have to be philosophers but Vergara also considered Escala an incompetent on military matters. At the battle of San Francisco, for example, Escala happily unfurled a banner of Our Lady of Carmen, proclaiming that it "had given us victory." Vergara, a Mason, demurred: "We owe more to our valour and our bayonets than what this good image can do for us," and then unsuccessfully urged the general to "attack quickly and vigorously" the fleeing enemy.[52]

Vergara, who held a commission in the National Guard and who had studied military history, actively participated in the war. He landed with the troops at Pisagua and explored the Peruvian interior, performing so well that Escala promoted him to the rank of lieutenant colonel, and appointed him to serve as Martiano Urriola's chief of staff. Vergara fought at the battles of San Francisco and Tarapacá. Indeed, disappointed because he was blamed for that ill-fated expedition, Vergara retired from the army in December 1879.

His respite proved short. Pinto begged Vergara to return to the front, claiming that Chile needed him to restore peace to the army of the north. The president had not exaggerated: when Vergara arrived he discovered that Escala and Sotomayor rarely spoke to each other but instead communicated through an intermediary. Vergara's job was to moderate the hostility which existed between the two men.[53] This task proved extremely arduous because Vergara did not always agree with Sotomayor. He considered Rafael's brother, Colonel Emilio Sotomayor, a lunatic and had urged the minister to dismiss him from the army. Vergara also felt alienated because the regular officers, resenting a civilian intruding into their affairs, referred to him as "cucalon." Although Vergara managed to charm Escala, by March he reported that he could not counteract the influence of Escala's coterie and urged the Moneda relieve the general of his command.[54]

Initially it appeared that Baquedano would prove more willing to work with civilians than Escala. Indeed, once reassured of the Moneda's support, the general cooperated with Sotomayor and Vergara. The relationship became a virtual love feast when the Moneda ordered Colonel Zubiría to Santiago.[55] But Sotomayor's death complicated the situation. Vergara, who following Escala's resignation had been elevated to the rank of commander of the cavalry, seemed a likely candidate to replace the fallen civilian. After all, *El Ferrocarrilito* indiscreetly observed, Escala was "an impossible general,"; Baquedano "maims Spanish" (apparently the general suffered from a speech impediment); Villagrán cannot say anything "which does not result in zero," while Urrutia "is crippled by rheumatism."[56] The only one left, therefore, was Vergara. Pinto, however, feared Vergara's impetuosity while political pressure within his cabinet forced the Moneda to divide the responsibility for directing the war among Vergara, Baquedano, and Velásquez.[57]

A triumvirate could not rule the empire of Rome and it proved equally incapable of administering the army of Chile. Baquedano slyly abolished the post of head of the cavalry thus leaving Vergara with his rank but no one to command. This petty act infuriated Vergara and led to increasingly frigid relations with Baquedano and Velásquez. While planning the attack on Tacna, Vergara had advocated an enveloping movement which, he argued, would not only defeat the enemy but also seal off his escape routes. Baquedano, a devotee of the *panache et gloire* school, preferred his usual frontal assault. Lamentably, Vergara proved quite prescient: although the Chileans triumphed at Tacna, the enemy again managed to retreat with many of its units intact. Outraged because Baquedano's victory at Tacna proved so costly, Vergara resigned his commission. The civilian could not remain on the sidelines: in July 1880, Pinto, with Santa María's support, appointed him minister of war.

The nomination aroused mixed responses. Some praised his selection, predicting that Vergara would rejuvenate the army and avoid many of the mistakes of the professional military. While many knew of the rift between the civilian minister and the generals, Vergara's supporters believed that these stories were exaggerated; the regulars would not, they argued, resent his occupying the post of minister of war. This prediction rang hollow. Máximo Lira wrote Pinto that both Baquedano and Velásquez loathed his candidate because of his unkind remarks about Tacna. Should Vergara become minister, Lira prophecized, not only the two generals but numerous artillery officers as well would resign. The public reaction proved equally depressing.[58] One critic alleged that the Moneda had selected Vergara in order to persecute the officer corps; another blamed Vergara for the disaster at Tarapacá, claiming that Chile triumphed at Tacna precisely because the military had ignored his advice, concluding that the civilian's presence spelled "misfortune and his absence a guarantee of success."[59]

Despite these complaints, and some heated congressional debates, Vergara became minister of war. Appalled by the army's lack of logistical support and inadequate transport system, Vergara worked long hours to remedy these defects. In October, after serving as Chile's delegate to the Arica peace conference, Vergara remained in the war zone, acting as *ministro de guerra en campaña*, formulating strategy.[60]

Whether in Santiago or the north, Vergara encountered difficulties. The navy's supporters claimed that the civilian official had slighted Condell, when he questioned the latter's stay in the capital on sick leave. "There is nothing more irritating to the heart than the ingratitude found today permeating the salons of the Moneda."[61] Vergara's relations with the army seemed equally uncongenial. Theoretically the minister should have fared better: he had, after all, shared the hardships of the earlier campaigns and had led troops in battle; moreover, he liked Baquedano, supporting him over Villagrán to command the army. Vergara's criticism of Baquedano's conduct of the battle of Tacna, however, had poisoned their relations; henceforth the men clashed on almost every issue. When Vergara requested that Baquedano dispatch his men for the north, the general threatened to resign. By December 1880, Baquedano warned Pinto that "where they fight only I command."[62]

The etiology of this conflict apparently goes deeper than mere pique over Vergara's version of the battle of Tacna. Altamirano noted that

Baquedano was paranoid, an attitude presumably cultivated by his civilian aide, Máximo Lira. A covey of admirers assured Baquedano that as the victorious general he would easily succeed Pinto to the presidency. Trying to control the general, Altamirano informed Baquedano that the officer who captured Lima would win the Moneda as well. The civilian attaché hoped that this prize would keep the general amenable if not tranquil for the rest of the war.[63] Unfortunately, Altamirano's strategy failed: the once humble warrior—the man who lived the spartan life, who used to breakfast simply in Santiago's *mercado central* at dawn—discovered his own grandeur. "His head is weak," wrote Altamirano, "his brain is small, and his glory has confused it." Riveros proved almost as difficult, challenging Vergara's authority.[64]

The fall of Lima did not sweeten the relationship. Vergara, arguing that Chile could ill afford to maintain a large military establishment and anxious to return the troops to their peacetime labors, wished to reduce the size of the army and the navy. A furious Baquedano stated that he would disobey any order which would strip his command of a single unit. Vergara, apparently willing to force the issue of who commanded in the north, ordered General Velásquez and his staff to sail to Arica where he wished them to draw up plans for an expedition on Arequipa.[65]

The minister did not randomly select Velásquez and his artillerymen. Soon after Lima's capture, a group of civilians and officers, including Velásquez, had dined in the Hotel Maury. Following the meal, one of the officers toasted Baquedano. A civilian, Adolfo Carrasco Albano, suggested that Vergara also merited a share of the credit for Chile's victory. Most of the participants either refused to drink to Vergara's health or insulted him for depreciating the role of the artillery during the battle of Tacna. Thus Velásquez provided Vergara with a particularly attractive choice for retaliation.[66]

The minister ordered Velásquez and his staff south a second time, noting specifically that he acted in the name of President Pinto. Baquedano again refused, claiming that he would not allow himself to be used to avenge Vergara's injured ego. Stating that the Moneda would have to choose between its minister or general, Vergara requested that Pinto reduce the size of the army, either disband the fleet or strip Riveros of his command, and finally delineate exactly the functions of both the general in chief as well as the *ministro de guerra en campaña*. Vergara warned that he was prepared to return to Santiago if Baquedano remained in Lima but the ultimatum proved unnecessary. Pinto sided with his minister, ordering the fleet to Valparaíso and giving Baquedano the choice of remaining in the north or returning to Chile with those units which were to be demobilized. The general, as Pinto predicted, accepted repatriation, leaving Vergara the master of the north.[67]

In April 1881, Vergara journeyed to Santiago to assume his post as minister of war. Some Chileans welcomed the civilian home, praising his contribution to the war effort and describing him as a selfless citizen who had galvanized an inert military into action. Others used the opportunity to attack Baquedano whose "disastrous plan for Chorillos and the great military confusion of Miraflores" had uselessly sacrificed Chile's soldiers.[68] Baquedano's boosters responded by arguing that only the general's presence had prevented Vergara from destroying the army and the navy. The anonymous "Colo Colo" alleged that Vergara had returned to Santiago to orchestrate the military's intervention in the forthcoming presidential election when the army would intimidate or even shoot those workers who wished to honor Baquedano.[69]

THE PRESIDENTIAL ELECTION OF 1881

Politics became an increasingly important factor in the relations of the Moneda and its military. Baquedano, it appeared, did not leave Lima simply over a policy disagreement with Vergara. Just after the Peruvian capital had fallen, Altamirano reported that the Conservatives, in conjunction with the Echaurrenista Liberals, had offered to nominate Baquedano for president. "Poor General," observed Altamirano, "they are going to do him a disservice with this. He could have returned home to universal applause and now, they are going to force half the nation to insult him."[70]

Altamirano's predictions rang true. Baquedano accepted the Conservative offer and his entry into the presidential campaign of 1881 exacerbated the already strained relations between civil and military authorities. A professional soldier had not resided in the Moneda since Manuel Bulnes had ruled Chile from 1841 to 1851. Although officers occupied seats in the legislature, none had participated in a presidential contest since the largely symbolic effort of General José María de la Cruz thirty years earlier. Thus, Baquedano's decision to seek the presidency not only violated recent precedent, it also antagonized large sectors of the civilian population.

Baquedano, his opponents argued, might have been a splendid soldier but this attribute failed to qualify him to lead a nation at peace. Many feared that the general's admitted lack of political sophistication would prevent him from understanding the political, economic, and diplomatic problems confronting the nation.[71] The less generous worried that Baquedano would become a gullible dupe of "Conservative and cheap" politicians who wanted to exploit his reputation for their own "Machiavellian designs."[72]

Since the Conservatives sought to capitalize on Baquedano's military reputation, the Liberal opposition concluded that demonstrating the general's incompetence would short circuit his candidacy. Lamentably, Baquedano's opponents had ample evidence to demonstrate that he was either a lucky bumbler or worse, a callous butcher. Journals repeatedly attributed Baquedano's success not to his military skills but to the "energy, valor, and inimitable heroism of our glorious soldiers," and the assistance, if not tutelage, of Sotomayor and Vergara.[73] *La Patria*, for example, recited the rosary of Baquedano's supposed military exploits, claiming that all, with the exception of Arica, which Lagos directed, were characterized by a "lack of plan or direction." Chorillos emerged as a "strategic blunder" because Baquedano not only had failed to capture the fleeing enemy, but because he had lost control of some of his troops who looted the city, an act which stained Chile's military honor. Had the general but followed Maturana's plan, *El Corvo* argued, the army would have suffered 50 percent fewer casualties. Any man whose errors caused 5,000 homes to be draped in mourning did not deserve the presidency.[74]

Eventually the political campaign focused not on Baquedano's war record but on the fear that he might militarize the nation. Chile, Baquedano's foes averred, owed its success to its democratic and essentially civilian institutions.[75] Bulnes might have served the nation well in the 1840s but the country had changed. Electing Baquedano in 1881 would empower a caudillo who would convert the nation into a barracks, substitute personal caprice for the rule of law, and infect Chile with the the same cancer of militarism which had so devastated Peru and Bolivia.[76] The opposition revived the question of Baquedano's mistreatment of *El Mercurio*'s correspondent, not it noted, "a solid guarantee for public freedom." *El Ñuble* claimed that the general's election would signal a return to slavery, an end to education for the working class, restrictions on political activity, and the suffocation of freedom of thought.[77] Liberal Chileans simply could not trust that Baquedano would abjure dictatorial behavior and abide by civilian customs. To substantiate this allegation, some newspapers claimed that the general might call upon military colleagues to intervene in the election.[78]

Portions of the nation believed that the general's military career had so insulated him from political life that they doubted that he understood how the government functioned. Thus, they feared that if confronted with a complicated problem President Baquedano would seek the counsel either of men who wished to restore clerical influence or his military cronies.[79] Others described Baquedano as the stalking horse of a Conservative-ultramontane clique, "the black militia and the party of the soutanne," who would use the general to usher in a new age of intolerance.[80]

Opposition newspapers often described the general as a representative of the Pelucon aristocracy or the Santiago oligarchy and happily noted that Baquedano refused to stop at a victory arch constructed in his honor by the workers of Santiago. This omission, they believed, clearly demonstrated that the general was simply the candidate of "the wealthy who have no popular mandate." Consequently, many urged the working class to repudiate the man who had so arrogantly disdained their attention, noting that Vergara, on the other hand, had accepted an honorary membership in a laborer's organization.[81]

The less genteel described the "candidate of the priest and the sword" as a balloon being inflated by a priest.[82] Some charged Baquedano with exploiting the dead hero Arturo Prat, an act they considered sacrilegious. Nor did the general's personal flaws escape mention. Baquedano apparently stuttered, an impediment which the tasteless *El Corvo* often lampooned, concluding that the ability to speak was the only characteristic which distinguished an animal from a man.[83] Aware that he would lose and doubtless wounded by the abuse, Baquedano withdrew from the presidential campaign. Many rejoiced, claiming that the general's decision to quit saved the Republic from a clerical military conspiracy. As its colleagues celebrated the triumph of the pen over the sword, *El Heraldo* hoped that other officers would learn from Baquedano to eschew politics and to concentrate instead on perfecting their military skills.[84]

Before Baquedano resigned, a group of his legislative devotees introduced a measure to strike a special medal in his honor and to promote their candidate to Captain General of the army, a rank heretofore bestowed only upon O'Higgins and Freire. Pinto had earlier submitted a somewhat less ambitious proposal to award Baquedano the salary and privileges of an officer commanding an expeditionary army. The general's supporters not only ridiculed Pinto's bill, they also wished to grant a special medal for Riveros in belated compensation for the Moneda's cavalier dismissal of that valiant sailor.[85]

José Balmaceda, obviously wishing to humiliate the general's promoters, berated them for rushing to honor Baquedano while forgetting the less exalted but still equally meritorious enlisted men. To rectify this oversight, he proposed the construction of a victory arch to sit astride Santiago's Alameda, which he wished to rename the Calle de Gloria. Atop the arch would stand the statues of Arturo Prat as well as other heroic figures. Angel Vicuña attacked Balmaceda's proposal, labeling it as yet another manifestation of the Moneda's hostility toward the military in general and toward Baquedano specifically. Not only had the government denigrated the army's contribution to the war, but alluding to the then ongoing election, it would have forced the military to "undertake a second campaign, not against the enemies of their motherland but, painful though it is to admit it, against the liberty of its citizens, against the most proud and prestigious leader who yesterday carried us to victory." Although Balmaceda withdrew his motion, his legislative colleagues still regarded the Conservative proposal excessive. The measure's advocates, likening Baquedano to General Wellington, unsuccessfully tried to force a vote. Instead, the Conservative backed measure passed to committee for additional study, a normal legislative procedure which Baquedano's boosters had tried to circumvent.

By the time the committee reported to the lower house, Baquedano had already quit the presidential race. Superficially its recommendation struck a balance between what the signatories considered the government's frugality and the legislature's fantasy. The committee awarded Baquedano the rank, salary, and privileges of a general commanding a field army as well as a medal to commemorate his triumph at Lima. The committee's members, at least half of whom supported Baquedano's abortive candidacy, also authorized the government to grant the general a prize of $100,000.

The last provision provoked the government's ire. Balmaceda objected to the cost of funding such largesse, complaining that it might set a precedent for other officers. Predictably the debate degenerated into a squabble between the general's patrons and the Moneda's followers. The legislature eventually revived Pinto's less ambitious measure which it passed after some quibbling. In a spasm of patriotic gratitude, the lower house granted Baquedano free postage as well as rail transport for life. The deputies also approved a similar measure which rewarded Riveros for his contributions. The Senate accepted the proposal but not until one member ungenerously carped that Baquedano's salary would be too high and that his travel as well as his postal privileges would cost the state too much money.[86]

THE 1881 MEMORIA

In 1881, Minister of War José Vergara issued his annual report to the legislature providing an overview on the condition of the miltary as well as his assessment of the recent conflict. Vergara noted that organizational problems in the army, an inadequate supply system as well as shortages of certain essential items, had hampered the final drive on Lima. These observations, while chaffing the professional military, paled beside Vergara's speculation that if Baquedano had outflanked Lima's defenses, as Maturana suggested, the nation would have saved some 2,000-3,000 lives. Vergara's *memoria* also defended his decision to demobilize partially the army and the fleet. The minister's report reopened the partially healed rift between the Moneda and the military. The civilians, it must be remembered, had insisted on reorganizing the army as well as creating a supply service. The minister not only emphasized this fact, but he offended Baquedano by openly attacking his sledge hammer tactics. Finally, Vergara reminded his readers that the oft lampooned *cucalones*, not the military, had directed the war. [87]

When the *memoria* appeared, *The Chilian Times* warned that since Chile had triumphed, "the less that is said about them [the various participants] the better."[88] This very sage advice unfortunately fell on deaf ears: Vergara's report instead unleashed a firestorm of controversy which predictably split along partisan lines. War, Zorobabel Rodríguez, argued, should be left to the soldiers; civilians merely "introduced into the military encampment the plague of politics, demoralization, discord, and internecine war."[89] Other anti-Vergara elements shrilly charged that the minister had slandered the regular officers in order to advance the political fortunes of his party or to indulge his apparently insatiable appetite for gratification.[90]

Vergara's motivations seem unclear. He subsequently admitted that he wished to demonstrate that the nation's civilian institutions and its ministers merited at least some small place in the sun of national adulation. Regardless of his intentions, Vergara managed to anatagonize almost every senior officer. Within months of the publication of his *memoria*, a wave of confessional literature inundated the nation. Ironically, it became a war by proxy for all but one of the various participants employed a literary champion to do their jousting.[91]

BAQUEDANO'S REVENGE

Predictably, the most offended officer was Baquedano who selected his former secretary, Máximo Lira, as his literary paladin. The civilian minister, Lira argued, had committed a multitude of sins: he protected antimilitary journalists, like Eloi Caviedes; he unfairly claimed credit for reforms instituted or proposed by Sotomayor; and, finally, he neglected his primary responsibility, that of providing the military with adequate logistical support, preferring instead to meddle in the conduct of the war.[92]

Although directed at Vergara, Lira's barbs struck instead the former president. Pinto fumed that Baquedano, contrary to his public statements, agreed to attack Lima only after both Vergara and the Moneda forced him to undertake this campaign. While Pinto did not vent his anger publically, Vergara proved less stoical: he retained Isidoro Errazuríz, editor of *La Patria* and a civilian who had served in the north as an advisor to the army, to respond. This proved a wise choice. The editor forcefully argued that without Sotomayor and Vergara, who had reorganized the military and created a supply system for the army of the north, the armed forces would never have been able to wage a war so far from Chile. Conversely, Baquedano was depicted as a butcher who uselessly sacrificed thousands of troops because of his penchant for attacking the enemy's center. "The General-in-Chief," Errazuríz concluded, "has acted according to the methods of seventeenth century physicians: bleed for all types of illnesses." [93]

THE PALADIN OF THE FLEET

While perhaps silencing Baquedano, Errazuríz would have to confront yet another opponent: Admiral Riveros. Vergara's report on the navy did not appear to be as provocative as his statements on the army. Nevertheless, the former fleet commander joined his military colleagues in criticizing Vergara's conduct of the war. Enlisting the services of Rafael Egaña, he published a book that sought to prove the importance of Riveros's contribution to Chile's maritime victories.[94]

Riveros provided his readers with a detailed litany of Vergara's sins of omission and commission. The minister, he alleged, had flaunted naval protocol and had ordered the fleet's units to various destinations without due regard for either their safety or their admiral's sensibilities. Vergara, he argued, should also bear the responsibility for the inept landing at Curayaco although the admiral generously allocated some of his opprobrium for Baquedano. It was also charged that Vergara demanded that his subordinates, including Riveros, follow his orders, a bizarre complaint from an officer who demanded the same obedience from his own men. The minister, the admiral continued, also meddled in the fleet's internal affairs, particularly in the disciplining of *Capítan de Fragata* Jorge Montt. Riveros, asserting that Montt had refused to provide an adequate explanation for certain activities, had ordered the junior officer confined to his room. Montt, employing some of his below deck language, refused, thus forcing the admiral to convene a court martial. Vergara indicated that he wanted a light sentence so that Montt could return to active duty as soon as possible. Believing that leniency would set a bad precedent, Riveros refused to heed Vergara's counsel. The minister, therefore, ordered Montt transferred to Valparaíso, out of the admiral's reach. Once in Chile, the authorities not only released Montt but promoted him as well, doubtless much to Riveros' acute displeasure.

Riveros published a second volume in order to prove he alone deserved the credit for capturing the *Huáscar* on 8 October 1879. Sotomayor's original plan had called for the flotilla, under the command of the admiral to push up from the south, drivng the enemy northward toward Latorre's squadron, which would catch the fleeing *Huáscar*. Riveros did not deny that Sotomayor had originated this strategy, but, he argued that it was fatally flawed. The minister had originally ordered Latorre's flotilla to station itself approximately fifty miles off of Mejillones. Riveros claimed that he suggested that the squadron move to within fifteen or twenty miles of the shore so that it could see the enemy more easily. As a consequence of this vital modification, Latorre's ships sighted the Peruvians and captured the *Huáscar*. Much to the admiral's ill concealed fury, Latorre had received the credit for modifying Sotomayor's plan and hence for the victory at Angamos. Riveros now demanded that Chile acknowledge his contribution although he somewhat ruefully admitted that he possessed no proof to support his allegations. He was sure, however, that there was a cabal at work, intent on depriving him, and parenthetically the entire navy, of the glory of Angamos.[95]

The admiral also became involved in a dispute over his conduct during the battle of 8 October, an issue which, for once, did not involve either Sotomayor or Vergara. Benjamín Vicuña Mackenna, whose pen often outdistanced his factual material, claimed that Riveros had arrived after the battle had started, that his ship handling had almost disastrous results, that he had unsuccessfully tried to ram the *Huáscar*, and finally that shells from the *Blanco Encalada* had accidentally struck Latorre's ship, the *Cochrane*.[96]

The admiral's hostility toward Latorre shriveled in comparison with his fury over Vicuña Mackenna's statements. Describing himself as the victim of unverified allegations, Riveros hinted that Latorre sought to blame the admiral for some of his own mistakes, for example, the attempted ramming of the Peruvian ironclad. Riveros also indicated that the *Cochrane* had violated naval etiquette by opening fire on the *Huáscar* first instead of waiting for the senior officer to initiate the hostilities. Somewhat incoherently, the admiral protested that even if a shell from his vessel had struck the *Cochrane*, it was not his fault because a ship's captain should not be responsible for the errors of his gun crews. Thus the admiral created a unique division of labor: he would claim only the successes of his command; the failures belonged to his subordinates. In his final literary non sequitur, the naval officer stated that even if all of Vicuña Mackenna's allegations were true, they still should not detract from his contributions to Chile's naval victories.[97]

Even prior to the publication of Vergara's *memoria* and Riveros' rejoinders, the admiral's popularity had waned. Some of the press had already noted that he had refused to promote Jorge Montt despite his splendid war record. While one paper admitted that it did not know the reason for this oversight, it suggested that Riveros should acknowledge Montt's heroism even if the junior officer had subsequently displeased his commander. The admiral also tarnished his image when he began dunning the Moneda for the prize money due him, as well as his crew, for the capture of various Peruvian naval and merchant vessels.[98] Riveros aggravated this situation when he subsequently asked for additional funds as a reward for the capture of the *Huáscar* and the *Pilcomayo*, a request which one newspaper labeled as "vulgar ambition."[99]

Most of Riveros's allegations appear to have been without foundation. The admiral, for example, was notorious for playing favorites, generally selecting men of lesser merit in preference to the most skilled officers who, he apparently believed, might then undermine his prestige. Consequently, Riveros ignored Latorre and actively persecuted Jorge Montt while placing his confidence in Manuel Thompson and Peña who, through impetuosity or simple incompetence, either died needlessly or endangered their commands.[100] The former fleet commander also failed to convince the nation that he had originated the navy's strategy at Angamos. The government's telegraph traffic, private correspondence, and the reports of eye witnesses all agreed that Latorre, not Riveros, suggested that the fleet move closer to the coast.[101] *La Epoca* even published some of these official documents, noting that they should suffice to "destroy the elegant but fragile structure which senor Riveros has constructed to serve as the temple of his glories." while the less strident *El Ferrocarril* sadly contrasted the publicity-hungry admiral with the dead Sotomayor whose only goal had been to serve silently but well the cause of Chile.[102]

Riveros fared no better at the hands of the Supreme Court which rejected the admiral's claim for prize money. The congress, Justice Ambrosio Montt noted, had already rewarded those men who had participated in that battle. The judge tartly observed that if the admiral wanted to make war into a business venture, he should bear the costs as well. Since the expenses easily exceeded the value of the ships he captured, Riveros deserved nothing.[103] The admiral did have one bit of luck: the issue of his ship's firing at and hitting the *Cochrane* faded away. This happy event occurred not because the charges lacked validity but because Latorre, apparently out of a sense of patriotism, decided to ignore the issue. Isidoro Errazuríz, who did not have to spend the rest of his life in the navy, felt no restraints about flaying Riveros by reviving the memory of a "certain 250-pound shell."[104]

THE RETURN OF WILLIAMS

Although the 1881 memoria did not even mention him, Admiral Williams Rebolledo nonetheless joined the chorus of maligned officers who published their memoirs in 1882. Apparently Williams reacted in this fashion because his principal antagonist, Rafael Sotomayor, had died. Thus, the admiral believed that he could vindicate his career without fear of reprisal.

Williams's accounts, syndicated in the national press, stressed one theme: Pinto, through his agent Sotomayor, had betrayed the admiral by issuing contradictory orders, by starving the fleet logistically, and by abandoning the naval commander when the government's ill conceived plans miscarried. Williams even complained that the enemy was uncooperative. Yet, when addressing certain specific issues, Williams, became enmeshed in his own deceit.

The admiral, for example, alleged that it was he who wanted to attack Callao at the onset of the war despite the evidence which indicated that the Moneda proposed this plan and that Williams had rejected in preference to blockading Iquique. Williams also tried to defend his abortive sally against Callao, arguing that the Moneda had specifically ordered him to undertake that mission. He forgot to mention that Santiago had originally made this request six weeks before the admiral decided to react. Williams also defended his decision not to attack the enemy vessels found lying at anchor in Peruvian harbor. The admiral, retrospectively citing the example of Manuel Thompson who died in February, 1880, after a shell from one of Arica's shore batteries struck his ship, concluded it would have been suicidal to attack ships protected by Callao's coastal cannons in May, 1879. Williams's explanation for abandoning the Iquique blockade also lacked foundation. The officer claimed that he had received only verbal instructions to terminate the quarantine and that he had refused to obey these orders until he received written confirmation. When these instructions did not arrive, he nonetheless departed for Antofagasta, citing damage to his ships and "other [unspecified] difficulties."

The admiral's articles went on to argue that he was the victim of a "well-directed" conspiracy engineered by "the parasites who surround the seat of power." When the capture of the *Rimac* threatened the government's safety, it threw the hapless commander to the mob, a fate he stoically endured in the name of a higher virtue: patriotism. Williams lacked only Golgotha to make his articles into a passion play. The admiral's Judas was Sotomayor who had betrayed him by concocting false tales to ruin the naval officer.[105]

Williams's literary efforts did not resurrect his career. Indeed, *El Ferrocarril* became incensed because he had defamed the dead Sotomayor. The admiral, it argued, would have served the nation better had he followed the civilian hero's advice, advice which proved more accurate than the naval officer's judgment. Apparently aware that he had erred by attacking the dead minister, Williams deleted the anti-Sotomayor passages from his book. The expurgated volume, however, still failed to impress the public.[106]

In large measure, these shrill, harpy-like attacks often misfired. The formerly pro-Baquedano *La Epoca* denounced Lira's attack on Vergara.[107] Another journal, while easily acknowledging the contributions of Baquedano and Riveros, could not understand why these men refused to share some of the glory with Vergara or why they became so angered by the latter's *memoria* which, it noted, merely reflected his perspective on the war. After comparing the various rebuttals, the newspaper concluded that Vergara did indeed merit the nation's gratitude and that his opponents had indulged in avoidable petty feuds.[108] A Santiago journal predicted that when passions cooled "the figure of the minister will be distinguished as the only man who comprehended the extent of that tremendous undertaking and who beforehand would have tried to remove the difficulties and problems which have limited its implementation."[109] Certainly Vergara's reputation did not seem to suffer. A meeting was held in Valparaíso's Teatro Nacional where various speakers praised him as a civilian willing to sacrifice his interests on behalf of the war.[110]

CONCLUSION

Vergara's *memoria* constituted the final skirmish between the military and civilians over the war issue. Each side fervently claimed that it alone should rightfully take the credit for leading Chile to victory. In a sense, both were correct: clearly the professional military and navy officers had directed those campaigns which resulted in triumph. Just as obviously, however, without civilians, like Vergara and Sotomayor, who created and operated the logistical system, the military could not have absorbed the new recruits, equipped them, transported them to the war zone, or supplied their needs once they reached the front.

Unfortunately, the professional military had not recognized the changing nature of warfare. Armies could no longer live off the land, particularly a land so bleak as the northern nitrate deserts. Henceforth, logistics would prove almost as important as valor to win a war. Through no fault of their own, moreover, the army and the navy were unprepared for a conflict. Economic hardship had reduced their budgets; the army's traditional mission—keeping the Indians at bay—did not prepare it for a modern war; and administrative sclerosis had ossified the military establishment, ensuring that the most political and often the least competent would retain their posts. Chile, in 1879, resembled France on the eve of its conflict with Prussia or the United States prior to the Spanish-American War: a nation whose armed forces were not only unprepared for war but which were also unready to fight the type of struggle they would have to wage.

Normally, once aware of the nature of the military conflict, the armed forces would have replaced their least efficient members with new leaders. This is what happened to the Union Army and might have happened in France had the Prussians not crushed Napoleon so quickly. Unfortunately, this personnel change did not transpire in Chile because the officers who should have been dismissed used their political connections to protect their careers. Thus, the Moneda had no choice but to intervene: first to provide the technical support the armed forces required but could not generate from their existing bureaucracy, and then, in order to give direction to the various campaigns when the high command had demonstrated its lack of skill. Had the military contained a highly trained officer corps capable of providing logistical services, civilians might not have intervened. The Chilean armed forces, however, could not meet alone the challenge of the war, forcing the government to become more intimately involved, and thus precipitating the struggle between the *cucalones* and the *militares*.

It is not surprising that Santa María also instituted a program to reform the armed forces deciding, with ample justification, to enshrine Prussian military dogma as the Chilean army's new religion. While this program represented a commitment to ensuring Chile's dominance over the Pacific Basin, the president might also have believed that a domesticated and professional military would not pose the same problems for his successor as it did during the War of the Pacific.

4

The Pen and the Sword

> Military men are the scourge of the world.
> Guy de Maupassant
>
> Dedicated to work and to a productive peace Chile showed the face of a hardworking people.
> "Preliminares del gran día."
> J. Arroyo

The Chilean armed forces did not gracefully accept civilian domination. Indeed, as the earlier chapter demonstrated, the professional officers unsuccessfully attempted to direct the various campaigns without consulting the Moneda. Regrettably, the military's disdain for civilians also extended to Chile's laws. Rather than respect the nation's legal institutions, the officer corps cavalierly attempted to abridge the Constitution. Eventually this situation became so acute that the Moneda as well as the judiciary had to intervene actively to protect Chile's civilian institutions.

Traditionally, almost like unwanted relatives, the professional military remained closeted in their barracks or in a line of outposts located in the rain forest of Arauco, isolated from the mainstream of Chilean society. This alienation, however, was more than a question of distance. Some of the most senior commanders entered the military either directly as cadets or rose through the ranks; while these gentlemen commanded the respect of their men, the civilians often denigrated the officer corps, excluding it from "good society."[1] The War of the Pacific brought the armed forces into closer contact with civilian society, an encounter which often generally began with contempt and concluded with loathing.

TOWN VERSUS GOWN

The friction between the civilians and the military existed on two levels. The least vexing problem consisted of the chafing between the population and the army. In a sense, such confrontations were predictable and not particularly momentous. Traditionally, Chile recruited its enlisted personnel from the lower class, but even diluting the army with the more genteel civilian volunteers or elements of the newly mobilized National Guard did not substantially improve the conduct of the troops. *La Discusión*, for example, carped about a soldier of the Batallón Ñuble, "drunk as a lord" weaving down the streets of Chillán. Other, more serious problems developed. Soldiers accidentally injured civilians during training exercises or inadvertently spread disease to the nearby garrison towns. Occasionally, violence erupted as when, for example, some elements of the Batallón Carampangue mutinied, causing injuries and upsetting the local community. In Chillán, riots occurred. Sometimes even the best of intentions miscarried; Lebu's priest, Father Pedro Vivano, used his pulpit and some extremely "unchristian" language, to denounce a National Guard band whose playing drowned out his sermons.[2]

The relationship between the civilians and their military guests seemed, at best, ambivalent. Quillota's merchants rejoiced upon learning that their town might be selected as a site to locate a garrison since the troops would stimulate the local economy, reviving "the small industries which are the mainstay of the working class." The Moneda eventually selected Quillota over a nearby town on the provision that it assume the cost of building a barracks, a task the city happily undertook. Not every inhabitant proved so hospitable: the abbot of the local monastery refused to billet any soldiers for fear that they would ruin his garden. Quillota, however, suffered few, if any inconveniences. The local press appeared content with the soldiers' behavior even when recruits took to the streets to protest the food provided by a local caterer. Surprisingly, many of the local townspeople sympathized with the troops, considering their reaction quite reasonable.[3]

Clearly not all cities enjoyed such a positive experiences. Initiallly San Felipe's merchant population was delighted to learn that their city would house 1,200 men of the Regimiento Valparaíso. The vendors of *aguardiente* and *chicha* immediately raised their prices—and doubtless watered their stock—in anticipation of the troops' arrival. Yet when the local newspaper complained about the way some soldiers acted, a group of junior officers destroyed its press. Happily for San Felipe, the Regimiento Rancagua, which followed in the Valparaíso's wake, behaved more elegantly, and its band entertained the local population.[4]

Violence, unfortunately, became commonplace. In Chillán, troops, including some deserters, fought the police and looted stores. "If the military would only return these men to their units," noted one newspaper, "all would benefit: tranquility for the people and morality for the army."[5] In Valparaíso and San Bernardo, troops battled each other, other units, or the authorities. Soldiers, as well as their officers, also brawled with the civilian population, sometimes inflicting serious injuries. Occasionally, the rough housing became homicidal. An officer from the Batallón Linares, for example, apparently believing that his honor had been sullied, murdered a vendor in Rancagua's railroad depot.[6] Various towns lived in fear of recently discharged soldiers who sometimes used their newly acquired military skills to terrorize them. "If they keep discharging men without pay," rued a provincial journalist, "you will have to carry a revolver if one wants to go out at night."[7]

Nevertheless, the civilian population refused to stigmatize an entire army because of the excesses of a few drunks or deserters. Of course, economic gain may also have encouraged this charitable attitude. San Bernardo's monthly income from the troops averaged $6,000-$8,000, a not inconsiderable sum. Thus, perhaps those who lived in garrison towns accepted disruptions as the price they had to pay for the privilege of fleecing the troops by selling them adulterated alcohol or gulling them with fraudulent schemes to buy their way out of the army.[8]

The officer corps did not always enjoy a good reputation either. The press fumed that so many officers abused their sick leave privileges—a right not given to enlisted personnel—that Santiago looked like the capital of a nation at peace. Eventually, the situation became so scandalous that the government ordered convalescing officers either to submit to a weekly medical examination or to return to their units.[9] This abuse constituted a minor problem which paled before issues which seriously aggravated civilian military relations.

GENERALS VERSUS POLITICIANS

One of the myths about pre-war Chile was that Santiago's armed forces were professional, proficient, and apolitical. These statements appear exaggerated if not completely erroneous. If professionalism signified advancement based upon merit, then Chile's military became professional, if at all, only on the eve of the War of the Pacific. In September 1878, the legislature instituted a system which granted promotions based upon years of service. Time in grade constituted the sole factor in granting two thirds of the advancements up to the rank of colonel; only in the remaining one third of the cases could the government consider merit or distinguished service as criteria for promotion. As a result, Chile's military marched in lock step, with seniority not skill, exercising the most decisive influence.[10]

As an institution, the army might have defended the state in 1851 and 1859, but not all its officers were so faithful. Manuel Montt dismissed Manuel Baquedano from the army for meddling in politics, and only an amnesty saved Justo Arteaga from the firing squad for his participation in the 1851 revolt. Such activity did not cease with Montt's departure from the presidency in 1861. Evidence indicates that the military considered rebelling in 1876 because it believed that Errazuríz had blatantly intervened in the recent presidential election.[11] While perhaps apocryphal, the government did exile some men and apparently punished a group of officers, including General Escala and General Venegas, for supporting Pinto's opponent.[12]

The lack of an established standard for promotion encouraged officers to perform political favors to advance their careers. *La Discusión* correctly predicted that the Moneda would promote Baquedano as a reward for helping its candidate win the 1876 presidential election. Pedro Lagos won his colonelcy by manipulating Mulchen's elections three years later. Sometimes, dabbling in politics could also prove risky. Estanislao del Canto, for example, was serving as *gobernador* of Cañete when he received a letter ordering him to prevent the election of Máximo Errazuríz and Cornelio Saavedra. Del Canto complied and sent his subordinates into the countryside to "conquer the will of the electorate." However, although Saavedra lost in Cañete, he won in another congressional district, and eventually became minister of war. Remembering his earlier defeat, Saavedra first disbanded and then re-created del Canto's unit under a new commander, Lieutenent Colonel Gregorio Urrutia, who proceeded to persecute his protector's electoral enemies. Consequently, elections often signalled the purge of various officers or the reassignment of the more docile. The navy also suffered from similar upheavals, leading various officers to resign in disgust.[13]

Numerous military men also served either in the legislature or in some executive capacity, governing either a province or a *departamento*. In 1879, all of Chile's *generales de division*, three of the five *generales de brigada*, and at least four of seven colonels either occupied a seat in the Congress or had worked for the Moneda. This activity allowed the officers to form strategic friendships with civilian politicians. Estanislao del Canto and Patricio Lynch, for example, asked their connections to obtain them a better posting when the war began.[14] Similarly, political parties used their power and that of the press to protect their military members in order to present them as candidates in future elections.

Predictably, a large number of those professional officers occupying legislative seats used their civilian occupations to enhance their military careers. In January 1881, congressman and former general, José Villagrán, requested that his legislative colleagues investigate why General Baquedano had relieved him of command during the final push on Lima.[15] Villagrán's interpolation evoked a mixed public reaction. Some of the press appeared distressed that the general had lost his command but others warned that granting Villagrán's request would undermine military morale, a singularly unwise act with the army of the north literally besieging Lima. *La Patria*, observing that other former commanders had silently if not stoically accepted a similar fate, became upset that Villagrán appealed his dismissal to the legislature. Even citizen Villagrán, it argued, would agree that he was acting "as an impossible subordinate whom neither General Villagrán . . . nor General Baquedano would have tolerated."[16]

Most of the deputies shared *La Patria*'s disdain, agreeing that neither precedent nor the law permitted the lower house to consider Villagrán's request. Ricardo Letelier argued that initiating a congressional investigation would confer on the chamber's military members excessive power and would encourage future acts of insubordination. Any remedy, he stated, should be sought within the army's system of military justice. Still others claimed that legislative action might be construed as a lack of confidence in Baquedano. Hence, the chamber rejected Villagrán's proposal.[17]

Politics also warped the promotion process. G.G., an anonymous correspondent, angrily noted that officers still advanced their careers not in combat but "in domestic service, in political service, as courtesans, bending their spirit until they have lost the first prerequisite of a military man: integrity of character."[18] These soldiers, he bemoaned, although thriving in the hot house of politics, wilted on the field of battle. Thus, the promotion system rewarded the officer who served not the "nation but the minister," those, in short, who had cultivated the manly art of political groveling. With elections scheduled for 1881, few believed that the abuses would cease. It was, as one noted, an "incontrovertible truth that an election produced more promotions than a battle."[19] Ironically, while some of the press criticized the Moneda for ignoring the 1878 law, various newspapers nonetheless favored certain officers who, they believed, merited reward. *Los Tiempos*, observing that Juan Martínez, commander of the Regimiento Atacama, had lost two sons in battle, wondered if Pinto would require the sacrifice of yet another heir before promoting the bereaved father to colonel.[20]

In July 1880, the promotion issue became a matter of legislative interest as the Senate debated which officers should receive higher ranks. The discussion became quite hostile, particularly when the senators considered the cases of lieutenent colonels José Luis Ortiz and Ricardo Castro, officers who had earlier threatened to resign when they did not receive a promotion which they believed they deserved. Their fit of pique, occurring in the midst of a war, so antagonized various legislators that even though the upper chamber eventually promoted the two men, the vote was far from unanimous and, in the case of Ortiz, required two ballots before it was approved. Other candidates also aroused opposition in the Senate and the question of promotions became sometimes quite acrimonious.[21]

The Ortiz and Castro debates raised an important point: how could the government reward officers who did not possess enough seniority to occupy a high rank. Thus Senator Alejandro Reyes proposed suspending the 1878 promotion law in order to appoint men to fill vacancies created by battlefield casualties and because he believed that it discriminated against National Guard officers. The Senate overwhelmingly passed the Reyes proposal which, however, received only a lukewarm reception in the lower house. The legislators, perhaps convinced by Enrique MacIver's argument that abolishing the 1878 promotion law would revive the old excesses, rejected the Senate's proposal.

This act precipitated a mini-constitutional crisis. The upper house refused to accept defeat, vowing that it would continue to resubmit the measure until the Chamber of Deputies accepted it. Valentin Lastarria, warning that they must do something to break the stalemate, proposed suspending the 1878 legislation for the duration of the war. This compromise finally became law.

Lastarria's measure brought only a respite. A year later, nine antigovernment deputies suggested increasing the number of generals in the army's table of organization. The measure's sponsors also used the opportunity to hint strongly that Pedro Lagos, Orozimbo Barbosa, and José Velasquez merited not only promotions but also special gold medals as compensation for having endured a government directed campaign of neglect if not outright persecution.[22] Although this suggestion failed, it indicated that politicians tried to intervene in the military process. Unfortunately, these disputes often obscured the primary issue confronting Chile—the war—and instead involved the government and its officer corps in matters which dissipated their energies while arousing frustration if not overt hostility.

THE MILITARY VERSUS THE PRESS

Sometimes civil-military strife raised constitutional issues such as restricting the right of a free press. Neither good taste nor fear of legal retribution restrained Chile's newspapers in peacetime. And unfortunately, the onset of the war did not curb the journalists' zeal. Indeed, the press published so much sensitive information that Aníbal Pinto once lamented "to know what is happening in Chile, the Peruvian government only has to subscribe to our newspapers."[23] One periodical called for censorship as well as a public boycott of those journals which proved too garrulous.[24] Despite these complaints, the Moneda refused to muzzle the news media. It did request, however, that the editors be more circumspect when describing military troops movements.

The military authorities reacted in a more direct manner. In San Felipe, Clemente Suarez, a writer for *El Censor*, wrote unkindly about the conduct of the officers and men of the Regimiento Valparaíso. A group of young subalterns, complained to the newspaper's editor. When the latter refused to retract Suarez's editorials, the officers destroyed the paper's printing press. Although the Intendent, Blest Gana, supported *El Censor*'s editor, the newspaper's colleagues proved unsympathetic, dismissing Suarez as a "hunchbacked dwarf" whose condition embittered him. Another journal apparently sought to excuse the officers' conduct by claiming that they were merely responding to the provocation of a "worthless rag" while *El Correo de Quillota* urged the press, in the name of patriotism, to ignore "the defects and flaws which our heroic defenders might possess."[25]

In September the conflict between the pen and the sword sharpened. Elio Caviedez, a correspondent for the prestigious *El Mercurio*, arrived in Arica to report on the war. Although he carried the proper accreditation, including permission from the minister of war, the military authorities arrested the correspondent for entering the war zone illegally. General Baquedano defended this act, alleging that Caviedez had not only prematurely disclosed official information, but that he had defamed the military thus fomenting discord within the army.

El Mercurio alleged that the general had jailed Caviedez because he had critized Baquedano's direction of the battle of Tacna. The newspaper tartly contrasted the officer's hostile reaction with that of Vergara who, under similar circumstances, had remained silent. The violation of Caviedez's civil liberties evoked strong antimilitary attitudes in some of the press, and many newspapers which had earlier dismissed the *Censor* incident, now protested vigorously.[26] After all, Caviedez was no hunchback and his employer, Agustín Edwards, was a man of great wealth. "La prensa de Valparaíso," noting that Caviedez's only offense was that he "had expressed frankly his opinion . . . about the military's direction of the Chilean army," hoped that other newspapers woud also protest Baquedano's action.[27] This appeal enjoyed some success: La Patria denounced the general for misusing his authority, concluding that for the first time the Chilean press had to endure the abuse which in Peru had become standard. *Las Novedades*, while willing to acknowledge the Pope's infallibility, would not confer the same right on "our military leaders."[28] Various provincial newspapers like *La Libertad* claimed that Baquedano's efforts represented the military's attempt to "kill one of the most important and unquestionable achievements of modern times: the right of the press" while *La Patria* called for the Moneda to force the general to release Caviedez.[29]

Of course, Baquedano was not the first officer to act so arbitrarily. In March 1880, General Escala expelled some reporters for entering the war zone on a ship specifically reserved for the military but in this case, the method of transportation, not the newsmen's personal sentiments, precipitated the incident. Escala, moreover, did not attempt to defend his actions. He candidly admitted that he disliked reporters because they lied, played favorites—of which he was not one—while denigrating his role in the war. The general, unlike Baquedano, merely expelled those whom he abhorred or feared; his successor jailed them, an act which stimulated hostility if not fear. Even *El Correo de Quillota*, which had earlier pleaded for the public to tolerate the military's foibles, believed that Baquedano had acted out of a sense of pique.[30]

Not all of the press, however, shared *El Mercurio*'s outrage. *El Independiente*, for example, argued that since military law ruled the war zone, Baquedano had acted correctly against what he considered a disruptive influence. Consequently, not even the minister of war could intervene since "there should be no overriding authority over the general in chief . . . as long as he commands, he should exercise [power] within the bounds established by military law." *El Nuevo Ferrocarril*, which earlier had denounced *El Mercurio*'s correspondents as a "group of vulgar and ambitious individuals who possess neither the bravery nor the competence demonstrated on the field of battle," accused the journalists of slurring the regular army officers in order to enhance the reputation of Valparaíso's National Guard units. "Anti Cucalon" maintained that the nitrate interests disliked Baquedano and that Edwards's friendship with Vergara dictated *El Mercurio*'s editorial policy. This charge may have possessed a kernel of truth because Edwards did request Vergara to intercede on behalf of his employee, a petition which apparently resulted in Caviedez's freedom.[31]

The military clashed with the press again, in 1883, when an army zone commander arrested the editor of *La Industria* who was accused of revealing troop movements, thus endangering the lives of the troops, and of communicating with a Bolivian officer who worked as a correspondent for a La Paz newspaper. While admitting that he corresponded with Bolivia—as did other Chileans—he claimed that his editorials were balanced statements devoid of any intent to spread false information or rumour. The paper stipulated that it had published news of troop movements but only after they had become widely known. *La Industria*'s plight did not win widespread support from its colleagues who demanded that the paper should state clearly its loyalties.[32]

THE ADMIRAL AND THE COURTS

Patricio Lynch was a paradox: half-English, half-Peruvian, part-time sailor, part time general, the "Red Prince," as he was called, had enjoyed an eclectic but stormy professional career. Graduating from the *Escuela Militar*, he served in the navy during the War of the Peruvian Bolivian Confederation. At the conclusion of that conflict, Lynch was seconded to the British fleet, fighting in the naval engagements of the Opium Wars where earned the respect of his superiors. Enticed back to Chile, he commanded a ship during the 1851 Revolution. While loyal to the government, he apparently did not act ferociously enough for President Montt who dismissed him from the navy. Lynch remained "on the beach" until the 1865 war with Spain brought him back to active duty. Although an experienced officer, command of a vessel eluded him. Instead he served as Maritime Governor of Valparaíso and later as an attaché to the Ministry of War and the Navy. While he was promoted to *Capitán de Navío*, he apparently managed to antagonize his colleagues and superiors because when the War of the Pacific erupted, Lynch could not find a berth on a man-of-war. Instead, he became the head of the naval transport service. Later, he served as Political and Military Commander of Tarapacá. In 1880, Lynch led the punitive expedition against Peru's northern coast and three months later, still a naval officer, he commanded an army division in the final assault on Lima. Finally, in May 1881, Lynch became commander-in-chief of Chile's expeditionary forces with the responsibility of administering what remained of Peru.[33]

The Red Prince attracted enormous notoriety. His promotion to vice admiral apparently upset various colleagues, including his former commander, Riveros. His occupation policies angered the civilian population who condemned Lynch for not acting more ruthlessly and for failing to eradicate Peruvian resistance. While this criticism was directed mainly against Lynch's war policy, or the lack of it, the press also became upset by his activities as a civil administrator. Some newspapers, for example, denounced the admiral for selling John Thomas North 40,000 tons of guano, apparently at below market prices, hinting strongly that the officer retained a portion of the sale price; others claimed that Lynch had performed similar services for the Grace interests. A series of articles claimed that the admiral had corrupted the army and lowered its morale. One author unfavorably compared Lynch's lenient treatment of the Peruvians with the draconian punishments he imposed on Chile's soldiers for committing minor offenses. The admiral, it was claimed, had become a corrupt proconsul who, for sexual favors or money, ignored Peruvian resistance, even if it caused the death of Chilean troops.[34] Despite the gravity of such charges, the public did not become as outraged as it would by what subsequently became known as the Letelier incident.

At the outbreak of the war, Ambrosio Letelier seemed just another of Chile's regular officers. Although he served in the military for approximately fifteen years and had reached a relatively distinguished rank, initially he did not participate in the war's military campaigns. This failure may not have been Letelier's fault: like many of his contemporaries, he spent March and early April 1879, manipulating the congressional elections on behalf of the government.[35] By 1880, however, he was serving as a staff officer in Antofagasta and the following year participated in the assault on Lima.

Following the fall of that city, and acting on the orders of General Pedro Lagos, Letelier led a punitive expedition into Peru's interior. By May, news began filtering back to Lima, indicating that Letelier's men were terrorizing not only the local population, which perhaps would have been acceptable to Chileans, but also various foreign residents. Lynch, infuriated by Letelier's conduct and believing that he had exceeded his authority, ordered him to return to the Peruvian capital. Letelier, apparently ignored this command, which the admiral then repeated, presumably with more emphasis.

Letelier's column finally straggled back to Lima in July. Lynch alleged that the troops had arrived in wretched physical condition, often without their horses and poorly disciplined, yet with their pockets filled with money. Letelier, claiming that he was acting under verbal authorization, had imposed taxes on the Peruvian towns which he had occupied. The colonel had also generously distributed some of these funds among his men as prizes. Lynch ordered Letelier, as well as his subordinates, detained. A court of inquiry investigating the charges concluded that the officers had illegally levied imposts on the hapless Peruvians, extorted funds from an Italian born naturalized Peruvian citizen, and, had failed to obey Lynch's order to return to Lima in a timely fashion.

In 1882, a military court, composed of high ranking officers, discovered that Letelier's expedition had collected approximately $180,000, some of it through extortion. The colonel's generosity proved less than even-handed, while he had distributed some of the funds to his men, the court determined that a substantial portion had remained in Letelier's pockets. Thus the court stripped him of his rank, ordered him to jail for six years, and levied a fine of approximately $102,000, the amount Letelier had been accused of misappropriating. The colonel's subordinates received similar sentences which Lynch subsequently confirmed.[36]

Normally, this event would not have attracted the attention of the Chilean public. Letelier, however, appealed his conviction to the Supreme Court in Santiago, where his attorney, Roberto Murillo, argued that Lynch had denied the colonel's appeal without studying the evidence and that this action had deprived Letelier of his civil rights. The fact that both men were officers serving abroad did not permit the admiral to deny Letelier due process. Thus the Supreme Court, Murillo averred, should assert its jurisdiction and remove the entire matter from the clumsy hands of military justice.[37]

Murillo's entreaties achieved their purpose: in May 1881, the Supreme Court chastized Lynch for his actions and agreed that the defendants could appeal to a court located in Chile even if the cause of action had occurred outside of the nation's boundaries. The court, moreover, affirmed its right to review the case, a prerogative which, it claimed, Lynch had illegally sought to usurp. Judges, it noted, not soldiers, should administer justice in Chile. Lynch violently disagreed, requesting the Council of State to confirm his authority. The protection of the 1833 Constitution, he argued, remained confined solely to Chile. Once outside the nation, the president became the sole source of law and, as his delegate, the commander of Chile's expeditionary army enjoyed rights which no civilian court could abridge. The admiral observed, moreover, that legal precedent restricted the authority of appeal courts exclusively to Chilean territory while the military court system permitted appeals only for causes of action which originated within their jurisdiction. Since Lima did not fall within the ambit of Chile's military legal system, the commanding general constituted the last recourse. In short, neither the Constitution nor the court system enjoyed any validity in Peru; only Admiral Lynch enjoyed such power, a power which he correctly exercised when he confirmed the sentence of Lima's military tribunal.[38]

The admiral's legal pretentions upset some of the press which began to describe Letelier as a victim of Lynch's caprice or of his religious bigotry. *El Padre Cobos* demanded that the Moneda persecute Lynch for his numerous blunders, reviving the charge that he had stolen $1,500,000. It also suggested that Lynch could better serve the nation by being stationed either at sea or in Peru's interior. Others interpreted the issue as a struggle between civil and military authorities over who should rule the north, a conflict which *El Ferrocarril* hoped would not lead to the military's abridging the right of due process. *La Patria*, which described Lynch as an alley cat with the ego of a lion, concluded that the admiral threatened the administration of justice. Increasingly, it feared that the armed forces would encroach on civilian authority. In the same vein, *El Correo de Quillota* sarcastically hailed the creation of a fourth branch of government: *el poder Lynch*—a form of absolute power, arbitrarily exercised, and one from which no appeal existed.[39]

Eventually the Council of State agreed that Lynch had usurped the prerogatives of the courts: the Supreme Court enjoyed jurisdiction because the cause of action involved the army of occupation whose actions were always subject to the rule of law. Chile's citizens, when in the service of the motherland, enjoyed the protection of the 1833 Constitution regardless of where they lived. Therefore, in October 1883, the high court overturned Letelier's conviction, rejecting Lynch's contention that the war had endowed him with extraordinary power. While a field commander might clearly issue orders to regulate discipline, the admiral simply could not "dictate orders ... suspending not only pre-existing laws ... but also constitutional precepts, absorbing and annulling the attributes of public powers."[40] Letelier, however, did not escape unscathed: the court ordered the Corte Marcial of Santiago to retry him.

It appears that perhaps personal animosity, not legal issues, had inspired the admiral to act so vindictively. Letelier had worked earlier with Colonel Lagos and, in mid-May, 1881, Letelier suggested attacking the Peruvian interior which, he believed, would separate Lima from La Paz and thus hasten the end of the war. The admiral opposed this tactic and may have resented Letelier's meddling, particularly when the press praised Letelier and Lagos for pressing the war so energetically. This theory gains substance because one of Letelier's codefendents was Anacleto Lagos, a relative of Lynch's arch rival, Colonel Pedro Lagos. Old pre-war political grudges also may have influenced the situation. Letelier, Lagos, and Basilio Romero as well as Lynch participated in manipulating the 1879 congressional elections. It is conceivable that they may have alienated the admiral who, three years and thousands of miles later, would exact his revenge. Regardless of its origin, the conflict between Lynch and the courts brought into focus the struggle between the civilian government and the military. Numerous Chileans considered the Supreme Court verdict a victory of the *cucalones* over the *militares*.[41]

CONCLUSION

Although Chile vanquished its enemies, it did not emerge from the conflict imbued with a sense of gratitude toward its professional military. A variety of factors produced this reaction. From the onset of the war, the officer corps had not satisfied the nation's expectations. Various men had squandered almost as much energy protecting their careers as they had fighting the enemy. A certain antimilitary bias began to permeate the nation, a hostility rooted in a repugnance toward officers who squabbled over promotions, who resigned their commissions out of pique when the country needed their services, who overstayed their sick leave while the enlisted men suffered in the north, who jailed newspaper correspondents or destroyed printing presses, and who abridged, if not obliterated the legal process. The Treaty of Ancón could not erase these memories. After a sober analysis of the various battles, numerous Chileans concluded that the nation owed its triumph solely to its "rotos" who successfully overcame not only a ferocious enemy but their own officers' "ineptitude."[42] Not surprisingly, some advocated that the symbol of triumph should not be a statue of a general on a horse but a monument to the previously ignored, if not denigrated, "roto chileno" who had made victory possible. One newspaper compared this warrior, inspired solely by a wholesome love of the motherland, with the "bastard ambitions" of the others.[43]

Chile's image of itself may also have colored the country's attitude toward its military. Chileans considered themselves unique: a racially homogeneous, Catholic nation of citizens voluntarily submitted themselves to the rule of law. Admittedly not a paragon of democracy, Chile had nonetheless escaped internal upheaval because its government functioned adequately. Thus, while its neighbors had squandered their energies and largesse by indulging in homicidal internecine strife, Chile had quietly devoted its energies to developing its resources. Overcoming the economic and political obstacles had forged and tested the collective Chilean personality, endowing it with the strength to vanquish its foreign enemies. England may have won the Napoleonic Wars on the "playing fields of Eton" but Chile conquered Peru and Bolivia because it first triumphed in "the struggles of peace, of work, and of civilization" not because of its martial virtues.[44]

5

El Pago de Chile

> For its Tommy this, an' Tommy that,
> an' "chuck him out, the brute!"
> But it's "Savior of 'is country" when
> the guns begin to shoot.
> "Tommy." R. Kipling

> Beloved and adored Motherland,
> I wonder, why unloving mother,
> are you rewarding so badly
> One who is giving his life for thee.
> "Los hijos de Chile quejandose a su
> Madre Patria." by Bernardo
> Guajardo

Purging the officer corps of incompetents and prodding the survivors into action solved only a few of the Moneda's problems. The government still had to confront the issue of obtaining recruits as well as providing the armed forces with rations, munitions, and medical care. Chile, however, was no more prepared for dealing with these manpower and logistical problems than it was ready to prosecute the war. Unlike France or Germany, for example, the Moneda did not possess the legal authority to draft soldiers and the armed forces lacked a supply corps to equip the army or the navy. Once again the government had to improvise, hastily creating a mechanism not only to obtain troops but also to provide logistical support. In addition, it had to devise a system for granting pensions to the maimed and to the families of those who perished on the battlefields of the War of the Pacific.

RECRUITING WOES

Enticing men to join the military constituted one of the Moneda's most urgent wartime problems. The government could not conscript individuals because Chilean law explicitly prohibited forced military service. Thus, the administration had three alternatives: it could appeal for volunteers; it could authorize the payment of a bounty, an *enganche*, to attract recruits; or it could mobilize the National Guard.

Few institutions aroused so much loathing as did the *Guardia Nacional*. These territorial reserve units existed throughout Chile and the law required all able-bodied men to participate. Predictably, the influential either avoided service or acted as officers. Thus the hapless enlisted men had to spend Sundays and as well as civic holidays, their only days of rest, aimlessly marching and countermarching while their commanders, encumbered only by a ceremonial sword, stood about in poses of studied nonchalance. Cynics described the militia as nothing more than "bands of music . . . , many soldiers, many bayonets, and much powder burned on independence day."[1] For numerous workers, however, the Guard absorbed so much time, energy, and income that they fled Chile to avoid service.

Few contemporary observers could discover any military value in the *Guardia*: its obsolete equipment threatened no one but the user; the level of training appeared almost nonexistent; and budget cuts reduced the number of units. The militia, some claimed, devoured substantial government revenues for the questionable purpose of restraining a potentially unruly populous during elections. Thus rather than acting as "the sentinel against foreign invasion and a defense against an enemy who might wish to treat upon our soil, in reality, [the militia] pursues the weak and sacrifices the unfortunate."[2]

Although the Moneda was unwilling to mobilize the reserves, perhaps fearful of disrupting the economy, it could appeal for volunteers. Initially, during the first days of the conflict, many patriotic men stepped forward to rally around the flag and one woman deservedly earned the title of "Spartan Mother" because her seven sons joined the army.[3] Reluctance, however, quickly replaced the early enthusiasm. Enlistments did not match expectations. Local newspapers suggested that the Moneda seek its volunteers elsewhere. Provincial officials predicted that a loss of manpower would cripple their economies. In a few cases, the minister of war reprimanded certain intendents for failing to cooperate in various recruitment drives.[4]

A variety of forces inhibited volunteering. Scholars and contemporary observers have often described Chile as a unified country whose citizens possessed a highly developed sense of national identity. This picture is simply without foundation. In 1861, "Atropos" noted that the *roto* owed his allegiance and affection only to the *fundo* where he was born; little outside of the *hacienda* on which he worked interested him. Eighteen years may have altered this situation but it seems unlikely. Where would the *roto*, who composed the majority of the nation, learn about Chile: in a non-existent school? From a book which he could not read? At best, provincial, not national sentiments, predominated. Guardsmen rarely volunteered to fight in the north, particularly if they had to serve under officers they did not know.[5] In comparison to Bolivia or Peru, Chile may have appeared to be a nation state but in truth, most of its rural populace had little notion that they lived in a country called Chile; this lack of nationalism made it difficult to obtain recruits.

Even if some citizens glowed with patriotic fervor, family men could ill afford to indulge in the luxury of nationalism. Troops received wretched pay and the government had not yet created a system to provide a stipend to supplement the paltry salaries of the soldiers. Volunteering, therefore, might benefit Chile but it beggared the working man's wife and children.[6]

The Moneda tried to entice men into the military by offering a bonus, a tactic that often failed because the recruiters often did not receive enough funds to pay the bounty. As a result, various officials quickly discovered a less expensive and more efficient method of obtaining soldiers: the press gang. Recruiters spread through Chile with the speed and often the same consequences as smallpox. The countryside soon felt the presence of these dragoons. In Chillán, for example, recruiters from the Zapadores, Regimiento Valparaíso, and the Regimiento Esmeralda arrived simultaneously. Within a short time the local press accused a Major Coke of poaching on men already selected by his rivals. Given this level of competition, peasants and others quite wisely refused to come to market to sell their produce, fearful of being snatched into the army.[7]

Rather than rail futilely against forced recruiting, some Chileans used this device in a constructive manner. Instead of drafting the conscientious farmer, miner, or artisan—a move would not only paralyze the economy but also hurt the soldier's dependents—they suggested that the recruiters instead impress the vagrant, the town drunk, or what one official described as "bad citizens but good soldiers": the local criminal who had already demonstrated a vocation for mayhem.[8] This solution accomplished two goals: the military would gain recruits and the towns would lose some of its least desirable inhabitants. The authorities, aware that the absence of these men would scarcely provoke a controversy, happily complied. Talca's police, for example, began collecting transients as well as petty criminals for service in the army, delighting many who praised the authorities for freeing "us . . . from the terrible plague of vagrants who fill our streets."[9]

Inevitably, the press gangs turned their attention to the honest citizen. In San Carlos, the recruiters broke into homes at night, carrying off the men. Police arrested anyone walking Chillán's streets after 10 P.M., sending them to join the Carabineros de Yungay. Not surprisingly, recruiters housed their charges in jail to await transportation or sent them north under armed guard.[10]

Eventually, the activities of the press gang attracted the attention of the legislature when Carlos Walker Martínez reported that he had seen recruiters literally run to ground hapless citizens and then remove them, "as if a herd of cattle, under a corporal's whip and, like slaves, to serve a cause which they did not understand." Such treatment, he argued, violated their individual rights, endangered the Chilean economy, and produced uninspired soldiers. "Are we, Mister Minister," he asked, "in Chile or Russia?"[11]

"Mister Minister," García de la Huerta, claimed that although the government could mobilize the National Guard, no one had to serve involuntarily in the army of the north. The authorities, he argued, could and did force citizens to enroll in territorial units because the Constitution mandated such service. But he explicitly denied that he had authorized the use of violence, blaming this problem on an overzealous commander he had ordered to cease employing these methods.

The minister's explanations apparently pacified the congress until Luis Urzua introduced a letter indicating that the authorities of Molina had quartered its local Guard unit in an isolated home, performed a cursory medical examination, and then shipped the men to the army of the north. The seizure of *inquilinos* in nearby Talca, outraged another deputy, Ambrosio Montt, who lamented that the lower class suffered the most from this treatment. Continued forced recruiting, he warned, would only make the war unpopular with the masses.

To remedy this situation, Montt proposed that the legislature outlaw the press gang and hold responsible the president and his minister for any future recruiting abuses. The deputy's proposal unleashed a wave of criticism. Clemente Fabres, whose love of civil liberties did not extend to religious dissidents, nonetheless wanted to censure the Liberal ministry while his cohort, Walker Martínez, sought to use the motion to force a change in war policy. Some legislators, claiming that a censure motion would delay the prosecution of the campaign, tabled the proposal. In late July, Urzúa returned with another horror report of recruiters using weapons to hunt down the luckless draftees. Montt therefore revived his measure, which the legislature again defeated.[12]

Perhaps encouraged by the rejection of the measure, the press gangs became more bold. In San Antonio, recruiters entered a *fundo* carrying off all the *inquilinos*, including the *mayordomo*. A school boy, pursued by *enganchadores*, took refuge in a stranger's house, thereby saving himself but later exposing his savior to the reprisals of the police. Both the student and the Good Samaritan were fortunate; others died while resisting the press gang.¹³ No one seemed safe, "Like a band of voracious vultures," the recruiters take "boys from schools, the old, servants, unregistered citizens, soldiers on leave...."¹⁴ In Constitución, the authorities unleashed dogs to pursue "as if ferocious beasts, the poor peasants who live in the mountains and the thick forests of that departamento."¹⁵

Not all *enganchadores* employed such crude tactics. In Santa Juana, the recruiters arrived with a band whose sweet music, they hoped, would entice the *rotos* into the plaza where they would be harvested. Quillota's judges graciously offered local drunks a Hobson's choice of jail or the army. Apparently the men opted for the latter because the next day "they all happily marched to the barracks."¹⁶ Sometimes violent methods misfired. In San Carlos, the police invaded a "low place" and arrested its patrons. When a physician examined the potential recruits, he discovered a woman who had disguised herself as a man, apparently to savor the seamier pleasures of the dark side of life.¹⁷

Recruiters did not always encounter Gandhi-like passivity. The *fundo* San Gabriel provided a refuge for those unwilling to serve in Linares's Compañía Movilizada. *Hacendados* sometimes tried to prevent the authorities from taking their peons, a tactic which did not always succeed. In Palpal, the owner of a farm managed to stop *enganchadores* from taking twenty men. To prevent bloodshed, however, he had to allow them to seize four hapless souls whom they brought, trussed up like criminals, to Chillán. Some recruiters refused to compromise: in Itata they stabbed one man and shot at another when the latter questioned their authority. Some good hearted individuals did help to save peons from the military. Santa Juana's *subdelegado* and the head of the civic guard warned the local men about the recruiters while in Coronel, a Señor Apolonio went from house to house urging the men to flee to the mountains. Thus, when the recruiters arrived, they discovered only five men, all missing either a limb or an eye. A few commanders refused to accept conscripts: Captain Cortés of the Escuadrón Movilizada Freire released all those who had been illegally recruited. Some of the influential used their connections to secure the release of those trapped by the recruiters. In one instance two individuals, falsely arrested as vagrants in Coronel, were saved. One group of rescued men, however, had to walk back from Concepción— and a few from as far away as Santiago—before reaching their homes in the Lota area. Of course, not all the stories had such happy endings: in Aconcagua the authorities seized two men, one an invalid and the other over military age. The former, despite his medical disability, was sent north; the old man was put to work constructing a road in front of the *subdelegado's* office.[18]

Despite the numerous abuses, one journalist considered the press gang "a good and wise method, quite worthy of applause," especially when it was directed against those of dubious antecedents. *El Correo de Quillota* praised conscription as a marvelous tool for eradicating drunkeness and vagrancy: "Today," it noted,"very few drunks can be found and those few remaining are careful not to attract attention to themselves." The town, moreover, benefited almost as much as the unwilling draftee's family which received a government allotment—perhaps the first time that their menfolk had earned a salary. Another example, rhapsodized the paper, "of how the war has accomplished something good . . . serving profitably as a school of morality and providing a wonderful lesson to our working class." Doubtless this same spirit of concerned duty motivated *La Voz de Itata* to inform the authorities about the well known vagrant, Mateo R.: "You would," it admonished,"be doing a service to him and to many by making him come forward."[19]

Predictably, recruiting became a vehicle for corruption. People who harbored grudges or who owed money denounced their enemies or creditors to the *enganchadores*. Venal officials used their power to avenge past slights or to extort future concessions, livestock, personal favors, or cash in return for exemptions. People, noted one journal, would pay anything to avoid becoming "cannon fodder" for the north.[20] Not all the corrupt acted so honestly. Melipilla's authorities arrested two men who, posing as recruiters had first captured men and then graciously released them in return for money or livestock. Occasionally courts prosecuted officials who had committed recruiting abuses, including one exconvict whom the *subdelegado* of Gualleco employed as an *enganchador*.[21]

The arrival of recruiters often precipitated a frenzied flight of the local population. Peasants, terrorized by the prospect of military service, fled to the cities where they hoped to envelop themselves in the cloak of urban anonymity. This tactic failed: the police merely shifted the locus of their activity to the center of town. Miners often deserted the coalpits for the countryside where farmers also hid. The exodus of large numbers of men deprived the mines and farms of labor and also paralyzed commerce.[22] After the local officials completed recruiting in Chillán, the town was described as "without movement or business transactions, the fields are without work, the houses are empty, their owners hidden in the mountains."²³ Sometimes special hardships developed. Quillota was devastated to learn that one of the town's two barbers—unfortunately the good one—had gone north; Itata lost a portion of its police force. Since honest men did not dare work, for fear of being drafted, they became instead criminals to support themselves and their families.²⁴ Yet, while "our countryside, mines, and factories, our sources of wealth are . . . becoming deserts, without movement, abandoned . . . because [the laborers] have marched off to the fields of cannon, bullets, smoke, and death," the wealthy young rentiers filled cafes.²⁵

Some *hacendados* acted as if the forced drafts hurt them more than the impressed. In Linares, for example, one agriculturist attempted to prevent the formation of a militia unit in order to guarantee himself a steady supply of labor. Conversely, Miguel Barros Moran, a *terrateniente* serving in the legislature, generously offered his farm laborers to defend the motherland. Mulchen's landowners tried to reconcile their economic and patriotic instincts. José Miguel de la Jara, claiming that they should subordinate everything to the motherland, suggested that the *hacendados* should choose those *inquilinos* who would serve in the army. Within minutes his audience had selected 105 men, taking first bachelors and then those whose absence would work the least hardship on their families. The newspaper praised de la Jara's solution as "a simple and patriotic way of raising soldiers without resorting to violence or abuse which upsets us because it injures those interests and guarantees which our constitution grants us."²⁶

The renewal of forced recruiting inspired Valentin Letelier to denounce this practice in the Chamber of Deputies. With Lima under Chilean control, the minister of the interior became a bit saucy, replying that the government had to balance the individual's rights against the needs of the state. Forced recruiting, he added, had been authorized only "for vagrants who are unemployed." Although he repudiated violent methods, he admitted that had the recruiters not used force, they could not have raised an army of 70,000 men. Clemente Fabres, echoing public opinion, criticized Recabarren's methods, which the deputy claimed, had failed because instead of drafting "the vagrants, the drunks, and criminals," the press gangs seized honest workers. Simply conscripting "just the drunks," the deputy claimed, "could have raised an army of more than 50,000."

The debate failed to prevent additional abuses. The war seemed on the verge of a happy conclusion; the task of preventing forced recruiting seemed too complex. Doubtless many deputies shared the feelings of Barros Moran who considered the press gang both a fact of life and of war and who, with the generosity of one who did not have to serve, had "impassively watched" as the recruiters carried his *inquilinos* off to war.[27]

Thus, as forced recruiting continued through 1883, the police still watched for the staggering drunk or the footloose vagrant whose disappearance would not provoke a congressional debate. A favorite source of able bodies remained the jailhouse. Unfortunately, convicts rarely made the best soldiers. In one case, they flung one of their comrades off a troop ship because he was winning at cards too regularly. Local authorities continued abusing their powers, forcibly carrying off the hapless mechanic, the *inquilino*, and occasionally the disabled veteran. Men still died resisting the recruiters, intendants still traded draft exemptions for votes. Sometimes the draftees ended up serving in the forest of Arauco instead of the Peruvian altiplano.[28] The provinces protested, citing economic hardship and complaining that the recruiters should seek greener pastures, always elsewhere. "And why," questioned one newspaper, "does the government want soldiers? To carry them to the slaughter house? In order to take them to die, of fever, of *tercianas*, and other epidemics? Have not the Chilean people seen enough Chilean bodies?"[29]

SOLDIERING

Chilean military life would test the mettle of sterner stuff than the summer soldier or the sunshine patriot. Even the most zealous nationalist blanched at the regimen of boredom, wretched food, inadequate clothing, and squalid barracks. Military discipline bordered on the savage: generous doses of the lash for the disobedient and the firing squad for the incorrigible. Statistically, those who volunteered in hopes of winning glory on the battlefield were more likely to succumb to an intestinal or venereal disease, a respiratory infection, or one of the pernicious fevers which infested the Peruvian heartland.[30]

Chile did not deliberately set out to mistreat its troops but the government lacked the financial resources and the administrative means to provide food, clothing, and medical care. Consequently, the Moneda relied on civilians to improvise a quartermaster and medical corps. It also appealed for contributions to defray the cost of the military campaigns. In a sense, the struggle against Peru and Bolivia resembled a charity drive more than a military contest. The War of the Pacific was not waged by a centralized state which controlled the nation's economic resources: it was a war of voluntarism.

Fortunately, the public responded positively, providing the government with money, and gifts ranging from livestock to tobacco. In April 1879, Pinto authorized provincial authorities to collect these donations and remit them to the Tesorerías Fiscales which would deposit them in a special account. Some weeks later, some of Santiago's leading citizens organized the *Junta Central de Subsidios para la Guerra* to collect funds to support the war effort, organize hospitals, and to assist the families of the war dead as well as those still serving in the military. The Moneda subsequently founded a *Junta Central de Donativos para la Guerra* to supervise and coordinate the nationwide collection of charitable contributions.

This organization raised and dispersed substantial sums from a variety of sources. The Junta equipped three ambulance units which it donated to the army, the first of these contingents it received. Sister organizations, like Talca's *Sociedad Protectora* and a local branch of the *Junta de Subsidios*, also donated money and food to the families of needy servicemen. These groups also provided other services: Santiago's *Sociedad Protectora* hired a lawyer to help soldiers' families prepare the forms needed to secure pensions. By July 1881, the *Comité Central de Donativos* had amassed approximately $100,000 pesos, portions of which it distributed to help the families of the war wounded as well as the troops.

Some of this money purchased food for the soldiers when the Moneda encountered difficulties providing adequate rations. Soldiers traditionally carp about their food. In the Chilean case, these complaints seem eminently reasonable in part because of the rations' monotony—beef jerky, flour, and hard tack—and also because of their paucity. The Chilean army did not possess a supply system, having abolished its quartermaster corps in the 1840s. Thus, the military initially relied upon civilian contractors who often sold the armed forces such wretched rations that some cooks threw them out rather than serve them. To remedy this situation, Santiago created the *Intendencia Jeneral del Ejército i Marina*. Its first director, Francisco Echaurren, failed to resolve the problem because General Arteaga, preferring to use civilian sutlers, refused to cooperate with the Moneda's appointee. Almost five months elapsed before Echaurren could formulate a standard field ration, but since Arteaga would not even inform him how many men he commanded, the civilian could not institute his supply system. Not surprisingly, Echaurren resigned.[31]

Although his replacement, Vicente Dávila Larraín, enjoyed more success, he still had to deal with civilian provisioners who, like the battleship *Potemkin*'s victualers, supplied "wormy meat, old beans, and nitrate instead of salt."[32] Troops also failed to receive the firewood needed to cook their rations let alone onions or potatoes, treasured by one officer, "as if they were gold." Even when rations proved edible and abundant, the lack of a transportation system prevented them from reaching the troops who had to slaughter their mules for food.

As a result, soldiers often purchased additional food from civilians who either demanded excessive prices or who discounted the paper money with which the government paid its troops. Either way, the men suffered: one soldier spent half his salary just on supplementary food. This situation outraged the press which complained that the government stinted on rations while paying enormous salaries to its higher ranking civilian employees.[33]

Just as Chile lacked a quartermaster corps, it also did not possess a medical service. Prior to the war, the army relied upon civilian doctors and hospitals to care for its Santiago garrison. Those unfortunates stationed in the southern forts remained "at the mercy of nature" when, in 1878, economy measures forced the dismantling of their extremely primitive and unprofessionally staffed medical system. Thus when the war erupted, the Chilean army had over 5,000 men stationed in the littoral without a military surgeon to care for them; those who fell ill had to depend on their comrades to cure them.[34]

To remedy this situation, the Moneda organized a *Comisión Sanitaria*, placing it under the authority of the *Intendent Jeneral del Ejército i Armada*, with the express mandate to create, staff, train, and equip a medical corps for the army. This effort proved a tremendous undertaking because of tje logistical problems and the shortage of trained medical personnel. Unfortunately, even when the *Junta* overcame these difficulties, the military neglected to use properly its medical resources. General Arteaga, perhaps a devotee of homeopathy, neglected to send physicians or medical equipment to Antofagasta while General Escala forgot to find a place for medical personnel, supplies, or ambulances on the transports when he attacked Pisagua. Consequently, many men perished not because of their wounds but from exposure. In addition, the authorities often did not treat the injured immediately but instead evacuated them to military hospitals located in Chile. Many times the wounded had to travel two to three days, sometimes on the deck of a transport, before receiving medical attention. Not surprisingly, at least half of the eighty-six survivors of the battles of San Francisco and Tarapacá who reached Coquimbo, arrived with gangrenous wounds which required amputation. To prevent a recurrence of this event, the *Junta de Donativos* established hospitals in the occupied territories as well as increasing their number in northern and central Chile.

Building facilities alone could not compensate for the almost criminal negligence with which the injured were treated. The wounded often arrived in Chile, without fanfare, to march, sometimes under guard, to a hospital while enemy prisoners rode through the city on coaches. The government also halved the pay as well as the rations allowance for hospitalized troops. This action not only hurt the convalescing soliders but also their financial dependents. Initially, hospitals even charged the wounded, or their unit, for the medical care they dispensed. Only in November 1879 did the government assume financial responsibility for such services. Apparently the authorities also distinguished between those troops who suffered battle-connected injuries and those who required medical attention for other reasons. The former received their medical care for free; the latter had to pay. Once discharged from the hospital, the soldier often discovered that the army had stopped paying either his salary or allowances and, in some cases, both. Thus maimed men, often clad only in the tattered remnants of their uniforms, would expose their mutilated bodies in order to cadge money from a passersby.[35] After a troop ship disgorged a cargo of "ragged and sick soldiers" many of Valparaíso's inhabitants, who earlier had celebrated the army's victories with fireworks and champagne, now fled at the sight of these "mutilated servants of the motherland."[36]

The final offensive in the early summer of 1881 strained an already tautly streched medical delivery system. Although the government created various provincial hospitals, the pressure proved too much. Troops arrived in Chile improperly fed, thirsty to find there were no hospital beds for them. The *Itata* docked carrying only one physician and five nurses to care for 400 men, many of whom suffered from fever. Because of this shortage of medical personnel and facilities, the overworked staff had to perform emergency amputations. The lucky just lost a limb; the less fortunate perished. It might have been wiser, noted one journalist, to keep the wounded in Lima rather than for them to die of neglect enroute or in a Chilean hospital.[37]

El Estandarte Católico called upon Santiago's citizens to supplement the government's efforts: the rich should donate money; the woman should sew; and the poor could offer their personal service. However, since so many *Santiaguinos* had left for their summer vacations it was doubted that many would volunteer. Thus, the wounded continued to arrive at Santiago's hospitals via trolley car. Those sent to provincial facilities often rode in third class train compartments. Even the best of intentions sometimes misfired: all of Talca turned out to welcome its heroic wounded but the train arrived with its precious cargo left behind in Santiago.[38]

The demand for hospital space forced the authorities to discharge patients prematurely thus filling the city with half well men. One correspondent reported seeing two troopers, both veterans of Tacna, begging on Santiago's streets. When one man's wound began to bleed, he sought to re-enter a hospital only to discover that no beds were available. Rather than remain in the capital, he turned to panhandling in hopes of obtaining passage to his home, Concepción, where "at least he would not die like a dog."[39]

Not all experiences proved so grim. San Felipe collected $700 for medical care for those hospitalized in its infirmary. In contrast to their earlier meager rations, the hospital offered each soldier four meals a day and, should he request it, another as well. Curicó welcomed its wounded guests with soup, milk, ice cream, and cigarettes. Chillán provided money; and while Limache organized concerts and entertainment for the convalescing troops.[40]

Soldiering not only endangered a recruit's health, it also jeopardized his family's survival. The departure of the wage earner into the military drastically reduced his dependents' standard of living. A private in the infantry or cavalry, for example, earned only $11 per month, less than a peon's wages. Although the government provided a subsidy of $3-$4 per month, a *mesada*, this sum alone could not sustain a family. Clearly soldiers had to remit part of their pay home to maintain their wives and children.

But, just as the Moneda lacked the expertise to meet the technical requirements of the war, it also possessed neither the financial resources nor the institutions to pay its troops. Local officials, facing large military payrolls, often did not have enough funds and had to appeal to the capital for help. Sometimes the Moneda ordered the local *aduana* to deliver the money to provincial administrators so they could pay the soldiers. But when the custom house's coffers were empty, the government either had to authorize a special payment or, in a few cases, simply borrow the money from private individuals or appeal for charitable contributions.

When this finance system failed, the government stopped paying both salaries or *mesadas*. Thus men like Abraham Quiroz, a soldier from Quillota, wrote numerous letters home inquiring whether his father had received his allotment or asking if his family could send him money either because he had not received his pay or the army required him to purchase certain items. Trooper Quiroz and others observed that the government did not begin paying him on a regular basis until the end of 1882. Consequently, sometimes the only money the troops received arrived as a result of the generosity of private individuals or communities who often donated to units originating from their area.[41]

Again the wounded suffered more than the healthy because the government sharply reduced the salaries of hospitalized soldiers. If a trooper died or became permanently disabled, the military stopped paying both his *mesada* and his wages, thus reducing his family from subsistence to poverty. The dependents of officers could at least obtain a pension under an 1855 measure, but enlisted personnel enjoyed no similar protection. By the end of 1879 when, after the battles of San Francisco and Tarapacá, the casualty rate soared and the press began complaining about the suffering endured by the families of the troops, it was clear that the Moneda had to alter the situation.[42]

In December 1879, Pinto introduced a measure to grant to the families of soldiers killed in battle a temporary pension equal to two-thirds of the deceased's salary. The heirs of officers could either accept this award or receive the payments authorized by their own pension legislation. Some congressmen wished to increase the benefits; others sought to table the Pinto proposal although, as Felix Echeverría observed, delay would cause a hardship: he had already seen the families of dead soldiers begging in the streets. While this heartrendering scene inspired Echeverría to speak, it did not stimulate his generosity because he proposed reducing the pension benefits. Such parsimony outraged some of his colleagues, among them Enrique Tocornal, who quite accurately characterized the president's suggestion as an act of justice not charity. Tocornal's anger, however, failed to convince the lower house which, following Echeverría's lead, authorized only half pay to the families of the war dead. The Senate proved equally mean and the emasculated Pinto proposal became law in December 1879.[43]

The legislation verged on the grotesque because it failed to include those men who died of natural causes while serving in the armed forces. Of course, it mattered not at all to the families whether their fathers, husbands, or sons succumbed to the bullet, the bayonet, or the bacillus: their means of support had evaporated and with him the possibility of sustaining themselves. Given the standard of Chilean military medicine of the time, the virulence as well as the prevalence of disease, and the lack of any concept of hygiene, such "natural" fatalities far outnumbered battlefield deaths.

The press condemned the measure, denouncing it as niggardly and demanded adequate compensation for the "noble rotos" who spilled their blood for the motherland. Typically, even those who were supposedly covered by the provisions of the December law failed to receive their benefits. Many had to beg or live in "misery," leading *Los Tiempos* to wonder whether "while our soldiers risk their lives in the north, if their families are perishing from hunger?"[44]

Injustices also developed because the pension law demanded extensive documentation that often exceeded the ability of illiterate peasants to prepare and submit. Government officers often did not keep convenient hours or operated far from the provincial homes of the needy. The offices, moreover, had to wait for the Moneda to remit the funds before they could pay any benefits. Of course, these reasons provided little consolation to the long lines of women and children who waited for hours, often in the sun, simply to receive their just due. Tragically, some of the bureaucrats deliberately delayed the paperwork to convince the exhausted family to sell its pension rights for a fifth of its value and thereby obtain a guaranteed income for life. This corruption even reached down to the guards who charged people a fee simply to obtain entry into the official's august presence.[45]

The various defects in the pension measure inspired efforts at reform. In mid-1880, Echeverría sought to amend the 1879 legislation to include men who had died of non-battle-connected causes. The lower house's comisión de guerra i marina opposed any alterations, claiming that they would strain the treasury as well as become a method which would allow people to cheat the government.[46] Echeverría begged his colleagues to reconsider before rushing off to their *haciendas* or seaside resorts leaving "those who have given the motherland glory, honor, and fortune, deprived of the most basic requirements or subjected to the cruel martyrdom of not being able to work, lacking even food."[47] Portions of the press also became indignant, demanding that the government cease economizing by starving the families of the war dead. One critic likened Chile to a cruel stepmother, noting that one woman received a pension of but $3.33 per month for which her son had to perish. "Enough, it is not possible that one's heart should not react to so much misery." El Padre Cobos, tired of seeing soldiers starve and orphans die, declared that the government's preoccupation with the needs of the rich, at the expense of the families of the war's heroes, could drive one to embrace either Communism or Nihilism.[48]

Finally, in June 1881, the minister of justice, Manuel García de la Huerta, informed his colleagues that a congressional committee had taken the pension issue under consideration. But, when nothing materialized, Eulojio Allendes proposed that the government grant the family of those who died a one-time payment equal to their monthly stipend for two and a half years; the crippled would receive their entire salary for life.

The committee sidestepped Allendes's suggestion but, perhaps shamed, it finally submitted its own version of how Chile should reward the families of those who died and the maimed. Officers and enlisted men who suffered a complete disability would receive their full salaries for life. Partially disabled officers were awarded a sum equal to their pay for ten years, while the lower ranks acquired a pension based on two-thirds of their salary. The measure also included funds for the widows and children of the war dead and, under certain conditions, widowed mothers as well. The families of officers killed in action could either remain under the protection of the 1855 pension law or accept the payments established by the new proposal; the heirs of the deceased would recieve a stipend equal to 50 percent of his salary. This proposal also established institutions to train, either in agriculture or mining, the sons of the dead or disabled; the daughters would obtain a more genteel education in two schools especially created for them. The measure also finally provided some compensation to the families of those men who died from non-battle-connected causes by granting them the payment of three months' salary.[49]

Having introduced this proposal, the legislature permitted it to languish because, as *Padre Cobos* claimed, "nitrate barons, bankers, and guano merchants" controlled the Congress.[50] During the initial discussion, various deputies carped that the proposed benefits to the war-wounded seemed too generous. Luis Urzúa, for one, observed that a blind veteran should not be considered permanently disabled because he could always earn his living by playing a musical instrument. Matte also learned that crippled workers could happily subsist on very little and thus would prefer to draw a small pension to rejoining the labor force. Not all shared this attitude: Abdón Cifuentes and Manuel Hurtado considered such haggling unseemly. Lamenting that a government which had spent the nation's blood so prodigally should suddenly become so parsimonious with its treasure, Hurtado labeled the quibbling about the duration of the disabilities "stingy . . . sordid . . . and unjust."[51]

The chamber still refused to extend pension benefits to those who suffered a non-combat-connected injury and rebuffed an attempt to increase the pensions for the partially disabled. Some deputies became upset because the new bill excluded illegitimate children and provided so little assistance to widowed mothers. Clemente Fabres feared that granting natural children the same rights as those born in wedlock "would introduce immorality into our laws which cannot be tolerated." Class distinctions also remained. Nicolás González Julio would not bestow the same pension benefits on both officers and enlisted men because, he argued, the latter's families could always supplement their income by working in industry or enrolling their children in state educational institutions, alternatives not acceptable to an officer's survivors.[52]

The legislature continued to ignore the compensation issue until Luis Urzúa, reporting that he had seen a wounded verteran die in a Santiago gutter, "perhaps because he had no money," forced his colleagues to confront the issue. Urzúa's tale, however, loosened only the deputies' tongues not their purse strings. The congressmen rejected a proposal to grant pension benefits to the families of officers who died of exhaustion during the northern campaign. They also opposed an attempt to increase the compensation granted to a private's widow: the families of such a class, various members reasoned, could always work. Not completely devoid of generosity, the legislators did authorize a pension for illegitimate children, providing the fathers had left no other heirs.[53]

The Senate proved equally mean. Benjamín Vicuña Mackenna denounced the deputies' proposal, describing the amount of money allocated for the widows and orphans as "simply absurd." The senator became particularly incensed when he discovered that the measure would reduce the benefits already authorized for war heroes like Ramírez and Santa Cruz, fuming that the proposal "would take the bread from the mouths of the nation's most self sacrificing servants." Melchor Concha i Toro supported his colleague, noting that it would cost the Moneda but a few pesos per month to restore these benefits. "Those," he added, "who did not stint with their blood have the right not to have others stint on their reward." A chastened upper house restored the money to the families of Chile's most distinguished war dead; it refused, nevertheless to increase the benefits for the less famous but perhaps still deserving. The press, noting that the legislature had granted a pension to the family of Rafael Sotomayor, futilely argued that the Congress should not deny similar benefits to those who also had died from natural causes while in the service of the motherland. The appeal fell on deaf ears: in December 1881, the legislature approved the new pension measure's final version.

Unfortunately, the 1881 law suffered from many of the same defects as its predecessor: the disabled or soldiers' families still could not collect their pensions or their *mesadas*. Although the army ordered its civilian staff to work extra hours and holidays, apparently many government officials would not obey a directive that instructed them to prepare pension petitions free of charge. Desperate, some individuals simply sold their benefits to pawn brokers for a fraction of their value.[54] "How sad is the pago de Chile. What cruel greed."[55] *El Precursor*, a newspaper which claimed to represent the lower classes, denounced the 1881 bill as "the law of misery" which utterly failed to care adequately for the permanently injured or the families of those who died. This situation developed, it argued," because of the ruling class's "unpardonable indolence . . . its criminal lack of concern."[56]

HOMECOMING

The Moneda mustered out the victorious troops with its traditional lack of grace, granting each soldier to receive a demobilization payment equal to three months salary. This prize was a less than generous sum—$33, or approximately $1.25 per month for those privates who managed to survive the war from its onset until April 1881—although it pleased Atacama's merchants who were delighted at the prospect of these funds stimulating the local economy. Some Chileans considered the demobilization bonus ludicrously inadequate and suggested that local municipalities supplement it. Self-preservation as well as patriotism may have inspired this suggestion. *La Libertad*, claiming that recently discharged troops had looted stores in Santiago, argued that Talca might avoid a similar experience by greeting its returning soldiers with at least a hot meal and some type of reward.[57]

Numerous normally grim provincial towns gussied themselves up to welcome their returning sons. Quillota constructed a triumphal arch, decorated its streets, and warmed up the municipal band. *El Ñuble* called upon Chillán to "abjure its usual apathy ... to shake off this crushing trancelike state and prepare a decent celebration for their men.[59] Perhaps heeding *La Libertad*'s injunction, local authorities prepared gargantuan meals. Quillota's unit devoured 600 *empanadas*, one steer, three sheep, two kinds of salad, with wine for the enlisted men and champagne for the officers. The celebrations did not always materialize as planned. The unit en route to Chillán traveled so packed together that the men had to relieve themselves standing in place. "The odor was so unbearable that the officers could not eat for over twenty hours. If our soldiers were coolies perhaps they would be treated with more consideration."[59]

The same problems that had earlier plagued the payment of the troops apparently did not abate; units still failed to receive their demobilization payment. The men of the Rejimiento Valaparaiso and Batallón Navales were simply left without funds while the troops of the Batallón Valdivia trekked from one government office to another searching for their mustering-out pay. Not surprisingly, the desperate men resorted to begging or, in some cases, to crime to sustain themselves. The families of the mutilated or the deceased also suffered because they received no pensions; the government still stopped the salaries and *mesadas* of those hospitalized. Not without reason did *El Corvo* print a cartoon showing a mutilated soldier, who had left home promising to buy his children clothes upon his return, now reduced to begging after the army had discharged him.[60]

The nation, which had lavished such a lukewarm welcome upon the returning war heroes, was even less reverential toward its war dead. Earlier, the press had complained that the authorities had transported the cadavers of soldiers on open carts through the city to dump them, often without a casket, unceremoniously into a grave. This situation became a scandal in Valparaiso where dead officers went to their tombs unnoted and unmourned. Upset by this inattention, a group of artisans began paying for their funerals and provided a hearse and a delegation to accompany each body to the cemetery. A Señor Vivaceta also began appearing at each of these ceremonies, paying $6.00 for each internment, apparently for certain unspecified niceties. Those who died in the war were entitled to receive a free burial but Vivaceta's generosity ensured that the dead officers did not become "just scraps which should be flung into a common grave." *La Patria* praised the activities of the *Sociedad de Artesanos* "for accompanying [each casket] to the cemetery with more pomp than the most important officer." The paper urged that henceforth the city's volunteer fire companies should provide some attendants and, perhaps shamed by the contributions of the workers, the newspaper began publishing free death notices.[61]

COMPENSATING THE HEROES

After Lima fell, some Chileans again raised the issue of granting the veterans with something more substantial than a paltry three months' pay. No longer could the state plead poverty, and even if it did, the nation had to recognize the contribution of its heroic defenders. As "Un patriota" tritely observed, "one should render unto Caesar what is Caesar's."[62] Some, like *El Padre Cobos*, called upon Santa María to reward the "*rotos*" by offering them education, protection, and an opportunity to improve themselves by providing them work. Should the president do this, the newspaper promised, he would be the first leader to work for the benefit of the people of Chile. *El Ferrocarril*, which could hardly be considered a radical journal, also suggested that the Moneda should either absorb the returning troops by fomenting public works projects or by granting the men land in the south.[63]

Ramón Barros Luco had earlier proposed that the Moneda use the newly liberated Indian territories to reward the men of the victorious army and navy. While this measure evoked some support in the press, the legislature, which did not consider the proposal until January 1881, condemned it to the oblivion of a special congressional committee from which it did not emerge. This action distressed various Chileans who noted that Argentina had enticed *inquilinos* to migrate beyond the cordillera simply by offering them what Chile possessed but would not give: free land.[64]

Eulojio Allendes recommended that the legislature award a bonus of six months' salary to each veteran. Participating in a battle or sustaining a wound would give the former soldier an additional three months' pay.

Thus, a trooper who had fought in numerous encounters or who had suffered various wounds could receive a substantial sum. Perhaps because it was so generous, the legislature sent the measure to another committee for intensive study. Allendes's colleague, Diego Elizondo, also tried to compensate the victorious hosts, by proposing that the government grant each veteran a cash settlement based on the man's military rank. The state could finance this bonus by levying a tax on nitrate and guano as well as by issuing another $12,000,000 in paper money. Such a measure, he argued, would not only justly reward the efforts of Chile's citizen soldiers, it would also stimulate the economy by a massive infusion of capital. Manuel Carvallo, who had earlier denounced the failure to grant benefits to veterans as "Shylokismo," supported Elizondo's proposal. The legislature, however, decided to consider it only after a congressional committee had studied it. Like the Barros measure, the Elizondo bill disappeared into the legislative process and with it went any prospect of rewarding the veterans.

Only a few individuals won the support of the treasury. One group consisted of important generals and admirals, generally those with strong political connections, whose protectors apparently believed that these commanders should reap the benefits sowed by their men. As one newspaper noted, however, it did not seem fair to reward certain favored officers while doing nothing for the enlisted personnel. This complaint did not alter the situation: the only recipients of the legislature's largesse, other than the most senior commanders, were those who died, generally fighting in titanic struggles and against enormously unfair odds: Prat at Iquique, Ramírez at Tarapacá, and finally the men of Concepción. Even the heroic dead did not receive their posthumous reward without a struggle. Pinto introduced a measure to award a pension to the family of Rafael Sotomayor who had beggared himself on behalf of Chile. Although Jovino Novoa, a fellow National deputy supported the bill, describing the dead statesman as "the highest personification of civic heroism," not all congressmen seemed so enthusiastic. Eventually the measure won approval but it did not pass unanimously.[65]

Even the pension awarded to the family of Arturo Prat, perhaps the war's pre-eminent hero, became a political football. Juan Mackenna wished to double the family's benefits to $500 per month, since the original pension, he claimed, could barely sustain Prat's heirs. The legislative committee supported Mackenna's action, warning that unless the lower house agreed, people would denounce Chile as "cheap." The Senate, however, tabled the motion. It required a petition, signed by over fifty deputies, to shame the upper house into action.[66] The fast response, as well as the size of the pension, was reserved only for the famous: a private's widow still had to wait for months to received her mite.

The Congress also neglected the war-wounded. In 1880, Luis Jordan suggested that Chile construct a *Cuartel de Invalidos* (a veteran's hospital) where those whom the war had crippled could live at state expense without having to earn a living by "showing themselves, like live but mutilated trophies of the glory which they have provided the nation." Intitially, a committee rejected the proposal, claiming that the nation already provided adequate support. It also argued that the government should not initiate such a project because it did not know precisely how many soldiers might require this special care. The public, however, supported the idea and in July 883, Jordan revived his proposal. Again, the *comisión de guerra* opposed the measure. This time it knew exactly how many soldiers—2,010—comprised this class of the war-mutilated. Now, however, the committee vetoed the proposal because it would force the men to live apart from their families, who often needed their pensions to survive. Those crippled but not institutionalized also suffered. Only in 1882 did the government hire the services of a technician to provide prosthetic devices for those the war had maimed. This news infuriated Tocornal, who seemed more upset by seeing the mutilated walk the streets than by the suffering the veterans had to endure.

Orphans fared only slightly better than the widows or the wounded. Both the *Asilo de la Patria* as well as the *Asilo de la Purísima*—institutions for the care of the children of former officers—had a waiting list of children seeking entry. Consequently, Carlos Walker Martínez and Luis Urzuá became distressed when they learned that the Senate rejected funding the *Asilo de la Purísima*. Instead of rewarding the meritorious, one noted, the upper house concentrated its efforts on supporting a bloated bureaucracy and awarding the "comfortable classes medals, honors, promotions, and nice gifts." At the behest of the two legislators, the Chamber of Deputies mustered enough votes to override the Senate's action and to fund the orphanage for another year.

Even when it cost very little, the legislature often refused to recognize the efforts of the most worthy. In 1881, Pinto called upon the Congress to acknowledge formally the contribution of those civilians who had provided valuable assistance in supporting the war effort. The *comisión de guerra i marina* considered the president's list too short and it rejected his proposal because the deputies wanted to add the name of other deserving people. When the congressmen debated the measure in secret session, the Pinto bill disappeared.[67]

The Congress only became generous when it allocated medals. In 1880, it authorized the granting of a decoration to those men who had participated in the various battles which had occurred from the onset of the war until the capture of Arica. Even this proposal became mired in patriotic rhetoric and financial frugality. The legislature, for example, defeated a suggestion that it grant both a medal and a pension of $12 per year to each soldier. It was also strongly opposed to Enrique MacIver's suggestion that the battle of Tarapacá should be excluded from the list of approved battles. The debate became so acrimonious that the president of the Congress temporarily had to suspend the session. Eventually, the deputies approved the measure and included not only the battle of Tarapaca but also Los Anjeles and Sama. Congress would subsequently strike another medal to reward those men who captured Chorillos and Miraflores. Consistent with its tradition of generosity toward the spectacularly heroic, the legislature quickly authorized double pensions for the families of those men who perished at the battle of Concepción. Santiago would not reward the survivors of the War of the Pacific until 1906.[68]

CONCLUSION

Clearly Chile was less than generous toward its citizen soldiers and this lack of concern troubled many Chileans. *El Padre Cobos* denounced a nation for not keeping faith with its former soldiers:

> The President of the Republic, his ministers of state, the legislators, the bankers, the millionaires, all those who have economized on their blood, all those who have become richer at the cost of the people, sleep on their very soft couches... [while] ... the widows and the orphans of our brave ones, the war mutilated, and the poor, those who have brought to the altar of the motherland their widowhood, the loss of their parents, their tears, their blood ... these people have no bread to eat nor a bundle of rags with which to clothe their thin limbs ... Ah, Chilean motherland, I bless thee ... because a son cannot, and should not, curse his mother.[69]

While perhaps harsh, this quotation reflects a legitimate discontent. Clearly the legislature, more than Chile's two presidents, must bear the responsibility for failing to provide adequately for those men who fought and died, who suffered permanent injuries, or who simply survived. Exceptions to this niggardliness existed—Echeverría, Elizondo, Allendes—men who unsuccessfully sought to convince their colleagues to reward the veterans more generously. But the Congress merely mirrored the attitudes of the affluent from whose ranks came the men who occupied the legislature.

Certainly the wealthy did not enjoy a reputation for generosity in Chile. *La Esperanza* even compared them to a guillotine. Again, exceptions existed: Agustín Edwards donated enormous sums to numerous charitable endeavors and purchased military equipment as well. He even granted interest free loans to the Moneda so that it could buy armaments in Europe.[7] But Edwards was so atypical that one newspaper urged "that the other capitalists of Chile imitate the noble example of Señor Edwards and stop dissipating their fortunes on dances and tertulias, banquets, and dinners" but instead donate it to the war effort.[71]

Perhaps we should not judge Chile's wealthy too harshly. Many of them regarded the entire nation as a *hacienda* and its citizens *inquilinos*. Not surprisingly, the upper class did not contemplate rewarding the troops upon their return: the men had simply performed their duties. And, just as a *hacendado* did not provide special compensation for bringing in the harvest, he did not consider compensating the men for participating in the war. In fairness, this attitude did not stigmatize Chile alone but seemed typical of most nineteenth century rural nations. What does emerge as significant, however, is that the nameless "rotos," who merited so much and received so little, performed so well on behalf of a nation which only belatedly, and then ungenerously, honored them for their participation in the War of the Pacific.

6

The Economic Consequences of the War

> We cannot agree ... that all consumption which is not directly reproductive ... for instance that of war—is absolutely injurious without qualification.... Strictly speaking, material wealth may have been consumed unproductively, but this consumption may, nevertheless, stimulate manufacturers to extraordinary exertions, and lead to new discoveries and improvements especially to an increase of productive powers.
> Friedrich List

By consuming raw materials as well as finished products, a prolonged war can have a severe impact even upon developed nations. Chile's economy, based almost exclusively on the production of commodities and suffering from endogenous flaws, proved to be particularly vulnerable. Regrettably for Santiago, the conflict began when the productive capacity of its mines, industries, and farms was still recovering from the crippling effects of a worldwide depression. The ensuing military campaigns not only used up large quantities of foodstuffs and manufactured goods, they also absorbed manpower, hindering the country's ability to produce either for export or domestic markets. The armed struggle with the allies, however, did not constitute the only factor which affected the nation's economic development. Natural forces, like the weather, in conjunction with international market conditions, and the vagaries of world demand proved to be perhaps equally if not more destructive than the enemy. Thus, although the conflict might have had an impact on various economic sectors, it is not the only element to be considered when analyzing Chile's economic growth during the War of the Pacific.

AGRICULTURE AND THE WAR OF THE PACIFIC

Chilean agriculture had not dramatically changed since the early nineteenth century: a small land-owning clique dominated the rural power structure while the peasant, the *inquilino*, provided the muscle that filled the pockets of his employer. In return for a minimal salary, primitive housing, and some niggardly perquisites—the right of free pasturage and firewood, for instance—the peon constituted a resident labor force which, as the years advanced, had to accept increasingly onerous duties.

The *inquilino*, unlike a serf, could always leave his employer, but in a nation where arable land was particularly scarce, the threat of eviction became the *terrateniente*'s ultimate weapon. Thus, the patron could still exercise enormous power. Indeed, observers often likened the *hacendado* not to a feudal knight but to a monarch since the landlord often controlled the local militia unit as well as political office. *Hacendados* could even order their mayordomos to whip the *inquilinos* and not without reason that one contemporary advised: "If someone wishes to live like a king and to enjoy royal honors, become if you can, a *hacendado* and at that moment your dreams will come true."[1]

Generally *inquilinos* lived in rustic squalor surrounding the opulent *casa grande*. Largely compensated in kind, the cash salary—sometimes paid in scrip rather than specie—often passed from patron to *inquilino* and back to the patron via the infamous *hacienda* store. Isolated on the *fundo*, the tenant could generate little if any affection for Chile; his *patria* was the *hacienda* on which he was born and where, if he were lucky enough not to be evicted, he would die. Marcial González defended this system, claiming that the condition of the rural masses had actually improved, but *The Chilian Times*, which did not have a vested interest in the social structure, sounded less sanguine, finding "the land monopolized by a few proprietors interested only in getting in the largest possible return, irrespective of future depreciation. The soil is tilled by a race of serfs, in all but name, housed, fed, and treated like cattle; who, having no hope for the future or care for the present, are indifferent to both their own and their employer's interests."²

Once the premier agricultural producer of the Pacific Coast, Chile's farming sector had lost its vigor. The emergence, first of California, then of Australia and Argentina, in conjunction with increased activity from the American Middle West and Europe, eroded Chile's pre-eminence. Wheat, the nation's principal export crop, no longer could compete successfully against foreign grains: Chile had become a marginal producer, existing on the fringes of the world economy, waiting for some disaster—a war, a drought, a plant disease, or a pestilence—in order to make a profit. The Depression of the 1870s, combined with a glut of American grains, dashed these limited expectations. Even if a market existed, the Chilean farmer could not have satisfied world demand: the winters of 1877 and 1878 devastated Chile's agriculture, converting the *haciendas* into lakes. Not only could Santiago not export cereals, it had to import them to feed its citizens.³

In late 1878, however, the seedlings appeared healthy in the southern grain provinces and, with the exception of a few complaints about plant disease, harvesting began without incident. The results appeared gratifying although various farmers complained about their yields. Still, as *La Discusion* noted, *hacendados* always complained. The statistics indicate that the yield for wheat, barley, potatoes, and beans did, in fact, increase; only corn and *arveja* production declined.⁴

The war did not adversely affect the 1879 harvest. Chilean troops occupied Antofagasta after the onset of reaping and the outbreak of hostilities occurred after most of the harvesting had been completed. Prices moderated, much as they had in the past, although one newspaper believed that they might rise once the army began to purchase wheat to feed the troops. These expectations proved false: prices fell in the south; in Talca, sales declined so drastically that various small firms went bankrupt; and Rengo's business activity declined to a twelve-year low.⁵

Still, on the whole, the agricultural sector prospered. Indeed, as Table 1 demonstrates, 1879's harvest perhaps proved too abundant. Farmers, compensating for the terrible year of 1878, had planted large quantities of wheat. The weather reacted generously, producing bumper crops and thus depressing prices. "In 1878, we died from languor, in 1879, wheat is dying from plenty. A similar phenomenon has befallen before all those who exaggeratedly based all their hopes on a single crop. Harvesters, sowers, and producers ... should learn from this lesson."⁶

Many *hacendados* continued to ignore such counsel and increased the amount of acreage dedicated to wheat. In late 1879 and early 1880, this policy seemed quite prescient. The 1879 harvest of Great Britain, the principal purchaser of Chile's wheat, fell to its lowest level since the Napoleonic Wars. The Continent fared no better: London's *Economist* estimated that 1879 would be Europe's worst harvest in thirty years. Chilean wheat quickly commanded between 54 and 55 shillings per 480 pounds on the London Corn Market, Nirvana for those who read, with almost ghoulish pleasure, the reports about Europe's wretched farm yields. It was the old scenario replayed: Chilean *hacendados* successfully capitalizing on poor world economic conditions. Fortunately for Chile, Europe's 1880 harvest was disappointing. England, which had initially predicted more generous yields, discovered that it had been too optimistic. And, while France and the Low Countries enjoyed good harvests, Germany and, more important, Russia did not. Thus Chilean wheat brought high prices during the latter part of 1880.[7]

Logically, the war should have adversely affected agriculture in 1880. Yet, although thousands of men were serving in the army, harvests, with the exception of barley and potatoes, actually increased. Of course not all the districts enjoyed this good fortune. In the extreme south, where rains hampered the reaping, *El Araucano* claimed that some *hacendados* lost 50 percent of their crops. The owners of small parcels of land, who had to delay their reaping until they had helped their patrons, suffered even more. By April, Arauco's governor reported that crop yields would be a third less than that of the previous year, a lament repeated in Canete, Valdivia, and Concepcion.[8]

Again in 1881 many grain-producing nations produced only average harvests and Britain faced a wheat shortage.[9] Regrettably, Chile could not capitalize on the Continent's misfortune because its agricultural sector had also fallen victim to climatic caprice. The winter of 1880 painfully resembled that of 1878 when heavy storms had inundated Chile. Coronel and Quirihue, for example, endured months of constant precipitation. By the end of 1880, Santiago had suffered through sixty-five days of rain, more than the combined totals of 1878 and 1879. These storms not only devastated farm lands but also destroyed forage, killed livestock, severed road, rail, and telegraph communications, and leveled buildings.[10] (see Table 2). Obviously the crops could not escape such widescale devastation. *El Curicano* estimated that only 30 percent of the farmers would enjoy average crops; for the remainder the yields would range from bad to very bad. Not without reason did various observers conclude that the winter of 1880 had damaged Chile more than the combined efforts of Peru and Bolivia.[11]

The disastrous harvest of 1881 and the harsh winter that followed revived memories of the famine of 1877. Fearful that 1882 would be a repeat of the previous year, Concepción's bishop ordered his priests to pray for a bountiful harvest. Apparently these appeals failed: rain either delayed the reaping or destroyed the crops. Other areas suffered from a drought although enough precipitation fell in time to make the year "more mediocre than good."[12] In some cases, wind damaged the crops. The losses varied: in Lebu, they were estimated at between 33 and 50 percent; Chiloé's situation appeared more ominous: the local community had lost a quarter of its potato crop and the population's plight became so precarious that it petitioned both the municipal and the national government, for help to stave off starvation. The situation was equally bleak on mainland Chile. The unwelcome combination of precipitation and wind had virtually destroyed many crops. For Osorno, 1882 would be "a year of austerity, scarcity, and perhaps misery for the neediest of society."[13]

Ironically, prosperity did not reward those who managed, despite the terrible weather, to reap what they had sowed. A bountiful harvest often depressed prices in certain locales, and millers refused to accept wheat as a deposit. These meager returns appeared to be a cruel hoax, particularly for farmers who had spent enormous amounts of money to complete the harvest before the rains began to fall.[14]

In 1882, every important grain-producing nation experienced boom times; even England's farmers shared in nature's largesse, reaping their best harvest in seven years.[15] With Europe's silos full, Chilean wheat was no longer necessary to the Continental grain market. Again, however, Chile's agriculturists were spared to problem of having to compete on the world cereal exchanges. If 1882 had been indecently generous with rain, 1883 was the year of near drought, and farmers who had earlier cursed the precipitation, now futilely pleaded for it to return. Fires often ravaged what escaped the burning sun. Not surprisingly, yields declined in almost every category. Indeed, 1883's harvest rivaled that of 1878 as one of the least bountiful in Chile's recent agrarian history and *El Bío Bío* predicted that the poor would have to buy their food "for its weight in gold." Not without reason did one provincial newspaper note: "Misery is invading all the small homes of the peasants in our *departamento* in the most terrible way."[16]

II

As Table 1 indicates, productivity fluctuated during the War of the Pacific. As we have seen, these variations could be partly attributed to the whim of the weather. The military, however, also conscripted thousands of men into the armed forces, a loss which must have exacerbated the already difficult task of finding peons to work the land.

Labor shortages had bedeviled peacetime Chile as well. In 1878, the government offered free rail passage to peons in order to alleviate labor shortages in the south. The National Society of Agriculture (NSA) rejected the proposal; free transportation, it warned, would simply encourage gainfully employed men to desert their families in order to seek their future in the unexplored south.

At the same time that the Moneda wished to send men south, labor contractors were recruiting peons to work in Peru. Invoking nationalism, one newspaper counseled that it would be better to "beg for a piece of bread in Chile then to go to die of hunger or a horrible disease in a foreign land." Despite this warning, 150 men departed for Peru, a move which the press declared, was motivated, not by a lack of work, but by the proverbial wanderlust of the Chilean.[17]

Still, while Peru enticed men north, *hacendados* south of the Bío Bío fearfully had to wait for the arrival of workers before initiating the harvest. In Chillán, peons deserted urban projects to work on the farms while Ovalle's miners, apparently following the local tradition, abandoned their underground tasks. Thus, since labor shortages plagued the harvest in peacetime, the onset of the war should have strained an already fragile labor system. Certainly by the end of 1880, various southern and central cities complained that an inadequate supply of workers had so delayed sowing and harvesting, that the crops were damaged. In some cases, the situation became quite desperate: *El Chilote* predicted that the lack of peons would precipitate a famine while another newspaper fretted that the war would simply absorb Quillota's entire male population.[18]

The appearance of press gangs often upset the *hacendados* who needed the peon's labor and sometimes the peasants shared their patron's antipathy: in Cauquenes, a group of harvesters jumped into a river to avoid conscription. Occasionally, however, a peon happily deserted his rural master to "brandish his cherished corvo [a knife peculiar to Chile] against the Cholos."[19]

Whether seduced by patriotism or the recruiting sergeant, a lack of rural labor plagued the harvest of 1881.[20] The fall of Lima should have eased, if not ended, the shortage of manpower, but in fact, the exact opposite appears to have occurred: the need for agrarian labor remained unsatisfied even after the government began to demobilize various military units.

In part these shortages continued because the press gangs still roamed the countryside seeking fresh bodies to flesh out the disease depleted ranks of the army of occupation. In Putaendo, for example, the arrival of recruiters precipitated the wholesale flight of the town's male population. Curico's press became rightly indignant, noting the stupidity of one branch of government recruiting soldiers while another official agency was simultaneously discharging them.[21]

Throughout 1882, the military periodically competed with the *hacendado* for labor. Given the reduced size of the army, these levies should not have affected the size of the work force, but still the shortages persisted. Various provincial papers grumbled about the inadequate labor supply while *La Esperanza* lamented that one could no longer hire an artisan, a peon, or a servant, "even if he were offered his weight in gold."[22] These manpower problems persisted even when the war entered its passive phase. In Casablanca, a community near Valparaíso, harvests came to a standstill because farmers could find no one willing to work their fields. Although recruiting for the army ended in August 1883, labor shortages persisted even through early 1884 when Peru had capitulated and peace with Bolivia appeared imminent.[23]

It is interesting to speculate on the reasons behind the scarcity of labor even after the return of peace. In part, it was quite simple: the *hacendado* no longer monopolized rural labor. The military, particularly since it had won glory in the war, offered an alternative to the peon. The *salitreras* and *guaneras* of the north also competed with the landowner, holding out the inducement of more generous wages and a freer life style than that of the rural worker. Often overlooked, however, was the impact of the various public work projects, the construction of the railroads, and the process of urbanization on the rural economy which enticed peons off the farms. In Quillota, for example, workers could earn 75–80 cents per day and even these wages proved inadequate to lure men to participate in the construction of the Monastery of the Good Sheperd. As one journalist noted: "Since a year ago, Quillota could provide employment to a large number of workers because those presently available are scarcely enough to satisfy the most pressing needs of the moment."[24]

Some peons simply refused to return to their old prewar occupations. Perhaps after having participated in the great adventure of the war, they would not accept the old paternalism. A few, apparently applying their newly acquired martial skills, became thieves. Others simply joined the ever growing vagrant population, living "in a heap, primarily near the chinganas," in places like Chillán's Calle de la Independencia. A few became beggars, flooding the urban centers, particularly Santiago. The situation became so desperate in Osorno that when the military demobilized some soldiers, the local press demanded that the authorities jail them if the men did not begin to work immediately.[25]

Even those who returned to a civilian occupation did so halfheartedly. A Senate labor committee estimated that farmers lost 132 work days annually, 52 of these just to *San Lunes*, the "Devil's favorite Saint." The binge began on Sunday and extended into Monday. Tuesday was spent recovering from Monday, and only by Wednesday, and not always then, could the peon begin to function, laboring until Saturday when the cycle of drunkeness started anew. In a nation where free trade and unrestrained commercial activity enjoyed an almost mystical reverence, some newspapers tentatively suggested that the government restrict the sale of alcohol to reduce public drunkeness; others recommended the closure of bars on Sundays and urged employers not to hire people who did not report for work on Monday. San Fernando's police hit upon a more efficient if not felicitous solution: it began to raid the bars on Calle Jiménez, arresting the "luneros." Henceforth, it was hoped, workers would confine their social activities to the Sabbath. *La Araucania* suggested a more profitable and less draconian solution: the authorities should fine laborers who drank on work days, thereby ensuring the local treasury a virtually inexhaustible source of revenue.[26]

Faced with the need for labor, *hacendados* emulated the military's *enganchadores* by invading other agricultural districts in order to recruit workers. In 1883, one farmer journeyed north to hire 400 peons in order to complete his harvest. Often desperate, particularly when confronted with an impending natural disaster like a storm, or believing that their profit margins could support it, farmers increased wages. Still shortages became so acute that farm hands could command 80 cents a day, plus food, and even "lazy workers" could earn good wages. Yet, groused one journalist, improving salaries did not always achieve the desired result because "The worker does what he wants. Consequently the amount of work is halved and, at twice the price, or what is the same, the cost of production is quadruple normal." In some areas wage demands became so prohibitive that "More than one farmer in our *departamento* has preferred to delay his work, although the weather might intervene dangerously . . . to punish him for his lack of prudence."[27]

Despite the complaints, the amount of land under cultivation increased during the war, indicating that *hacendados* discovered a way to resolve their labor shortages. Many landowners appear to have embraced mechanization because imports of farm machines increased substantially during the war and local factories also manufactured similar tools. As early as 1880, a Curicó newspaper noted that "there is almost not one fairly comfortable farmer who does not possess a good thresher." Four years later, *La Araucania* reported seeing over eighty steam driven threshers as well as an additional ninety-six, drawn by animals, plus some reapers. Without these machines, a paper noted, farmers would have cultivated but 10 percent of their land and would have lost half the harvest. Not all agriculturists could afford machines but even the less fortunate could rent them from their more affluent neighbors. For that reason some have argued that it was mechanization that permitted the expansion of Chilean agriculture during the critical war years.[28]

If machines were unavailable or were too costly, farmers discovered alternatives. Copiapó's *fundos* hired enemy prisoners of war: others employed women. The integration of the latter into the rural labor force often had an unexpected effect: it deprived the rural bourgeoisie of their maids who henceforth not only could earn 40 cents a day but also have their evenings free as well.[29]

Although the agricultural sector functioned, and in some years even prospered, the war apparently did not alter its organic structure. As the *Boletín de la Sociedad Nacional de Agricultura* (BSNA) noted, a few families still monopolized most of the nation's arable land. Unemployment continued to plague the countryside where only 26 percent of the men and 14 percent of the women between fifteen and seventy-five worked. Various forces created this situation: inclement weather limited worker's access to the land; the lack of steady employment did not instill habits of work; alcoholism and vagrancy—which came first is still unclear—encouraged absenteeism.[30]

Some argued that bettering the lot of the people—improved working conditions, increased salaries, and expanded educational opportunities—might increase productivity. Others suggested that Chileans would not work regardless of the salary. According to one observer only 1 percent saved their pay; the rest merely drank it up. The more optimistic, however, believed that schools might inculcate a love of work and a sense of frugality in the rural masses. Others endorsed a proposal by Ramón Barros Luco to give returning veterans land in the newly opened Indian terrority.[31]

Apparently the condition of the *hacendado* also worsened during the war as his profit margins declined. *La Epoca,* after assessing the plight of Chile's agrarian sector, the varying exchange rates, the difficulty in obtaining shipping, and increased foreign competition, concluded: "The wheat trade in our nation is in its death throes and will receive the coup de grace the day the exchange rates reach par." The newspaper's assessment appeared accurate. Labor constituted approximately 50 percent of the cost of production and even a mediocre crop could prove disastrous. The National Society of Agriculture and others counseled both intensive agricultural techniques—the application of scientific methods, fertilizers, and farm machines—as well as crop diversification in order to compensate for increased labor costs. *La Epoca* also urged that Chile return to pastoral activities so that it might become the principal meat producer of the Pacific Basin. "Less wheat and more animals," it argued, should be the farmer's motto. Unfortunately, any change required massive infusions of capital, capital which farmers invested not in increasing the soil's fertility but in buildings, fences, roads, or the acquisition of a Santiago town house. Numerous *hacendados*, moreover, preferred to put their farm-derived profits into mining, forgetting, as the BSNA lamented, that their *fundos* represented a potential bonanza.[32]

When the war began, Santiago prohibited the sale of foodstuffs to the allies. This policy infuriated some farmers who claimed that it would depress the price of wheat. Chile might be at war but business was business. Their protests seemed premature because the enemy easily subverted this embargo using Ecuador, which, as the middleman, dramatically increased its imports of wheat and flour during 1879 and 1880. Once Lima fell, trade patterns reverted to their prewar patterns. Despite the flow of goods into Bolivia through Arica, La Paz remained isolated.[33]

With the slowdown in the war, farmers had hoped that trade would return to normal. The NSA, for instance, believed that Peru would soon be exchanging its sugar for Chilean wheat. Bolivia, it argued, would also benefit from a resumption of trade with Santiago. Foreign competition, particularly from the United States, however, threatened Chile's agricultural markets. Argentina, moreover, sought to muscle into the Pacific trade by developing its interior to link up with Bolivia. Farm interests reacted strenuously to this Platine incursion: some demanded that the Moneda guarantee that Chilean wheat should continue to enter Bolivia and the littoral ports duty free. Others wanted agricultural concessions included as part of a permanent peace treaty. Various individuals also urged the Moneda to imitate Argentina by building an extensive rail system into the Bolivian heartland. Such an act would ensure that La Paz could continue to use the Pacific as its economic lifeline to the world.[34]

Agriculture did obtain one important concession during the war: the abolition of the tobacco *estanco* in 1881. For years Chileans had debated ending this government monopoly. Opponents correctly argued that the prohibition of the domestic cultivation of this crop only enriched smugglers and agricultural bootleggers. Suppressing this prohibition, they promised, would diversify agriculture, restrict the flow of foreign exchange earmarked to pay for tobacco imports, and create a new export crop as well as a domestic industry that would employ many women and children.

Predictably the minister of finance warned that he could not easily replace the revenue so essential to pay for the war. The legislature compromised: it abolished the *estanco* but, in order to compensate the government for this loss of income, it levied an impost on those farms that had escaped taxation because they earned less than $100 per year. Contrary to the pessimists' predictions, tobacco production flourished in Chile. Imports of foreign leaf declined substantially below prewar levels.

Indeed, Chile became a tobacco exporter. An increase in the purchase of foreign cigarette paper indicated that the domestic tobacco industry was prospering.[35]

The constant hectoring about crop diversification finally yielded some positive results. By 1882, the amount of land dedicated to the raising of wheat declined from its prewar levels in favor of other foodstuffs. Crops of a commercial nature also became more popular: the acreage devoted to the cultivation of linseed and hemp increased by 415 and 115 percent respectively from 1877 to 1882. (See Tables 3 and 4) The expansion of viticulture (Tables 5 to 7) as well as the production of *aguardiente* and *chicha* increased the pace of diversification. Importation of wines varied: whites remained popular but the consumption of reds declined enormously. Purchases of foreign *aguardiente* decreased although the intake of beer remained strong particularly in the arid north. As in the case of tobacco, the alcohol industry enjoyed a moderate success in foreign markets, particularly in the newly annexed northern lands. In Chile's case, its products followed not only the flag but the palate.

Assessing the impact of the War of the Pacific on Chilean agriculture, like morality, is a question of perspective. What base year should be used as the measuring stick: 1878, when the floods came, or 1879, when farmers prospered? There is no platonic standard which can be uniformly applied: nevertheless some conclusions do emerge. The war affected agriculture because it had an impact on all of Chilean society. It restricted exports by limiting trade and consuming foodstuffs which normally would have been sold abroad. It disrupted transportation, subordinating the railroads, as well as commercial shipping, to the military.[36] But having noted these effects, it does not appear that the war seriously hindered agricultural development. In 1879 and 1880, when more men were under arms than at any time during the five-year conflict, the amount of land under cultivation slipped in 1879 by less than 1 percent below the level of 1878; in 1880 it actually increased by 6 percent (Table 8). As the Table 9 indicates, the effect varied, particularly from crop to crop. Productivity fluctuated more violently but this was more a function of climatic conditions than of the war. Indeed, had it not been for the increase in the amount of land under cultivation, the bad harvests of 1881 and 1883 would have been worse. Thus, the levels of farm output generally prospered or, at least, remained the same during the struggle. Only rarely did crop output fall and, even then, it cannot be attributed exclusively to the struggle. Thus the war's impact on agriculture appears, at most, to have been minimal.

THE MINING SECTOR AND THE WAR

The *fundos* may have given their owners the good life and prestige but it was the picturesquely named mining camps—like Lomas Bayas or Judio Muerto, located in the arid desolation of the north—that produced the real wealth in Chile. Since 1832, when Chileans began to exploit the silver deposits of Chañarcillo, mining had supplied the treasury most of its revenues. Unfortunately, the Depression of the 1870s curtailed the industrial consumption of copper, Chile's principal mineral export while the adoption of monometallism, first by Germany and then by other nations, simultaneously reduced international demand for silver, Santiago's other mining product. Metal prices declined, in copper's case quite drastically, from 84 in 1875 to 58 in 1878. (Table 10): the fall of silver seemed only slight less precipitious, dropping from 56 7/8 shillings per ounce to 52 9/16 in the same time period. Obviously, even had the war not erupted, 1879 would not have been an auspicious year for the mining industry. Coquimbo's copper pits, barely able to sustain production, had dismissed many of their employees. The workers fled the smelting center of Guayacán and the once frenetically active Chañarcillo became "languid, silent, its work areas with only a few workers, its mines barely producing."[37]

Logically, the war should have been the coup de grace to the moribund mining sector. Located close to the locus of military activity, the copper and silver fields offered a tempting target for the recruiting sergeant. And the statements of a local historian can be believed, many miners happily rushed to enlist. By the end of 1879, Atacama's intendent noted that his province had contributed two battalions as well as replacements for a total of 1,730 soldiers whose absence should have subtantially reduced mineral production.[38]

Yet, as in the case of agriculture, the war's impact appears to be mixed. While the exports of copper ingots in 1879 almost equaled prewar levels, the production of ore, *minerales del cobre*, declined drastically from 1,411,098 to 81,100 tons. This decrease resulted not from any interruption in mining activities but from the embargo on trade with the allies. Since the early 1870s, Chile had imported enormous quantities of copper ore from both Bolivia and Peru. An April 1879 government edict prohibited this commerce, reducing the flow of ore from approximately 7,400,000 kilos in 1878 to slightly more than than 99,000 the following year. Domestic levels of production also varied: the principal mining provinces, with the exception of Coquimbo, yielded more copper in 1879 than during the previous year. In some ways the conflict benefited the mining sector. Fears of a war-induced shortage halted the slide in copper's value on the world market. When it became clear, however, that the struggle would not seriously interrupt the flow of the red metal, international prices first declined, than stabilized in October, and eventually settled at a level 15 percent higher at the year's end. (Table 11)

Thus, copper mining flourished. The British consul noted the extensive coastal trade bringing copper ore to Lota for smelting and coal to Coquimbo for use in its metal processing plants. The north's economy benefited from the fact that it sold its products for hard currency while paying the miners in the less esteemed, and less valuable, paper peso.[39] Not all provinces shared the prosperity uniformly. In Santiago, Valparaíso, Aconcagua, and Atacama, yields increased but the amount of metal extracted often declined. Only Coquimbo's output dropped, although the amount of metal produced increased, indicating perhaps that the ore smelted contained more minerals.

By January 1880, it seemed as if good times had indeed returned. "Chile's sails billowed," rhapsodized one newspaper, but the prosperity quickly became becalmed.[40] By March, prices fell to 61£ per ton, and remained there for the rest of the year. Exports of *barra* and *ejes* also dropped. Domestic production enjoyed mixed results: while Atacama's yields rose substantially, those of Aconcagua declined. In Coquimbo ore production increased but not that of the finished metal. Indeed, had it not been for an increase in Santiago's output, due in part to the mines of Las Condes, the nation's total yield would have plummeted even lower. Some might have concluded that the war had finally seriously affected the mining sector.

Certainly the recruiting sergeant had arrived. Indeed, by early 1880, *El Constituyente* feared that unless the government restrained the press gangs' activities, they would "ruin mining and with it, commerce." Mine owners begged officials to stop the draft because, they argued, it deprived them of essential workers. The press complained that Atacama had contributed a disproportionately large share of men—1,800, about 14 percent of the total male population—and warned that a proposed mobilization of the National Guard would remove another 1,398 individuals from the province. By August, so many men had left the area that some mines ceased functioning, a phenomenon which apparently was not confined solely to Copiapó.[41]

Not all of those who departed Coquimbo joined the army. Many elected to seek their fortune in the newly opened *salitreras* of Taltal and Aguas Blancas. Regardless of their destination, be it the front or the nitrate fields, the effect seemed almost fatal. Caldera became virtually a ghost town: its commercial life was moribund and by 8 P.M., its streets were deserted. Henceforth, labor became more scarce and, as the British consuls of Coquimbo and Caldera noted, manpower costs increased.[42]

Yet, not all of the decline in copper's productivity could be blamed on the lack of labor. The same heavy rains which had ravaged the south in 1880 also devastated the north, flooding its mines, killing its citizens, and severing Tongoy's railroad as well as the crucial Coquimbo-Ovalle spur. Over 360 mm of rain fell in Serena, almost 300 percent more than in 1879 and five times as much as in 1878.[43] Unfortunately, 1881 brought no relief. Over 230 mm of rain fell, slightly less than in 1880, but still well above the average of the prewar years. Domestic production of copper ore dropped sharply: 75 percent in Aconcagua and 66 percent in Coquimbo. Of the three principal copper-producing provinces, only Atacama enjoyed an increase in its yield. (See Tables 12 and 13)

This decline was due, doubtless, more to natural phenomena than to the war which, by 1881, had become less active. Many mines remained filled with water and in Coquimbo additional rain prevented the reopening of the various pits. The flooding of the Rojas and Délano coal mine in Coronel also hurt the mining sector. Although all but two of the mine's 2,500 workers escaped—they were above ground celebrating Chile's independence day—the damage proved extensive. The owners closed their operation, forcing some 6,000 to 8,000 people who either worked in the coal pits or who relied on the mines for a livelihood, to seek their fortune in Talcahuano or Lota. Though far from the copper mines, this disaster also adversely affected the metallurgical industry. Smelters had to absorb an increase of 30 percent in fuel costs and the elevated prices of processing may also have reduced the demand for ore.[44]

War-related labor shortages, aggravated by the Panama Canal Project, the lure of the *salitreras*, and periodic outbreaks of disease, hobbled the mining sector. Hundreds fled from the Norte Chico to Antofagasta where they hoped to work. Sometimes these dreams failed to materialize: Taltal's *salitreras*, which initially lured so many, became paralyzed, depriving the migrants of their newly found jobs. *El Constituyente* suggested that the government could defuse a potentially dangerous social situation, as well as alleviate Atacama's labor shortage, by recruiting men in the idle nitrate fields.[45]

During 1882 and 1883, a dozen new mining corporations, many employing the latest technology, sought to resurrect their holdings in the Norte Chico and the Atacama. Those who feared the return of another Caracoles Bubble, with its frenetic speculation, had no cause for alarm: production increased substantially in Aconcagua, Atacama, and Coquimbo. The corporations, however, had little reason for happiness: international copper prices, which rose toward the end of 1881, slipped in 1882, forcing the miners "into mourning because this fatal news had dashed to the ground the castles which they had built." Despite this setback, copper interests persevered and productivity in the Norte Chico increased. Net yields, however, with the exception of Atacama, often remained below earlier levels of production: the attempt to revive the faltering copper industry had largely aborted.

Severe structural defects had prevented copper's resurrection. The mining code, unkindly described as a throwback to the colonial period, discouraged the investment of foreign as well as domestic capital, thus preventing the mines from modernizing. The communications system, moreover, hindered the movement of ore to the smelter as well as supplies into the mining camps. High interest rates, fluctuating prices, and cut-throat competition curtailed capital formation.[46] The state compounded an already desperate situation by levying high taxes on the export of the metal as well as the importation of items the miners required. Until these problems were remedied, "the miner [remains] a *mitayo* and the State an *encomendero*."[47]

Demobilization did not end the labor shortages. It was not as if there were no workers; on the contrary, idle hands abounded, clogging the streets or the dank *chinganas*. But the miners, like the agrarian proletariat, refused to return to the shafts and open pits. The local press advised that the owners should recruit men in the nitrate fields or counseled local officials to launch a campaign to convince people that Tarapacá's *salitreras* were not the promised land. One editorial even suggested that employers could hire and retain workers if they paid higher salaries and provided safer, if not more congenial, working conditions. A more traditional source advised the police to roust the vagrants out of the bars and into the mines. Ironically, Tarapacá did not fare much better: *El Veintiuno de Mayo* begged the government to discharge the army in the north rather than transport them back where they had enlisted. Otherwise they would have to import the Chinese who only wished to eat rice and smoke opium. Although some mine owners mechanized, others hectored to the government, requesting free rail transportation to bring men north to the copper pits.[48]

Regrettably, even when a labor force existed, it was improperly exploited. Chile's mines employed a system known as *pirquén*. Indeed, the *pirquinero* was to copper and silver what the share-cropper was to the *hacienda*: an inefficient worker who extracted "only the most profitable part of the ore" leaving the rest behind; in short, a slash and burn miner. The government's mine inspectors criticized the owners for employing this system but, they noted, for these men, the mine is "a hacienda which should require no fertilizer or labor: the pirquineros are their beasts of burden who are delegated the task of making the *fundo* produce without cost or labor."[49]

Thus, Chile's mining and smelting interests became mired in a vicious economic spiral. The mines produced mainly low grade ores which, when processed, yielded less copper. At the same time, labor shortages drove up wages by 75 to 150 percent between 1878 and 1883. Consequently, mining costs increased while output declined. Owners, moreover, could not recoup their expenses: by 1884, increased competition from the United States and Spain had depressed the copper market to its lowest point since early 1879. Not without reason did the Sociedad de Mineria funereally pronounce: "the exploitation of copper . . . is obviously prostrate and in an extremely grave and threatened condition."[50]

Silver suffered the same unkind fate as copper. The world's financial circles, with the exception of a few East Indians and the vocal North American Populists, had spurned silver in favor of gold, depressing its value and undermining its popularity (see Table 10). In addition to declining demand, labor shortages, inclement weather, disruptions in the transportation system, and reductions in coal output limited production. Still exports, except for the year of 1881, remained well above their prewar levels and the number of silver mines increased sharply in 1883, particularly in the Atacama where production reached its highest point in years (see Tables 14 and 15).

Despite its problems, silver had one substantial advantage over copper. Even if the world rejected it as specie, Chileans would happily pay a premium for silver coins. Unfortunately, silver became more difficult to extract. Although this problem varied from area to area, miners increasingly had to dig deeper, and at greater cost, to find the metal. In Chañarcillo, five mines had shafts over 500 meters deep and one reached the 680-meter level. To survive, mine owners had to purchase more sophisticated and costly equipment, which required substantial investment capital few possessed. The only bright spot was the discovery of a new chemical process which converted heretofore worthless slag heaps into a valuable resource. On the whole, however, although silver miners suffered during the War of the Pacific many of their problems were attributable to structural defects in the entire mining sector, not to the conflict.[51]

If the copper and silver mines suffered an economic recession during the War of the Pacific, lowly coal prospered. The growth of war related domestic industries, in conjunction with the greater consumption by the fleet, stimulated coal production by 26 percent in 1879 alone. Coronel, the center of coal mining, rejoiced in this increased activity (see Table 11). The following year, the mine's yield, as well as the work force,

The Economic Consequences of the War

declined. While it is hard to isolate a single cause, clearly the war exercised a decisive influence. The coal pits, located in the south, became a focus of recruiting activity and, unlike other areas, this province had to endure the efforts of the army's recruiting sergeant and the navy's press gang. When, as transpired in Coronel, both groups began to fish in the same water, the local populace fled the area, thereby disrupting the economy.[52]

Even after this spontaneous flight of population, one newspaper calculated that the area had contributed approximately 700 men to the military by early 1880 and, since many had been illegally recruited, miners refused to enter Coronel for fear of being impressed. The nearby *departamento* of Lautaro had sent 2,000 soldiers off to the war, and the recruiting, both legal and extralegal, continued into the next year.[53]

Although the work force in the coal pits decreased by 40 percent during 1880, the entire decline cannot be attributed solely to the war. Miners may well have sought more lucrative employment in the north, and others may perhaps have turned to agricultural pursuits. Although the causes for the drop in employment remain unclear, the results proved disastrous: commercial life stagnated. "The poor cannot earn enough not even to eat," wrote one paper which blamed this dilemma on the war. The same malaise afflicted not only Talcahuano but Coronel which resembled "a large school during vacation." Employment did not rise in 1881, in part because of the Rojas and Délano mine disaster. During the following year, 1882, the work force grew dramatically, indicating perhaps that the recruiters had become more restrained. Generally, the coal industry did not enjoy the bounty of peace. While the Cousiño family's Lota complex boomed, Coronel remained depressed, apparently still the victim of the unexpected closure of the Delano mine.[54]

Smelting was one of the few sectors of the mining economy to prosper during the War of the Pacific (see Tables 16 and 17). During the 1870s, Chile's metallurgical processing sector expanded and two centers of activity emerged: Guayacán located in the north and Lota, whose proximity to the southern coal pits and easy access to the sealanes endowed this grim provincial city with enormous commercial advantages. Indeed, before the onset of the war, Lota's manufacturing enterprises had made it one of Chile's most industrialized centers.[55]

Although the war may have interrupted the mines' output, it did not deprive the metal processors of their labor force. Even in 1880, when the conflict had dragooned so many men, employment at the smelters remained slightly above its 1879 levels. Only in six departments did the number of employees decline and in one of these, Ovalle, the drop may have been the result of weather-induced damage rather than a war-related labor shortage. Conversely, employment rose in five departamentos. Thus, while the ore-processing sectors of the mining industry suffered, the ancillary portion, smelting, thrived.

Although the metallurgical industry remained intact, mining's future appeared ineluctably grim. Chile had lost its dominant position as the world's premier producer of copper. Even when Chile's mines increased their level of activity, the nation's proportionate share of the world market declined.

The industry suffered from a variety of organic flaws. The mining code restricted development and the *aduana* not only taxed imports required by the miners, but it also levied an impost on the export of copper, increasing its cost and thus reducing its ability to compete on the world market. Some claimed that the lode of copper had disappeared but this judgment missed the mark: the mines were not depleted, one simply had to dig deeper to find the ore. This effort, however, required technology and therefore capital. While a few far-sighted individuals made such expenditures, these men apparently constituted a minority among the mining profession.[56] The provincial press flayed capitalists for investing their funds not in the mines but in the cities, the farming sector, or the banks whose rate of return was higher and the degree of security greater. "Money," wrote a newspaper, "is the best dynamite and the sharpest crowbar to perforate the mountain."[57]

The legislature somewhat belatedly sought to remedy the plight of the mining industry when in 1882 it debated abolishing the export tax on copper. Opponents described this impost as "anti-economic" since it was levied without considering the cost of production. Thus, a company could lose money and still have to pay the tax. Its abolition would permit the nation's mines to compete with foreign rivals and would encourage marginal enterprises to renew their activities.

The minister of the treasury, as always, opposed rescinding the tax, claiming that it was not the propitious moment to take such a momentous step. This assertion apparently struck a responsive chord because the Senate rejected the lower house's attempt to end the levy. Despite this rebuff, Francisco Gandarillas resurrected the measure in 1884. This time the minister of the treasury, Ramón Barros Luco, supported the proposal, seeking to substitute a *patente* tax for the export impost. Given the support of the government, the legislature managed to eke out a majority to delete the export tax from the *lei de contribuciones*.[58]

Although dissimilar, miners and farmers shared common perceptions. Both considered themselves overtaxed and undercapitalized. Both believed that they received few, if any, benefits from government. Both argued that they merited a special place in Chilean society: the farmer because he incarnated rural virtues; the miner because he was in the vanguard of technology.[59] Fantasies aside, both were also the victims of the world economy, the changing patterns of consumption, variable weather conditions, and the harsh rules of the law of supply and demand.

Assessing the impact of the war on mining is, at best, difficult. Exports of copper ingots rarely surpassed prewar levels but again this decline cannot be attributed simply to the outbreak of the war. Some of the problems afflicting mining—the failure to invest and foreign competition—appear systemic. Other factors such as the declining prices, the disastrous storms, although transitory, nonetheless strongly influenced the economy. Clearly the war absorbed labor but so did the opening of the *guaneras* and the *salitreras*. Indeed, the latter may have proved more seductive to the labor force than the clarion call of the military. Yet, the war's influence should not be overemphasized. During 1883, when the war had virtually ceased and the military need for manpower fell dramatically, the amount of copper produced, sometimes dropped below the level of 1879 and 1880 (see Tables 11 and 13).

In summation, the war did not cripple mining; Chile's copper and silver industries were moribund even before 1879. Productivity had declined and, as the figures for the coastal traffic indicate, the copper industry had come to rely increasingly on the occupied territories as a source of ore. Before the signing of the Treaty of Ancón, for example, the amount of copper imported into Chile from Bolivia surpassed the output of the mines of Aconcagua, a situation which worsened each year. Certainly the conflict adversely affected the traditional mining sector. Yet, increased foreign competition, uncertain world demand, and undercapitalization may have had exercised a greater impact. Victory gave Chile Antofagasta from which it would extract so much copper in the future. (Chuquicamata is located in this region.) But the same victory also assured the nation a monopoly on nitrate whose allure proved a stronger incentive for development than the silver and copper fields of Old Chile.

THE WAR AND THE INDUSTRIAL SECTOR

Francisco Encina argued that the War of the Pacific enhanced Chile's industrial capability.[60] This conclusion, like many, appears at best partially correct. Chile had abandoned free trade in the 1860s, preferring to insulate selected industries behind protective tariffs. In 1872, the legislature passed an omnibus *aduana* code which sought to reconcile two seemingly contradictory goals: collecting revenues for the government and fomenting the creation of domestic industry by permitting raw materials and certain other items—like tools and machinery—to enter Chile duty free. Six years later, new *aduana* regulations increased the number of categories of duty-free raw materials and machine tools and curtailed the entry of manufactured goods through increased import taxes. Consequently, when the war began Chile already had factories established and functioning.[61]

Unfortunately, few of these industries could be easily adapted for military purposes. Some, like the foundaries of Carlos Klein or Lever and Murphy and the government-owned Maestranza of the Southern Railroad, could fabricate some types of machinery, work metals, and repair boilers. Under the direction of Colonel Maturana and a civilian, Diego Hall, the Maestranza not only manufactured approximately 600 artillery shells for Chile's imported cannons and for captured enemy equipment— which it retooled—it also fabricated armor plate and reworked the boilers for various naval vessels. Another Maestranza employee, an engineer named Sellinger, even designed a torpedo boat.[62]

Other civilian enterprises provided interim assistance until equipment purchased in Europe could arrive. Otto Klein's Rancagua factory manufactured cartridges for small arms while Gustavo Aderman produced artillery shells. These activities complemented the efforts of the army's arsenal which initially was not prepared for war and then, as a consequence of an industrial accident, blew up in 1880. Repaired and equipped with French machinery, it began to produce materiel for the military. Despite these accomplishments, national industry's contribution to the war effort appears to have been limited. The government purchased most of the heavy equipment abroad.[63] Local factories, however, could and apparently did manufacture large amounts of ammunition, particularly for small arms, which undoubtedly helped Chile's army.

Domestic factories produced certain other material for the military. Tomé's Bellavista Factory wove cloth for uniforms as well as blankets and ponchos. The Fábrica de Paños de Tomé, which opened its doors in April 1879, manufactured some 15,000 ponchos in addition to over 120,000 meters of woolen material. By 1881, Bellavista, perhaps because it installed electric lights, could weave 8,000 meters of cloth per month. Tiffou Hermanos and Lecassie filled an order for 6,000 pairs of boots, an assignment which it completed with the help of the prisoners from the local penitentiary. Incarcerated felons also manufactured mattresses as well as other equipment for the armed forces while civilian laborers provided saddles.[64]

Not all local industries shared in the wartime prosperity. On the contrary, tax records indicate that a substantial number of factories ceased functioning during the first months of the war. A variety of forces might have precipitated this decline. The war disrupted internal communications because items needed for the military certainly had priority over those intended for the civilian consumer. The induction of large numbers of men into the armed forces also must have dampened the need for traditional consumer goods. Certainly the public's purchasing power declined because the level of military salaries remained below those paid to civilians. Regardless of its etiology, the decline becalmed not only factories but almost every type of business establishment, from a tannery to the confectioner. (Tables 18 and 19)

The situation improved after 1880 and industrial activity quickened. The shoe industry, for example, enjoyed great favor. Chileans extolled the virtues of domestic shoewear—*El Padre Cobos* claimed it was so sturdy it would last the "Wandering Jew" a year. One prominent bootmaker, Mariano Vuletich, described as a Chilean possessing the activity of a Frenchman, the intelligence of a German, the punctuality of an Englishman, and the entrepreneurial spirit of an American, employed over 500 people and produced footwear ranging from the most simple to the more refined.[65]

The area of the economy which quenched the nation's thirst for beer and alcohol also prospered. And, perhaps eager to capitalize on this boom, the Cousiño's Lota complex opened a factory to produce bottles. The abolition of the estanco encouraged the tobacco industry. Schleger, Gubler i Cia. founded a factory in Chillán which employed some fifty people. As booze begat bottles, cigarettes stimulated a related enterprise: matches. One factory, working in conjunction with the inmates of Rancagua's jail—who manufactured the boxes—began operating in 1881. This proved a felicitous arrangement: the city could defray a portion of the cost of maintaining its prisoners while the local poor, particularly the women and children, found gainful employment. Indeed, according to the local press, the factory needed even more workers. Perhaps aware that previous match factories had not fared well, the government granted the Compañía Nacional de Fósforos and anyone else interested in opening a similar concern, import concessions for a period of ten years. The establishment of local industry, while gladdening the nationalist, often proved less gratifying to some inhabitants. One poor soul, revolted by the stench emitted by Curepto's soap factory, demanded that it move, describing the concern as "simply a device which dissolves pigs, dogs, and whatever is given to the manufacturer."[66]

Generally it was not until 1881, and sometimes later, that the number of factories and commercial enterprises equalled their prewar levels (see Tables 18 and 19). Imports of the raw materials required to fuel Chile's industries had fallen during the first months of the war, rebounded partially in 1880, and then increased after Lima's capture (see Table 20). The importation of machinery followed a similar pattern. As Table 20 indicates, most of the consumer related industries acquired their capital equipment before the onset of the war; only the metallurgical sectors imported large amounts of machinery, undoubtedly because they could be used for the military. Even then, as in the case of other machine imports, the actual numbers generally increased only after 1880 (see Table 21).

The level of exports apparently followed the same course (Table 22). The factories established prior to the conflict apparently prospered during the 1870s. Then, probably as a consequence of the world depression, they ceased exporting significant quantities of goods. Exports apparently bottomed out in the first years of the war, not recovering essentially until after 1880. Most of the material manufactured locally—shoes, sweets, soap, ready made clothing, sacks, and noodles—flowed to New Chile, the area seized during the war, although the nation apparently also retained some of its pre-war markets as well.

While the nation's domestic industries grew, Chile still continued to import consumer goods (see Table 23). Yet, as the tables indicate, the entry of certain items often declined and in some cases, shoes—for example—rather substantially. Yet, the nation seemed to be in a transitional stage, producing items for export while simultaneously patronizing overseas manufacturers. The annexation of Tarapacá and Antofagasta, as well as the acquisition of the temporary sovereignty over Tacna and Arica, permitted Chile to internalize some of its former overseas markets. Heavily populated with large numbers of adults already integrated into the economy, the north should have provided Chile with a secure market and a potential for future economic growth. As we shall see, however, the nation failed to capitalize on this opportunity.

The War of the Pacific not only unleashed a wave of chauvinism, it accentuated its economic counterpart: protectionism. To call the prevailing attitudes of the time xenophobic may be perhaps too harsh, it is nevertheless true that foreign participation in the nation's economy became the subject of hostile criticism. The press objected to aliens working in government-owned factores, arguing that Chileans possessed the requisite skills. The activities of foreign corporations, particularly insurance companies, angered many as did the fact that these companies' dividends were remitted abroad rather than in Chile. The news media demanded that the state implement "Chilean laws for the Chileans;"⁶⁷ capitalists were beseeched not to invest their funds not abroad, which was "the ruin of the nation," but in Chile, in order to make the country as self sufficient as possible.⁶⁸ Some urged that the Moneda, in the interest of stimulating national industries, should give preference to goods produced locally, even if these proved more expensive than imports. Otherwise, as *El Ferrocarril* noted, "The great results which our military victories achieved would be lost for our benefit if they are not translated into energetic industrial vitality." *La Patria* claimed that Chileans would happily pay a 20 percent premium for domestically produced items if this policy would result in the creation of local industries. "Chile," it argued, "would never be a happy nation as long as it lacks industries and manufacturers."⁶⁹

Various individuals demanded that the government ensure maritime as well as naval supremacy over the Pacific Basin by subsidizing a national merchant fleet through monetary grants and laws requiring that a certain portion of each crew had to be Chilean. Ignacio Gana praised the services of the merchant navy without which, he claimed, Chile's war effort would have been paralyzed. Yet the nation still needed more ships than could be guaranteed by the Compañía Inglesa de Vapores which he described, was exercising a "monopoly of the strongest to the death of the weakest." Given the international situation, Chile required a larger merchant fleet.⁷⁰

An important change occurred: free trade, once a revered doctrine, became the object of hostility if not disdain. *El Padre Cobos*, with its usual lack of taste, described the economic theory's adherents as leeches sucking the blood from a supine and naked woman bearing the name "La República." Chile would have to cease being a raw material producer, particularly since its share of these resources had begun to decline. The war had demonstrated the nation's abilities; not to capitalize on these assets in peacetime would be criminal.⁷¹

Other considerations, both military and theoretical, stimulated protectionist sentiment. The recent conflict had revealed Chile's dependence on foreign arms manufacturers which the creation of a domestic weapons industries would diminish. For some, industrialism provided a solution to social problems. The forced repatriation of Chileans living in Peru and Bolivia had earlier unsettled the labor market, a condition which the demobilization of 25,000 veterans would surely aggravate. Many quite reasonably feared that a return to the high unemployment that characterized prewar Chile might unleash widespread unrest. Thus, industrialization emerged as the solution. Endowed with the requisite raw materials inhabited by a heroic as well as an intelligent population, Chileans believed that their nation could become an industrial power. Local factories would not only unleash a cornucopia of excellent finished products, they would stanch the flight of Chileans abroad, provide an opportunity for the landless peon and the urban poor, and cure unemployment "the gangrene that is threatening the nation's health," perhaps thereby avoiding a social upheaval.[72]

Increasingly, many visualized the state as the principal force to achieve this goal since the government possessed the means to train people in new technical skills. Its purchases of domestically manufactured goods would prove to the local capitalists that they could safely invest in national industries, converting each factory into "fountains of general welfare."[73] *El Padre Cobos* even urged that the state open factories in order to employ the returning veterans, offering them an alternative to a life of crime or the dismal prospect of starvation. The more restrained urged less radical but nonetheless viable suggestions: the state should provide technical education, grant monopolies to those who would create needed industries, patronize national factories, and increase tariff protection.[74]

Preoccupied with the conduct of the war, the legislature neglected the issue of protectionism; in a sense, however, it did not have to address the question. Early in the war, the lower house had instituted a 10 percent surcharge on items already paying imposts of 15 or 25 percent. This new levy represented a substantial proportional increase in the existing level of taxation. A subsequent decree required that all import duties be paid in hard currency. The differential between the *peso fuerte*—specie—and the paper peso fluctuated. Each month the president adjusted the amount charged. As Table 24 indicates, during the years 1880 and 1881, this levy reached almost 40 percent. Thus an item might sometimes have to pay an additional amount, essentially doubling the original tariff. This measure, then, certainly restricted the flow of goods into Chile. The British consul, for example, observed that the higher tariffs had helped the sale of spirits, wines, carriages, saddles, boots and even shoes in Coquimbo. Indeed, Chilean beer even supplanted its English competition.[75]

Lamentably, Chile's enthusiasm for its own national products had all the constancy of a feckless lover: the public tended not to patronize local industries. Sometimes this was because domestic items cost more to manufacture, a factor that generally cooled the ardor of even the most passionate economic nationalist. Snobbery encouraged various individuals to purchase foreign goods instead of locally produced products. The state did not act more nobly, ordering uniforms, saddles, and shoes from European manufacturers. These actions infuriated the press which argued that "the government has the duty to protect national industry." Occasionally, these protests restrained the Moneda from preferring foreign goods over those fabricated domestically, but unfortunately such successes were rare.[76]

In 1881, for example, the Senate debated the appropriation of $340,000 to purchase 4 locomotives and 100 cars for the Southern Railroad. Informed that the local maestranza could fabricate this equipment, the *comisión de hacienda* stipulated that 50 percent of the rail cars should be acquired from domestic manufacturers if they proved to be of the same quality and could be delivered in the same time period as those manufactured abroad. Various senators supported the proposal, among them Luis Urzúa who argued that the measure would employ the working class and thus provide an opportunity for social mobility. The minister of the interior, José Vergara, claimed that it would prove more costly than imported rolling stock and convinced the Senate to reject the proposal.[77]

Despite this setback, Chilean heavy industry enjoyed some success. A team of three men labored for five months to construct the locomotive *La Chilena* at a cost of $15,869.43. Although it rested upon European wheels and axles and its boiler included imported material, the rest of the engine was fabricated locally. Chilean firms bid and won contracts to build the bridges of wood and iron over the Calera, Itata, and Maipo rivers—492, 352, and 800 meters long respectively—as well as the Maule River. The latter contract contained a clause specifying that preference would be given to local producers, over foreigners, only if their bids "were equal or almost equal," otherwise, the lowest bidder would win the contract. The specifications for the other bids did not include this provision: the firms which won the competitions did so because they could outbid their foreign manufacturers.[78]

The legislature also passed certain measures favoring the creation of various domestic industries. Yet these never emerged as a substantial sector of the economy, at least not during the War of the Pacific. Despite its potential, Chile's heavy equipment producers never developed into a powerful industry. One newspaper despaired that the government had chosen to "help certain favorites of those in power who, with the collection of a commission of a certain percentage, long to amass a fortune at the cost of the country's laboring class and to hell with the future of the national industry."[79]

Not all the problems facing industry could be attributed to the government. Ironically, the very forces which brought joy to the hard money proponents hurt domestic manufacturers. As the purchasing power of the paper peso increased, the differential between it and the *peso fuerte* declined, making foreign goods more competitive. This drop began in 1881 and generally the surcharge generally remained below 10 percent for the next two years.

Many manufacturers also lacked capital. While there was a substantial increase in the number of corporations between 1879 and 1884, most of the investments flowed either into the mining or transportation sector (Table 25). Those involved in industry came in a poor fourth, faring only slightly better than agriculture. Local capitalists apparently preferred to invest in potentially more lucrative and less risky enterprises than a factory which had to compete against foreigners.

The equity market also siphoned off capital from potential industrial development. Stocks offered certain obvious advantages: liquidity, limited risk, a potential for capital appreciation, and dividend income. In addition, the stock and bond market advanced rather substantially during 1880 and 1881 when local industry was the most protected (Tables 26 and 27). One might well wonder what would have happened if the capital had been invested in Chile's manufacturing sector rather than a stock portfolio. Banks hindered industrialization largely because they refused to lend large sums of money for long periods of time, a policy which starved industry of needed capital.[80] Finally, geography also conspired against industrialization. European traders may have found it cheaper to transport consumer goods from the Old World than Chilean producers from the nation's Central Valley. Foreigners enjoyed a substantial advantage: on the return trip they could carry *salitre* back to Europe; local industrialists, however, had nothing valuable to transport from New Chile back to the lands in the south.

The statistics indicate that the War of the Pacific apparently did not stimulate Chile's industrial growth. Most of the nation's factories, perhaps responding to the protectionist 1872 Aduana Code, were established prior to the onset of the conflict. Imports of raw materials, as well as machinery, fell dramatically during the active phase of the struggle and did not recover until after Lima's capture in early 1881. Chilean exports of manufactured goods followed a similar pattern: prosperity in the mid-1870s, depression, and then recovery after 1880.

If not the war, then what stimulated the growth in industrial output? Two forces may have encouraged the post-1880 industrial development. One, of course, was the creation of a new growth pole in the captured provinces of the north, what we have chosen to call, New Chile. The population centers of the *salitreras*, largely dependent upon the south for survival, constituted a major consumer market for Chilean products. A revived urban economic sector, in conjunction with an ambitious public works program, also played a significant role. From 1875 to 1885, Chile's urban population increased dramatically (see Table 28). Four demographic clusters developed: in the north, around the traditional mining centers and the newly opened *salitreras*; in the south, where new cities grew on land once dominated by the Indians; around Santiago and Valparaíso; and finally, on the Concepción-Talcahuano axis. These emerging centers required new residences and commercial buildings to house their expanding populations. Santiago's numbers increased by 40 percent and; consequently, the amount of building permits issued during the war rose substantially (see Table 29). Similar expansion occurred elsewhere: in Traigen, in the south, there was a housing boom, a phenomenon which also occurred in Curepto as well.[81] Throughout Chile, municipal and provincial governments paved roads, installed water, lighting, and sewer systems, built plazas and parks, beautified areas, and planted trees.[82] As a consequence of this urban expansion, the building trades mushroomed, employing large numbers of men and using locally produced products.

The construction and maintenance of the nation's rail and road system both consumed products and employed casual labor. Chile's road network rarely managed to survive the long harsh winters. Periodically, severe storms, like those of 1877, 1878, and 1880, washed away roads, bridges, telegraph, and rail lines. During the lean years of the late 1870s, a parsimonious Moneda did little more than patch the most tattered of the highways. And, of course, the onset of the war prolonged this period of neglect as the military absorbed the lion's share of the budget. Thus, throughout the war, despite the numerous complaints of provincial officials and private citizens, the communications system suffered from economic malnutrition.

The reduction in the level of hostilities freed funds for these needed repairs (see Table 30). The Moneda, as well as the local government, often bolstered by the contributions of private citizens, embarked upon a binge of road building and repair which absorbed large sums of money as well as labor. A road gang working on the Las Condes highway employed 500 men. The pay scale appeared high and responded to the demands of the market place: within a three-month period in the 1880s, wages increased from 32 to 40 cents a day; in less than a year, a peon was earning between 50 and 60 cents per day. (Apparently, these positions were highly prized because a group of workers, seeking employment, attacked a road gang, disrupting their efforts.) These public works projects, then, absorbed large amounts of labor—which might explain where the peons had gone rather than return to the farm or the mine—and undoubtedly stimulatied the economy as well.[83]

Thus one could argue that the War of the Pacific indirectly encouraged the development of Chile's industries. Victory permitted the annexation of the north, which in turn provided a new market for Chilean products. In addition, the revenues generated by the nitrate industry funded the government's public works projects, which both used locally produced items as well as employed large numbers of people who became consumers. This was not a proximate causal process: the industries did not develop to meet the needs of wartime Chile. On the contrary, it appears that the onset of the struggle disrupted the process of industrialization which could only regain its momentum with the return of peace.

THE WAR AND THE NITRATE INDUSTRY

Chile's *salitreras* expanded rapidly during the period 1879-1884. Before the war, Taltal and Aguas Blancas, located in Old Chile, the area south of the twenty-fourth parallel, contained the nation's nitrate mines. The annexation of the Atacama incorporated the fields of Antofagasta and Toco. Finally, with the conquest of Tarapacá, the richest prize of all, the mines of Peru fell into the nation's grasp, thus ensuring Chile a world monopoly.

Rather than forming an organic whole, the various *salitreras* differed in natural resources, transportation networks, and historical development as well as economic potential. Aguas Blancas and Taltal were developed in the early 1870s. Isolated from the rest of Chile, without adequate water supplies or access to a decent transportation system, these two mining areas did not produce a substantial amount of nitrate until late 1879. The distance from the coast, inadequate transportation, the lack of both water and a work force crippled these areas. Although the Chilean government had granted various concessions, the cost of production in Aguas Blancas and Taltal still averaged 100 and 75 percent higher respectively than in Tarapacá.[84]

Despite this inauspicious situation, people flooded north, attracted by the prospect of work. This massive exodus depopulated portions of the south. What started as a brillant venture, however, quickly lost it glitter. Taltal's *salitreras* became saturated with people while its level of production declined. The imposition of an export tax aggravated the economic situation. Local producers simply could not earn a profit after paying the cost of production, transportation, and then the new impost. Mines ceased functioning, commerce closed its doors, beggars filled the avenues. The local authorities, fearful that the miners might abandon begging in favor of more direct action, requested troops to police the city. This precaution proved providential: in late 1881, the unemployed workers took to the streets, threatening not only the government and their former employers, but all those who advised calm in the face of such unfortunate conditions.[85]

One deputy sought to alleviate the plight of Old Chile's *salitreras* by exempting them from taxation until a rail line could be constructed connecting the interior with the coast. While the *comisión de hacienda* supported protecting local industry, it opposed this measure because it favored one group of Chileans over their domestic rivals. The committee agreed that Taltal and Aguas Blancas labored under difficult circumstances but that the state should not try to equalize conditions among competing economic interests.

When conditions degenerated, the *salitreros* of Aguas Blancas beseeched the legislature for relief. Arguing that they should not be victimized because the nation had the good fortune to capture the nitrate fields of Peru and Bolivia, they sought two measures: an exemption from the export tax until March 1882 and a 50 percent reduction in the export tax until the completion of the railroad to the coast. Carlos Walker Martínez, inspired by the efforts of these individuals, introduced a formal proposal incorporating these demands. Again the deputies appeared unimpressed: "If it [Aguas Blancas] dies, it dies by itself, and the Congress is not obliged to preserve those who cannot live except at the expense of others." Not completely callous, the legislature accepted the minister of the interior's compromise by halving the export tax until June 1882. The Congress also authorized the construction of a rail line connecting Aguas Blancas with Antofagasta.

Capitalizing on this unexpected outburst of generosity, the *salitreros* of Taltal submitted their own petition requesting help. Seven hundred workers, it noted "pulse through the streets, bearing menacing countenances, demanding salaries which cannot be paid because the *salitreras* are paralyzed, [and] the owners have nothing with which to satisfy their obligations. Meanwhile men beg for bread and their families cry out from misery." Invoking the name of its 10,000 inhabitants, the petitioners sought for tax relief. While the Senate seemed compliant, various deputies complained that the proposal was too costly and that the industry was already moribund. The Minister of Finance Aldunate, however, supported the proposal, noting that it would provide temporary relief for a limited time. Blessed with this lukewarm benediction, the measure cleared both chambers.

The fall in the world price of nitrates hurt Old Chile's *salitreros* who felt overwhelmed by the burden of taxation, capital expenditures, the high price of food, and the cost of labor. A few legislators resented that the state should help the nascent match industry of Rancagua while it neglected the *salitreros* who also employed numerous Chileans, including women and children. The legislature eventually granted some concessions to the mines of Taltal and Aguas Blancas but to no avail: the lower prices that nitrate commanded could not defray the higher costs of labor, food, taxes, or needed capital expenditures. Production plummeted and the *salitreras* of Old Chile ceased contributing materially to the nation's nitrate sector.[86]

Antofagasta would share this same bleak fate. The province contained two centers of nitrate production. Toco, located inland near the port of Tocopilla, was the poorest in the region. Developed in the early 1870s by Chilean capitalists, it labored under substantial handicaps, particularly its geographical isolation, which increased the cost of transportation and provisioning. Most of the local miners barely eked out a living in a land noted for its lack of generosity. The Compañía de Salitres y Ferrocarril seemed more favored, possessing adequate nitrate deposits located close enough to the surface so that mining posed no special problems, and a developed transportation system.[87]

Despite these advantages, Antofagasta's situation appeared untenable. Initially it prospered: exports increased, its fields worked at capacity. But the imposition of the export tax devastated the region. "The people disappeared and the steam ships are inadequate to contain the emigrants who flee terrified from the hunger and desolation which comes to engulf them." Like its southern neighbors, the Compañía de Salitres could not compete and petitioned the government to grant it a concession to extend a railroad into Bolivia's interior as well as grant it a subvention.[88]

Tarapacá clearly constituted the gem of the nitrate empire. The most developed, it produced the lion's share of Chile's *salitre*. Military victory may have given the Santiago control of Lima's *salitreras* but it did not confer legal ownership. The nitrate mines still belonged to Peru; possession without legal title tainted the situation and complicated Chile's attempts to tax the export of this commodity. It was like a civil marriage: the appearance of propriety would not suffice; without the blessing of the church, the union lacked validity.

Unraveling ownership proved a difficult task. In the 1860s and early 1870s, private capital, part of it Chilean, had developed Peru's *salitreras*. Caught between the enormous expenditures for public works and a parsimonious oligarchy, Peru's President Manuel Pardo increased the export tax on nitrates, delighted that this act, which could regulate market conditions, would not hurt Peru. Having hit upon this congenial solution, Pardo established a government monopoly to control the sale of nitrates. In 1875, hagridden by financial problems, Peru expropriated the *salitreras*. Many of the property owners did not object too strenuously: the nitrate market had collapsed, hence they could not believe that they had lost any bonanza.

Initially, Lima used the nitrate mines as collateral for a £7,000,000 loan, 3,000,000 of which would finance needed public works while the remainder would liquidate the costs of the nationalization of the *salitreras*. Unfortunately, the government could not implement this plan. Instead, it took title to the mines, issuing the former owners interest bearing certificates, that were to serve as trust deeds, and which it promised to redeem in two years. While the government legally owned the mines, it did not work them: the former owners continued to operate the *salitreras*, functioning under a quota system that sought to obtain the maximum profits by regulating production.[89]

At first, Santiago did not agonize over the question of ownership. Anxious to obtain revenues, it sought to sell the nitrate that had accumulated during the blockade of Iquique and Pisagua. The *salitreros*, however, refused to cooperate, not out of any affection for Lima but because the Peruvian government threatened to levy an enormous fine on any nitrate miner who acceded to the Moneda's demands. Tired of legalistic niceties, Santiago seized the nitrate, selling it at public auction. The various mining companies, led by the powerful House of Gibbs as well as other prominent *salitreros* like Gildemesiter and Campbell, protested. Lima's capture ended the threat of Peruvian reprisals against any *salitrero* who would work his mine under Chilean control. The revival of production, however, did not solve the state's dilemma. The foreign certificate holders requested that Santiago exchange the Peruvian paper for Chilean government bonds. But if the government accepted this demand, it would have burdened the nation with a debt of $31,000,000.[90]

In 1880 Pinto appointed a congressional committee to study the problem and to offer solutions. The men, citing Chile's historic affection for free trade and Lima's disastrous mismanagement of the *salitreras*, unanimously urged the abolition of the Peruvian nitrate monopoly. Instead, it suggested that the courts supervise the return of the mines to private hands; henceforth, the *salitreras* would function unfettered by government regulation.[91]

The dismantling of the monopoly delighted many. Chile, one argued, had triumphed in the war "under the banner of liberty and progress," whose colors would inspire it in the postwar struggle as well. Economic liberty, which had brought prosperity to Chile, would make the arid wasteland of Tarapacá flower, whereas the retention of the monopoly system would have eventually corrupted the nation's public morality.

Pinto empaneled a second congressional committee to study how to dismember the monopoly and return the *salitreras* to private hands. Acting on its recommendation, the government in June 1881, authorized granting title of the mines to individuals who could produce 75 percent of the certificates issued for each *salitrera* as well as a cash deposit for the remaining amount. The Moneda subsequently liberalized its terms and in 1882 it permitted the sale of any company whose ownership remained unclaimed.[92]

Many have subsequently lamented that the government relinquished a monopoly that would have enriched the state. Two powerful considerations made such a decision quite predictable if not rational. Nineteenth-century Chileans, while willing to grant some lukewarm protection to industry, simply could not imagine the state administering an industry. When in the past the government had become involved in certain enterprises, like the tobacco *estanco*, it invariably demonstrated an unparalleled ineptitude. Thus, the concept of the state competing in the market place was anathema. The government instead should stand out for its "purity and simplicity of administration." The return of the nitrate *oficinas*, even to enemy nationals, not only indicated the measure of Chile's greatness but the reinstitution of free trade would offer local capital and labor new opportunities. Thus, ideology, in conjunction with past experience, encouraged the Moneda to cede the *salitreras* to private hands, "an economic and political solution which is perfectly in accord with the aspirations and the needs of our nation."[93]

As noted, various foreign *salitreros*, many of whom enjoyed close relations with their governments, demanded that Chile redeem the Peruvian nitrate certificates. This suggestion was not outlandish. Santiago, on the other hand, wanted the pleasure of ownership but balked at the painful prospect of assuming the outstanding debt. Already bogged down in a war, the Moneda could ill afford to finance the purchase of the nitrate shares. Thus, it washed its hands of the sordid issue, letting those who held the paper squabble among themselves over the ownership. Chile, in the meantime, would simply tax the *salitreras* and hope that all would prosper.[94]

And, of course, prosper they did (see Tables 31 and 32). In 1881, the government supervised the return of the nitrate mines to their new owners. The results would have gladdened the heart of Adam Smith: by 1882 the level of exports and employment had increased twofold over the previous two years. Most of this expansion occurred in Tarapacá whose nitrate deposits were richer than its competition to the south and which also possessed a more highly developed rail system. Indeed, by 1884 the tonnage of *salitre* exported through the ports of Antofagasta and Tocopilla constituted only 16 percent of the nation's total nitrate production.

Despite its advantages, Tarapacá's situation appeared less than idyllic. It too suffered from labor shortages and miners complained about the high prices charged by the local railroad—a situation which proved particularly vexing when the price of *salitre* began to decline on the world market. This problem became worse, forcing some, particularly the smaller producers, to protest the dual burden of the export levy and the high rail fares. The introduction of the Shanks process, however, substantially lowered production costs while permitting the refining of lower grade nitrates, and various *salitreros* rushed to incorporate this new technology. But the process and the general revival of the industry miscarried. Increased production saturated a market that no longer required so much nitrate, particularly when Europe's sugar beet industry suffered a recession. The world market price declined, leading to the formation of the First Nitrate Combination, a cartel that sought to regulate production in order to limit the decline in the market place. Thus, the Chileans learned a sad lesson: the *salitre* monopoly could not buffer one against the realities of the world economy.

The nation's economic future appeared splendid because the state still controlled the production of a highly prized commodity; in fact, however, although the nitrates were Chilean, the mine owners were not. Foreigners, particularly the British, had cleverly purchased the nitrate certificates at a fraction of their value when it appeared that Peru would repudiate them. Chile's decision to return the mines to private enterprise, while ideologically consistent with the nation's past, merely wrenched the nitrate monopoly from out of the hands of the Peruvian state into the control of English capitalists.[95]

CONCLUSION

The Chilean economy grew at an uneven rate between 1879 and 1884. This disparity in development cannot be attributed solely to the war. Agriculture, although victimized by labor shortages and inclement weather, expanded during the conflict, perhaps because it markets remained intact. Beset by similar problems, mining could not resurrect itself faced with an increase in the costs of production and a concurrent decline in the market value of its products. Industrial growth also occurred but this expansion does not appear to have been related to the war. The base for a manufacturing sector already existed and while the war perhaps stimulated certain industries—like textiles or shoes—the greatest surge of growth took place after the fall of Lima and thus is related to the growth of the urban sector and the expansion of public works projects. The surcharge on the paper peso also encouraged the consumption of domestic products more than war-induced shortages. Nitrates proved a congenial asset that in the long run stimulated the economy by providing Chile a captive population who consumed large quantities of domestically produced items. The revenues generated, moreover, became the nation's single most important source of income until the 1920s. Thus, although the War of the Pacific might have influenced various economic sectors by depriving them of labor, the impact of the conflict seems limited when compared to the distortions created by natural forces, such as the weather and the caprice of world demand and prices.

7

Greenbacks and Nitrates

> Anybody has a right to evade taxes if he can get away with it. No citizen has a moral obligation to assist in maintaining the government.
> J. Pierpont Morgan

The onset of the War of the Pacific forced the Moneda to spend enormous sums to pay the military and to purchase supplies and equipment. It quickly became apparent, however, that Chile's tax system, like many of the nation's prewar civilian and military institutions, was incapable of satisfying the country's financial requirements. Since the existing tax system could not generate sufficient revenues, the Moneda had to improvise stop-gap measures in order to fund the war. In comparison with its other difficulties, these problems appeared trivial; yet, without adequate funding, Santiago would lose the conflict as surely as if the allies defeated its troops on the field of battle.

As Table 33 indicates, Chile's tax system, like that of many nineteenth-century nations, rested squarely on the custom house. This method possessed certain obvious advantages: it functioned smoothly; it could identify and collect imposts quickly; and it provided the government with a fluctuating but nonetheless constant stream of funds.

The railroads constituted the next largest source of income although their operating expenses proved more costly than maintaining the bureaucratic staff of the *aduana*. The tobacco monopoly, the *estanco*, also proved a relatively lucrative source of funds, contributing about 10 percent of the state's annual income. Three other imposts completed the government's financial repertoire: the *alcabala*, a tax levied on the sale or transfer of real estate as well as certain other types of property; the *patente*, an impost charged for the exercising of a profession or operating a business; and the *agrícola*, a tax of approximately 9 percent imposed on all farms valued at more than $100. These taxes yielded approximately 12 percent of the nation's ordinary income.

One trait distinguished Chile's tax system: it lacked any sense of discrimination. Rich or poor, man or woman—all paid at the same rate regardless of their assets or income. The treasury never inquired into the economic status of the taxpayer or whether his endeavors produced a profit. Indeed, the only place where Chileans enjoyed full equality was not the courts of law but in the offices of the tax collector. Predictably, few favored the existing method of collecting revenues, precisely because it failed to impose a greater share for the funding of the government on the shoulders of the affluent.[1]

THE IMPOSITION OF THE INCOME TAX

The economic depression of the 1870s forced the Moneda to become more creative in discovering new sources of revenue. After having reduced its budget, Santiago moved to tax gifts and inheritances in 1877. These levies, although modest, constituted a sharp break with tradition and, because they fell essentially upon the wealthy, they represented a move toward a more equitable tax system. After much haggling, the *herencia*—an impost on estates—became law in 1878. Politics, however, had stymied the passage of a more radical measure: the imposition of a tax on income. The deteriorating economic situation, however, forced the minister of the treasury, Julio Zegers, to resurrect the idea in late 1878. Although the Chamber of Deputies accepted Zegers' initiative, the measure stalled in the Senate. Economic necessity and public pressure, however, forced the legislature to revive the proposal. Meeting in secret, the Senate approved the imposition of a 3 percent levy on earnings derived from capital invested in real estate, certain types of securities, and all income exceeding $300. Although a few senators, while supporting the taxation of interest income, objected to levying an impost on salaries, the new minister of finance, Augusto Matte, citing the economic demands of the war, prevailed.[2]

The passage of this levy, the *haberes,* aroused mixed reactions. The banks groused that the new law unfairly taxed them twice, once on the notes they issued and again on their reserves. Others complained that the measure not only fell on industry but also on its employees. Indeed, *La*

Esmeralda feared that the 3 percent impost on income would prove so confiscatory that the people would stop working.[3] Not all Chileans shared this apocalyptic view, many considering the *haberes* eminently fair: henceforth the capitalist and the rentier would have to bear at least a portion of the nation's tax burden. Talca's *La Opinión* even argued for a special war tax, to fall on "those who have too much and not take the bread from the mouths [of the poor]."[4]

The income tax began generating income immediately, and by 1880 the minister of finance predicted that it would produce about $600,000. Because he disliked certain aspects in the law—the differential in payment due to the source of income and the residence of the taxpayer—he suggested that the legislature remedy these defects. Subsequent ministers also proposed the abrogation of the double taxation on banks as well as instituting a system to ensure that private employees would pay their taxes like those in the public sector. Indeed, widescale tax evasion emerged as the principal flaw in the *haberes* tax. In 1882 the minister, as well as local authorities in Santiago, admitted that most private citizens successfully avoided paying this impost. To remedy this situation, he suggested creating a list of taxpayers, levying penalties for nonpayment, and making all taxes direct and progressive.

Perhaps inspired by these complaints, the legislature reformed the law by exempting the salaries of public employees from the *haberes* measure. Even the president sought to end the tax on salaries while retaining it on income from capital, changes which eventually occurred after the conclusion of the war. Despite its defects, the *haberes* tax represented a movement toward the modernization of Chile's fiscal system. For the first time, rentiers and those who derived their income from capital investment had to contribute toward the nation's maintenance.[5] Yet, while productive, neither the *haberes* nor the *herencia* could finance even a portion of the war.

THE *ADUANA* AND THE WAR

Traditionally, the government would have increased the customs' taxes in order to cover any war-induced financial shortages, but this alternative no longer existed: the government, in order to cover a budgetary deficit in 1877, imposed a 10 percent surcharge on imports paying duties of 15 or 25 percent. Continuous economic difficulties forced the legislature to renew this levy the following year.[6] Thus, by the onset of the war, Santiago had already exhausted many of its traditional financial nostrums (see Table 34).

President Pinto unexpectedly demonstrated some ingenuity when, in

July 1879, he requested a law which would require importers to pay their *aduana* duties in hard currency. Those who did not have the specie could pay their taxes in paper pesos. But Santiago, however, was not naive: it levied a surcharge, to be adjusted monthly, equal to the difference between the silver peso, worth 38 pence, and the paper note. Some opponents feared that this measure would increase the cost of imported necessities. Noting the absurdity of a government printing paper money and then coyly refusing to accept it, Luis Urzuá suggested that the Moneda either economize or discover a new source of revenue. Other deputies warned that Pinto's proposal would unleash a plague of pauperism on Chile; Félix Echeverría predicted that the bill would kill the proverbial golden goose. The minister of finance, Augusto Matte, however, insisted on the measure, asserting that this proposal would fall essentially on the wealthy. And, he added, if he but had the strength, he would "impose on the powerful and the strong the main weight of public taxation."[7]

Matte's statements did not endear the minister to those deputies who insisted that reducing expenditures would obviate the necessity for more taxes. Zorobabel Rodríguez, always in the vanguard of enlightened thought, suggested that the government economize by ceasing to fund public education. In order to demonstrate that he was even handed, he also favored withdrawing public support from the Church. If these measures failed, he advocated halving the Ministry of Justice's budget. Anything, obviously, seemed preferable to raising the price of imported goods when paper money had already pushed up the cost of living.

The more prescient believed that the tax, by increasing the cost of imports, would make domestic products, no matter how shoddy, more attractive. The suggested levy also enjoyed other benefits: it would prove easy to collect; it encompassed a large mass of tax payers; and, best of all, it fell generally not on the poor but on the wealthy. Finally, the measure, by balancing the budget, would strengthen the value of paper money. Tagle Arrate shared some of these sentiments and in addition noted that the proposal, by reducing the consumption of foreign goods, would stimulate national industries and thus provide employment for Chileans.

The Chamber of Deputies approved the Pinto proposal but the Senate proved more hostile. Melchor Concha i Toro described the measure as inflationary, particularly because it increased the cost of living for the working class. The comisión de hacienda concluded that the legislation created a dual monetary system: one for the importer and another for the producer. It also doubted that the measure would achieve the desired result. Consequently, it offered a substitute motion which sought to distribute the burden of future devaluation evenly throughout the entire tax system rather than place it exclusively on the *aduana*. After some rather byzantine calculations, the comisión concluded that the differential between the paper and silver peso equaled 12 percent. Thus, it proposed to increase by that amount all taxes: the *agrícola, patente, herencia, haberes* as well as the *aduana*'s impost. Should that suggestion fail to attract the support of the Senate, the committee moved to increase the existing tariffs by a flat 30 percent. Various senators, intimating that the comisión's suggestions verged on the unintelligible if not ludicrous, rejected its proposal. The legislators then repudiated the comisión's substitute motions, accepting instead the deputies' version with but one emendation: henceforth, 5 percent of the specie collected from the customhouse would be allocated to the amortization of paper money.[8]

The surcharge on paper money proved a clever resource. It did not require the creation of new bureaucracies nor even the expansion of the old. It also became a valuable accessory: in 1881, for example, it produced 18.7 percent of the total revenues raised from the taxation of imports into Chile. Nevertheless, it too proved unequal to the task of financing the war.

THE NITRATE TAX

In its frenetic search for revenues, the Moneda eventually turned to what some claimed had originally sparked the confrontation with Bolivia: nitrates. The president requested a tax of 10 percent on the profits obtained from the mining of silver, copper, and *salitre*—a measure, he believed, would yield about $400,000 annually. This proposal aroused substantial antipathy because it fell upon the weakest sectors of the mining economy: copper and silver. Others objected to the mechanics of the legislation because they feared it could easily be subverted by a clever individual. Ironically, a few deputies even considered the levying of such a tax illegal because it violated the exemptions previously granted by the Bolivian government in 1874. This argument outraged numerous legislators: deputies like Vergara Donoso, Walker Martínez, and Enrique Tocornal responded that since the war had benefited the Compañía de Salitres it too must contribute to the nation. Even Zorobabel Rodríguez, who generally preferred economy in government to taxation, supported the attempt to levy an impost on nitrates.[9]

The public had agitated for such a tax even before the president's proposal reached the legislative floor. *El Estandarte Católico*, noting that Chile did not fight wars to enrich the House of Gibbs and Edwards, demanded that the Antofagasta company contribute, and contribute generously, to the war effort. The issue became particularly volatile when some of the press alleged that the blockade of Iquique, by cutting off shipments of Peruvian nitrate, had enriched the *salitreros* of Antofagasta, a charge which various legislators repeated with ill-disguised anger.[10]

Some deputies considered the president's suggestion clumsy; others became upset because Pinto did not grant some concessions to the newly opened *salitreras* in Old Chile—those of Taltal and Aguas Blancas, which could not compete as effectively against the richer fields to the north. As a result, Ramón Barros Luco offered a substitute motion to correct both defects: he suggested a tax of $1 per 100 kilos of nitrate exported through the port of Antofagasta while exempting the *salitreras* of Old Chile from this impost for two years. The lower house rejected Pinto's proposal, calling instead for a tax of 20 percent on the net profits obtained from the sale of each quintal of 100 pounds of nitrate mined and exported in Antofagasta. This measure not only increased Pinto's original level of taxation, it fell exclusively on the reluctant back of the Compañía de Salitres y Ferrocarril.[11]

Although the company's journalistic and legislative defenders fretted that too much taxation would destroy the industry, public opinion favored such stern measures. *El Nuevo Ferrocarril*, noting that the nitrate interests of Antofagasta sought to influence the government, confidently predicted that the president would not dare to "contravene so openly the wishes of the nation."[12] Various news journals claimed that the Edwards family suborned representatives of the press, but warned that while "it is very easy to pay for an article or any type of message, it will prove more difficult to obtain the same favors from a body as respectable as the Chilean senate."[13]

Initially, it appeared that this prediction would miss its mark. The Senate's comisión de hacienda reduced the tax rate to 10 percent on the profits obtained from the sale of nitrate whose cost of production the committee arbitrarily set at $1.65 for each 46 kilos. Thus, the new measure had halved the tax rate while increasing slightly the cost of production. The committee's composition may have influenced its decision. One member, Marcial González, was an enthusiastic booster of free trade; another, Lorenzo Claro, was a Montt Varista deputy alleged to have close ties to the Edwards clan.

If these men believed that they could successfully gut the bill, their colleagues quickly disabused them of this notion. Most senators advocated the imposition of taxes, particularly on the property of the Compañía de Salitres, while supporting the temporary exclusion of the area south of the twenty-fourth parallel. Since charges of collusion permeated the debates, various senators turned the upper house into a confessional, announcing either that they had financial interests in the Compañía de

Salitres or that they were tied, by marriage, blood, or friendship to those who did. Having bared their breasts, the legislators began to discuss the essential issue: how much taxation could they impose without throttling the *salitreras*. Some called for special concessions, either for the Compañía de Salitres or the mines in old Chile, others opposed these same privileges, arguing that the constitution required uniform taxation; still another bloc objected to the mechanics of the comisión de hacienda's plan. Benjamín Vicuña Mackenna cut off the debates when he suggested that the government impose a simple export tax of 50 cents per quintal mined. The Senate subsequently reduced this amount to 40 cents while also seeking to exempt the Compañía de Salitres from paying both the *haberes* and *patente*. The lower house, however, accepted the imposition of an export tax but refused to ratify the Senate's concessions on the income and license imposts. Eventually, the Senate acceded to the demands of the deputies thus giving Chile a new weapon in its fiscal arsenal.[14]

It is difficult to determine if genuine economic differences or issues of personal gain motivated the legislature. Chile's past experience with direct taxation had proven less than satisfactory, a lesson which the *haberes* measure underscored. Consequently, the legislature's passage of an export tax, rather than an impost on net profits, does not seem either surprising or unwise. Similarly, the arguments over the level of taxation also seem genuine. The Congress erroneously believed that Peru would eventually participate again in the nitrate trade. Once the mines of Tarapacá began to function, Chilean *salitreras*, encumbered by a heavy export tax, would suffer the same fate as the copper mines: a loss of markets in a highly competitive trade. Thus, the legislators would have to impose enough taxation to fund the war effort without, as one senator noted, smothering those industries "still in diapers."[15] Perhaps the law of 12 September 1879 accomplished this purpose. Santiago had acquired a tax easy to calculate and collect: those who hated the Compañía de Salitres seemed equally content.

The conquest of Tarapacá in late 1879 opened that area's *salitreras* for exploitation. Indeed, as one of his first acts, the victorious Chilean general levied a tariff of $1.50 for each metric quintal of nitrate exported. Control of the northern territory, in conjunction with the occupation of Antofagasta and the ownership of the *salitreras* of Old Chile, assured Santiago a monopoly on the world production of nitrates. The opportunities seemed boundless and Vitalicio Lopez, perhaps voicing the sentiment of many, urged his fellow countrymen to extract the maximum profit from monopoly. The revenues, he reminded them, would liquidate the national debt, improve education, expand the rail system, and pacify the south. Indeed, he not only favored the retention of the cartel, he wished to expand it to include all of Chile's *salitreras*. Some devotees of free trade, however, urged that private individuals develop the nitrate fields. No disagreement existed on the issue of the $1.50 tax: Chileans endorsed it, particularly since it fell on the European consumer purchasing nitrates from the former mines of Peru.[16]

The *salitreros* of Antofagasta and Old Chile acutely feared that they might be subject to the same levy as those miners of Tarapacá. Obviously, the domestic producers preferred a system which taxed their competition at a rate almost four times higher than their own. Thus, the interests associated with Antofagasta began agitating for the treasury not to impose a uniform tax on all the *salitreras*, a request which some believed would be granted because the "owners of Antofagasta are influencial (sic) men."[17] Support for retaining the dual tax system also developed in the press. Justo Arteaga Alemparte warned that the levying of a high tariff on the export of Chile's nitrates would destroy that industry just as it had ruined the copper mines. The result, he predicted, would be wholesale emigration, empty factories, full jails, and banditry, "the precursors of a social war."[18] Others claimed that it would not be fair to tax equally all the mining areas: God had not endowed the *salitreras* of the south with as much water and nitrates as those of Tarapacá; their transportation system, moreover, was not as developed. Thus, abolition of the two tier tax system not only would destroy Chilean mining interests, it seemed a sacrilege as well.[19]

In early 1880, the government convened a legislative committee to investigate the condition of the nitrate industry and to make its recommendations on future policy. The members, arguing on the basis of Chile's historic affection for free trade as well as the poor experience of both the Peruvian and Chilean governments' participation in business, unanimously urged the abolition of the Peruvian nitrate monopoly and the return of the *salitreras* to private hands. The committee also called for the imposition of a tax of $2.20 for each 100 kilos of nitrates exported. While admitting that the tax appeared high, the comisión observed that it would fall primarily on the foreign consumer, that it would not adversely affect the domestic cost of goods, and that it would not hamper mining productivity. Thus it "least wounds the productive power and best serves the national interests."[20]

Perhaps aware of the unpopularity, in certain quarters at least, of the uniform tax, the comisión defended its measure arguing that it could not devise an impost which could take into account regional differences. It also opposed establishing a tax system which granted privileges to certain elements. Chile, it noted, should produce the greatest amount of nitrates at the lowest possible cost in order to fill the government's coffers. Those areas which could not compete would either adjust or fail.[21]

The abolition of the nitrate monopoly delighted many. Chile had succeeded in war, "under the banner of liberty and progress" and it would triumph in the area of peace and economic development under the same colors. Henceforth, the entire nation, including Tarapacá, would prosper under a regime of economic liberty. Conversely, retaining the cartel might eventually corrupt Chile's public morality.[22]

While Pinto may have supported the abolition of the monopoly, he did not endorse completely the committee's recommendations. Thus, he retained the uniform tax but his proposal sought to levy a tax of $2.00 per 100 kilos of nitrate exported as well as a 60 cent impost for each 100 kilos of iodine. Some opponents warned that excessive taxation would reduce world consumption, indirectly encouraging the purchase of alternatives like guano. Others argued that the uniform tax favored Tarapacá over Chilean miners. A few critics questioned the government's right to tax the *salitreras* of Antofagasta which, they claimed, still enjoyed the exemption granted by Bolivia. Increased taxation, noted others, would not simply hurt the nitrate interests but those enterprises in Chile which provided them with agricultural and industrial products. The tone of criticism became shrill: the Moneda was described as unleashing an economic pogrom against the valiant miners of Antofagasta; *El Mercurio* denounced the attempt to tax all equally as communism while comparing the unobtrusive Pinto to Atilla the Hun.[23]

The advocates of a uniform tax admitted that their proposal suffered from certain inequities. Yet, an impost based on local differences, no matter how attractive in theory, would prove virtually impossible to administer. A direct tax on a mining company's profits offered no viable alternative since any reasonably devious individual could evade it. Rather than grumble, chided one commentator, the southern *salitreros* should invest the profits they reaped during the blockade of Iquique in a good rail system which would permit them to compete more effectively. After all, concluded one deputy, the miners of Antofagasta merited no special consideration over those Chileans working in Tarapacá.[24]

Some legislators supported the uniform tax because they loathed the Edwards family whose Antofagasta holdings would benefit from the two-tier system.[25] Such concessions, others argued, would create a "privileged caste, upon whom the laws would not fall" while exempting them from "the burdens which weigh upon the more vulgar Chilean."[26] Although others admitted that the Edwards's interests had contributed generously to the war effort, they had also profited and hence should bear a greater portion of the economic responsibility. If they could flout the law, the "omnipotent will of a few rich, enslaving everything, corrupting all, will make a joke and a mockery of our sovereignty."[27] A letter from "Varios comerciantes de Valparaíso" reported that the powerful family had bought the services of *La Patria* and *El Mercurio* in order to seduce the public. The greedy financier's efforts, noted *El Nuevo Ferrocarril*, "only merits to be answered ... with the very expressive gesture which the Chileans have."[28]

Eventually the Chamber of Deputies approved a levy of $2.00 per 100 kilos of nitrate mined in the area north of the twenty-fourth parallel. The Senate's finance committee, claiming that this rate of taxation would hobble the nitrate miners, reduced the export tariff by 70 cents. Eventually a compromise emerged: the full Senate lowered the tax to $1.60, less than Pinto had wanted but more than its comisión de hacienda would grant. The *salitreras* of Aguas Blancas and Taltal retained their tax exempt status until 1881 and received a vague promise that the government would construct a railroad to improve their access to the sea. Protectors of the Antofagasta interests also obtained a provision relieving those corporations that produced nitrates from paying the *haberes* tax. The Chamber of Deputies considered some of these modifications unpalatable but the minister of finance, citing intense economic need, chided them into accepting the Senate's proposal: it became law in October.[29]

The passage of the nitrate export tax surprised many. Powerful forces had done everything, including trying to buy votes in the Chamber of Deputies, to stop the nitrate levy from becoming law. Even the normally blase *Chilian Times* appeared stunned: "Large sums of money and the influence of many of the most important men in the country have failed to prevent the bill from passing by a very large majority. Nearly all the papers in the country had been bought in vain; influence, generally so potent in this country, could do nothing."[30] *La Patria*'s Timonel happily reported that the tax had panicked those few unfortunates whose portfolios still contained stock in the Compañía de Salitres.[31]

Despite the black predictions, the nitrate industry prospered. Exports spiraled upward and the taxes they generated became a bonanza for the Moneda. Within four years, exports doubled and the revenues increased by approximately 500 percent. *Salitre* provided the Moneda with roughly 26 percent of its ordinary revenues and, in conjunction with the other measures, helped finance the drive on Lima.

CHILE ENTERS THE GREENBACK ERA

Regrettably. the imposition of new taxes, no matter how generous, could not fill the state's coffers as quickly as the war emptied them. The conflict not only disrupted communications, it also deprived Chile of its two traditional trading partners, Peru and Bolivia. Thus, customs revenues suffered substantial contractions. Frenetically searching for a new source of income, the nation discovered a felicitous solution: paper money.

Numerous nations had resorted to the printing of paper notes as a war time expedient. The United States issued greenbacks in early 1862 when its resources could no longer sustain the needs of both the civilian and the military. Washington turned to paper, however, only after it had been beggared by the war; since Chile began the struggle virtually insolvent, it had to decree the use of paper money almost with the same breath with which it ordered its troops to occupy the north.

Few questioned the need to resort to paper notes, only who would print them: the government or the banks. Under the influence of the French economist, Courcelle Seneuil, Chile abdicated many of its responsibilities to private enterprise. An 1865 law, for example, permitted credit institutions to issue bank notes equal to 150 percent of their reserves. Despite the inherent risks of such legislation, the system seemed to function. The banks pumped their newly printed notes into the silver mines of Caracoles as well as a series of often improbable economic schemes. Neither alternative proved a clever investment: the mines either exhausted their deposits or what they produced went unsold when the world market for silver dried up as a consequence of the onset of monometallism. Many of the coroporations founded during the fever of speculation collapsed when the Caracoles bubble burst.

Eventually, these unwise investments began to take their toll of the various overenthusiastic credit institutions. In October 1877, the Banco Thomas failed; the following January, the Banco del Pobre collapsed, raising questions about the nation's financial system. The Banco de la Unión, for example, barely survived a run on its cash reserves.

Chile's economic stability appeared almost as shaky as the nation's credit institutions. During the presidency of Federico Errazuríz (1871-1876), the Moneda embarked upon an ambitious but expensive public works program. Keen to complete the various projects, the government borrowed from domestic as well as foreign creditors. This solution only complicated the nation's economic plight: it increased the amount of money remitted abroad, thus straining an already taut economy.

During the depression of the 1870s imports as well as exports declined, reducing the income from the *aduana*. In order to obtain funds, the government turned to the nation's banks, borrowing $2,525,000 at 9 percent interest. In return for this loan, the government decreed that henceforth the banks' notes must be accepted as payment for all debts. In addition, the credit institutions acquired the right to issue bank notes equal to four times their loan subscription.

This was the banks' last coup. A month later, in July 1878, President

Pinto learned that the Banco Nacional could not convert its notes from paper to specie. Unfortunately, this financial dryrot permeated the entire system: all but one of Chile's banks was insolvent. Informed that only swift action could save the country from economic collapse, the legislature declared that henceforth banks would no longer have to convert their notes into specie upon demand.[32]

Although this law saved Chile from financial chaos, it outraged many citizens. To a few, the inconvertibility measure literally amounted to legal robbery: the banks had accepted specie and henceforth could return to the depositor notes of dubious value and questionable provenance. Some Chileans restrained their anger, fearful that it might precipitate widespread violence. The collapse of the Banco del Pobre had unsettled many and at least one deputy subsequently remarked that, had it been a larger bank, rioting might have erupted. A flyer appeared in Santiago denouncing the inconvertibility law as a measure conceived by the "owners of power," and predicting that more repression would follow. "Before this happens," the broadsheet exorted, "to arms, Chileans. The hour has arrived."[33]

Despite their decrepit condition, when the war erupted Pinto turned to the credit institutions for economic assistance. In return for an interest free loan of approximately $6,000,000, the Moneda promised to give its creditors bonds equal to the amount borrowed; this, in turn, would guarantee the inconvertible notes issued under the earlier legislation. In addition, the inconvertible notes would be exempt from the 4 percent tax as well as other limitations, including the conversion requirement. Ironically, the banks had nothing to lend but the same worthless paper which had earlier aroused such disdain. The financiers, however, rejected this offer which the minister of finance, Julio Zegers, considered a reasonable as well as a decent compromise. Although a blow to the Moneda, the refusal of the banks to help may have saved the government political problems. Even before the onset of the war some of the press had called for restrictions on the influence of credit institutions and the creation of a central bank.[34]

Unable to borrow, the Moneda had to print its own paper. A decree of 8 May 1879 authorized regional functionaries to issue $6,000,000 worth of "vales de tesoro," in denominations of $1,000 and bearing no interest; henceforth it would have to be accepted as legal tender.[35] Eventually, the government promised, it would find a source of revenue to redeem this paper. Until then, however, the greenback era had arrived in Chile.

The government's decision to print its own paper money did not anger the public. On the contrary, noted *Las Novedades*, for too long the banks had blackmailed the nation, driving up interest rates while lowering the value of the Chilean peso. And, the newspaper noted, it doubted if this exploitive behavior would cease in war time. "Enough of this Judaism," it argued, "the government must issue paper money."[36] Others favored the Moneda's printing *vales* because, unlike borrowing, it did not siphon money out of the economy and thereby reduce the nation's productive capacity. Prudently employed, government backed paper could replace scarce specie and complement the bank's notes.[37]

While some diehards still opposed the treasury's action, no less a personage than Z. Rodríguez, the doyen of free trade, supported the Moneda's issuing notes. Such a step, he argued, would sever the ties of the government "with the institutions of credit . . . ties which the public regards with distaste." The banks would doubtless demand 9 percent for a loan while state backed money would be interest-free. Under the aegis of the Moneda, moreover, the nation could return to the metallic standard more rapidly than if left in the hands of the banks. Rodríguez, who had denounced the credit institutions when they sought the protection of the inconvertibility legislation, also reasoned that the government's assumption of printing money would allow the banks to operate more freely. The dynamics of the market place would force the credit institutions "to consecrate themselves immediately to the work of prosperity and enriching the nation, prospering and enriching themselves at the same time."[38]

Because the $6,000,000 emitted under the law of April 1879 proved woefully inadequate, Pinto, on 20 August 1879, petitioned the legislature to authorize the issue of an additional $6,000,000 in *vales del tesoro*, henceforth, to be considered legal tender. While various legislators accepted the measure without demur, others, like Pedro Cuadra, inquired how the government planned to redeem this paper. The minister of treasury, Augusto Matte, argued that Chile's agricultural and mineral exports would generate enough revenue to convert, albeit slowly, the *vales* into specie. He also mentioned the imposition of new taxes. The minister encountered one enthusiastic supporter: Luis Urzúa. The fiery Montt Varista deputy argued that past borrowing had absorbed so much capital that it had paralyzed Chile's economic expansion. He warmly endorsed the proposal to issue more paper money, arguing that it would revive the sluggish economy.[39] Perhaps convinced by Urzúa's rhetoric, the legislature, with a few minor modifications, passed the measure which became law on 28 August 1879; by the end of the year, the treasury had issued $12,000,000 in paper scrip.

Slowly, the government's notes gained popularity. Some Chileans began to hale the *vales* as the nation's economic savior. The emission of paper notes, it was claimed, had lowered interest rates while stimulating economic growth. Loans, on the other hand, benefitted no one; they only absorbed capital while increasing the cost of imports. Even the normally conservative *El Independiente* tepidly supported paper money over borrowing, provided that it remained within reasonable limits. Otherwise, it warned, the scrip became devalued, specie fled the nation, and prices increased.[40]

In late 1879, Pinto again sought funds to prosecute the war as well as construct a drydock in Talcahuano. This time, he requested $6,000,000, $4,000,000 in *vales* and the extension of an earlier authorization to borrow the remainder. During the ensuing debates, Manuel Novoa, a National, Ricardo Letelier, a Liberal, and to a lesser extent, José Manuel Balmaceda emerged as the advocates of paper money, which they argued, saved the state money, reduced the interest rates, and capitalized Chile's industries. Not all the legislators waxed so enthusiastic: Enrique MacIver compared the *vales* to the mercury used to cure syphilis; a little bit was fine but too much would kill the patient.[41]

The issue took on a populist tone. One writer argued that the bankers had controlled the government and, through the system of borrowing, wished "again to enslave Chile so that they could, as before, usurp its sovereign powers." The credit institutions opposed government scrip because it undermined their power and reduced their profits. Another observer wryly noted that while the financial corporations lacked the economic resources to print paper money, they questioned the government's right to exercise the same right. Yet, the treasury's paper had liberated the nation from the banks' control while leading it to victory over the allies. *El Nuevo Ferrocarril* called upon the legislature to start acting like Chileans, not Jewish financiers, by authorizing more paper money. "Señores shareholders, go with God: leave Chile with its rights intact; if you wish to emit [paper], find the guarantee in order to deposit it in the hands of the state." Throughout the long debates, the hostility did not abate. When the value of the Chilean peso fell on the international market, one writer attributed the decline to the banks'attempts to undermine the nation's paper money. Surely the time has come, he noted, "to remove the direction of the state's economic affairs from the priests and the acolytes of usury."[42]

As the public discussed the issue, the proponents of paper money worked against the loan authorization. Arguing that the economy could easily absorb more *vales*—particularly since the conquest of Tarapacá—Novoa and José Tagle Arrate proposed a substitute motion which cancelled the loan authorization and called instead for the government to emit the entire sum in paper. Surprisingly, the lower house approved this measure.[43] This vote marked a turning point in Chile's economic history:

the advocates of paper money had successfully asserted the right of the state to issue notes instead of private institutions.

The upper house rejected the substitute motion and approved instead Pinto's original request. This rebuff did not distress Urzuá who, claiming that the nation would thrive with more paper, lamented that the government had not discovered this salutary expedient earlier. "Blessed be the war," he cried, "for it, as well as paper money, has brought prosperity to Chile." Others shared Urzuá's enthusiasm. Domingo Arteaga Alemparte agreed that Chile could readily absorb additional government notes which would merely stimulate the economy. Failure to support paper money would betray the heroic lower class; conversely, extending the loan proposal would be like Esau selling his birthright to Jacob. Perhaps because Matte promised not to seek a loan until the paper money had been exhausted, the deputies refused to override the Senate's objections and grudgingly approved Pinto's original proposal on 3 January 1880.[44]

The passage of the January loan authorization did not deter the advocates of government *vales*. Eventually, they knew, Pinto would again have to seek funds, and they would have another opportunity to argue their cause. In June 1880, the president petitioned the legislature to grant him the right to borrow $3,000,000 and to print an equivalent amount of paper.[45]

The ensuing debates, which lasted through the winter, represented the culmination of the struggle between the elements favoring *vales* and those who advocated recourse to the banks. Proponents of government paper enjoyed certain advantages: the credit institutions' record of defaults, the adoption of inconvertibility, and the high interest rates had alienated numerous Chileans. The financiers, they alleged, working through their legislative toadies—men like the nefarious Matte and the incompetent if not immoral Alfonso—wanted to enslave the nation.[46] One journalist likened Chile to Christ's tunic which was being "torn to pieces by the traffickers and usurers of its treasury."[47] Floating another loan would indenture Chile; repudiation would break the ties of exploitation. The nation, claimed another, was fighting a two front war: one against Peru and Bolivia the second "against the banks and the usurers who wish to impose upon it the law of their capital."[48]

Loans siphoned money from the economy, strangling industry and enriching only the capitalists. Conversely, government paper, in addition to emancipating the country from men like Matte and his minions, would revive the economy, stimulate the nation's industries, and encourage consumption while developing the nation's natural resources. Paper money benefited the lower classes by providing them with employment just as renewal of the loans would condemn the poor to widespread starvation. "Do not lend your authority and support to bring down on this nation a social crisis like that from which we escaped in 1878," begged Urzuá, "Think ... about the consequences of the convulsions of misery and save the nation from the disasters of the feudal epoch."[49] Francisco Vergara Donoso harkened back to prewar Chile when masses of the unemployed flooded Santiago. "It was something like a social danger," he noted, which the war and paper money had averted. If Chile wished to avoid a repetition of these social and economic problems, it had to provide the workers with bread and employment: only paper money could accomplish these goals. A writer in *El Ferrocarril* echoed this sentiment: "If the loan is adopted [the people] will clamor against the influence of the banks and the capitalists, a clamor which is not a good idea to start."[50]

Some defenders of paper money denied that government *vales* would lower the peso's value, blaming any decline on extraneous factors—the war or the scheming of the banks—not to the nature of paper money. Others, like Novoa, admitted that depreciation would occur but argued that this decline would hurt only the rich who already had profitted from the war. In short, paper money simply redressed past injustices whereas capital exploited the workers. Now the lower classes would finally benefit: " Does not capital live by the sweat or even the misery of labor? And by chance are not labor's efforts as meritorious as those of capital?" Indeed, since depreciation fell essentially on imports, it indirectly taxed the wealthy.[51]

Doubters still remained. Luis Aldunate feared that the resulting inflation would prove twice as costly as paying the interest charges on a loan. The measure, moreover, constituted a form of legalized robbery on behalf of the debtor class. The finance minister calculated that the interest, repayable in paper money, would cost $420,000 while the depreciation, which he estimated at 9 percent, would come to $2,790,000.[52]

Typical of Chilean politics, Alfonso's proposal unleashed a spate of others. In June 1880, Tagle Arrate proposed to authorize the president to issue, subject to some earlier legislation, $6,000,000 in *vales de tesoro*. He subsequently withdrew his motion in favor of one by Letelier which not only favored the emission of $6,000,000 in *vales* but also contained an important clause: two months after the implementation of his measure, no form of paper currency, except that issued by the government, would be accepted as legal tender in Chile. Thus this proposal represented a radical attempt to strip the banks of their ability to print notes. Rather late in the debates Urzuá, "in the name of the working class," proposed a measure to grant Pinto the right to issue $8,000,000 in *vales*, two million more than originally requested, and to annul the authorization to float a loan previously granted by the law of 10 January 1880. His proposal called for the deposit of these *vales*, in government vaults, at 5 percent interest, and a provision for their eventual withdrawal from the monetary system. Urzuá claimed that his suggestion originated with the Conservative Clementé Fabres and that he introduced it "on behalf of those disinherited men who have neither hacienda nor home, only a glance toward the heavens and their great and dearly beloved motherland."[53]

Juan de Dios Vial offered a counterproposal that rejected any attempt to issue more government paper money and instead permitted the president to borrow $6,000,000. Finally, almost as a compromise stood Alfonso's modest proposal: the president could print $3,000,000 while also receiving authorization to borrow an equal amount from private sources. During subsequent debates, Ramón Barros Luco sought to reconcile the various measures. He suggested that the government issue the entire $6,000,000 in paper but that it should also accept on deposit up to half that amount, on which it would pay 5 percent interest. Thus, the measure served two masters: the government would not have to borrow but it would also try to prevent the supersaturation of the monetary system. After days of debate, the chamber rejected all of the various proposals except that of Barros Luco; his proposal, however, barely managed to obtain a three-vote majority. Yet his measure still represented a victory for the advocates of government notes over the proponents of the bank loan.

This time the Senate did not defeat the proposal. Alfonso fairly presented the measure, which no longer even vaguely resembled his proposal of June 1880. He argued, however, that the new version enjoyed two advantages: it satisfied the economic needs of the war while the deposit provision allowed the reduction of the amount of paper in circulation. The antibank forces sought to stiffen the measure. Lorenzo Claro introduced two emendations: he suggested that the treasury accept up to $6,000,000 on deposit in order to minimize depreciation and, more significant, he wished to prohibit the banks from printing their own notes. Other senators, claiming that Pinto's request seemed inadequate to finance the war called for a doubling to $12,000,000 of the amount originally requested. Although the upper house rejected Claro's alterations, it did increase the authorization.

Alfonso dutifully carried the Senate's motion to the Chamber of Deputies where he admitted that since the government had already spent the $6,000,000 it had originally sought, the additional funds might prove useful. He also argued that the provision for depositing money in the treasury would reduce the inflationary aspects of the measure, thereby successfully reconciling the interests of the state, the consumer, the working class, and those who lived on a daily wage.[54]

Not all the advocates of paper money supported the Senate's version. Letelier claimed that the deposit requirement benefited the nation's financial institutions: "the reserves of the banks will be placed on deposit in the treasury of the nation, earning interest, and the bankers will remain, like the arbiters of the situation, picking up the emission and retiring their deposits, and thus they will create a tyrannical and restricted situation."[55] This argument apparently swayed some legislators because the lower house divided evenly on the Senate's proposal. In the ensuing discussion, deputies like Letelier, Tagle Arrate, and Agustín Edwards, the head of the banking clan, as well as Donoso argued that the measure subsidized the credit institutions because it allowed them to deposit their own notes in government repositories and earn interest. Urzuá declaimed, "With the Senate's adoption of this method, we have left the welfare or the ruin of the state in the hands of the great capitalists; on them will depend whether industry, commerce, and work will prosper or succumb." Despite such impassioned rhetoric, on 11 August 1880, the measure won a scant four vote majority in the lower house.[56]

While passage of the measure may have alleviated some of Chile's financial woes, it did not please the general public. Some feared that it would precipitate a destructive inflation. Calling for "less glory and more bread, if the glory consists of cheating the people with golden excuses and happy stories," *El Progreso* accused the legislature of undermining Chile's prestige with "thousands of parcels of paper money."[57] *The Chilian Times* warned, "A score more millions of paper money and we shall rival the Peruvian quotation: 6 d [pence] per dollar." On the other hand, *El Constituyente* echoed the sentiments of the antibanking elements, claiming that the credit institutions, not the nation, benefited from the August 1880 law. The newspaper even claimed that the financiers had converted their paper into specie, which they remitted to Europe, leaving the Chileans, "like the Peruvians," with the paper.[58]

The printing of so much money flooded the financial markets with cash, albeit, of dubious parentage. As predicted, bank deposits increased and interests rates declined. One wag remarked that the Moneda had initiated a war of economic liberation. Chile, noted another, had been emancipated "from the forces of usury . . . [which] are today in full retreat."[59] Debtors, particularly those who owed money to the Caja de Crédito Hipotecario (a government-sponsored land bank), took advantage of the situation to renegotiate their loans at a lower rate. Bonds bearing in excess of 5 percent interest—more than that authorized by the law of 25 August 1880—soared; stocks, especially those of the banks, also showed a healthy increase. The onset of the abortive Arica peace conference depressed the stockmarket while the happy news that the war would continue elated the Bourse. "For our speculators, the war should prove to be a paradise, an increase in capital and wealth, which should also be translated into an increase in the value of the paper representing them."[60]

With the economy so engorged with money, it is not surprising that Alfonso decided to use the authorization extended by the law of January 1880 and float a loan. The antibank hostility still had not abated. Novoa stated that the minister had violated the sense of the legislature which earlier had rejected the idea of borrowing from the nation's credit institutions. Unlike early 1879, the bankers seemed willing to lend the government the needed $2,000,000 at 6 percent interest. *El Ferrocarril*, perhaps still furious at the banks' earlier unpatriotic niggardliness, objected to the government resorting to this device. Instead, the newspaper suggested that the Moneda raise the money through a popular subscription thereby accomplishing two objectives: providing the potential bondholders with a good income and reducing the nation's dependence on the banks. Apparently, even the minister of finance shared these sentiments because he allowed the public to purchase the bond issue which quickly became oversubscribed.[61]

The Senate proved remarkably prescient about the administration's underestimation of the cost of the war. By December 1880, Pinto returned yet again to the legislature to request permission to raise another $12,000,000. Alfonso explained that the government was spending $3,000,000 per month both to fund normal civilian functions and to carry the war to the enemy. Since the nation's monthly revenue amounted to but $1,750,000, the minister sagely concluded that the government would soon run out of money.

Although Novoa endorsed Alfonso's request, he opposed the measure because the treasury would have to pay interest to those individuals who deposited their funds in the treasury vaults. Labeling this proposal a "monstrosity," he concluded that the minister's suggestion was "really a loan at interest ranging from 3, 4, or at the highest, 5 percent" which would provide the banks with an annual income of $600,000. "Nothing," he demanded, "for the favorites of fortune. Everything for the widows, the orphans, and the glorious wounded of our heroic army."[62]

The minister responded that the interest provision seemed essential because it would absorb the excess money in circulation. Unlike Novoa, he did not consider his measure a loan and defended his legislation on the grounds that it would pay the interest in depreciated paper not specie. Either necessity or Alfonso's curious logic convinced the Chamber of

Deputies to approve his request. The Senate, sensing the financial urgency, agreed virtually without discussion.[63]

Perhaps bolstered by new sources of revenue, the Moneda never requested permission to print more paper money. The approval of the law of 7 January 1881, however, did not appease the antibank forces. In June Letelier noted that the interest payments on the *vales* deposited in the government's treasury cost the Moneda $600,000, approximately half the yield of the *agrícola* tax. Denouncing this as a gift to the banks, he moved that henceforth government offices should accept only notes printed by the treasury. The comisión de hacienda demurred, arguing that such a proposal violated previous arrangements with the banks. More than the sanctity of contractual obligations motivated the committee. It did not "wish to establish a government monopoly to issue paper money in conflict with the laws of the nation and in contradiction of universally known economic principles." Thus, while the comisión's members sought a return to specie and the convertibility of bank notes, they opposed the idea that only the government should print currency. This act, it claimed, was inconsistent with the functions of government and "should be under the direction of private initiative and the action as well as indispensable liberty of industry."[64]

The comisión de hacienda had earlier also rejected a proposal by Juan de Dios Vial who wanted all contracts to stipulate whether payments should be made in specie or paper *vales*. The committee opposed his suggestion, claiming quite correctly that it would not only violate earlier laws, but that it would establish a dual monetary system. The deputies repeated the by now accepted litany—stigmatizing paper money as a useful wartime expedient—and concluding with a promise to abjure it once peace and economic prosperity had returned.

Novoa still retained his fanatical devotion to paper money. While other legislators predicted the arrival of a financial Day of Judgment—when all the paper *vales* would be destroyed and metallic currency resurrected—the deputy remained an apostate. He constantly proposed schemes to keep the *vales* in circulation, steadfastly believing that their demise would destroy the national industries and increase the cost of living. Thus, the deputy opposed allocating funds to pay for the destruction of outstanding paper notes. Always innovative, he suggested that Peru be made responsible for redeeming in gold the paper money Chile had issued during the war. He also sought to prohibit banks from printing notes in small denominations, which would have effectively crippled them from competing with government *vales*, as well as to impose a tax on the amount of the money they issued.[65]

Novoa was not the only paper bug. In the Senate, his fellow Montt

Varista, Lorenzo Claro, also opposed the extension of the law of 5 January 1881 because it permitted credit institutions to earn 5 percent interest on the notes they deposited in the government treasury. He too considered the 1881 legislation not an emission of *vales* but a loan. He repeated his earlier demand that the state rescind the right of the banks to print paper notes. The minister of finance, Luis Alduante, apparently shared some of Claro's antipathy for the financial institutions. He noted, however, that the state could not violate its contractual obligations with the banks without paying them substantial compensation. Once Chile returned to the gold standard, he argued, the Moneda would recapture this right. In the interim, he supported the 1881 law, reassured that since Tarapacá had already absorbed so many *vales*—he estimated about $11,000,000—that the emission would not prove indigestible to Chile's economy.[66]

The various debates authorizing the issuing of paper money reveal that many of those Chileans who favored the government *vale* did so convinced that it was the only way to stimulate the economy and to assert the dominance of the state over the private banks. These elements remembered, perhaps too well, the fiasco which precipitated the 1878 declaration of inconvertibility and, quite reasonably, refused to entrust the nation's economic future to the financiers. No one political party monopolized this doctrine; the men who fought for the right of the Moneda to print its own notes represented all the existing ideological factions and their actions enjoyed the support of the nation. A letter, published in *El Bío Bío*, for example, praised those "patriotic legislators [for] shaking off the disastrous tutelage of the banks."[67] (Tables 35 and 36 trace money supply and bank activity from 1878 to 1883).

The hostility toward the nation's credit institutions was rooted in their abuse of the 1865 banking legislation. Elements of the press complained that the banks had seduced Chile into a life of ostentation and luxury. Then, in 1878, the legislature had to rescue the banks, but at the cost of enslaving the nation to the capitalists, of "exploiting the poor in favor of the rich."[68] A dual standard of conduct had emerged: the banks, which had greedily overextended themselves during the Caracoles Bubble, still retained the right to print paper money; the businessman, no matter how solvent, could not issue *fichas*.[69] Despite their wretched performance, the financiers still enjoyed unrestricted power. As one deputy noted, "Our great credit institutions, which have thoughtlessly opened their vaults to the greedy hands of the great speculators, suddenly find themselves on the verge of bankruptcy . . . the abuse of credit, which thrust the nation toward this alluring precipice, now threatens to put it into an abyss where it will disappear completely. Not a few Chileans feared the banks. *La Opinión* opposed a merger between the Banco de Valparaíso and the Banco Nacional, worrying that they would then intentionally increase interest rates to the detriment of the nation's businessmen and the poor.[70] Apparently the financiers worried with ample reason about their reputations. In April 1879, they refused to lend money to the government. Weeks later, they publically attacked the *haberes* tax, claiming that it unfairly discriminated against them. Already incensed by the reckless behavior of the nation's financial institutions, this niggardly lack of patriotism perhaps radicalized many legislators to move against the banks. Necessity forced Pinto to use paper money. The desire to free the country from an unhealthy dependence on the banks in conjunction with the wish to stimulate the economy and help the lower classes, encouraged sectors of the country to adopt the *vale*. Consequently, paper money, thrust into their hands accidently, would help to change Chilean society as well as to finance the nation's epic struggle against Peru and Bolivia.[71]

The Chilean tax system, following the imposition of the *salitre* tax, was not altered dramatically throughout the remainder of the war. The legislature regularly renewed the 10 percent surcharge on the *aduana* tax although some senators complained that this levy contributed to inflation and discriminated against consumers. The minister of finance, José Alfonso, while stating his antipathy to the measure, nonetheless favored its retention, claiming it helped defray the costs of the war. The following year, when the measure came up for renewal, various legislators raised the familiar but nonetheless valid arguments to oppose the surcharge. Francisco Puelma believed that the burden of taxation seemed to fall lightly, if at all, upon agriculture and urban property owners while "commerce has been taxed enormously and those industries, like nitrate, for example, it can be said, appear almost moribund." Pedro Cuadra disarmingly agreed, noting the various fiscal defects and inequities. Still, he argued, the surcharge was not so evil because it fell mainly upon luxury imports while providing the government funds for the war. Thus the legislature retained the surcharge.[72]

Despite the various attempts at diversification, the treasury continued to rely on the indirect tax for its sustenance. While the impost on the export of *salitre* provided a growing portion of the government's income, a substantial tax burden still fell on imports, leading *The Chilian Times* to conclude that while the poor and the merchant suffered "landowners and capitalists are not taxed in proportion to their means."[73] This sentiment gained currency. One rural journalist observed that the small vendor of potatoes paid with his blood during the war and 20 to 30 percent of his income in peace while the wealthy escaped taxation. Despite the complaints, these generic flaws in the tax system survived: the administration refused to distinguish between the pawn shop and the factory when it came time to collect revenues.⁷⁴

No one party or group was responsible for this situation, although each critic had his favorite target. Some blamed the Montt Varistas for talking the most about reform and doing the least. *El Padre Cobos* focused on the Conservatives who, it suggested, deliberately aborted any tax reform so they could earn interest on the money they would otherwise have to pay to the government. Observing that the productive members of society had to pay taxes, the newspaper suggested that the Moneda should also rifle the pocketbook of the clergy who, it argued, did not work. Others criticized the government's "Jewish spirit" which thrived on the "sweat of the poor." The nation's fiscal system, lacking a coherent basis in economic theory, blindly taxed without inquiring into the nature of the individual enterprise: the large *hacendado* and the farmer earning less than $25 annually both had to pay the *agrícola*. "The tax system," noted one critic, "is the executioner of the small and a dear friend of the important."⁷⁵ Worse yet, few could discover any benefit accruing from the payment of taxes: the all-absorbing treasury merely sopped up the money, paralyzing the economy.⁷⁶

Despite these complaints, certain positive changes occurred during the war. After much haggling, the legislature, in order to streamline business negotiations, abolished the *alcabala* on the rental of property. At the same time, it imposed this same impost on the transfer of foreign owned ships. This about-face, it averred, would encourage aliens to register their vessels under the Chilean flag thereby enhancing the nation's maritime resources. Unfortunately, a subsequent attempt to suspend for a decade the collection of the *alcabala* failed. Thus the nation could not completely eradicate the remnants of its colonial past from its tax structure.⁷⁷

While the government might have protected the national merchant marine, it did not act so benevolently when dealing with the moribund copper industry. Noting Chile's declining share of the world market, Francisco Vergara called for the abrogation of the export tax on the red metal. The deputy's reasoning appeared impeccable: the impost increased the cost of production, thus making Chilean copper more expensive than its competition. The Senate's comisión de hacienda, while proposing some relief, did not act so generously. Rather than abolish the tax, it proposed to halve it. As usual the minister of hacienda replied that the copper industry did not merit special consideration. And, despite the protests of various senators, this accountant's argument carried the day. Eventually the copper industry obtained tax relief but only months after the signing of the Treaty of Ancón.[78]

CONCLUSION

Chile's prewar fiscal system, like the other parts of the nation's administration, intially could not satisfy the needs of a nation involved in war. The government tried a variety of means to generate the needed income but these failed to provide enough funds. Consequently, Santiago had to resort to paper money to bridge the fiscal gap until the capture of the *salitreras*, and the imposition of the nitrate tax, could fund the government adequately. Without the combination of the government's paper and the nitrates, Santiago's war effort would have aborted.

Once the *salitre* revenues began to flow south, they not only financed the nation's crusade against the allies but also permitted the state to modernize its tax structure by abolishing certain regressive imposts. Unfortunately, the legislature, perhaps understandably, also discarded the *haberes* and the *herencia*, the first levies which introduced direct taxation into Chile. *Salitre* and the greenback, while providing a temporary solution to the nation's economic needs, would subsequently distort Chile's economic growth, spawning a monocultural economy and inflation. Yet, for a brief moment, the two measures produced enough money to permit the country to fight and to win the War of the Pacific.

8

Life on the Homefront

> There were no signs in [Chile's] capital that such a fearful struggle existed. The thoroughfares even had an everyday look about them: there were no crowds, no placards, and, above all, no soldiers swaggering about the streets.
> R. Nelson Boyd

Clearly the War of the Pacific influenced, often enormously, various aspects of Chilean life. The conflict forced a reassertion of executive power, revisions in the tax system, and altered the patterns of economic growth. Similarly, the struggle in the north provided the rural masses an opportunity—one that many would doubtless have preferred to have avoided—to put aside their more banal pursuits in order to participate in the great adventure of war. Although we know something of the lives of the soldiers, the plight of those who remained behind still remains to be told. What impact, if any, did the War of the Pacific have on a developing nation like Chile? Did civilian society live unaffected by the firestorm of the north or did the prolonged war mark the nation in an indelible fashion?

Nineteenth-century Chile was an agrarian nation most of whose population lived on *fundos* located mainly in the Central Valley. Largely illiterate and isolated, the majority of Chileans were unaware of the struggle in the north. Indeed, unless the *enganchadores* visited their area, the average *inquilino* knew little and probably cared less about the war. The urban areas, with a more literate population and with access to the latest news, seemed more concerned with the conflict. Yet, perhaps because of the enormous distance separating the nation and the front, even this interest flagged.

The War of the Pacific did not dramatically alter Chilean society. Women may have worn dresses with a military motif but this was a temporary fashion: Chile, unlike Felix Krull's Prussia, did not internalize martial habits. As a foreign visitor noted, the conflict rarely intruded into people's lives.[1] When it did, it had a kaleidoscopic quality: a glimpse of Peruvian officers enroute to their comfortable captivity in San Bernardo; an exposition of military trophies including a collection of bullets extracted from the Chilean wounded after the Battle of Tacna; the arrival of two lions, looted from Lima's zoo, for Santiago's menagerie.[2]

Technology, not the conflict with Peru, altered the quality of Chilean urban life. Valparaíso and Santiago installed a telephone system linking first various government offices and then eventually private individuals. Provincial cities seemed content with the less sophisticated instruments. When the telegraph reached Puerto Montt, local officials held a dance to celebrate "this manifestation of progress." Although willing to modernize, municipal governments often neglected to pave the streets, forcing people to live in a miasma of dust in the summer while the onset of winter signified muddy roads or washed out highways which isolated not only provincial cities but even neighborhoods within Santiago.[3] City residents yearned not only for macadamized avenues but also potable water and sewers which promised a healthier standard of living. Illuminating a city's streets increased security and allowed people to venture abroad at night. Conversely, periodic blackouts provided the thieves limitless opportunities to steal. Unfortunately, the cost of gas lighting proved so onerous that many merchants could ill afford to remain open at night, thus giving the downtown section a deserted appearance. Some towns installed electric lights rather than the more noxious gas and soon lights began to blink on throughout Chile.[4]

Some aspects of urban life remained the same. Despite the demand for labor, beggars, many exhibiting gruesome wounds or injuries, clogged each city, sometimes actually launching themselves at the passersby. Local governments tried to outlaw this activity though the more compassionate suggested that the needy should seek help from the local *hospicio*, the poor house. Yet if the *hospicio* offered the same abysmal accommodations as the municipal hospital, the poor were indeed wiser to remain on the streets. Religious organizations and various *ollas del pobre*, soup kitchens, distributed food, and provided funds for paying rent. One charity offered daycare for working mothers but it would accept only females, forcing some women to dress their sons as girls in order to gain entry. Despite their heroic efforts and countless bazaars, the volunteers could not raise enough money to moderate such extensive poverty. One *olla del pobre* on Valparaíso's Calle Merced finally had to close because of the lack of funds.[5]

In addition to mendicants, towns had to contend with packs of dogs, some rabid, which occasionally attacked people on the street. An Englishman named McNaughton shot at one of these animals but struck instead a little girl; portions of Lota's population carried sticks to ward off these beasts. To restore order, cities hired men to feed strychnine pellets to the local canine population. Although most supported this solution, one journalist considered it immoral and inefficient; instead, he recommended that the government fine those whose dogs strayed off their property. Lautaro implemented such a law, charging the owner for maintaining his animal while it remained in official custody; the fee for wayward pigs, however, was higher. Strychnine, although offering one cure for the canine plague, sometimes miscarried. Poisoners indiscriminately killed any dog, including those penned up or with known owners. Even when discreetly conducted, a campaign of extermination left in its wake countless dead hounds littering the streets. These remains posed a serious health hazard, particularly when pigs, like those which lived by Santiago's Mapocho River, began eating the carcasses. Consequently, the authorities threatened to fine anyone who sold the canine-enriched pork to the public.[6]

Urban traffic, in addition to tainted meat, endangered the public's health. Coachmen careened through the streets at breakneck speeds. In Santiago bullock-drawn trollies, often driven by profane women conductors, menaced not only the rider, who often received his change in "money not coined in the Moneda," but also the pedestrian.[7] In other towns, the problems remained those of an essentially agrarian society: a bull gored a passerby in Valdivia, oxen ran untended in Lota, while people rode their horses on the sidewalk in Chillán or galloped too rapidly through the streets of San Fernando.[8]

The quality of city life varied: Antofagasta contained a newspaper but no school; Lebu had a primary school but wanted a *liceo*. Some towns did not possess doctors or even a barber; others enjoyed only the temporary succor of a dentist. In Talca many houses still lacked street addresses. Curicó needed a morgue because the authorities buried corpses often without identifying the cadaver. Copiapó wished for a library while Valparaíso's library required money to bind its rapidly disintegrating books. A few deficiencies contained an enormous potential for disaster. Osorno, whose buildings were almost entirely of wood, did not employ a fire department.[9]

The ability of a municipality to provide essential services often depended upon the willingness of its inhabitants to donate funds or the skill of the local government in raising revenues. Unfortunately, to accomplish the latter, the municipality had to petition the Moneda for permission to undertake most projects, to collect the taxes to finance them, and sometimes for a subsidy to complete them. As the minister of interior observed, however, the war absorbed Santiago's energies and financial resources to the detriment of local needs. Chile, in short, lacked the infrastructure and resources to fight a war, conduct the affairs of the national government, and resolve provincial or municipal problems.[10]

The Moneda, for example, literally ran out of money during the War of the Pacific. This problem resulted not so much from the conflict but the 1878 declaration of inconvertibility which, among its numerous consequences, caused specie virtually to disappear from circulation. The absence of money paralyzed the economy; commercial life either stagnated or simply came to a halt; factory owners, farmers, and even the Moneda could not pay their employees.[11]

The few who possessed specie had to pay the exact amount for their purchases. When no change existed, individuals had to leave their cash in stores and draw upon it, like a bank, until it was exhausted. The prominent, of course, could easily obtain credit whereas the poor could not. Specie became not a medium of exchange but a commodity. Coins, particularly those of gold, commanded a premium of 45 to 50 percent. Despite this crisis, the government continued to permit the export of silver which, one journal described as a "hemorrhage which is destroying our financial structure."[12]

Various innovative concerns began to fabricate money: the famous *fichas* or *vales*, scrip. Teodoro López of Chillán manufactured chits of zinc while his neighbors, including the brewer Carlos Andwanter, employed other materials. Lota Schwager, for example, minted a green piece of cardboard, arbitrarily endowing it with a value of 25 cents. Local merchants rejected the latter, not because they did not have confidence in the mining company, but because the *ficha* disintegrated after four days of use. Perhaps because of their durability, the *vales* of Carboniferos de Puchoco, as well as those of Rojas and Deláno, enjoyed a wider acceptance.[13]

Fichas became quite widespread. In Quillota one was smothered in paper as speculators refused to part with their specie for fear of never seeing it again. San Fernando's commercial houses also issued scrip while *La Voz de Itata* suggested that each merchant be authorized to print $50 worth of chits, providing that he would accept the *vales* of his competitor. Unfortunately not all the commercial establishments honored the *fichas* and thus people ran the risk of being cheated.[14]

The minting of *fichas* often also became a lucrative endeavor. Commercial houses deposited their capital in local banks where it earned interest, while issuing scrip. Other stores would accept the paper of their competitors, at a discount of 25 percent, and then sell back the depreciated paper at its face value to the issuer. In the north, wealthy merchants used the lack of small change to monopolize local trade and to force the poor to borrow at high interest rates to purchase necessities. Banks also profited by levying a 4 percent surcharge to change money while the counterfeiters diversified their activities, reproducing not only the government's money, the bank's notes, but also scrip.[15]

Although it clearly violated the law, some government officials requested that local commercial houses print *fichas*, which they used to purchase food for the army's recruits. Santiago frantically sought to satisfy the need for currency but when the treasury sent a shipment of money to some desperate town, speculators or hoarders quickly absorbed it. Anxious to resolve this problem, the Moneda requested legislative permission to fabricate $2,000,000 in small change. Unfortunately, this step did not bring relief because the ship carrying the minting machines was lost at sea.[16]

Thus *fichas* continued to circulate—some so filthy that people only reluctantly accepted them, others so worn that the holder could barely discern the demonination. A Cauquenes official, conceding that the "cure is to a certain point worse than the evil it seeks to remedy," prohibited the printing of more *fichas*. His action appears to have been isolated. In Osorno only *vales* existed, a situation which the local press blamed on one Juan Anselmo Mangano who apparently printed them at will. This condition persisted until the onset of the racing season in 1881: these races attracted enough big spenders that the city was able to re-enter the money economy. Eventually, the state claimed it had brought its monetary output in line with demand, but provincial officials periodically requested shipments of money indicating that the "contagious evil" of *fichas* continued to bedevil isolated areas of Chile.[17]

Other commodities, in addition to specie, also became dear. Food prices initially increased because both the European market as well as the Chilean army competed for foodstuffs, a rivalry that, while enriching the farmer, impoverished the consumer. The size of a loaf bread, the staple of the Chilean diet, contracted. Attributing this shrinkage to the war, one wag argued that instead of calling bread "pan frances" it should instead be dubbed "pan peruano."[18] Some blamed the increase on the high taxes levied on the bakers; others attributed it to the rising cost of labor. When heavy rains flooded the fields and destroyed the crops, prices for some commodities doubled, inflicting great hardship on the poor.[19]

Scarcities afflicted Chile throughout the war. Wood and charcoal, for instance, proved extremely difficult to obtain. This fuel shortage could clearly be attributed to the conflict: the *carboneros* refused to enter Lota, fearing they might attract the eye of the recruiting sergeant or suffer an enemy bombardment. As a result, charcoal became quite dear, even in the heart of Chile's coal mining region.[20]

Meat, which apparently had comprised a substantial portion of the poor's diet, became increasingly expensive. In Valparaíso, the cost of cuts "thinner than a Jew, and . . . nauseating to serve," rose by 20 percent within a few days.[21] Some blamed the higher prices on the heavy winter which closed the mountain passes from Argentina; others attributed the increased cost to the imposition of an export tax, levied by the provincial government of San Juan, on cattle destined for Chile. Unfortunately, domestic production of beef declined because the same heavy rains that devastated Chile's agriculture decimated its livestock population as well.[22]

But the press also blamed local butchers for the meat shortages. In Quillota, for example, the slaughter houses manipulated prices by regulating the amount of cattle dressed for market. Price fixing became quite common throughout Chile, precipitating an increase in the number of illegal slaughterhouses. Meat prices rose dramatically and, in a sense, the War of the Pacific clearly marked a culinary watershed: meat became a luxury not a staple and henceforth poor Chileans were condemned to a perpetual Lenten diet.[23]

Prices for other foodstuffs—wheat, milk, sugar, coffee, rice, and fat—increased as well. A few journalists ascribed the rise to exchange rates which, they alleged, made imported goods more dear. Others blamed it on inflationary paper money, the government's imposition of new taxes, or its demand that importers pay duties in specie. Another contributory factor was the food processor who gouged the consumer by adulterating—often with dangerous substances—his milk, oil, liquor, or coffee; who sold horsemeat as beef or parasite-infested pork; who often gave short weight. The press denounced these individuals, warning that the people will exact "a terrible justice . . . against those who independently try to strangle them . . . with usury and profit. Be careful."[24]

Yet, as tables 37 to 39 indicate, wholesale prices fluctuated minimally. Wheat, flour, corn, and barley remained relatively stable, although products related to cattle—meat, cheese, *charqui*, and fat—increased substantially. Judging from comments in the press, however, retail prices soared. In 1881, for example, *La Patria* estimated that since the onset of the war the cost of flour accelerated by 14 percent, sugar by 21 percent, meat by half, while coffee, tea, and clothing rose by 75 percent. During the same period, *El Ferrocarril* reported that the price of wheat climbed almost 22 percent, and that for sugar and clothes jumped by 60 percent. Three years later, *El Mercurio*, using 1877 as a base year, compared clothing prices and concluded that costs had increased at least 9 percent for a short jacket and 25 percent for a summer frock coat. Unfortunately, the journalists did not provide data to support these allegations. Adolfo Latorre (see Table 40) created a price index which indicated dramatic changes, but if one drops meat from his equation, the increases seem moderate.[25] Thus although the cost of living, the higher prices cannot be attributed solely to the war; domestic inflation also played a significant role.

On the other hand, the higher prices did not reduce the life style of the wealthy. Women purchased extravagant hats, each costing $40. After Christmas, the wealthy deserted the cities either for their *fundos* or a fashionable coastal resort. This lemminglike rush for the seashore became so pronounced that traffic jams developed around the capital's main railway station because "half of Santiago has gone . . . and the other half is packing its bags in order to follow the same path."[26]

Not everyone, for geographical as well as personal reasons, visited beach resorts. Chillán's thermal baths enjoyed such a spurt of popularity that four guests shared a room and the local hotel had to hire additional coaches to transport their clientele. The less affluent or more timorous settled for vacation spots—San Bernardo, Limache, Quillota, Los Andes —closer to the large urban centers but still far from the toiling masses. Those unhappy few who remained lamented that the summer exodus had emptied the larger cities, making them into deserts where nothing "not even a decent stabbing occurred." Thus, although the War of the Pacific may have disrupted Peru's existence, noted one journalist, it did not alter Chilean migratory patterns.[27]

Holy Week precipitated another exodus from Santiago and Valparaíso. Traditionally the Church enjoyed the support of various officials willing to prohibit Santiago's merchants from working on the sabbath and arrested people for witchcraft in the south. Not unexpectedly, Chile agonized during Lent: naval vessels lowered their flags to half mast; and until 1880, military units marched in the Good Friday procession; business slowed: and municipalities sometimes restricted wheeled traffic. During this season, young girls often filled the streets, visiting various churchs where the sermons became so harsh that the largely female congregations cried "oceans of tears, screaming like goats, to the point that people walking a block away from the church [could] hear them."[28] The end of Holy Week brought a return of the vacationers and of the invitations to "tomar una tasita de té."[29]

Of course, the poor could not flee the cities. For them, the free baths on the Mapocho River constituted their only vacation. Indeed, one of the many blights on the worker's existence was that the cities provided few legal and healthy diversions. Santiago's large parks, the Quinta Normal—an agricultural testing station and exposition site which also housed the municipal zoo—and Cerro Santa Lucía, charged an entry fee except on Thursdays when everyone was working. Various newspapers rightly protested that the city's poor should be allowed to enter the Quinta Normal and the Cerro free of charge. Still, many cities contained Plaza de Armas, miniscule green zones where municipal or military bands played, where the middle-aged escaped the summer heat and where the young eyed each other across a tattered square as they participated in the *paseo*, a courting rite unique to Hispanic culture. Regrettably some towns lacked even these minimal pleasures. In Osorno the women had to go to bed "with the chickens," because the town could not raise enough money to hire a band for the *paseo*.

Ethnic communities scrupulously maintained their life styles. The French colony celebrated Bastille Day while the English not only played cricket but also steeplechased. Valparaíso's Anglo-Saxon population even formed a hunt club until, having apparently annihilated the local fox population, it disbanded.[30]

Winter restricted, if not ended, many activities. Resort towns closed down, wistfully yearning for the beautiful people who once strolled their *paseos* while the swank retreated to their clubs, housed in such institutions as Santiago's Club de la Unión or San Felipe's Hotel Frances. Those who lusted after cultural entertainment, flocked to the Teatro Municipal, which auctioned its seats to the highest bidder. In 1881, the sale raised $51,900 with Jorge Ross and José Ortíz each paying $1,710 for their theater boxes. Still, the price might have been worth it: the innovative theater had installed a cloak room where the ladies might adjust their hair and put on their jackets. Regrettably, the shows did not always match the building's conveniences. A performance of *La Traviata* so upset the local audience that a newspaper critic warned singers that they were trying the audience's patience. Theatergoing, while perhaps uplifting, sometimes jeopardized one's life. One young lady fainted in the Teatro Municipal. Someone, mistaking a call for water as a scream of "fire," almost started a stampede for the exit. Happily, in that instance, the crowd did not panic, but during a party celebrating Santa María's inauguration, a woman's dress caught on fire, nearly precipitating a riot when the guests discovered that the authorities had locked the doors.[31]

Smaller cities also supported the arts. Local individuals or traveling troupes gave violin recitals, concerts, *zarzuelas*, and dramatic performances. Los Anjeles boasted of the arrival of a piano teacher. Although resort towns, like San Bernardo, organized concerts and plays for their summer guests, these activities stopped when the tourist season ended. Poor weather and wretched roads made it extremely difficult for provincial cities to sustain an intellectual life. As a Puerto Montt newspaper suggested, when winter arrived, people should plan to spend their time with their families.[32]

Attempts to "civilize" the provinces sometimes miscarried. Invariably, townspeople preferred the less genteel efforts of "the Cuban magician" —whose performance raised $100 for a local hospital—to a more "uplifting" event. The arrival of a company of jugglers, rued one newspaper, easily attracted people, "But announce a dramatic company or a *zarzuela*, and all the pocketbooks remain closed."[33] Lota ignored a theatrical performance but two thousand miners deserted the coal pits to trudge miles to witness a public execution. Similarly a thousand spectators gathered at 8:30 A.M. to watch the shooting of four men in Talcahuano. The sloppy performance of the firing squad—one prisoner required two rifle shots and a coup de grâce before expiring—and the vulgar tone of the proceedings caused *The Chilian Times* to suggest private executions and replacing the gun with the rope, which it claimed, dispatched the victim more humanely and efficiently.[34] Public lashings also provided some diversion although sometimes these events became depressing, particularly if the criminals screamed while being flogged. In Concepción, the scene so appalled a correspondent that he took to his bed for a day.[35]

Blood sports like cockfights also enjoyed wide currency. This pastime, although perhaps unaesthetic, did not damage the working class as much as the innumerable bars, the infamous *chinganas*, which infested Chile like lice. In 1875, Dr. Adolfo Murillo observed that "to earn, not enough to eat but to drink . . . seems . . . to be the motto of the great majority of the lower class."[36] Observers rightly complained that these drinking establishments drained the worker's pocketbook, ruined his health, and thereby indirectly destroyed his family. Few towns escaped the pernicious influence of "these schools of crime" which functioned, apparently nonstop, much to the distress of those hapless citizens who lived next door.[37]

Fortunately there were some diversions, like religious holidays, which provided alternatives for entertainment. Carnival, however, unleashed a wave of raucous behavior. People filled the streets, dousing each other with liquids of unknown origin and composition—a tradition which ruined many a dress and inconvenienced pedestrians. Others threw flour, making Valparaíso's streets look as if snow had fallen. Lent saddened everyone, not simply because it signalled the onset of austerity, but because it ended a period of freedom when even dour mothers "wink at remembering their own past."[38] Although offering occasions for merriment, religious holidays, like Christmas, sometimes degenerated into violence. Thus festivals could become dangerous: at Carelmapu, two people died celebrating the feast of the Candelaria.[39]

While Chileans commemorated patriotic events, the anniversary of their independence day, the *deiziocho de setiembre*, became the secular calendar's longest celebration. The nation devoted four or sometimes five days to fireworks, dancing, and drinking that occasionally degenerated into brawling. The war's victories also provided opportunities for rejoicing. Santiago celebrated for three days when Tacna fell. The high point was a large balloon—forty meters in circumference and decorated with the names of the principal heroes—which showered the city with colored paper and little flags. When Arica capitulated, a Chinese merchant in Santiago sold close to 2 million rockets and firecrackers.[40]

The conflict spawned a new pantheon of heroic figures for the nation to venerate. In Santiago, handkerchiefs appeared, decorated with the portraits of the heroes of Angamos and Iquique. One newspaper objected to this vulgarization of these men, predicting that soon the president's picture would appear on a matchbox and "even a facsimile of some minister (pardon me for saying it) on a urinal."[41]

Not surprisingly, 1881 emerged as the premier year for patriotic celebrations. When, after weeks of anxious anticipation, Chileans learned that Lima had fallen, the nation erupted into a paroxysm of joy, fireworks, and band music. Six thousand rejoiced in Santiago; in Valparaíso, the citizens ignited enormous amounts of fireworks and the bars quickly ran out of liquor. Commercial life ceased functioning when the port's workers abandoned their jobs to mark the happy event. But as many of Chillán's inhabitants celebrated, thieves robbed their homes.[42]

Quite properly, the nation exerted a special effort to mark the return of its army. Valparaíso enjoyed the honor of being the first city to welcome the men. Committees there visited homes, distributing flags and bunting, which they urged the owners to fly from their homes if they did not wish their patriotism questioned. So many anxious relatives saturated the port that many had to sleep in hotel saloons and dining rooms. Other provincial cities held similar festivities, albeit on a less grand scale, when the men returned for demobilization. Sometimes, however, the civilian expectations were frustrated. In January 1880, Luis Uribe, Prat's executive officer on the *Esmeralda,* returned to Santiago after being freed from Peruvian captivity. A fire company, a band, and a large crowd, led by Benjamín Vicuña Makenna, awaited his arrival at Santiago's rail depot. As the train slowed to a stop, the band began playing and, as the crowd surged forward to cheer one of Chile's premiere heroes, the conductor announced that Uribe was not onboard.[43]

It is difficult to assess how the war affected Chile's social life. *El*

Curicano observed that the Christmas celebrations of 1880, which coincided with the final drive on Lima, lacked a certain élan. A journalist in a southern city made a similar observation, although he was pleased; a quiet holiday meant that the lower orders would not commit any excesses.[44] Perhaps the smaller towns, because of their size, felt the war's impact more than the larger cities. One provincial journalist speculated on the whereabouts of "the elegant youth who filled the *paseos* and the saloons of our society."[45] Curicó's press asked the police not to close the town's all night restaurants so that "our city, which already lacks so many people who have left for the army, will not become a real cemetery at night."[46] Yet while these towns complained about the slow pace, Valparaíso's *chinganas* celebrated from early Friday evening until Monday morning, closing only when the singers were exhausted and the patrons' pocketbooks were empty. Masked balls continued to attract crowds who ceased dancing only after the beer ran out. As one newspaper observed, people seemed to enjoy themselves "making it hard to believe that we are at war and that thirty thousand of our brothers are now, at this moment, risking their lives."[47] A dance craze seized the capital and Santiago's *gente decente* still entertained. Indeed, one newspaper suggested that people gave more parties, perhaps believing that these social events, by reducing tension and providing honest diversions, contributed to the war effort. Clearly social life continued unabated except when some military disaster, like the sinking of the *Covadonga* or the publication of long casualty lists after Arica, forced the cancellation of a scheduled dance. Thus, for some ladies, the fall of Lima caused not elation but great sadness because it signified an end to the balls and the disappearance of so many handsome eligible young officers.[48]

The closest the conflict ever came to touching the nation was the explosion of Santiago's arsenal in January 1880. This disaster rained shot, shell, and debris on nearby homes, converting the luckless residents into "cannon fodder," and scaring large numbers of people into flight from the city. Normally, however, unless a family member served in the north or lived next to a powder mill, the average Chilean could live untouched by the struggle. Not without reason one contemporary concluded that the onset of the smallpox epidemic caused more disruption than did the war.[49]

While not slowing the tempo of the nation's social whirl, the War of the Pacific altered the level and pattern of criminal activities. Before April 1879 an epidemic of lawlessness infected Chile. Armed bands ravaged agricultural communities, attacking *fundos*, extorting protection money from *hacendados*, stealing livestock, terrorizing peasants enroute to market, and murdering *inquilinos*.[50]

City life proved equally dangerous. People converted homes into *chinganas* or worse, brothels, both of which attracted boisterous crowds and prostitutes who subjected the local residents either to abusive language or indecent proposals. Sometimes passions clouded the judgment. When one Santiago maid opened the door at 6 A.M. to take out the garbage, six well-dressed gentlemen entered, seeking female companionship. The owner managed to evict his unexpected guests, but only after a physical struggle. But the noise of the *chinganas* and the misplaced passion of the whoremonger paled in comparison with the wave of violence which gripped the cities. Entire neighborhoods, not simply one street, lived in fear when criminals moved in and took over the area, a problem that afflicted provincial centers as well as the capital.[51]

The police could not halt the violence. Indeed, many citizens claimed that when not indulging in criminal activity themselves, the constabulary acted capriciously, arresting people for minor offenses. For a variety of reasons, in part economic, few men wished to become policemen. Chillán, for example, had twenty vacancies but applicants considered the pay of $12 per week inadequate to support a family. Those who enlisted often lacked education, or were delinquents or allies of the criminals they promised to pursue. Many abused their authority, wielding their clubs too generously and indiscriminately for minor offenses. Loathed by the public and poorly armed, the constabularly lacked the support, the training, the skills, or the inclination to stop the criminals.[52]

Certainly the authorities possessed a curious set of priorities. During the same period that Manuel Jesus Ramírez was serving fifteen days in San Bernardo's jail for disobeying his mother, the authorities found three corpses, all the victims of violent crime, littering the city's streets. In truth, the underpaid, untrained, and undermanned police could not defend themselves, let alone the public, against their criminal opponents. The problem resulted in part because the justice system failed to punish miscreants efficiently. Thieves, if apprehended, easily escaped from the flimsy jails in which they temporarily resided. If they chose to remain in custody and were convicted, the Council of State reduced their sentences to a fraction of its original severity. If the judiciary punished the criminal by lashing him, the felon might subsequently retaliate against the executioner.[53] The onset of the war, moreover, strained an already overburdened police because some cities used their constabulary to create military contingents which the government mobilized for active duty. In desperation, the virtually defenseless municipalities ordered their volunteer fire brigades to fill in for the police.[54]

With the police off defending the nation, violence should have increased. Yet, criminal activity only slightly accelerated until the winter of

1879, when it precipitiously declined, inaugurating almost two years of comparative tranquility (see Table 41 and Figure 1). This unexpected blessing can be traced to the government's unofficial policy of forced recruitment. As noted earlier, local authorities impressed the indigent, the vagrant, and the criminal, converting once turbulent areas into islands of quiet.[55]

Sadly, the disbanding of the army in the north allowed criminals to return to their prewar occupations. Provincial newspapers warned that demobilization would initiate a resurgence of lawlessness, particularly if the veterans could not find jobs. This prediction quickly materialized when Chillán's press reported that the newest thieves were exsoldiers recently discharged from a local regiment. Consequently, while the nation certainly rejoiced when their soldiers returned home, their happiness must have dissipated when they realized that the war, ironically, had brought them more domestic security than the restoration of peace.[56]

Indeed, beginning in mid-1881, bandits again devastated the countryside, raiding *haciendas*, stealing animals, and even seizing agricultural products already loaded on trains. Urban areas remained dangerous: "In the plaza, the street, and the mountains people feel neither tranquil nor safe," wrote *El Eco de Taltal*—a description which seemed to apply everywhere. Criminals robbed the citizens of Santiago in broad daylight; in Chillán thieves attacked a woman, taking all her possessions including her clothes. One newspaper estimated that, in only one year, bullet and stab wounds hospitalized 3,000 Chileans, one-third of whom would die. Yet, in the midst of this carnage, Copiapó's police arrested two men for sodomizing a sheep.[57]

Some towns tried to frustrate the thieves by declaring a curfew of 11 P.M.; others allowed the police to detain anyone they considered suspicious. This technique did not always work. For instance, while Chillán's police put two workers in the jail for the night—where they were robbed—bandits attacked a nearby *fundo* and killed its owner. Some Chileans believed that heavy jail sentences might retard criminality, citing the success of a particularly harsh Lebu judge. A journalist for *The Chilian Times* disagreed, calling for more flogging, gleefully writing that even a hardened criminal pleaded for mercy when confronted with the prospect of receiving thirty lashes.[59]

Happily, the mounting level of violence did not return to its prewar level. In part this moderation might be attributed to the persistence of the recruiting sergeant who still needed bodies for the army of occupation. The economic situation had also drastically changed. The depression of the 1870s had forced many to turn to crime out of economic need. The expansion of the nitrate fields and the creation of various public work projects provided an alternative source of employment, thus reducing the level of illegal activity.

Although the mines and construction projects opened new alternatives for the worker, they complicated the situation for the *hacendado* who before the war had monopolized the labor market. Another force also eroded the landowner's dominance: contractors of the Panama Canal project actively recruited workers in Chile. The De Lesseps' undertaking, however, revived memories of the thousands who had left Chile, never to return, to build Peru's railroads. Despite appeals to patriotism and warnings of the press and the clergy, that they would face an "almost sure death," many peons nonetheless departed for the Isthmus to work on the Canal.[60]

Many observers recognized that the exodus to Panama was a repudiation of Chile's rural conditions. Clearly the peons had changed: they would not accept the old salaries of "50, 40, or 30 cents a day because they have been tempted with promises of being paid one or more pesos." Indeed, *El Ñuble* blamed not De Lesseps's gold but the greedy landowners for causing "the emigration of workingmen which has occurred this year." One newspaper became furious that the nation which produced such fine laborers would not reward them accordingly, a situation which another expected to remain the same "until the Chilean boss abandons the path of vexing and criminal exploitation."[61]

Improving conditions of the agrarian working class might staunch the demographic hemorrhage but few *hacendados* would consider this alternative and fewer still adopted it. The *Boletín de la Sociedad Nacional de Agricultura* blamed the terrible plight of the rural lower classes on poor treatment, abysmal working conditions, and inadequate rations. Salaries, it noted, suffered a 50 percent reduction in real purchasing power but landlords still refused to increase wages. In Chile, the journal continued, unlike in advanced farming nations like the United States, *inquilinos* were treated as things and not human beings.[62]

Rather than improve the lot of their tenants, the *terratenientes* discovered another expedient to remedy their labor shortages: immigration. Proponents of importing foreign labor argued that the new arrivals would bring not only strong arms but also needed skills and, perhaps, capital. Citing the experiences of the United States and Argentina, advocates also pointed to the German settlements in Valdivia and Llanquihue which had spearheaded the development of Chile's south.[63]

This solution did not enchant those who concluded that immigration projects merely obscured the basic issue: the wretched status of the nation's peasantry. Even *El Independiente* joined the anti-immigration chorus and Zorbabel Rodríguez, who generally opposed all forms of government intervention, nonetheless called for the Moneda to improve the lot of the working class. The *hacendados* erred, he claimed, when they complained about not finding enough willing hands: they simply wanted "laborers who will work for the same nominal salary of 20 or 30 cents, plus a ration of beans, that prevailed before the war." If the rural landowners paid higher wages, they would have more than enough peons. Instead, the landlords hoped that government sponsored immigration projects would provide them with cheap labor. Rather than trying to save agriculture by oppressing the lower class, the *terratenientes*, he argued, should modernize their farms, introduce new techniques, and provide their *inquilinos* homes "suitable for civilized and Christian men." *El Padre Cobos* shared this belief, alleging that "the bastard ambitions of a group of miserable speculators" supported immigration projects as a way of depressing the cost of labor. Instead of the state allocating money to defray the cost of immigration, it should use these funds to help Chileans. The journal even suggested offering prizes to families who had raised a majority of their children to the age of 15 or 20. "Chile for the Chileans and Chileans for Chile," the paper urged.[64]

Chauvinism also motivated the opposition to immigrants. Chileans, while conveniently forgetting their own mixed racial background, traditionaly had disparaged their Andean neighbors for being Indians, blacks, or *zambos,* a prejudice which the war had only reinforced. The immigration proposal, however, not only threatened to dilute the country's purported racial purity, but to introduce crime, disease, and pauperism as well. As Rodríguez intoned, no immigrant could match a Chilean created by its own "sons, each time more strong, more Chilean."[65]

Rather than lure foreigners, one journal called for "protection for the proletariat and the national worker" while its colleagues argued that the Chileans who conquered the southern lands were being displaced or victimized by their new foreign neighbors. A few suggested providing demobilized soldiers with farms in the south and Ramón Barros Luco even introduced a measure to implement this program. Unfortunately, speculators purchased these lands in hopes of making a profit when the Central Valley's railroad came south.[66]

Thus, Chile's situation appeared curious. Its employers clamored for laborers while beggars, many quite healthy in appearance, clogged its cities and criminal activity escalated. "It seems strange that we should have so many bandits and so few working but . . . this is what is happening," leading one journalist to conclude that "the Chilean working class is inclined by instinct to assault, robbery, and murder."[67]

Many contemporaries concluded that the nation lacked workers not because the working class was lazy or inherently criminal but because too few lived long enough to join the labor force. If landlords would "treat their dependents less like cattle, provide them decent housing to ward off poor weather, and exert themselves to get all their children properly vaccinated, each census might exhibit a marked increased in population."[68] Until then, however, Chile's farmlands would remain underpopulated.

The urban situation appeared equally bleak. Most Chilean cities looked and apparently smelled like cess pits. People defecated on the streets, irreverently urinated on the walls of churches, and threw their garbage and offal everywhere. Many urban poor lived in *conventillos*— rows of squat tenements with dirt floors and few windows, facing each other across an open drainage ditch—"really sewers"—where the central patio served as privy and refuse heap. Contemporaries reported that these terrible accommodations were where the "aristocracy of the poor" lived. The less fortunate, their animals, and their friends shared homes built below street level. These hovels were without windows or floor, where the inhabitants slept six to a bed beneath a roof that leaked.

Fumes from foundries, butcher shops, tanneries, pig sties, and factories often became so powerful that pedestrians had to press a camphor-soaked hankerchief to their noses. Some urged the planting of eucalyptus trees to mask the stench. Regrettably, attempts to construct sewers and potable water systems often encountered technical problems. Valparaíso, for example, found it difficult to install a sanitation system because the city rested on sand. Consequently, breweries often used polluted water; a bakery in the port drew its water from a well which adjoined a privy. In Lebu, water drained from the cemetery into the town's drinking supply. Regardless of the source, the failure to dispose of these human or animal wastes literally poisoned the nation.[69]

Disease, the logical result of the lack of sanitation, decimated Chile's population. Scarlet fever, whooping cough, and measles scourged the young; syphilis decimated their parents; smallpox democratically annihilated both generations. *Viruela* epidemics had afflicted Chile before but a particularly virulent form returned during the war, killing more Chileans than the allies. This new outbreak began with the onset of 1880 and rapidly spread throughout the country; for three years Chile endured this cruel affliction.[70]

The number of patients quickly outstripped the nation's medical facilities, including those, like Santiago's Hospital San Vicente de Paul, which also cared for the war wounded. *El Comercio* reported that not one street in San Felipe had escaped the epidemic and noted that the local hospital had to turn away smallpox victims. At first some local officials had housed *viruela* patients in hospital wards where they invariably infected their neighbors. Eventually the victims were deposited in a lazarette, a polite name for a charnal house, where as many as 90 percent died. The level of care varied. Many facilities lacked supplies. Others, like Chillán's lazarette, was staffed by two attendants, "more knowledgable about killing than curing."[71] Employing a doctor did not always guarantee better care. Lota hired a Dr. Mariano Guzmán, who often stood half a block away from the lazarette shouting medical instructions to the facility's staff. Conditions within the lazarettes were overcrowded and filthy. The structures, sometimes hastily constructed, generally required repairs, and occasionally collapsed on the already suffering patients.[72] Various municipalities, however, did not possess even the most primitive facilities. San Bernardo, noted one observer, contained "no lazarette, no doctor, except for a phamarcist, consequently the ill, . . . were treated in an open clearing, under trees or even under a rock." Meanwhile, the entire province of Arauco had but one dispensary and a single physician; the poor, as a result, "died in the most deplorable state of abandonment." Some cities hastily constructed lazarettes but because they lacked the funds to hire doctors, many of the patients expired from inadequate care.[73]

The law required confinement in a lazarette. The public, however, quite rightly described these institutions as warehouses of death that one entered "in search of . . . health but from which few escaped with their lives." Not suprisingly, people often refused to inform the medical authorities if one of their family contracted smallpox. Government policies also frustrated official attempts at isolating *viruela* victims. Santiago's health authorities, for example, specified that parents had to provide food as well as an adult to accompany any child under the age of six confined to a lazarette. This regulation, however, imposed hardship on the poor. The victim's father had to work and the mother could not institutionalize the sick infant without deserting the rest of her family. Consequently, the parents would not hospitalize their sick child. Valparaíso's laws were more grotesque. The port's elders demanded that landlords evict any family if one of its members contracted smallpox. Thus, instead of stopping the contagion, health regulations forced the family into the street, where they could infect others.[74]

Lazarettes not only endangered the ill, they also contaminated the areas where they were located. Santiago's Barrio Maestranza, for example, fearing contagion, requested that the government move that "permanent focus of infection" to the Hospital San Salvador which stood on the outskirts of town.[75] One did not have to live next to a lazarette to suffer. In Santiago, an open drainage ditch first passed through the San

Borja pest house and then flowed into a nearby residential neighborhood.[76]

Predictably those who succumbed to smallpox received even less reverence than the living. Perhaps this indifference represented a psychological defense against the high mortality rate, because for a time Chile resembled Europe caught in the grip of the black death. People carried cadavers on long poles through the streets of Lebu. Municipal hearses, which often doubled as garbage carts, traveled through urban centers, sometimes at lunch hour, with the naked limbs of the deceased exposed. In one case, a body dropped off of a wagon and might have remained unnoticed had some children not alerted the driver. Eventually people requested that the officials show, if not respect for the dead, then sensitivity toward the living by avoiding the centers of town when transporting the dead to a cemetery. Santiago established certain routes for its death wagon when the epidemic forced it to work during the day rather than, as apparently had been the custom, at night.[77]

On its return trip from the cemetery, the hearse sometimes carried new smallpox victims to the lazarette, but not before the driver stopped enroute for a drink. Those who operated the death wagons enjoyed a certain immunity. Chillán's driver not only seized a house, knowing that its owner would not dare evict him, but also parked his cart in front of the homes of those individuals with whom he was feuding.[78]

If the lazarette appeared to be a medieval pest house, the cemetery resembled a Bosch engraving. Many burial grounds lacked adequate space so that the gravediggers had to throw away the remains of the old corpses before they buried the newest victims. Frequently the authorities did not inter the cadavers deep enough allowing dogs to rummage among the bodies to feast upon the remains. One canine even carried the head of a smallpox victim into town where it was found on the street. Thieves violated graves to steal the clothes or jewelry. Other families, seeking to avoid the payment of burial fees, entered clandestinely to bury their loved ones in illegal plots while rivers, swollen by heavy rains, overflowed their banks, uncovering bodies. When the weather turned dry, and the wind blew across the cemetery, the stench of decaying flesh filled the air.[79]

Rather than passively wait for its population to perish, some municipalities tried to stem the epidemic. Local governments ordered its citizens to sweep the streets and clear the communal drainage canals, told landlords and renters to clean their homes, and even appointed inspectors to ensure compliance. The police distributed disinfectant for the poor to use in order to wash their homes; Lota's main employer, the coal company, sanitized the residences of its workers. But these campaigns invariably faltered and then sputtered to a feeble end. Copiapó's authorities stopped picking up the garbage, forcing a newspaper to note that "there are certain barrios in this town which are simply privies ... more cleanliness for God's sake." "Either more attention is paid to the public," noted *El Independiente*, "or contagion ... and the ten plagues of Egypt will do everything possible to make a city of the dead on both banks of the Mapocho."[80]

Some Chileans advocated a balanced diet, regular hours, and keeping one's feet dry; others recommended sweating, generous doses of water, salt, lemon, or vinegar, the ventilating of one's clothes or purging to stave off the pox. A few believed that frequent bathing might ward off infection, consequently, *La Revista del Sur* urged people to wash twice a day, a suggestion which Curicó's newspaper seconded. Regrettably, most municipalities did not possess the necessary facilities. Santiago's public baths lacked dressing rooms and only provided waste water, hardly an antiseptic solution, for bathing. *The Chilian Times* denounced Valparaíso's town fathers for appropriating funds to build "toy parks and toy gardens" but not for providing sanitary facilities for the poor.[81]

Many wisely ignored these nostrums in preference for a more well-known solution: vaccination. Physicians as well as lay people urged that all Chileans be immunized and suggested that either the Moneda or municipalities support a program of preventive medicine. Various government agencies hired full-time vaccinators whose services became so popular during the epidemic that they had to hire medical students to meet the demand. Rather than wait for patients, organizations like the Junta Central de Vacuna sent vaccinators into Santiago's most populated neighborhoods in order to bring Dr. Jenner's solution to the people. Apparently other communities adopted similar policies. Rancagua's residents became angry when the vaccinator would not visit the school.[82]

Despite the empirical evidence and the enthusiastic recommendation of the press, many Chileans still spurned immunization. A few doubted that the vaccine worked—not an unwarranted conclusion since occasionally some shipments of serum failed. Others claimed that the injection transmitted syphilis, a canard which physicians futilely tried to refute.[83]

The health crisis demonstrated the inability of the Moneda to resolve pressing social and economic problems. Various Chileans became angry that so many of their compatriots perished, a majority unnecessarily, because they received inadequate care as children or lived in such squalor as adults. *The Chilian Times* calculated that smallpox alone killed 10,000 annually and cost the nation $10,000,000 in lost productivity. While others might quibble about the newspaper's figures, they agreed that this self-inflicted genocide had to stop. The authorities launched vaccination campaigns: Santiago's Intendent requested that the local bishop tell his parishioners to accept innoculations.[84] Santa María demanded compulsory vaccination, a proposal one journal believed would save thousands from death thus increasing the nation's "wealth and glory."[85]

The legislature, however, refused to authorize mandatory innoculations. During the 1878 smallpox epidemic, the Chamber of Deputies passed a measure instituting mandatory vaccination for students enrolled in state schools or residing in its institutions: for the military; for prisoners in jails; and hospital patients. The legislation languished until the 1880 epidemic made the lower house forward the measure to the Senate for its approval. During these debates, Benjamín Vicuña Mackenna convinced his colleagues to enact a measure requiring the vaccination of all Chileans. The upper house approved Vicuña Mackenna's suggestions and returned the drastically amended proposal to the Chamber of Deputies for its approval.

Predictably Zorobabel Rodríguez, who also opposed regulating either the dishonest pawnbroker or the diseased prostitute, believed that Vicuña Mackenna's proposal restricted a citizen's freedom of choice. Rather than require vaccination, he suggested that the legislature grant a bounty of 50 cents to individuals who voluntarily accepted immunization. The Liberal *El Ferrocarril*, while admitting that only humanitarian considerations had motivated the Vicuña Mackenna proposal, nonetheless considered it "a draconian resurrection, in the name of hygiene," of oppressive techniques earlier used on behalf of "the state or an exclusive church." Chile's health problems were due to the "climate and custom," neither one of which could be resolved by the passage of an undemocratic law. The clerical press shared this opinion. While favoring legislation which prohibited individuals from working on Sundays or religious holidays, and while opposing attempts to protect the religious nonconformist, *El Estandarte Católico* hypocritically concluded that mandatory vaccination violated a citizen's liberties.[86]

The bill's legislative opponents used a variety of scare tactics to discredit the proposal claiming that innoculations either did not protect the recipient or that they transmitted syphilis. The government had admitted that some of its serum had failed, although it noted that no one had suffered any adverse effect and certainly not a venereal disease. Still, the damage was done: various provincial officials refused to administer the serum, forcing the desperate poor to inoculate themselves with a substitute.[87]

Advocates of mandatory vaccination, including the physicians Adolfo Murillo and Augusto Orrego Luco, staunchly defended the program.

Dismissing the notion that an innoculation spread venereal disease, they also tried to counter the allegation of Luis Jordan that forced vaccination constituted "a trampling of the sainted right of property." Even Adam Smith, noted one physician-deputy, allowed the state to intervene in the affairs of an individual under certain circumstances. But, Murillo and Orrego Luco failed to convince their colleagues. Not only did the syphilis canard remain intact, the issue of personal liberty emerged as the focal point of the argument. Ricardo Letelier feared that the government, which earlier had capitalized on the issue of public necessity to intervene in the nation's political life, would use the health issue to usurp more power. Such government involvement, moreover, would kill—although not perhaps as painfully as smallpox—individual initiative, "the basis and the seedbed of all progress." For Letelier the choice was quite clear: "The ravages of smallpox are nothing in comparison to what would transpire from that other plague which bears the name of authoritarianism." Letelier's speech convinced his colleagues to reject the Vicuña Mackenna amendments, thus protecting *viruela* from the ogre of big government.[88]

Antipathy to state participation permeated other aspects of Chilean society. Venereal disease permeated Chile. To counter this problem, the Intendant of Valparaíso, Eulogio Altamirano, proposed licensing prostitutes, permitting only the healthy to practice their trade. Again, however, the issue took on more than moral or public health implications. *El Independiente*'s Rodríguez considered the health regulations an unwarranted intrusion by the state to limit individual freedom. The Church attacked the suggestion, indicating that licensing gave the state's imprimatur to illicit sex. This clerical opposition failed to convince *El Padre Cobos* which published a cartoon portraying women and children thanking Altamirano while a pox-disfigured priest raged in the corner. A similar reluctance to grant the police broader powers permitted the owners of pawn shops to cheat their clientele by undervaluing their merchandise while demanding 5 percent interest per month.[89]

The war highlighted the inequities in Chile. *El Independiente* denounced the *conventillo* owners who reaped generous profits from their slum properties but who refused to make needed repairs. Various individuals excoriated a system which permitted the poor to live in wretched hovels, heavily taxed their foodstuffs, and denied them access to decent recreation. The state had to build housing in neighborhoods with paved streets and adequate illumination, to lower taxes on items consumed by the poor, and to provide medical care. Such proposals even enjoyed the support of *El Independiente* although it, like *La Libertad*, believed that private enterprise, not the state, should participate in some of these projects.[90]

Reformers also called for the state to grant the peasantry lands in the south, "the only just, logical thing; a most decent and useful act which would end *inquilinaje*, and with it the great cancer which for some time has corroded us more and more—vagrancy, banditry, and the other plague: emigration."[91] The government, moreover, should create a special ministry to direct the creation and administration of public services, to help those "who live unprotected and oppressed by the rich hacendados, the users of the sweat and labor of the patient *inquilino*," to alter the agrarian system which forced people from the farm either to starve in the city or migrate.[92] Others suggested that the government might also guarantee the working class a safer work environment. *La Epoca* praised an intendent who, by limiting the work day, ensured that "our children do not serve merely to sow cemeteries but instead give life to industry and develop the thousand resources of this fertile and unexploited land." The lash and good works, noted E. Fosten Recabarren, were but a "drop of water which barely sufficed to quench the burning throats of a voracious pauperism."[93]

Education, moreover, became an increasingly important issue. Expanding schools would not only permit members of the lower class to improve themselves but would create a cadre of technicians whose skills would end Chile's dependence upon foreign workers. Many advocated educating women although others warned against the dangers of mixing the sexes in the classroom. Coeducation might work in the United States, but not, according to one observer, in Chile where the lower classes would threaten innocent young girls. "Honor and virtue," noted *La Esperanza*, "are worth more than knowing how to read and write."[94]

The various solutions—better living conditions, the creation of more hospitals, improved education, industrialization—all required the active participation of the Moneda. Unfortunately, these reforms seemed beyond the reach of the government. In the Chile of the 1880s, the state might poison dogs, but it would not protect the citizen against the dangers posed by humans. *La Patria*, hardly a radical journal, wondered why the state punished those who murder with a knife but still allowed people to rent filthy homes "which were really branch offices for smallpox and death."[95]

Unless the Moneda instituted change, warned a journalist, internal unrest would convulse the nation. What will transpire, inquired *El Nuevo Ferrocarril*, when 25,000 men "highly skilled in handling weapons and used to following the first blast of the trumpet" return to Chile and face starvation. Such fears proved illusory. Worker organizations existed, although on a limited scale. Most provided a combination of cultural activities and economic assistance. In Bulnes, for example, workers organized both a night school as well as an aid society.[96] Although not extensively organized, labor seemed increasingly aware that it possessed unique goals and different tastes. The workers admired Manuel Rodríguez and Juan Aldea not O'Higgins and Prat; they supported the candidacy of a Sr. Lazarte to the national legislature because he promised to address their special interests and elected Isais Francisco Ramírez to Chillán's municipal council; they were urged to unite in order to protect themselves from ruthless businessmen who would import Chinese labor into Chile, thus depressing salaries.[97]

Sometimes, the workers violently manifested their dissatisfaction. The most notorious dispute occurred in Toco where a group of nitrate workers rebelled, killing the local manager and forcing the government to dispatch troops to pacify the *salitrero*. Stevedores struck in Iquique, and in depressed Taltal, 300 miners marched through the streets demanding their salaries.[98] Labor unrest spread throughout the nation. Lota's coal miners stopped working, much to the distress of the local press which blamed the dispute on malcontents. To the north, in Concepción, railway workers struck, claiming that they had been shortchanged. Even bucolic *fundos* suffered: a group of apparently drunken peons refused to work, and at another *hacienda* an exsoldier protested the inadequate and poor rations his patron provided.[99]

It is evident that although the war might have enlivened the nation's life, it did not appear to alter it dramatically. Chile, of course, was not engaged in "total war." The enemy did not attack economic targets; large numbers of people avoided military service; the naval war did not interdict the flow of imports; rationing did not exist. The social status quo ante bellum remained intact: those with money lived well; those who suffered, probably would have done so whether or not Chile went to war. Still, the conflict may have started some subtle changes. The returning soldiers had discovered their own worth. After having traveled thousands of miles to participate in a great undertaking, many veterans would no longer accept passively their old subservience. The lower class discovered for the first time a life independent of the *fundo* and a force within themselves which had permitted them not only to defeat Peru but also to alter their own destinies.

The nation, or at least part of it, suddenly discovered the virtues of the lower class and a growing number recognized their truly desperate plight. Regrettably, the social critics could not institute the needed reforms. The obvious solutions—better housing, the creation of more hospitals, improved education, and industrialization—all required the active participation of the state. And unfortunately, the government lacked the mechanisms, the funds, or the inclination to institute such changes. Chile remained a laissez faire nation which still financed its war, paved its streets, and built its hospitals with voluntary donations. Still, the awareness which developed during the War of the Pacific would emerge years later as the *cuestión social*—an issue involved with improving the lot of the lower classes—and inspire other Chileans to alter drastically the nature of their society.

9

The Politics of War

> Politics is war without bloodshed; war is politics with bloodshed.
> Mao Tse Tung

One of the most enduring myths was that prewar Chile possessed a sophisticated and representative political system which not only accurately reflected the will of the nation but also permitted the Moneda to respond more efficiently than the allies to the demands of the war. It was claimed, moreover, that Chilean politicians constituted a loyal opposition who abstained from partisan activity in order to permit the government to direct unhindered various military and naval campaigns. These allegations, like those which proclaimed Chile's vaunted military prowess, are simply without substance.

It is true that Aníbal Pinto managed to complete his term of office while the leaders of Peru and Bolivia did not enjoy such a happy fate. Manuel Prado, for example, unable to cope with the political opposition, handed power to a successor and abandoned Peru in November 1879. The frenetic Nicolás Piérola quickly overthrew Prado's replacement, ruling Peru, first from Lima and then from the altiplano until he too decamped for a foriegn exile, leaving his nation to become a prize for rival caudillos. Bolivia fared only slightly better. Daza was in the field when he received a telegram informing him that the army no longer supported his administration. Warned that he risked assassination if he returned to La Paz, Daza wisely retired. His successor, General Narciso Campero, would occupy the unsteady presidential throne throughout the remainder of the war.

Thus not without reason did Chile appear to be a paragon of political virtue. Even in the midst of the Bolivian crisis, congressional elections occurred on schedule. In 1881, the nation selected a new president, Domingo Santa María, and the following year, elected another Congress. Superficially, at least, the republic appeared stable, democratic, and capable of surviving the most trying circumstances. Yet, beneath the facade of legality and apparent respect for the constituion, there existed a political system teetering on the edge of collapse, driven to the point of paralysis by partisan bickering, and afflicted with many of the flaws subsequently attributed to the Parliamentary Regime. By indulging in self-serving, anti-government interpolations, the political opposition distracted the Moneda, thus prolonging, at great cost to the nation, Chile's involvement in the War of the Pacific.

THE POLITICAL DANCECARD

Ostensibly five political parties existed in Chile: the Conservatives, the Nationals or Montt Varistas, the Liberals, the Liberal Democrats, and the Radicals. Despite their impressive names, these organizations lacked "ideas, convictions, or doctrine"; principles and morality were ballast to be jettisoned in case of political expedience; party discipline was lax if not nonexistent.[1] Only the Conservatives controlled their members, a device which permitted them to wield more power than their numbers warranted. The rest of the parties had fragmented into numerous wings destroying the notion of political unity or cohesion.

Essentially two blocs emerged out of this political Babel: those in power, the various wings of the Liberal party; and those striving to replace them. For the first time, the Liberals seemed in danger of losing their control. Personal factions developed—the *Errazuristas*, the *Ricardistas*, or the *Echaurrenistas* who coalesced respectively around the former president, Federico Errazuríz, Ricardo Letelier, a prominent deputy from Talca, and Francisco Echaurren, former intendent of Valparaíso. Other elements also coexisted under the umbrella of Liberalism: the moderates, who favored some vague reforms; the *independistas*, who apparently wanted more reforms but never specified how many; and the *liberales de gobierno*, the administration's followers. When Liberal unity frayed, the party's leaders had to go outside the party circle to obtain support. In Pinto's government, at least initially, this meant forging alliances preferably with the Nationals, occasionally with the Radicals, but never with the Conservatives.

The Conservatives, once the nation's most powerful party, had lost their grip on the Moneda decades past. When it had ruled, the clerical party wielded power in an extremely authoritarian manner; once out in the political cold, it advocated administrative decentralization, reducing the power of the executive branch, and, of course, continuing state support for the Church. The National party, or Montt Varistas, was created by two men: Manuel Montt, former president and still politically active until his death in the late 1870s, and his former protegé, Antonio Varas. A secular version of the Conservatives, they sought to retain the Portalian state without having to pay homage to the Catholic Church. Over the years, however, the lines distinguishing the National party from its contemporaries had blurred; instead of advocating firm political ideals, it had degenerated into an epicence clique that one journalist described as, "ni chicha ni limonada."² Another essentially personalist organization was the Liberal Democratic party, which owed its origin to Benjamín Vicuña Mackenna's anger at not receiving the presidential nomination in 1876. Composed of renegade Liberals, it functioned without articulating, except in the vaguest terms, either its goals or purpose. The Radical party, perhaps because it was the youngest, had a definite idea of what it wished—the secularization of Chilean society—although, like the young, it lacked the finesse and the power to achieve this ideal.

Perhaps a strong man could have tamed these restive groups but Aníbal Pinto was no strong man. Handicapped by a singularly unimpressive demeanor and then plagued with the aureole of the hack politician, the new leader took office just as a terrible economic depression swept over the nation. Hamstrung by a balky economy and constantly sniped at by his political opposition, Pinto tried to put things in order but the caprice of the weather and world demand proved too powerful. By late 1878 various opposition political figures had ample cause for complaint: Pinto's dismal record on the economy, his increasingly hostile relations with the Church, and the Argentine crisis clearly demonstrated his administration's incompetence. The confrontation with Bolivia provided his enemies with an opportunity to depict Pinto as a weak, vacillating leader who cravenly permitted Chile's neighbors to break their obligations with impunity.

THE 1879 CONGRESSIONAL ELECTIONS AND THE WAR

Thus, by 1879 the national mood appeared quite depressed and by the summer many Chileans wondered if congressional elections would occur. Rumors abounded that the Conservative party would lead a rebellion, rumors which seemed quite credible given threats published in *El Estandarte Católico*. On the Left, *El Taller* warned that the nation's laborers would not tolerate intervention in the electoral process. If the government tried, it warned, "to prevent our triumph by force and illegality, we will use our own force to oppose it."³

Despite these threats, the government intervened. Minister of the

Interior Belisario Prats provided a functionary with a list of candidates on whose behalf the Liberal party should work, while appointing a "completely trustworthy officer," as interim governor to supervise the elections.[4] Manipulation apparently took two forms: some candidates preferred to buy public office, although Melchor Concha i Toro, a multimillionaire, was appalled to discover that he had to spend $1,500 if he wished to purchase the affection of Chillán's electorate. "This is too much," he declared, "the sacrifice is now too large, nevertheless do it if it is necessary."[5] Others, often the government, used the army, the police, the National Guard, or the local authorities to strongarm the voters.

Although the press constantly cited examples of the Moneda's intervention, all the political groups apparently indulged in similar behavior. Abdón Cifuentes, a Conservative deputy, requested that "the friends" avoid any activity which might hurt certain candidates.[6] Still, the government received the principal share of attention and it must have disheartened the nation to learn that in the midst of the Bolivian crisis, the Moneda had unleashed its troops, not to attack "a foreign enemy" but to pursue "the peaceful electors and defenseless citizens of Los Anjeles and Mulchen." The war became an election issue, allowing the opposition to accuse the Moneda of using the international dispute either to distract the masses or to mask its persecution of anti-government candidates. The Bolivian crisis thus became quite dear to the administration's foes who would first shame Pinto for not acting and then complain when he did.[7]

Toward the end of the campaign, the various parties frantically began forming coalitions, often with groups they had earlier denounced, in order to guarantee the election of their candidates. Although the Liberal party's candidates won a substantial portion of the contests, large numbers of the opposition, including the Conservatives, also triumphed, indicating that the charges of government intervention were perhaps overblown.[8] Given the fragile condition of the Liberal party, the election of a substantial number of hostile legislators promised to pose problems for Pinto and complicate, if not delay, the prosecution of the conflict.

Some political figures honestly disagreed with the government's war policy. Others, however, particularly the Conservatives, used the war to overturn a ministry, not in order to alter government policy, but to achieve power for themselves. From its onset, opposition politicians manipulated the Bolivian crisis to undermine Pinto's power. During the final days of the congressional campaign, the president acceded to public opinion and called the parliament into extraordinary session where the legislators, while unanimously supporting the president's call for a declaration of war, also seized the opportunity to criticize his government. This hostility did not end after the election. On 9 April 1879, for example,

Isidoro Errazuríz, in addition to requesting detailed information on the status of the fleet and the military, demanded to know why the army had not occupied the Loa Valley or attacked Iquique. When the minister of war, Cornelio Saavedra, pleaded for time, angry opposition deputies claimed that Saavedra could not respond because he had devoted his efforts not to preparing for the war, but to manipulating the election. Other ministers defended their policies, but they too failed to convince their opponents who also raised the issue of Prats's intervention in the electoral process. The purpose of the interpolation quickly emerged: the Conservatives wished to depose Prats's ministry as punishment for its political intervention and to gain a portfolio in a government of national unity. Although the pro-Moneda deputies defeated the censure motion, the failure to win a vote of confidence nonetheless distressed Belisario Prats. The remainder of the cabinet appeared almost as demoralized. Saavedra, for example, suggested that Pinto replace him, citing his ill health and a lack of self-confidence.[9]

Ironically, Pinto disapproved of his minister of the interior for opposing his policies, for favoring the declaration of war against the allies, and finally for his clumsy manipulation of the recent elections which alienated the president's allies in the Radical and Liberal parties. Consequently, although Prats survived the wrath of his colleagues, he could not escape the ire of Pinto who dismissed him in early April.[10]

THE VARAS MINISTRY

Selecting a Montt-Varista to form a new government seemed, if not inappropriate, then at least injudicious; but nevertheless the president chose Antonio Varas as his new minister of the interior. Certainly the politician enjoyed certain advantages: he was extremely experienced and, as a National, had not been involved in the various internecine struggles which convulsed the Liberal party. Aware that his involvement with Montt had made him one of the most despised men in Chile, Varas initially refused Pinto's offer, fearful that his presence might prove too divisive. Reassured by the president, Varas accepted the post, requesting that the president permit him to form a government of national unity which would include all the various political parties. Pinto, however, would not permit Conservatives to enter his administration, thus the new cabinet remained basically Liberal in affiliation if not ideology: Domingo Santa María served as foreign minister; the increasingly decrepit General Basilio Urrutia occupied the ministry of war while Jorge Huneeus and Augusto Matte held respectively the portfolios for justice and treasury.

Although at the onset of hostilities all the political parties had promised to abstain from partisan squabbling, they quickly reverted to their prewar truculence. Indeed, Pinto subsequently noted, "I did not have any illusions but I never believed that it would be like what I am now seeing. The feeling . . . in the bottom of my soul is very sad." The president's anxiety proved well founded: the Conservatives, were joined by Prats who, smarting over his recent dismissal, became a leader of the anti-government coalition. In one of the first meetings of the newly convened legislature, the Conservatives accused Urrutia of failing to provide adequate supplies to the troops and, two weeks later, used a secret session to demand information about the war and to defend Admiral Williams Rebolledo. Although presumably the debates focused on military topics, invariably the speakers managed to mention the government's policy of excluding the Conservative party. A more serious attack on the powers of the executive materialized when Tagle Arrate sought to have the Congress participate in the conduct of the war by appointing a team of three deputies to accompany the expeditionary forces. Although the lower house rejected the measure, it indicated that some legislators believed that they should not permit Pinto to direct the war unchaparoned.[11]

These legislative activities aroused increasing hostility. Government officials serving in the north lamented that narrow political interests continued to harrass the Moneda. Were it not for the battle of Iquique, noted José Alfonso, the ministry would have fallen as "if we do not have enough with this extremely difficult international conflict."[12] A sense of dread permeated Chile. Although the press requested that Pinto call the Congress into extraordinary session, the public's faith in its parliament evaporated when it saw that the deputies devoted most of June and July bickering over the credentials of the prospective legislators not the war. Thus, those who hoped that the newly elected Congress might provide direction to the war now despaired and in the late winter a pamphlet appeared urging Chileans to abandon temporarily their democratic institutions in favor of a dictatorship. Pinto appeared as distressed, noting that fruitless debates had diverted eight days of the ministry's attention from the conflict to answering congressional questions.[13]

Ironically, although they carped about the slow progress of the war, there was nothing of substance to denounce and consequently little opportunity for deposing the Varas ministry. The capture of the *Rimac*, therefore, was a godsend to the opposition because it stirred up anti-government sentiment. In Santiago, an angry crowd massed in front of the Congress to protest. When these elements refused to disperse and began stoning the police when they tried to end the demonstration, the municipality called up mounted units which rode into the crowds with sabers swinging. By the end of the evening, numerous policemen as well as civilians had been hospitalized. Anxious provincial officials inquired about the stability of the government and one even asked if a rebellion had occurred.[14]

For many, the *Rimac* riots revived memories of the civil wars of 1851 and 1859 because the demonstrations came uncomfortably close to an insurrection. The authorities limited public access to the neighborhood surrounding the congressional building while the Council of State pondered if it should limit the right of public assembly. Press accounts, including one claiming that Pinto had fled through the streets wearing a disguise, agitated the crowds which jeered and insulted the government's ministers, particularly Urrutia. Not surprisingly, opposition journalists used the *Rimac* incident to demand that the government resign.[15]

The Senate was the first to move against the Varas Ministry. Like the lower house, it had dissipated most of the winter debating the results of the congressional elections. In late July, however, José Manuel Encina, egged on by Prats, demanded that Varas answer certain questions about the direction of the war—a proposal which received the support of Benjamín Vicuña Mackenna who submitted a less extensive list of inquiries. The capture of the *Rimac*, of course, coincided with this debate, giving Encina and Prats additional reasons to discredit the ministry.

The Senate rejected the censure motion, apparently because many believed that it would slow not expedite the prosecution of the war. Still, the debates increased the pressure on the Varas government. Huneeus, seeking to pacify the upper house, suggested that Pinto dismiss Urrutia because he seemed incapable of tolerating the pressures of his office. The president refused, noting that replacing the general would prove too politically difficult. Pinto refused to abandon Varas or permit a Conservative to join his government. The president, however, lost control of the situation. Urrutia, in ill health and tired of the political abuse, resigned on 2 August. Aware that the legislature's animus toward the National party limited his ministry's effectiveness, although it had won a vote of confidence, Antonio Varas also quit. This move depressed Santa María who noted: "All the civic virtues have disappeared in our society and there are people who not only seek speculation in the midst of the crisis of war but take advantage of a disaster so it can be used to overthrow a ministry and to seize power."[16]

Even before the Senate began to debate the fate of the ministry, the Chamber of Deputies launched its own inquiry into the war. After Aníbal Las Casas failed to force both the ministers and the Council of State to attend the legislative sessions, the Conservative Zorobabel Rodríguez submitted a motion to condemn the government, alleging that the ministry did not accurately reflect a political consensus and that it had failed to direct the war either energetically or competently. Carlos Walker Martínez, supported his colleague's charges, criticizing the blockade of Iquique, the dismissal of General Arteaga, and what the deputy considered to be Santa María's illegal participation in the direction of the war.[17]

The endless debates to certify the election results and the constant interpolations alienated the public which tired of seeing politicians vying for power while "the affairs of the war are allowed to drift along in a crablike fashion to the great satisfaction of the enemy and the scandal of every well-wisher of the country." Thus, the rumor that Pinto would not convoke an extraordinary legislative session pleased *El Nuevo Ferrocarril* because the Congress hindered the war effort.[18]

THE RISE OF SANTA MARÍA

The opponents of the government had won only a partial victory: they may have ejected Varas but the new ministry did not include either the Conservatives or the followers of Prats. Instead, Pinto selected Domingo Santa María to serve as minister of interior, José Antonio Gandarillas, a Liberal *Errazurista*, as minister of justice, and Miguel Luis Amunátegui, an old line politician from the Matte wing of the Liberal party, as minister of foreign relations. For his minister of war, however, Santa María selected a National, Rafael Sotomayor, whose skill and experience made him suitable for this post even if his political affiliation did not. The new cabinet still did not inspire enormous confidence, in part because some Chileans believed it was less competent than the Varas ministry. Indeed, various journalists regretted Varas' departure, blaming it on the Conservatives, who had spitefully plunged the nation into political turmoil simply because they did not hold a ministerial portfolio. The Conservative press, of course, disagreed, attributing the recent political crisis to the Montt Varista failure to prosecute the war more vigorously.[19]

The new minister stressed that he would devote himself solely to the war and would not become the advocate of one party or philosophy. Although Carlos Walker Martínez claimed that he too would abstain from politics, the Conservative attacked the nomination of Sotomayor, claiming that he lacked both the skills for the post and the support of his fellow countrymen. Walker's hostility, however, clearly had its roots in Sotomayor's clashes with Escala.[20]

Santa María survived this attack and, unlike Varas, enjoyed a period of relative calm. In part, this respite was the result of a purge which cleansed the armed forces of its incompetent officers. These personnel changes did not go unchallenged, but once rid of these men, as well as others like the alcoholic Simpson, the military campaign proceeded, if not brillantly then unmarred at least by disaster.[21] Conservatives continued, of course, to harass the ministry. Carlos Walker Martínez tried to insert a demand that the Moneda attack Lima into a congressional motion stating the nation's appreciation of the military. Ironically, it was a dispute between ministers, not external pressure, which destroyed the Santa María ministry. The ostensible cause of the difficulty was a clash between Santa María and his minister of finance, Matte, over fiscal policy. Clearly, other forces were also at work. Santa María and Pinto, for example, opposed attacking Lima which the other ministers considered essential for Chile to triumph. Personality problems also surfaced: the death of Sotomayor left Santa María as the principal Liberal presidential candidate, a fact which sorely displeased Gandarillas. Thus, the confrontation over monetary policy merely precipitated a crisis which had been brewing for some time.[22] Indeed, many had expected a ministerial change since Sotomayor died; and a few even seemed pleased, believing that the government had ossified and thus required, "a kick between the coattails of their jacket" for it to regain momentum if not vigor.[23]

RECABARREN AND THE RADICALS

Pinto wanted Santa María to form another government but he refused, claiming that his presence would unleash enormous political opposition. Consequently partisan considerations forced Pinto to select a ministry which would not appear to favor one candidate over another in the forthcoming 1881 elections. The president, then, with some prompting from Santa María, included not only the Radical politician Manuel Recabarren to head the new ministry but another "red"—the name often given to the Radical party because of its anticlericalism—José Alfonso, who would serve as minister of finance. Liberals of various tones occupied the remaining posts: Melquíades Valderrama, foreign relations and Manuel García de la Huerta, justice. Originally, Pinto wished to appoint the poet, Eusebio Lillo as minister of war, but instead he wisely selected José Francisco Vergara. Despite the latter's battle experience and unquestioned military skill, the legislature threatened to censure him. Only when Vergara promised the Conservatives that he would push onto Lima did they agree to support him. Had partisan politics prevented him from serving as minister, the struggle of the war might have taken a different course.[24]

The appearance of the new government engendered more hostility than enthusiasm. Many Chileans regarded the Recabarren ministry as a coalition of mediocrities. *El Nuevo Ferrocarril*, for example, described the minister of the interior as an insipid dullard; it labeled García de la Huerta a political opportunist, and concluded that the cabinet did not reflect the legislature's political composition. "Don Aníbal [Pinto]," it noted, "as on numerous occasions, has not taken into account the dignity nor the interests of the nation."[25]

Unfortunately, Recabarren would not enjoy the same political good fortune of Santa María. Infuriated by the sinking of the *Loa*, which he chose to blame on the government, Luis Jordan proposed that the Chamber of Deputies cease funding the war. This bizarre suggestion offended even the most antigovernment legislators who, while delighted to support a censure motion, considered Jordan's proposal more harmful to Chile than the Recabarren ministry. When Jordan withdrew his motion, a colleague introduced it in another form, urging that the Congress table a finance measure until the ministry had responded to certain questions about the war. Although this proposal also failed, it discredited the legislature. *El Ferrocarril*, for example, denounced the Congress for delaying the funding of the government, which, it noted, only confused the nation while undoubtedly encouraging enemy resistance. The journalist resented that deputies could capriciously overturn ministries without bearing the responsibility for their deeds.[26]

These abortive motions demonstrated that an incipient parliamentarianism had taken hold in Chile. Legally, despite the constant references to a parliamentary system, the nation remained a presidential form of government with the cabinet responsible solely to the chief executive. Various Chileans, however, began demanding that the ministers should serve instead at the legislature's pleasure. In September 1880, José Manuel Balmaceda, for example, criticized the Recabarren government, not simply for the way that it conducted the war or for daring to consider entering into peace negotiations with Lima, but because it rested on a Radical minority for its support and hence it did not reflect accurately the political composition of the lower house. Thus Balmaceda, who would subsequently fall prey to a parliamentary rebellion in 1891, set the precedent for his own downfall when he called for replacing the Recabarren ministry with another one which "inspires the confidence of the nation and the parliamentary system." Antigovernment deputies, of course, happily seized the opportunity to criticize the Moneda's war policy, alleging that Santa María had ordered the government not to attack Lima until after the 1881 presidential elections.[27]

Balmaceda's censure motion upset many of his colleagues. Enrique MacIver, hardly a partisan of the Moneda, noted that it would be the first time that the legislature tried to overturn a ministry not for what it did or failed to do, but because of some grotesque notion of political representation. The cabinet, he observed, did not contain enough ministerial portfolios for each of the various factions of the Liberal party let alone the other parties, and warned that Chile was slipping into a type of parliamentarism where ministers will "arrive, be seen, and then leave and the administration will become anarchical." Other congressmen strenuously opposed the legislature's intervention in the executive's right to conduct the war.[28] The press seemed equally distressed. *El Ferrocarril* denounced legislators who "play with ministries like children play with their toys in order to satisfy the agitated nature of their tender years."[29] Another found Balmaceda's objections ingenuous, if not ludicrous, because two-thirds of the Congress had obtained their seats either through fraud or intervention. If Balmaceda's motion won, forming cabinets would be impossible and "the job would pass into the hands of the first one who might happen down the streets."[30] These predictions did not impress Walker Martínez who pointedly noted that better the opposition protest inside the legislature than outside in the streets. Recabarren's promise to mount an attack on Lima ended the debates, much to the relief of *El Heraldo* which lamented that the debate had deprived the nation of financial resources while slowing the prosecution of the war.[31] This episode would not be the last interpolation. Vicuña Mackenna, for example, launched yet another censure motion, criticizing the government's failure to pursue the war. Since Baquedano's army was within striking distance of Lima, the motion failed but not until it consumed the legislature's time and the nation's patience. The press, tired of politics as usual, considered the senator's motion singularly inappropriate, devisive, and indiscreet; it tartly noted that the Chamber of Deputies rarely managed to have a quorum for its meetings.[32]

The fall of Lima did not relieve the political pressure on the president. In April 1881, the Comisión Conservadora asked Pinto to call the legislature into extraordinary session. The commission, composed of seven congressmen who acted as the legislature's watchdog when that body was in recess, could, under exceptional circumstances, request a special congressional session. Distressed by the high cost of the occupation and the heavy casualty rate, the members submitted their petition to Pinto. The president, either fearful of political intrigue or jealous of his prerogatives, refused to act until the members first explained what circumstances prompted this petition and what issues the Comisión wished to place on the agenda.

Pinto's response outraged the committee's members who replied that they disliked the Moneda's policies and that they believed that the president should seek the legislature's advice and consent before it either acted on the war or opened peace negotiations. Although the government's representatives tried to dissuade them, the commission forwarded its request to the government.

The legislators also resented the president's demand that they explain their reasons for calling a session as well as define the scope of their debate, a request which they interpreted as the Moneda's attempt to limit the right of the Congress to oversee the war. The Comisión argued that it did not have to defend its decisions. A costly struggle still raged and the chief executive had to consult the legislature on how he planned to terminate the conflict and achieve a peace. This policy, it argued, seemed particularly appropriate since the government had consistently demonstrated its incompetence since the onset of the hostilities. Thus, the committee approved a measure stating simply that the Comisión Conservadora, exercising its constitutional prerogatives, wished to hold an extraordinary legislative session in order to discuss the war. Claiming that he could not discover any extraordinary circumstances which justified another congressional session, Pinto rejected this request. His decision would subsequently have serious repercussions.

Congress opened its regular term on 1 June 1881. Two days later, fifteen senators, either Conservatives or discontented Liberals like Prats or Vicuña Mackenna, introduced a motion to censure the government for refusing to grant the Comisión Conservadora's request for an extraordinary session and for not conducting the war in a manner the legislators deemed adequate. As usual, Vicuña Mackenna submitted a separate censure motion, stating that the Senate retained little, if any, confidence either in the ministry's ability to oversee the forthcoming presidential elections or to conclude the war successfully.

Although the government defended its Peruvian policy, its explanations did not mollify its legislative critics who insisted that the Congress had to share in directing the war. The Moneda, the critics feared, could not be trusted to subordinate its political needs for the good of the nation. Vicuña Mackenna, for example, charged that Vergara was planning to use the military to intervene on behalf of the government's candidate in the forthcoming presidential elections, thus converting Chile into a "hereditary and constitutional monarchy." At the same time, the Moneda continued to send troops into the pesthouse of Peru, to die fruitlessly of disease or to become corrupted by the Chinese. After almost a month of debate, the upper house barely defeated both censure motions, indicating the precarious state of the Recabarren ministry.

Surviving the Senate's censure motion did not guarantee Recabarren's ministry. On 21 June 1881, Luis Urzúa, one of the lower house's more obstreperous members, demanded that the government explain its failure to convoke the extraordinary session and its blatant intervention in the recent presidential campaign. Perhaps, the Moneda may have ridiculed Urzúa's proposal and expected that it would easily survive the censure motion. On June 30, however, the minister of finance, José Alfonso, requested that the legislature temporarily suspend the interpolation to consider instead the passage of the *lei de recursos*, which would expire on 5 July 1881.

The Chilean constitution had established a complicated system for funding the government. Ministers submitted their annual budgets, which the legislature, after some debate, invariably passed, thus permitting the government to make its expenditures. In addition, every eighteen months, the Chamber of Deputies also had to approve a measure which authorized the government to collect taxes. Thus, the Congress could deprive the government of funding in two ways: it could refuse to authorize a budget or it could, by rejecting the *lei de recursos*, cut off the Moneda's revenues. Consequently, when the Conservative Abdón Cifuentes refused to yield the floor and allow Alfonso to expedite his proposal, he threw the nation into a constitutional and financial crisis.

The government's plight became quite serious. It had only five days to obtain passage of the needed tax legislation but it could not act until the Chamber of Deputies voted on the pending censure motion. The Conservative opposition knew precisely what it was doing, coyly hinting that it could easily tie up the debate for weeks. In desperation, the Moneda called the legislature into a special session on 1 July, hoping that it could prod the interpolation toward a conclusion. Ricardo Letelier, however, questioned the legality of this procedure, arguing that since he had not received a formal invitation to attend the congressional session, the meeting was illegal. The Conservatives, describing the hastily called special legislative session as an attempt by the executive to repress them, frittered away the afternoon with procedural issues. That evening, when the chamber convened for another meeting, the opposition became so disruptive that the president of the Chamber of Deputies had to suspend the session.

Thus, the opposition successfully paralyzed the lower house in order to punish a ministry whose principal sin was that it would not offer portfolios to the Conservatives as well as other political factions, and that it presumably did not reflect the composition of the chamber. Both Letelier and Cifuentes, for example, denounced the government for remaining in office when they believed that it should resign even through it enjoyed a parliamentary majority. The possibility that their actions might deprive the Moneda of its ability to wage war did not impress the obstructionists. Better to lose money, Clemente Fabres piously intoned, than to "permit the national honor to suffer and perhaps put the nation's future in danger." Just before the expiration of the legislative term, the Conservatives graciously yielded the floor, permitting their colleagues to pass the *lei de recursos*. They had acted so nobly, they claimed, in the interests of the nation and indicated that if Recabarren and his ministers possessed similar instincts, they would resign.[33] The legislature's obstructionism outraged most of the press which accused the minority bloc of abusing its right. Conservative and antigovernment journals, however, defended the censure as not simply legally correct but as a "serious, dignified, and correct."[34] Recabarren's ministry persevered, leaving office with Pinto.

On 18 September 1881, Domingo Santa María entered the Moneda. The new leader bore little resemblance to his predecessor. Santa María had enjoyed a particularly active political career, possessed an agile mind albeit one sometimes hampered by a fiery temperament, a harsh character, and a disdain for those whom he considered *arribistas*. An admirer of Portales, he subsumed within himself the characteristics of his role model and, consequently, had little tolerence for opposition or dissent.

As his minister of the interior, Santa María selected José Francisco Vergara, as well as another Radical, Carlos Castellon, to serve as minister of war. Luis Aldunate, a Liberal, held the post of minister of finance while a National, José Eugenio Vergara, served as minister of justice. Surprisingly, the outspoken José Manuel Balmaceda won the post of minister of foreign affairs. The Vergara ministry lasted until February 1882 and fell because the minister of the interior and the president clashed over the conduct of the forthcoming congressional election. For two months Aldunate occupied Vergara's place until Balmaceda became minister of the interior, a post he held almost to the conclusion of the war.

To ensure that he would not have to face a contentious chamber, Santa María shamelessly intervened in the congressional elections of 1882, installing in the legislature men distinguished for their passive if not supine character. Unlike his predecessors, Santa María did not act spontaneously but planned his intervention in advance, ordering his underlings to falsify the voting lists long before election day dawned. Thus most of the Conservatives, apparently in search of notoriety, loudly abstained from the contest.[35]

Thanks to his foresight, Santa María escaped the sniping which plagued Pinto. The war and negotiating a peace ceased to preoccupy the legislature which instead became caught up in stripping the Church of its control over the civil registry, the rite of marriage, and the cemeteries. Occasionally, a deputy gingerly mentioned the stalemated conflict, that seemingly endless bloodbath which consumed Chilean blood and gold with obscene monotony. If questioned about the situation in the north, the minister of interior suggested that the deputies should pass on to more pressing matters. Benjamín Vicuña Mackenna, for example, once tried to interrogate the minister on the ongoing negotiations with Peru and to force the government to consider withdrawing the army from Lima to the south. His motion failed to carry and, forced to speak in secret session, he lost most of his national impact.[36]

Generally, the Moneda's war policies almost escaped congressional scrutiny, but its poor bookkeeping techniques exposed it to yet another interpolation. In 1882, the Comisión de Guerra discovered that the government had spent $34,000,000 more on the war than the legislature had authorized. Not one to fret over such practices, the minister simply asked the Congress to grant the government permission to spend the money it had already disbursed. Although the Senate acquiesced, perhaps considering the request a tidy solution to the problem, it offended Augusto Matte, former minister of finance and a banker, who objected to granting blanket approvals, noting that the Chamber of Deputies enjoyed a constitutional mandate to oversee expenditures.

Matte's interpolation ranged over two congressional terms and raised not only the constitutional issue of funding but also such topics as politics and the conduct of the war. More significantly, he opened the floodgates of repressed hostility. Enrique MacIver, for example, joined his colleague in denouncing the ministry and its attempt to debase the legislature. For the next month and a half, deputies denounced the government's political intervention, Lynch's occupation policy, as well as the war which was mired in a bloody stalemate.

Various ministers tried to evade the criticism by blaming the funding issue on a recalcitrant Chamber of Deputies while also defending their policy of continuing to occupy all of Peru rather than, as some suggested, retreating to the south. The minister of finance, Pedro Cuadra, argued that the government had exceeded its military budget every year since 1879, describing it as a chronic problem which he attributed to inadequate staffing and poor bookkeeping. The minister noted, moreover, that sometimes emergencies occurred which required immediate action and which simply could not be resolved if the Monea had to remain within very tight budgetary restrictions. These arguments failed to convince Matte, but faced with funding the war, the legislature authorized the ministry to spend the money it had already disbursed.[37]

PUBLIC DISENCHANTMENT

By 1883, Congress appeared as tired of the war as the general public. The request for yet another $6,000,000 distressed Antonio Varas who confessed that "as a Chilean and as a senator, I am sorry and I regret that this war still remains unresolved, that we should be calculating the cost for another year . . . it saddens me that Chile is still involved in a war that is already four years old and that we still do not know when it will end." The statement by the aged doyen encouraged a colleague, Francisco Puelma, to lament that he too had tired of mechanically authorizing expenditures for a conflict which seemed endless. Chile, he argued, could not live in a state of perpetual war and he, for one, would withhold his vote until the government explained the situation more fully. First Castellon and then Balmaceda tried to dispell the Senate's fear that Chile accepted war "like a chronic illness." The nation, the ministers noted, had no choice but to wait for the enemy to come to its senses. Until then, the Congress must continue to fund the war as a patriotic duty.[38]

Either because of the legislature's exhaustion or its desperate desire to end the war, the government obtained congressional ratification of the Peruvian peace treaty and the Bolivian truce without difficulty. The congressional committees approved the documents which their respective chambers accepted virtually without comment. Typical of the distrust that seemed to permeate the political climate, Francisco Puelma noted that he would have preferred a permanent peace treaty with Bolivia rather than a truce, because the president might use his extraordinary war powers to intervene in the electoral process. Having fulfilled its responsibilities, the legislature could return to the endless debates that stumbled on, from topic to topic, without resolution.[39]

By 1884, the nation seemed eminently displeased with its political system. *El Precursor*, complaining that the various parties either exploited or ignored the working class, warned that a rebellion would sweep the nation if reforms did not occur.[40] Even the bourgeois press concurred, lamenting the endless debates, the lack of public spirit, the "growing progress of the political gangrene which unfortunately is corroding the foundations of the electoral system that rules in this nation."[41] Predictably, the public lost faith in the government's ability to achieve a peace: "while in the north our brave soldiers die by the thousands, the victims of the terrible scourge of yellow fever, in the highest official places the leaders of the nation are occupied in weaving political webs with which to make more difficult our present situation."[42] Many accused the government not simply of political crimes but of unethically granting their friends public works contracts although they were not the lowest bidder. The legislature enjoyed less favor and was despised for its endless sterile debates that served no purpose and resolved no dilemma.[43]

This malaise cannot be attributed solely to the war but perhaps owes its origin to the proliferation of political factions devoid of ideological substance. As long as the electoral process remained subject to corruption, as long as provincial officials accepted an *inquilino*'s scribble as proof of literacy, and as long as candidates could buy votes for 20 cents, the nation would, of course, be ill served. Certainly by the end of the war, various journalists concluded that democracy did not function well in Chile and wondered if the nation should not seek some alternative.[44]

Clearly partisan politics influenced the course of the war. Opposition elements used parliamentary procedure to overturn ministries for committing the sin of not including them in the circle of power. Yet, these same elements exerted pressure to protect their friends who held commands in the army or navy. Similarly, they sought to intervene in the direction of the campaigns, trying to alter tactics and influence strategy. On balance, the intervention hindered rather than expedited the war. The countless hours of fruitless debate unnecessarily occupied the ministers' attention, costing days, perhaps weeks, which more profitably could have been used to fight the allies, not fend off the political opposition. Certainly the overthrow of the ministries must also have absorbed additional time as the new officials had to learn their trade before they could fulfill their mandate.

In a sense, the intense partisan atmosphere not only complicated the conduct of the war but also influenced the nation's political history. Santa María's massive intervention in the congressional elections of 1882 may have simply represented his political cynicism. Alternatively, he might have acted in this arbitrary fashion in the belief that only a docile legislature would permit him to formulate and implement military policies without harrassment. The absence of Carlos Walker Martínez and Abdón Cifuentes not only ended congressional obstructionism, but permitted the government to hold on until Peru's political leadership accepted a peace treaty.

Perhaps Chile's political system should be compared not to a platonic ideal but to the political reality of its neighbors. Unlike Peru, Bolivia, and Argentina, Chile had developed a system which transferred power with a minimum of unrest. The mechanism also selected men to hold government positions who, as we have seen, directed the war to a successful conclusion. Chile, torn by economic dislocation and social unrest, almost collapsed before the onset of the conflict. After 1879, the nation managed to function and its elected representatives successfully—sometimes too successfully—influenced government policy in directing the various campaigns. Despite constant harassment, the Moneda did not retaliate against its congressional critics; an opposition press flourished, again with perhaps mixed results; and people could meet freely. Chile, unlike other Latin American republics, did not become a dictatorship but retained its political system, a system that despite its flaws, managed to survive and led the nation to victory in the War of the Pacific.

10

The Quest for Peace

> Keeping guard in the sierra
> beseiged by montoneros
> they were at the end of the war
> the forgotten battalions
>   "Los Batallones Olvidados"

> It is far easier to make war than to make peace.
>   Georges Clemenceau

Negotiating a peace treaty at the bargaining table proved almost as elusive to the Moneda as securing a victory over the allies on the battlefield. Initially, it appeared that a diplomatic settlement was within easy reach: Santiago controlled Lima and La Paz had petulantly retreated into the altiplano; surely victory was within easy reach. This optimism foundered when Peru's leaders, encouraged by American diplomatic efforts, refused to sign any agreement that included territorial concessions. Indeed, Santiago had to wait until 1883 before it could withdraw its troops from the north. During this impasse, Peru organized guerilla bands to prosecute a war of attrition that lasted for almost three years, a war that consumed Chile's youth, its wealth, and eventually the patience of its citizens. This prolonged and unhappy campaign ultimately discouraged the public who, in turn, forced the Moneda to search for a means to stop the bloodshed.

Santiago must have been a joyous city in January 1881 because the capital had just learned that its troops had emerged victorious after a bitter and protracted struggle. All that remained for the Moneda was to sign a peace treaty and bring its sons home to labor in Chile's fields, mines, and factories.[1] Regrettably, this proved an elusive goal: since no one governed Peru, and thus could enforce a peace treaty, Santiago would continue to occupy the north, mired in an expensive and dirty guerrilla war.

THE CLARO INITIATIVE

Indeed, even before Lima's fall, various Chileans had struggled actively to end the war. In December 1879, Senator Lorenzo Claro wrote an open letter suggesting that the Moneda resolve the conflict diplomatically. Rather than attack Lima, "a mere question of vanity and popularity," Pinto should seek a stable peace by returning to Chile's prewar boundaries. To annex Tarapacá, he declared, was a misuse of the weapons "blessed by God." Santiago had gone to war to defend its treaty rights and to destroy the alliance not to acquire land. The government should remain in Tarapacá and the littoral, with the enemy bearing the cost of maintaining the occupation army only until the allies had paid an indemnity of £40,000–50,000. In addition, Peru and Bolivia would also have to foreswear rebuilding their navies for thirty years, grant Chile most favored nation status, and compensate those Chilean citizens whose property they had seized.[2]

Claro's modest proposal aroused enormous ire: one columnist described it as an "abortion . . . the product of an insane mind."[3] Eulojio Allendes became particularly incensed because Claro had disparaged the nation's military and the collective wisdom of the Chilean masses, "the voice of God," that demanded annexation. Since Lima precipitated the war, Santiago had the right to seize its territory which it deserved not only as a reward for punishing Peruvian perfidy but to assure a stable peace.[4]

Claro attempted to rebut these arguments. Lima, he claimed, lacked the financial resources and the manpower to threaten Santiago. Indeed, if the future followed the same course as the past, internal disputes would so devour Peru that Chile would require only a small army to keep it at bay. Thus, although dismayed that his statements had antagonized his colleagues, Claro still opposed annexation, claiming that the northern territory was so unhealthy and that its resources, including the nitrate mines, were too limited.[5]

Claro's amended statement failed to pacify Chile. Various journalists denounced him as a traitor, the agent of a small economic clique—one alleged it was the *salitreros* of Antofagasta—"who have forgotten that they are not the ones to whom Chile owes its honor and its present greatness."[6] Retaining Tarapacá, they argued, would deny Peru the economic means of financing a postwar rearmament while compensating Chile for its war debts. Anything less was "criminal, traitorous, and an infamy."[7]

"Argos," citing Claro's letter as proof of Chile's intellectual freedom, urged that the nation discuss his ideas with "moderation and respect."[8] Others seemed less tolerant: Santiago's citizens circulated a petition of protest, an act which *La Patria* suggested that the people of Valparaíso might profitably emulate. This proposal appeared positively libertarian in comparison to the call to lynch anyone who signed a statement opposing the annexation of Tarapacá.[9]

Justo Arteaga Alemparte, perhaps stimulated by Claro's proposal, introduced legislation to "retake what... the sweat, the labor, and the capital of our fellow countrymen had developed." Some deputies, while agreeing with Arteaga's measure, tabled the motion, fearing that annexation might precipitate a hostile reaction by European states. Conversely, Enrique MacIver openly opposed the measure, arguing that civilized nations did not use force to expand their boundaries even when, as in Chile's case, their nationals had developed the contested area. The lower house rejected Arteaga's legislation, apparently more out of fear of European intervention than in deference to MacIver's moralizing.[10] This rebuff scandalized many Chileans who considered their Congress too passive. Private, in particular foreign interests could not, they argued, stop annexation. In addition, outsiders would consider the integration of Tarapacá into Chile as a boon since annexation would clarify the legal situation.

Since December 1879, Tarapacá had existed in a legal limbo because theoretically Peruvian laws still applied even though Chile controlled the province. *Salitreros*, fearful of Lima's reprisals, refused to export, thereby hurting the Moneda, which urgently required the nitrate revenues to finance the war. Incorporating the disputed territory would resolve the ambiguity: the miners could again export and the Moneda would obtain a steady source of income. Chile also did not have to agonize over the issue of annexation: it deserved Tarapacá because its citizens and capital had transformed the arid lands into a bonanza and its ownership by Santiago would guarantee economic prosperity.[11]

Many argued for annexation on moral grounds. Assimilating the north meant the introduction of good government, liberty, and progress into a previously blighted area. Indeed, some contrasted a barbarous Peru with a Chile that represented the vanguard of western civilization. Strategic considerations influenced the pro-annexationist sentiment as well. Santiago needed Tarapacá for the same reasons that Germany required Alsace and Lorraine—as a buffer to protect the country's vulnerable

Central Valley. Returning the occupied territories not only jeopardized the nation's security, it also subjected those Chileans who might remain at the mercy of ruthless caudillos.[12] "The peace between Chile and its neighbors" required not a treaty but a good sentry."[13]

THE ARICA CONFERENCE

Claro's efforts did not end attempts to negotiate a peace settlement. Various European nations, intent on protecting their nationals' investments, had earlier offered their good offices. Chile accepted these overtures but the allies would not, preferring American mediation. Washington's diplomatic efforts, they believed, would save them from having to cede any property to Santiago. Although willing to accept a negotiated settlement, Peru and Bolivia insisted that Chile withdraw from all occupied lands as a precondition for discussing peace. Having captured this territory at great cost, Chile would not return to the status quo antebellum simply to open negotiations.

Initially, Washington had wisely refrained from involving itself in this diplomatic morass. But, as Chile's army advanced toward Lima, European nations became more restive and the United States more nervous. The American minister to Chile, Thomas Osborn, suggested that Washington might successfully offer its good offices to settle the war. Although Issac Christiancy, the U.S. representative in Lima, feared that Chile would still insist on retaining Tarapacá, he passed on his colleague's suggestion, hoping that Santiago might accept monetary reparations rather than land.

In July 1880, still fearing European intervention, Washington ordered its envoys to offer the warring nations U.S. mediation. Osborn convinced Pinto to accept America's good offices. And, when Chile agreed, Bolivia did so as well. Anxious to expedite the negotiations, Christiancy traveled to Santiago in order to confer with Osborn. The two diplomats spoke to Pinto, who still insisted that Chile must retain Tarapacá. For reasons best known to himself, Christiancy did not tell Piérola that Santiago demanded that Lima cede Tarapacá before it would negotiate. Chile believed that Peru recognized its territorial claims whereas Piérola presumed that Santiago knew that Lima would accept no preconditions before negotiating. Having thus informally set the stage for a diplomatic disaster, Washington officially offered in September 1880, to mediate the dispute.[14]

Although some Chileans, citing humanitarian reasons or diplomatic pressure, were willing to consider negotiations, few expected that the peace talks would succeed. On the contrary, many described the talks as a plot hatched by Peruvian Masons working through Chile's Radical party.[15] Certainly Pinto's selection of a poet as his chief negotiator did little to reassure the nation. As one journalist noted, however, no one wanted an end to the war except perhaps the wealthy, who would benefit from an increase in the peso's value which peace would bring.[16] Some futilely hoped that the legislature could derail the conference but, they lamented, "the rotten Congress," had cravenly capitulated to Pinto who "is carrying us to an abyss . . . the Peruvian torpedo is headed toward the ship of state and the vessel's captain is another Peña and his lieutenant is another Ferrari."[17]

While exaggerated, the public's fears were not without foundation. Most Chileans distrusted Peruvian diplomatic missions, particularly after the abortive Lavalle experience. Portions of the press considered the negotiations demeaning since Chile was on the verge of victory, or objected to the discussions because they paralyzed the nation's war effort.[18] Others believed that Chile would first have to depose Piérola before Peru's men of good will "could come out of their hiding places" to negotiate a settlement.[19] If so, then Chile might as well invade the north. Many doubted, moreover, that a subsequent Peruvian government would honor any peace treaty. Indeed, one journalist warned that Santiago would have to protect Piérola from his countrymen should he accede to the Moneda's demands.[20] Eventually the nation accepted the Moneda's participation in the American-sponsored conference, but only on the condition that it continue to prepare for attacking Lima: peace "through an active and energetic war."[21]

While Chileans disagreed about the advisability of negotiating, few doubted that the Moneda would have to annex Tarapacá and the Bolivian littoral. The country deserved the north in part because Chilean "blood had nationalized these conquered lands," but also because annexation constituted the only method the allies could pay their war reparations.[22] Peru and Bolivia were bankrupt, and it appeared unlikely that they would amass enough money to pay an indemnity. Cession of the desert, therefore, was payment in kind for forcing a conflict on Santiago. Ironically, some doubted that Tarapacá would generate enough revenue to defray the cost of maintaining an occupying army or pay the various pensions the nation would have to award to its victorious troops.[23]

Territorial concessions, alone, would not pacify the nation. Chile had to "emasculate" Lima to prevent a resurgence of Peruvian revanchism.[24] To accomplish this goal some demanded that Piérola demilitarize Callao; others wanted to force Peru to disband its army or navy or limit their size for up to thirty years. Annexation of Tacna and Arica was also mentioned as a way of providing the nation another buffer against future aggression.

One newspaper proposed that Bolivia receive a slice of Peru's coastline, for which it would have to compensate Lima, thus restoring its access to the sea. This Machiavellian proposal not only protected Chile but it might so poison Peruvian-Bolivian relations that they would never again conspire against Santiago.[25]

Some argued that Santiago needed Tarapacá not only to secure its boundaries but also to acquire "ample space for our industry, confidence for Chilean capital and labor."[26] Others called for a treaty provision to ensure that Chile's products could enter Peru and Bolivia duty free. This concession would ensure that California would not capture the Peruvian market "which is ours and which should continue being ours."[27] A restoration of trade would also show the allies that abstention from war could bring prosperity. And a wealthier Peru or Bolivia could more easily liquidate its debts, thereby allowing Chile to emerge richer and with the Pacific's most important port.[28]

The prospect of peace negotiations disturbed the legislature almost as much as it did the Chilean public. José Manuel Balmaceda chided the foreign minister, Melaquídades Valderrama, for considering negotiating without first consulting the Congress; he eventually proposed to censure the government for its peace initiative. Z. Rodríguez, fearful that the Moneda might conduct the peace negotiations as negligently as it had waged the war, submitted a proposal stating that "the opportune moment has not yet arrived for Chile to enter into peace negotiations much less offer them." Valderrama's melodramatic rebuttal—that his right hand should wither before it signed away Chile's rights—failed to impress Rodríguez. Chile, the latter alleged, had triumphed in spite of the government which had to "be pulled down the road of victory as one pulls an ox."[29]

Apprehensive that the president's charitable excesses, various legislators offered their own versions of a peace arrangement. Clearly Peru had to cede Tarapacá not simply because Chileans had developed that province, but because it had become essential for Santiago's "benefit, world prestige, and its future security." Other deputies believed that for Chile to eradicate Peruvian revanchism, Lima would have to dismantle its forts in Callao. Balmaceda considered this recommendation too faint-hearted and stated: "Our domination of the Pacific (I refer to the enemy's coast) must be complete." He urged the disbanding of Lima's fleet, the establishment of a naval base in the north, and the imposition of such heavy taxes that Peru could never reconstruct its navy.[30]

A few legislators either favored a negotiated settlement or critized the harsh nature of Chile's demands. Enrique MacIver sarcastically inquired whether the nation would again go to war if, years later, Peru decided to rebuild its fortifications at Callao. Rather than impose an unenforceable treaty, he suggested that the Moneda should strip Peru of its economic resources while devoting its efforts to making Chile prosperous, creating a strong government, and strengthening its fleet. Domestic development, not a draconian peace treaty, would ensure tranquility in the Pacific basin.[31]

Realizing that the legislature would tolerate negotations only if they did not paralyze the war effort, Recabarren promised that the Moneda would continue preparing to invade the north even as it discussed a peaceful resolution to the dispute. The minister's pledge pacified the legislature: the deputies grudgingly withdrew their various motions, including the censure motion, allowing the government to pursue its contradictory mission of talking peace while waging war.[32]

Pinto, surprised that Piérola would negotiate, particularly after the Lynch expedition and the bombardment of various Peruvian coastal towns, was privately less optimistic. Joaquín Godoy, Santiago's minister to Quito, warned his president that the Peruvian dictator would do anything but cede Tarapacá. Although anxious to end the war, Pinto was no fool. Intent on neutralizing Peru, he demanded a substantial monetary indemnity that, he hoped would force the enemy to sell its military equipment in order to liquidate its debts to Chile. The president's concerns seemed premature. The meeting was nearly not convened when it became known that Peru had accepted the American mediation only after Chile had agreed to attend the peace conference. This news infuriated various deputies who accused Valderrama of deceiving them, a complaint which the chamber chose to ignore so the peace talks could occur.[33]

The various delegates met on the USS *Lackawanna* in Arica's harbor on 22 October 1880. Chile's Lillo, Eulojio Altamirano, and José Vergara demanded Tarapacá and Atacama; an indemnity of $20,000,000; restoration of property taken from Chilean citizens; the surrender of the *Rimac*; dissolution of the 1873 alliance; and a Peruvian promise not to fortify Arica. If the allies accepted these terms, Chile would occupy Moquegua, Tacna, and Arica until they had paid the indemnity.

Santiago's demands pleased no one: the allies labeled them draconian whereas the Chilean public considered them exceedingly generous. When the Peruvian delegate tried to negotiate the demand for Tarapacá, Altamirano reported that his fellow countrymen would not support his government if it yielded on this point. Peru's political situation was, of course, virtually the same as Chile's. The negotiators never managed to agree on the issue of annexation and consequently, on 27 October, they broke off their discussions.[34]

Piérola's refusal to cede Tarapacá convinced many Chileans that he was insenstive to his nation's needs and that he had not negotiated in good faith. The collapse of the Arica conference, however, unleashed a flood of crocodile tears in Chile. The Doubting Thomases smirked and the bloodthirsty indulged their most martial fantasies. Santiago could now attack Lima rather than waste its time and energies discussing peace. Some faulted the United States, rightly criticizing its opposition to annexation.[35]

The failure of the talks depressed Pinto. Altamirano considered the entire episode a farce and blamed it on Piérola, who had deceived everyone into believing that he would cede Tarapacá. The Chilean delegate's appraisal missed the mark: in truth, the fault belonged to Christiancy, who had misled the Chileans. This fact could not shield Pinto or his ministers from their countrymen's anger. Still, concluded one critic, what could one expect from a government composed of individuals crippled by strange maladies and bizarre sexual proclivities, "whose cowardly tendencies and completely conciliatory and pacific spirit threatened to undo the accomplishments of Chile's heroic troops."[36] In retrospect, they argued, Santiago should never have attended the conference because it gave the allies time to reorganize and thus prolonged the struggle.[37]

THE PUBLIC'S VISION OF PEACE

The conquest of Lima did not moderate Chilean demands. On the contrary, because taking the north had cost the Moneda more money and lives, the price of peace had inflated along with the peso. In addition to the annexation of the littoral and Tarapacá, Chileans demanded Arica to insure their control over the sea lanes; Peru's disarmament; trade concessions; and the right to occupy temporarily certain lands until the allies implemented the peace agreement. The public urged Pinto not to relent: generosity invariably bred insolence and intransigence while a harsh occupation policy would force the enemy to face reality. Like Paris in 1871, Lima had to bite the bullet of territorial concessions and settle the conflict in order to begin the process of national reconstruction. Additional resistance, even passive, needlessly prolonged the agony of the war.[38]

The analogy to the Franco-Prussian war is not quite completely accurate: Bismarck, at least, had a Thiers; Pinto had no one with whom he might negotiate a peace treaty. Thanks to Baquedano, Piérola had escaped into the interior where he created a new government. Vowing to continue the struggle, the Peruvian divided the nation into three war zones: the north, under Admiral Lizardo Montero; a central portion, commanded by Juan Martín Echenique; and the southern sector, administered by Pedro del Solar. Initially, Pinto might well have been tempted to ignore Piérola. After all, the Peruvian leader enjoyed no legal mandate, having come to power by overthrowing Prado in 1879; isolated in the mountains, he must have appeared absurd to the victorious Chileans. Still, his regime resembled a common law marriage: although unsanctioned by law, it gained legality by its existence over time. The dictator's defense of Lima, moreover, had earned him widespread popularity of many Peruvians who elevated him to the status of hero. Thus, while the Moneda abominated him, Piérola's countrymen hailed the caudillo as their leader.[39]

Most Chileans, however, regarded the pugnacious Piérola as a comic opera figure, ridiculing his promise to continue the war. The Peruvian leader, they declared, was no Juárez; his nation was no Mexico; and Pinto was no Maximilian. Even if someone mounted a campaign of resistance, no Peruvian would heed his call to battle. One wit even suggested that Santiago place a bounty on the dictator's head, sure that some "cholo" would assassinate him for the reward. Nevertheless, the resilience of the dictator indicated that the war had not ended. Indeed, when the minister of war began to repatriate some military units, *El Curicano* warned that the act would "seriously injure the interests of the war" and undermine almost two years of sacrifice.[40]

Since Lima would not accept its fate as supinely as Versailles, the Moneda had to devise a Peruvian strategy. Simply pursuing Piérola's *montonero* supporters seemed fruitless.[41] Some journalists advocated besieging Arequipa, thereby eradicating the last pocket of enemy resistance and, at the same time, increasing La Paz's sense of isolation at the nominal cost of "a few more bodies."[42] Others, however, claimed that such an expedition could accomplish nothing; only the continued occupation of Lima would bring Peru to its knees.[43] "The war of the Comblain and the Krupp has ended . . . now we should start the war of the pocket book. Taxes will save us."[44]

In truth, most Chileans favored a strategy which spared the least both their population and their treasury. Unfortunately, proponents of the less strenuous approach failed to agree on what tactics to employ. The devotees of the "hand of iron . . . of fire and steel not sweets and endearments," suggested imposing martial law, executing Piérola's supporters, and billeting Chilean troops on the enemy's civilian population.[45] Others aimed at the enemy's billfold, demanding the levying of additional taxes to support Santiago's troops; confiscating the property of absentee Peruvians; uprooting the rail lines for use in Chile and accepting only silver as payment of Callao's customs' duties.[46] The government should simply loot Peru of "any element of work, of advancement, of progress so that its campaign of passive resistance will collapse." Just a "little Bismarckian policy," suggested *The Chilian Times*, "is all that is required to bring the notables of Lima to their senses."[47]

Opinions within the government mirrored those of Chilean society. Balmaceda, for example, favored coupling harsh rule with an assault on Arequipa in order to strangle Peru. Other national leaders, while they disliked Piérola, were not unwilling to discuss peace terms with him. But Altamirano, who apparently despised Piérola because of his conduct at Miraflores, was willing to parley with the caudillo only if the dictator could demonstrate that he enjoyed widespread support in Peru. Should this prove impossible, Altamirano suggested either reconvening Prado's old congress or creating a provisional government. The Peruvian dictator, however, seemed less amenable, demanding a return to the pre-1881 lines, foreign mediation, and personal guarantees for his envoy before he would discuss peace terms.[48]

ENTER GARCÍA CALDERÓN

One of Altamirano's suggestions materialized. The survivors of Peru's prewar political system created a rump assembly, the Junta de Notables, which despite its title, presumably represented the interests of all of Peru's social classes. Meeting in a private residence, they revived the 1860 Constitution and called for the convening of a congress to negotiate a truce with Chile. The 150-man junta also elected Francisco García Calderón Peru's provisional president on 22 February 1881.[49]

The new government excited little enthusiasm since few Chileans expected that its leaders would accede to the demands for territorial concessions. Altamirano concurred. The Chilean envoy argued that the García Calderón administration would have to possess a small measure of power in order to appear viable. Thus, the Moneda's troops would have to remain in Peru, at great cost to the nation, to prop up the newly created regime. Unfortunately, he noted, the alternatives confronting the Moneda appeared bleak: "Do we remain collecting the existing taxes? It is an unprofitable business. Do we meekly accept this passive resistance? We would look ridiculous." The situation, he warned, would certainly worsen and he doubted that García Calderón would cede any territory to Santiago. Chile's only alternative, he feared, was the imposition of a harsh occupation policy. Santa María seconded this suggestion: retaining the army in Lima cost Chile dearly and endangered the men's health. The government should instead use the fleet "to sow fear and terror [in order to] pressure Peru by all means possible."⁵⁰

Santiago did neither. Instead, it acted generously, providing the town of Magdalena to serve as Peru's Vichy. García Calderón formed a cabinet, called his legislature into session, and reconstituted the judiciary. Rather than conduct new congressional elections, the president simply reconvened the legislature that had functioned until Piérola seized power in 1879. While perhaps not devoid of legitimacy, the Magdalena Congress suffered from one grave flaw: most of its members' terms of office had expired, thus there was doubt about their right to hold office.

The new government had to face certain unpleasant realities including paying a tax of $1,000,000, which Chile had levied to defray the cost of occupying Peru. Despite this burden, the Magdalena government persisted, calling the Congress into session in May 1881. To correct the legislature's defects, García Calderón ordered elections to fill any vacancies, a process which lasted into June. The new body still did not accurately reflect the nation's political situation since its members came exclusively from those provinces occupied by the Chilean army. Despite its limited constituency, the parliament nonetheless elected García Calderón Peru's permanent president and, in a secret session, authorized him to initiate discussions to terminate the war.⁵¹

García Calderón, perhaps to demonstrate his administration's virility, tried to quash internal opposition. He requested and received weapons from the Chilean occupation forces in order to rearm the Peruvian army and extend his sphere of control. Lamentably, these efforts miscarried: once in the field, many of the Peruvian troops simply vanished, along with their newly issued weapons, into the ranks of the *montoneros*. García Calderón also failed to win either the heart or the mind of Colonel Andrés Cáceres who, after the collapse of Lima, had organized a center of resistance in the altiplano. García offered the officer the post of vice president, control of the central provinces, and continued command of his army. Cáceres rebuffed these inducements, claiming that only he, not García Calderón, should govern Peru.⁵²

While not unsympathetic to García Calderón's plight, the Moneda wanted to discuss peace terms with the Magdalena government. Like the public, the administration had increased its demands for an end to the war: Peru would have to make territorial concessions and pay the cost of maintaining the army that would occupy Tacna until the allies liquidated an indemnity of £4,000,000. In addition, Santiago wanted to levy a surcharge of $100,000 for each day that elapsed between the conclusion of the Arica conference and the signing of a permanent peace treaty. These terms were not merely draconian, they were unrealistic, because Peru did not possess the financial resources to satisfy them. Ironically, when the Chilean diplomats met García's envoys in March 1881, they never had an opportunity to present their conditions. The Peruvian delegate instead requested that Chile sign a formal armistice and either evacuate Lima or grant the Magdalena government control over the capital. The surprised Chileans refused and, when the Peruvians insisted, Santiago's delegation ended the talks. The failure to achieve peace distressed the Chilean press who suggested that Pinto end his lenient occupation policy and begin countering passive resistance "with resolute pressure."[53]

As part of that program, Colonel Pedro Lagos, Baquedano's successor, ordered a punitive raid into Peru's interior in April 1881. The Chilean units departed in mid-April and within weeks had captured Cerro de Pasco, an important mineral-producing center where they collected taxes and showed the flag.[54] This renewed military activity failed to dispel the growing sense of pessimism because as one deputy observed "The nation is becoming alarmed with the prolonged inaction and is beginning to look fearfully at the clouds tenaciously gathered on our horizon."[55]

In truth, it was the inability of the Magdalena government to pacify Peru that was prolonging an expensive war and depriving Chile of the fruits of its hard earned victory.[56] Unfortunately, the Moneda's confidence in García Calderón waned almost as fast as his army turned their coats. Many reluctantly concluded that García Calderón's power base remained confined to Magdalena's city limits. "The truth is, gentlemen," stated one legislator, "that the war has left a cadaver on our hands and what we should consider is what to do with it before it corrupts the healthy."[57]

Despite their whining, few deputies knew what to do. Clearly Chile could not withdraw unilaterally without undermining the García Calderón government. A partial retreat, perhaps to Arica, offered no solution since it would still require the nation to maintain a large army while depriving Santiago of the limited resources of Callao's *aduana*. It would be better for Chile to withdraw completely than to compromise in this fashion. Some advocated establishing a Chilean protectorate over Peru that would not only instill "habits of order, obedience, and work," but, once properly assimilated would permit the Moneda to end its occupation safely.[58] A few Chileans even called for annexation or partition of their defeated enemy. Others recommended that Chile should merely keep enough troops in Lima to exploit Callao's *aduana* while allowing the competing Peruvian caudillos to battle for leadership. When one finally emerged from this cockpit of political upheaval, the Moneda would negotiate with him.[59] The president tacitly rejected all these legislative innovations, preferring instead to hang on, fervently hoping for the best.

BLAINE'S FOLLY

A serious and potentially more dangerous complication developed on the diplomatic front: the possibility of American intervention. The election of James Garfield produced numerous changes in Washington including the appointment of James G. Blaine as secretary of state. The anglophobic Blaine appeared determined to use the War of the Pacific as an excuse to thwart what he perceived to be British imperialism, while simultaneously extending the mantle of the Monroe Doctrine to cloak South America.

Washington, unlike the European nations or even Santiago, recognized the García Calderón government. Christiancy had warned Blaine against taking this step, citing Piérola's popularity. This admonition proved one of the envoy's last official acts. Blaine, for unrelated reasons, replaced his ministers to Chile and Peru, sending Judson Kilpatrick to Santiago and Stephen Hurlburt, a particularly venal former Civil War general, to Lima. The new secretary of state, unlike his more staid predecessor, enthusiastically embarked upon a campaign to prevent what he believed to be a British-backed Chile from seizing Peru's land. Consequently, he instructed Hurlburt, as well as Kilpatrick, to convince Santiago to accept a monetary indemnity rather than territorial concessions. Hurlburt interpreted these instructions to read that he should become García Calderón's champion. In August 1881, the minister unilaterally proclaimed that Washington would recognize Chile's demand for territory only if Peru could not pay an indemnity. This promise, while probably delighting the Magdalena government, enraged the Moneda. Kilpatrick tried to neutralize his colleague's gaffe when Hurlburt announced in October that he had negotiated an agreement in which Peru granted the United States mining and rail concessions as well as a naval and a coaling station in the port of Chimbote. The idea that the U.S. might establish a protectorate over Peru began to seem quite plausible.[60]

Chileans found Hurlburt's behavior completely inappropriate; Santiago, they noted, could resolve its problems without foreign tutelage. Sure that Hurlburt had exceeded his authority, most Chileans seemed prepared to ignore him but the minister clearly compromised Washington. *El Padre Cobos*, for example, published a cartoon showing Uncle Sam wearing a dunce cap entitled "por intruso." Others found American opposition toward annexation peculiar, particularly from a nation that had aggressively extended its frontiers at its neighbor's expense.[61]

In July, Piérola convened an Asamblea Nacional in Ayacucho which named the dictator provisional president. The Peruvian then organized a cabinet, selecting General Andrés Cáceres as minister of war. The Chileans still held fast to García Calderón who tantalized them with the prospect of negotiating a peace settlement that would include territorial concessions. Washington's involvement or, more accurately, Hurlburt's unauthorized bluster surely stiffened Magdalena's resolve not to capitulate to Chile's demands.

García Calderón did not base his confidence solely on the statements of Blaine and Hurlburt; he relied as well on a series of offers to lend Peru the money it needed to pay a Chilean war indemnity. Throughout the struggle, Santiago had insisted that Lima had to cede territory because it lacked the financial resources to pay Chile's demand for reparations. Obtaining the funds from a third party would save García Calderón from mutilating his already mangled nation.

The first of these financial Good Samaritans was the Credit Industriel, a French enterprise with extremely powerful political connections in the U.S. legislature. The company offered to liquidate's Peru's foreign debt, provide Lima an income, and pay as well the proposed four to five million pound indemnity to Santiago. In return, Chile would return the occupied territory to Peru which, subject to an American protectorate, would allow the Credit Industriel to mine the area for an unspecified number of years. In February 1881, the company had offered this proposal to Evarts, Blaine's predecessor, who interpreted the measure as a way for Peru to avoid having to cede territory. But he repudiated the idea of any American involvement in the negotiations, although he transmitted the Credit Industriel's offer to his ministers serving in the belligerent nations.

Another alternative appeared, based on the claims of Alexander Cochet, a deceased French citizen. The latter's son, stating that the Peruvian government owed him $500,000,000, assigned this claim to an American concern which incorporated itself under the title of The Peruvian Company. Cochet's claims apparently lacked any merit but this did not prevent a notorious speculator, Jacob Shipherd, from advancing them in Washington. The Peruvian Company, unlike the Credit Industriel, did not make specific suggestions. Instead it sought U.S. intervention in order to prevent the cession of the nitrate provinces which consituted the corpus of its assets and, not incidentally, the means of liquidating Peru's liabilities.

A third litigant materialized. John Landreau was a naturalized American citizen, who advanced the claim of his brother and partner to certain nitrate and guano deposits located in the occupied lands. Like Cochet, Landreau had failed to prove his case in Peru's courts and now sought to avail himself of the aid of his adopted homeland. While these claimants eventually failed, they appeared to enjoy the support of both the American secretary of state and his minister in Peru, thus encouraging García Calderón to resist Chilean demands for territory.[62]

This unexpected opposition troubled the new president, Domingo Santa María, who, like his predecessor, demanded the cession of the nitrate lands. Indeed, his foreign minister, Balmaceda, added a new twist to the knife: in addition to Tarapacá, he insisted that Chile occupy Arica indefinitely in order to deprive Peru of a possible site from which it might launch a war of revenge. Fearing that Washington's involvement might have exaggerated García Calderón's sense of self-importance, the Moneda began to reel in the Peruvian leader's leash. On 26 September, General Lynch confiscated the Magdalena government's treasury. Two days later, he effectively ended García's control over his largely ceremonial army. Aware of the tightening net, the Peruvian leader met secretly with his legislature and suggested that it appoint Admiral Montero as vice president. García Calderón also published a letter affirming his refusal to cede land to Chile. He argued that this act would destroy his government and agitate irredentist sentiments. As always, he stated his willingness to pay reparations.

Ironically, Lynch's persecution of García Calderón increased the president's popularity. The forces in Arequipa, who had earlier pronounced him anathema, publicly stated their support, and Montero accepted the post of vice president, praising García Calderón's efforts to unify the Peruvian nation. As García Calderón's star rose, that of Piérola declined—particularly when Cáceres and his army joined the president's cause. Sensing that García Calderón was no longer malleable, Lynch arrested him in November, deporting him as well as members of his government and family to Chile.

With García Calderón in exile, a *junta patriotica* ruled Lima while the presidency, such as it was, passed to Montero. Piérola refused to recognize the admiral's authority but Cáceres did, leaving the dictator-president virtually friendless. Without support, he resigned in November 1881 and ordered his subordinates to ally themselves with Cáceres. Although temporarily stymied, Piérola did not renounce politics. He conferred with Jovino Novoa and Altamirano, Chile's diplomatic envoys, who had traveled north to speak with the Peruvian politician. Piérola offered to betray Cáceres, thus unifying Peru, if the Moneda accepted a peace treaty without territorial concessions. When the delegates refused, Piérola flounced off to New York, leaving Santiago again searching for some agreeable soul with whom it could negotiate.[63]

Perhaps aware of his plight, Santa María moderated his demands. In November Santiago considered signing an armistice with Peru that, while allowing Chile to occupy the disputed area, would not force Lima to recognize formally the loss of its sovereignty over Tarapacá. Eulojio Altamirano, noting the wretched state of the Peruvian economy, had earlier recommended that Chile either prepare for a long stay or withdraw to Tacna after first razing the north. Another plan, advanced by a Bolivian officer, appeared to be a variation of this idea: Chile and Peru would agree to a truce; Santiago would retreat to the Sama River, retaining its control over Tarapacá and Arica subject to some future permanent solution. This alternative, Santa María realized, still begged the key question of who in Peru would sign the truce. Precisely for this reason Novoa opposed the plan. After all, he argued, if Chile had to create a government in Lima merely to sign an armistice, it might as well make the same effort to form a regime willing to negotiate a permanent peace settlement.[64]

Thus, after months of effort, Chile had come full circle. It still controlled the Peruvian coastline but it had yet to find someone with whom it could parley. "We can say," observed one journalist, "that we are in a more mortifying situation than in the midst of the war."[65] Predictably, some Chileans still favored a military solution, naively believing that *montonero* resistance would collapse as soon as Santiago made an example of a captured guerilla leader. Even if the Moneda did not use this option, the nation demanded that the government should continue to exploit Peru's resources until Lima capitulated by, among its various concessions, ceding Tarapacá.[66]

If the arrest of García Calderón delighted the Chileans, it enraged various American officials. Hurlburt immediately recognized Montero as president while continuing to work to save Peru from mutilation, an exercise which *The Chilian Times* dismissed as giving a "little éclat to the orgies of the 'wake' that is being held over the corpse." The American minister became so enmeshed in Peru's domestic politics that he convinced Cáceres to recognize Montero as president. Blaine, who had publicly and privately repudiated Hurlburt's Chimbote agreement, interpreted the Moneda's incarceration of García Calderón as an insult to the United States. Rather than deal through his resident ministers—a wise choice given Hurlburt's partisan nature and Kilpatrick's declining health —he sent his son, Walker, as well as William Trescott, a career diplomat, to Chile to resolve the dispute. The two men received orders which virtually guaranteed a war if Santa María refused American arbitration. But the confrontation did not materialize: the bullet that assassinated James Garfield may also have prevented a war in South America.[67]

Chester Alan Arthur replaced James G. Blaine with Frederick Frelinghuysen who canceled his predecessor's instructions, ordering Walker

Blaine and Trescott instead to tread softly. When the two diplomats arrived in Santiago in January 1882, they received this news as well as Chile's terms: annexation of Tarapacá; an indemnity of $20,000,000 plus the right to occupy Arica for ten years. If Lima could not pay the reparations, Santiago would take Arica as well. The Moneda could make these demands with impunity since, even before Blaine and Trescott had arrived, Santa María's minister to the U.S. had informed the president that Washington had abandoned its bellicose stance. Peru had lost its protector.[68]

The Chilean public, unaware of this important policy change, naturally opposed American intervention, criticizing its insensitivity and its willingness to plunge unilaterally into matters which Santiago alone could resolve. Others could not understand Washington's refusal to accept Chile's right to annex land, a right which they considered nonnegotiable. Some claimed that speculators had influenced U.S. policy; others implicated Washington's ministers who, they believed, also had financial interests in resolving the dispute. Of all the possible villains, however, Blaine emerged as the most loathed. He had warped his nation's diplomatic policies and, in league with certain economic groups, supported García Calderón in order to make Peru "an emporium of North American power and wealth." Regardless of American motivation, Chile would resist, if necessary with European support, before it capitulated to the United States.[69]

Washington's acceptance of Santiago's territorial demands while abjuring armed intervention, indicated that Frelinghuysen had repudiated Blaine's policies. Meeting in Viña del Mar, the American envoys signed a document in February 1882, recognizing Chile's right to annex Tarapacá. For many Chileans, this concession came too late. Santa María, they believed, should reject American mediation efforts in preference to those of Europe, Chile's traditional trading partners. Henceforth the United States, particularly after Hurlburt's escapades, could not be trusted.[70]

THE RETURN TO FORCE

Since the Viña del Mar agreement protected Santa María's diplomatic flanks, the president decided to launch two military expeditions: one to capture Junín and thus destroy Cáceres, and a second to dislodge Colonel La Torre from his mountain retreat in Arequipa. Unfortunately, the government could not seize the offensive immediately: it had demobilized so many army units that it would have to find, train, and equip new recruits before unleashing another expedition. The opening of enlistment drives, however, pleased neither the war-weary public nor the legislature.⁷¹ Indeed, congressional pressure had become so great that the president cancelled the Arequipa expedition, deciding to attack only Cáceres.

Over the objections of Lynch, who warned that the onset of the rainy season would cause enormous problems, the expedition departed Lima on 1 January 1882. As predicted, weather conditions slowed Lynch's progress and permitted Cáceres to retreat into the interior. Rather than return to Lima, the army received orders to occupy the interior. For approximately the next six months, Chile's army of occupation seemed on the road to Calvary: fighting in the altiplano at 15,000 feet, in areas without roads, savaged by winds, rain, *soroche*, and constantly threatened by a hostile population. Virtually cut off from resupply, adrift in a hostile environment, the Chilean troops wandered aimlessly through the Peruvian highlands, showing the flag, levying taxes, and seeking, no matter how briefly, to impose Santiago's authority. When local communities resisted, Lynch's men exacted brutal reprisals—reprisals which produced temporary relief and created permanent hatred. Living off the land, without medical supplies, and hagridden by illness, many soldiers simply deserted rather than perish of disease or in an enemy ambush.

Eventually Santa María acceded to the army's pleas and allowed the expedition to withdraw to the coastal plains. Cáceres took advantage of the expedition's exposed position to harass the retreating Chileans. During the general withdrawal, Peruvian regulars trapped a force of seventy Chilean troops in the hamlet of la Concepción. The soldiers of the Regimento Chacabuco refused to surrender but instead resisted to the last man; their victors responded to this heroism by murdering the wounded and mutilating the dead.⁷² Although Chileans now consider Concepción a triumph, few felt so uplifted in 1882. At Concepción the motherland's sons had become "montonero cannon fodder," dying because of the "lack of foresight, the negligence, and the poor arrangements of the directors of the war."⁷³ And, like the battles of Iquique, Tarapacá, and Tacna, Concepción forced a reappraisal of the conduct of the war.

CHILE'S WAR OF ATTRITION

After 1881, most of the expeditionary force consisted of troops drawn from the marginal elements of Chilean society: criminals, those who lacked the "santos en la corte" to escape the press gangs, and the occasional adventurer. As long as these men suffered silently or perished in small numbers, few seemed to notice or care. Chile's press, particularly in the provinces, more preoccupied with curing constipation or preventing typhoid, gave no mention of the war unless it involved local men. The battle of Concepción, however, with its comparatively large loss of life, its spectacular heroism, and its gruesome consequences, brought the war home again. The nation had tired of bloody moral victories, of learning that its menfolk had perished in squalid altiplano hamlets bearing names few could spell and none but the mourners would remember. Many questioned why their soldiers had to succumb to disease without honor "in places which . . . could have been left alone without compromising the cause of Chile." Indeed, the public became openly hostile. *La Libertad*, for example, warned that towns like Talca "cannot remain continuously indifferent to the begging and the complaining of its soldiers who want to return home, not because they fear enemy bullets but because they do not want to die unexpectedly and treasonously murdered by epidemics."[74]

Some journalists, of course, used the battle to attack the government: there were charges that it tried to suppress the news and that its lenient occupation policies were responsible for high casualty rates. Others criticized a parsimonious administration for permitting the enemy to regroup unmolested, for not attacking Arequipa but sacrificing instead poorly equipped and outnumbered units for reasons as yet unknown. Since the fall of Lima, the Moneda seem incapable of deciding what to do with Peru. Many Chileans wondered who stationed the men of the Chacabuco in Concepción but, given the government's almost limitless incompetence, another seemed surprised that similar disaster had not occurred before and more often. Clearly the government had to change its politics in order to stop the loss of "money, the loss of prestige," and the military's demoralization. But, *El Ñuble* concluded, the government did not bear all the responsibility: the people were more concerned with the forthcoming *deiziocho* and the legislature with their clothes than with the death of Chile's young men. If the Congress continued in this fashion, "a terrible anathema will fall upon its heads if they do not know how to fulfill the nation's aspirations."[75]

Not surprisingly, many demanded that the Moneda exact harsh reprisals on Lima, complaining that the Limeños lived as well as Chileans "save for the loss of political and civil liberty to which Peru does not attach much importance." This generous occupation policy had to end: Chile had to show that war was not "cake and painted bread"; by "blood and fire we shall impose a peace with extermination."[76] The Moneda was caught in an untenable position: if it deserted Lima, Peru would collapse, yet continuing the occupation cost Chile $2,500,000 a year to provide its enemies the best government that ever ruled them.[77]

Beneath the bluster there existed a substratum of fear, an almost palpable anxiety. *El Estandarte Católico* speculated that Peruvian resistance, disease, and political dissent might cost Chile the war, and compared the enemy to some demonic force that God had visited upon the nation as punishment for Santa María's anti-clericalism.[78] While admittedly somewhat exaggerated, other news journals agreed. *El Independiente* tired of seeing Chileans, whose labor would have benefited the nation, perish uselessly in the altiplano. Others shrilly insisted that the stalemate had to end. Continuing the struggle "will hurt directly our interests and the most productive industries of the nation," noted one journal in arguing that the people wanted peace. The Peruvian question, warned *El Independiente*, will be "the cancer of our prosperity."[79]

The legislature appeared equally dispirited, although the abortive and costly summer offensive proved a boon to Santa María's opponents. Vicuña Mackenna maneuvered through a session of the senate a motion demanding either that the Moneda evacuate Lima and the nothern littoral or launch a more vigorous war. Novoa admitted that after four years of fighting, the nation did not seem to understand what direction the campaign should take. Yet, although displeased with the results of the recent effort, he still opposed retreating, which, he argued, would end any chance to annex Tarapacá. The legislature's attempt to initiate a withdrawal also upset some of the press which argued that the Congress should not meddle in the conduct of the war because . . . "we are now in the phase of reprisals and punishment," which would terminate the conflict on Chile's terms.[80]

THE RETURN TO THE BARGAINING TABLE

The bloody failure of the 1882 offensive so depressed Santa María that he seriously considered a proposal that Chile unilaterally retreat to the Sama River. As the president tartly noted, however, too many vested interests, opposed such a solution. A coalition of Chilean carpetbaggers, who staffed the occupation government, along with merchants and speculators opposed a withdrawal. "Within a short period of time," Santa María noted, "it will not be the Peruvians who will oppose peace but the Peruvianized Chileans." The president yearned to leave the north: the occupation required an army of 20,000 which, "if today does not cause worry, tomorrow will be a danger as well as a terrible waste of men and money." As before, Novoa rejected the notion of retreat. If Santiago withdrew, the enemy could simply use the fiscal structure established by Santiago to finance the creation of a new navy and military to launch at Chile. Novoa advocated patience until the American peace envoys had an opportunity to do their work.

Novoa's counsel rang true. The arrival of Washington's new minister revived the peace process. Dr. Cornelius Logan, who had served before in

Santiago, reached Chile in September 1882. Another career diplomat, James Partridge, went to Lima while George Maney took up residence in La Paz. Although the United States recognized Chile's claim to Tarapacá, it wished to convince Santa María to pay for the land Santiago would annex. American leverage, however, remained limited: it could only threaten to break diplomatic relations unless Chile acted more generously. While Logan tried to prise open Santiago's treasury, Partridge informed García Calderón that Washington would not help Peru unless it accepted most of Chile's reasonable demands.[81]

The Peruvian, perhaps tired of his confinement in Angol and realizing that he could no longer count on the United States, softened his position. García Calderón agreed to cede Tarapacá and the Lobos Islands but he refused to yield on Tacna or Arica. If Chile wanted the nitrate fields, moreover, it would have to take Tarapacá subject to all its outstanding debts. In addition, he demanded a six-month armistice and American mediation. Thus, although the exiled president finally accepted the loss of Peru's littoral, he would not grant the other essential Chilean demands. Logan, noting the Peruvian's intransigence, wrote to Montero seeking to obtain his acceptance of the terms which García Calderón had rejected.

Although the more cynical discounted the American's efforts, the news of the reopening of the negotiations delighted many Chileans. The situation had reached such a state, as one journalist observed, that "the point is to make peace, be it well done or not." His colleagues recognized that negotiating a treaty constituted but one part of the problem. They still had to convince Lima to accept an agreement that included the loss of its land.[82] As before, American diplomats worked at cross purposes. Inspired by Partridge, García Calderón stopped talking to Logan whom he accused of being a partisan of Santiago. Instead, the Peruvian leader tried to negotiate directly with Santa María. By this time, however, the Chilean president had found a new favorite with whom he could parley.[83]

THE PERUVIAN SAVIOR

Miguel Iglesias, a career soldier, had participated in the defense of Lima and was captured after the battle of Chorillos. Paroled after Miraflores, he retired to his *hacienda* until Admiral Montero appointed him a provincial administrator. In August 1882, Iglesias publicly called for negotiating a peace settlement with Chile. The general then convened a congress, the Asamblea del Norte, composed of delegates elected from the area he dominated, which met in Cajamarca in December.

Understandably, Cáceres, Montero, and García Calderón disapproved of Iglesias' actions. Despite their protests, the Asamblea del Norte authorized the general to seek a peace with Chile providing that the treaty did not jeopardize Peru's existence and that a constitutional Congress would ratify the agreement. After Iglesias—who began describing himself as the *Presidente Regenerador*—convened his legislature, Admiral Montero organized a Congress in Arequipa in April 1883. The indomitable General Cáceres, however, still constituted Santiago's most implacable enemy. Thus, while Santa María could safely ignore the landlocked admiral, whose deeds never matched his rhetoric, the Chilean leader would have to annihilate Cáceres if he wished to arrange a a peace treaty.

Although Iglesias's proclamations initially did not impress Novoa, he still forwarded them to the Moneda, especially after he learned that the general had tried to enlist Piérola's support against Montero. By November, the Chilean envoy endorsed the leader of Cajamarca as Santiago's best hope for peace. Neither Montero nor Cáceres, he noted, would support García Calderón; Piérola appeared equally friendless. Iglesias, however, "at least had the advantage of recognizing the need to sign a peace which included territorial concessions."[84] Santa María still remained skeptical: "I do not see how we can get peace either with Peru or Bolivia. Two crazy men rule these two exceptional and strange nations, and as Montero does not want peace, García Calderón is afraid, Cáceres is like the huanacos in the cordillera, and Iglesias has no power, I do not see how, nor when, we can arrange a settlement."[85]

Various events subsequently encouraged Santa María to alter his opinion. García Calderón's public refusal to accept a peace treaty proved that the exiled leader no longer was a serious statesman. The call of the Cajamarca Congress for a peace settlement, plus the defection of Colonel del Vento, a key Cáceres supporter, indicated that Iglesias might succeed. Consequently, Santa María ordered Lynch to help the Cajamarca government while dispatching Novoa to discuss peace terms with Iglesias' delegate, José de Lavalle.[86]

Although more tractable, Lavalle was not spineless. He reluctantly accepted the loss of Tarapacá, but he balked at surrendering Tacna. Rather than cede the territory, he proposed instead that Chile occupy the land until a plebiscite could determine it status. This artifice, he argued, would grant Chile temporary control of the north while mollifying Peruvian public opinion. But times had changed: Peru now sought and received concessions from Chile. Not only did Santiago agree to the plebiscite, it also accepted Tarapacá, subject to any debts which Peru might have contracted. Thus, after almost five years of intermittent war, both sides had finally negotiated a settlement. All that remained was for someone to eradicate Cáceres and Montero whose collective resistance stood in the war of the final resolution of the conflict.[87]

This tentative settlement, which years earlier would have outraged the public, now caused elation. By late 1882, most Chileans fervently wanted an end to a war which greedily consumed their taxes and their sons. Simply the rumor of a peace settlement, noted *El Constituyente* "calms somewhat a legitimate anxiety that exists in the public because of the bloody progress of the tremendous war which is already so fatal to us." The nation concluded that peace would usher in an era of economic progress: incomes would rise, taxes would fall, and Chile could begin to expand within its new frontiers.[88] Indeed, after five years of bloodletting, some forgot why Santiago had declared war and instead wondered how it could escape the abbatoir. Others accused the government of conducting the peace negotiations as maladroitly as it had directed the various campaigns, insisting that an unholy alliance—the military, the Moneda, the capitalists of both nations, as well as the bureaucrats staffing the occupation government in the north—deliberately obstructed the peace process because they benefited from the war. Another group appeared genuinely confused, attributing the continued hostilities not to Chilean greed but to Peruvian perversity.[89] Regardless of the causes, "the nation now wants [peace] and the government has to satisfy the country."[90]

Understandably then, the appearance of Iglesias seemed like the dawn of the millenium: someone had materialized who would assume the onus for Peru's earlier sins and would sign a peace treaty. Various Chileans feared, however, that the general's lack of popularity, as well as the strong possibility of a coup, militated against his success.[91] Still others hoped to improve the climate by moderating the peace terms. Logan's attempts to modify Chilean demands, for example, did not unleash a wave of protest. On the contrary, noted one observer, if Chile annexed too much Peruvian territory, Santa María should offer financial compensation as well as guarantee the rights of those people whose property fell under its control. Chile, henceforth, would treat Peru with "candor as an equal and with benevolence."[92] The Moneda was warned not to humiliate Lima which would be counterproductive for Peru, after all, "constitutes a vast market for our products, providing precious raw materials for our industry and a sensitive and honorable neighbor."[93] For Chile to extricate itself from "this swamp," it must not seek a treaty based on a preconceived ideal solution but "the best solution that the circumstances permit."[94] These forces therefore opposed the annexation of Tacna and Arica out of concern that the future plebiscite might provoke another war. Instead, Santiago should accept a monetary indemnity which Lima could liquidate by granting tax-free status to Chilean products entering Peru. The government, moreover, should neither impose onerous restrictions on Lima nor limit the size of its military. Not all felt so benevolent: Chile, *La*

Libertad caustically noted, was not Jesus; it did not have to turn the other cheek.[95]

The newspaper's fears proved illusory. Santa María reinforced his diplomatic overtures by ordering Lynch to provide Iglesias with weapons and permit the latter to replace the Chilean garrisons in La Libertad province. Cáceres, aware that he would eventually be attacked, launched an offensive designed to obliterate the Iglesias government and to destroy the isolated Chilean units, perhaps in hopes of weakening the Moneda's resolve.[96]

Fearful that Iglesias' government could not survive, Santa María decided to act. He recognized that attacking Arequipa attracted few partisans. Chile, as one critic noted, already had enough widows, orphans, and war dead. Instead, the president decided to direct his might against Cáceres, a move which the public endorsed although some questioned the wisdom of the Moneda trusting this mission to his minister of war.[97] Given the elusive nature of their prey, the Chileans prepared plans that they hoped would cover all the contingencies.

In early 1883, the Chilean forces returned to the altiplano again, determined to destroy Cáceres. The Peruvian proved as elusive as ever, crisscrossing the Andes in the dead of winter, and successfully eluding his pursuers. In July, however, the Chileans managed to ambush his expedition and annihilated his army at Huamachuco. With Cáceres at least temporarily neutralized, if only by default, Iglesias finally seemed to be the master of his own house.

Despite the protests of both Chileans residing in the north and some Peruvians, Santa María began to scale down his nation's presence. The president wanted to evacuate Peru before the summer fevers arrived "to bury us. If this calamity arrives, Peru might defend itself with this and there might not be any peace." Consequently, Santa María worked hard to buttress Iglesias, ordering Novoa to provide weapons and, if necessary, to neutralize the general's political opposition. "The strength of Iglesias will be superior the day he can dispense favors, grant incomes, and give food to the hungry."[98] Iglesias left Trujillo for the capital in September and one month later, Santiago officially recognized his government. The general paid dearly for this luxury: on 20 October 1883, he signed the treaty of peace at the seaside resort of Ancón.

Since Montero was not a party to the Treaty of Ancón, Santa María had to obtain his surrender by driving the admiral from his mountain fortress in Arequipa. Fortunately for Chile, the mere arrival of its troops stampeded the city's poor to rebel, and Montero with great wisdom decamped for a Bolivian asylum. On 29 October 1883, Santiago's occupation of the

Heavenly City of Peruvian patriotism ended Peru's involvement in the War of the Pacific.

BOLIVIA'S CAPITULATION

With Arequipa in Santiago's hands, the Moneda could finally devote some of its attention to La Paz. Since 1879, Chileans had expressed ambivalent feelings toward Bolivia, many regarding it as the instrument rather than the author of Peruvian deceit. These elements, therefore, advocated treating Bolivia leniently and even contemplated ceding it a strip of seacoast as compensation for its loss of the littoral. Others, however, considered Bolivia a nation inhabited by people who "live in a state of savagery, beset by all the vices of civilization, and without any of its advantages."[99] Although differing in their image of Bolivia, eventually both groups became furious when it refused to capitulate.[100] Economic considerations, however, necessarily tempered the fury.

Santiago became distressed when Bolivia used Argentina's rail and road network to obtain access to the Atlantic, ending its dependence on the Pacific Coast ports and frightening those Chileans who regarded Bolivia as their economic preserve.[101] Although a few dismissed the idea of a Buenos Aires–La Paz axis, others called on Santa María to grant Bolivia a sea coast and to build a railroad from Arica to the altiplano in order to entice La Paz to the peace table. Such a link would also ensure that Bolivia would remain in Chile's sphere of influence.[102]

Since Lima's 1881 collapse, various Bolivians too had questioned the wisdom of continuing the war, although General Campero continued to purchase additional military equipment and extended conscription to include new classes. The president's policies did not go unchallenged: Maríano Baptista and Ancieto Arce vociferously opposed a war that brought their nation so little comfort and so much grief. Despite their complaints, Campero insisted that Bolivia would remain faithful to its Peruvian ally, a feeling which apparently enjoyed widespread national support.

By 1882, while resisting the idea of signing a treaty which officially ceded their seacoast, they did consider a truce. This solution seemed ideal: it ended the fighting and yet let La Paz enjoy the illusion that it might someday regain its coastline. In October 1882, therefore, the Bolivian Senate formally expressed its hope that Campero would negotiate an armistice.

Maríano Baptista, one of the nation's two vice presidents, met with Eusebio Lillo in Tacna. The two men arranged a settlement which granted Chile the right to occupy Bolivia's littoral although it had not received legal title to the area. In addition to suspending the hostilities, the agreement also restored normal economic relations, allowing goods destined for Bolivia to enter through Arica where they would pay half the normal *aduana* duties. La Paz would, moreover, have the right to export its minerals through the same port. But Campero ultimately rejected the agreement apparently at the suggestion of the American minister, Charles Adams, who believed that the Blaine-Trescott mission would force Chile to moderate its demands. When the American diplomats capitulated to Santiago, Bolivia was left mired in a war which it did not want but from which it could not gracefully extricate itself.[103]

La Paz's refusal to accept the Lillo-Baptista agreement perplexed rather than angered the Chileans. Bolivia's economic future clearly lay in the Moneda's hands: Chilean interests could not only invest capital but would also teach their former enemies new skills, educating its lower class while Santiago exploited its neighbor's raw materials. Some even demanded that a peace treaty include a guarantee that Chilean capitalists would have access to all of Bolivia's resources. By 1883 an increasing number of Bolivians began considering any alternative to end the war, particularly when they saw Peru negotiating a peace settlement. After Ancón, even Campero recognized that the time had arrived for Bolivia to quit and thus he sent Belisario Salinas and Belisario Beoto to Chile to negotiate.[104]

While the collapse of Peru made Bolivia more agreeable, it increased Chilean intransigence. Santa María's only concession was his willingness to accept an armistice which did not confer on the victor legal title to Bolivia's littoral. When La Paz refused to accept this demand, apparently believing that Europe might save it from mutilation, Chile warned that it would invade the altiplano. Faced with this threat and aware that his nation wished to be rid of the war, Campero capitulated. In April 1884, his negotiators signed the armistice ending the state of war. Peace had finally come to the Pacific.

Epilogue: When the Laurel Leaves Begin to Wither

> The cannons have ceased thundering
> the trenchs are silent
> and along the roads of the north
> are returning Chile's battalions
> and squadrons.
> "Los viejos estandartes."

After its victory, Chile acquired the reputation of being a well-organized and powerful nation state. Various military historians and tacticians retrospectively discovered in the war a grandeur, a strategy, and a precision which, they claimed, made the Moneda's victory a virtual foregone conclusion. As has been demonstrated, however, the War of the Pacific revealed the immature and incomplete quality of the Chilean state: its inept military; its lack of political institutions and culture; and its inability to forge a sense of national consciousness. The 1879 struggle against the allies was a modern war, but it was fought by a society that had yet to evolve into a nation state. Instead of being a lark, as many have argued, the contest quickly degenerated into a nightmare of tedium, disease, and death that strained Chile's political institutions and avariciously consumed its economic as well as its human resources. Few Chileans remembered the early months of the war, when the nation lived in fear of Grau and the prospect of being crushed between the Peruvian-Bolivian hammer and the Argentine anvil. The anxiety and confusion were forgotten, replaced by a new and more congenial reality: Santiago had humbled its enemies, increased its territory by a third, and acquired a monopoly on the world's supply of nitrates. Clearly Chile's future was bright: affluent, militarily powerful, and confident, the Moneda controlled the west coast of South America in 1884.

This happy state endured but a short time. Chileans quickly learned that the Treaty of Ancón had caused almost as many problems as it resolved. In its haste to end the hostilties, Santiago agreed that it would occupy Tacna and Arica for ten years. In 1893, the Moneda was to oversee a plebisicite: the winner would receive title to the two provinces; the loser would be awarded a consolation prize of ten million pesos.

Less than the decade had elapsed when the government of José Manuel Balmaceda concluded that Santiago must retain Tacna and Arica in order to buffer the nitrate provinces and the Central Valley from a horde of Peruvian revanchists. Successive governments remained faithful to this new diplomatic policy, first stalling and then refusing to hold the plebisicite, which it knew Peru would win. The Moneda's intransigence not only infuriated Lima, which came to regard Tacna and Arica as some new Zion, but it also complicated Chile's relations with Bolivia.

La Paz had never signed a permanent peace treaty with Santiago: its 1884 agreement was merely an armistice. In addition, until a permament arrangement was made, Chile's control of Antofagasta remained conditional. Bolivia, of course, refused to grant its littoral to Chile unless it received an outlet to the Pacific Ocean. This left the Moneda with two alternatives: it could create a corridor through Chilean territory, which the nation would not tolerate, or it could grant Bolivia a seaport in either Tacna or Arica. Since the latter solution would force Peru to pay Chile's obligations, it appealed to Santiago. Nevertheless, because Santiago could not cede what it did not own, this option remained closed; until Peru yielded on the north, the Moneda could not reach an agreement with La Paz.

Time, moreover, was working against the Moneda. Chile had alienated the Latin American community, which resented its annexation of the land of its neighbors. They also bristled at the Moneda's refusal to abide by the treaty it had imposed upon Lima. Ironically, the vanquished acted as if they were anything but humble. Peru, infuriated by Santiago's refusal to abide by the Ancón arrangement, became increasingly hostile. Bolivia, seeing Chile's discomfiture, upped the diplomatic ante, seeking more generous peace terms. The Moneda might once have ignored Peru's fury and Bolivia's arrogance, but a new factor complicated its situation: the emergence of Argentina.

During most of the nineteenth century, Buenos Aires had tentatively tried to rule a nation riven by ideological and provincial disputes. After the 1860s, stability finally settled on the Platine Republic. Having put its

Epilogue: When the Laurel Leaves Begin to Wither

house in order, financed by the sale of grain and beef, and enriched by the arrival of thousands of immigrants, Argentina became a force in South America.

Logically, the emergence of a strong Argentina should not have caused problems for Chile. Both nations, however, were involved in a boundary dispute which by the last quarter of the nineteenth century had ripened into a full scale confrontation. Santiago, moreover, could no longer ignore the complaints from Buenos Aires. The latter had rearmed its large army and had purchased various naval vessels. Anxious to increase its leverage and to impress the Moneda, Buenos Aires made overtures to Peru and Bolivia, threatening to create an alliance which might undo Chile's recent successes.

The combination of Argentine expansionism as well as Peruvian-Bolivian revanchism forced the Moneda to undertake a costly rearmament program. Santiago hired a German military mission to retrain the army and purchased a variety of ironclads for the navy. The expanded military and refurbished fleet, however, could not assuage the feelings of anxiety. Having won the distinction of being King of the Hill, Santiago would have to spend millions for its armed forces and live during the remainder of the nineteenth century constantly looking over its shoulder, fearful that its neighbors to the north or the east would, either alone or in unison, strike at Chile (Table 42).

The War of the Pacific not only altered Santiago's relations with Peru and Bolivia, it changed various facets of the nation's economic life. Until 1885, the Moneda derived most of its income from the taxation of imports, a levy which fell largely upon the middle-and upper class-consumer (see Table 43). After the war, the northern *salitreras* provided the nation with new resources which, when taxed, generated millions in revenue for Chile. Indeed, by 1890, the sums produced by the nitrate tax constituted almost half of the Moneda's ordinary income (Table 44). Henceforth, the Chilean state's fiscal solvency would rest on the shifting sands of the nitrate pampas in the north. Iquique, once cursed as the Sodom and Gomarrah of the Pacific, became a thriving entrepôt, whose most prominent citizens wore the latest Paris fashions. The *salitreras* became a dependent of the Central Valley, relying upon the southern provinces for food, labor, and for supplies. The south, conversely, used the *salitreras* not only as a market for their products and as a dumping ground for their excess population, but also as a milch cow from which it extracted the wealth to develop both the Central Valley and the newly opened Indian territories in the rain forest.

Periodically, world economic conditions worsened, depressing the nitrate prices, and causing a contraction not only in the *saliteras* but in all of Chile. The combination of nitrate cartels and patience generally brought a return to prosperity to the *salitreras* and thus the country as a whole. Following the First World War, however, Franz Haber's formula for synthesizing ammonia became widespread, mortally wounding the nitrate industry. Although the Guggenheims managed to resuscitate the *salitreras*, the Great Depression completed the process of destruction: the great nitrate boom had ended. Happily for Chile, however, the northern deserts still yielded additional bounty for the economy. When *salitre* ceased to be prized, copper, wrenched from the open pit mines of the north, became the principal revenue source for the republic's treasury. Thus, Chile managed to live off the spoils of the War of the Pacific like a remittance man from an old inheritance.

The funds produced by the nitrate mines were absorbed in a variety of ways. Approximately one-third of the money paid for the cost of producing the *salitre*; another third was remitted to local as well as foreign investors to pay for interest and dividends; the remaining third went to the Chilean government.[1] If the money produced by nitrates had been used properly, the nation would have benefited; but it was not. Rather than develop the Chile's human resources, create industries, or enhance the existing infrastructure, the Moneda and the legislature squandered the funds generated by the *salitreras*. In 1879, Chile, like a substantial portion of the world, was suffering from the effects of a depression which had becalmed the economies of Europe and North America. Demand for raw materials had declined, severely curtailing the Moneda's income. Santiago tried to limit its expenditures but this tactic failed to achieve its purpose: the government's expenditures outstripped the nation's income. Thus, the legislature eventually had to impose levies which directly taxed an individual's income, the *haberes*, as well as the voluntary and intestate transfer of wealth, the *herencia*. For the first time, the burden of taxation fell upon the often unwilling shoulders of the affluent. Certainly these new taxes broke with tradition, and if carried to their logical conclusion, the *herencia* and *haberes* might have matured into genuinely progressive taxes while providing relief for the poorer elements of Chilean society.

Nitrates, however, aborted this movement for tax reform. As Table 4 indicates, the conquest of the *salitreras* completely distorted Chile's tax structure by placing the lion's share of the burden of taxation on the foreign consumer; revenues from import taxes declined. Using the income from nitrates, the legislature and the president abolished not only the *haberes* and the *herencia* but also the tax on land, the *agrícola*, the business license fee, the *patente*, and the transfer tax, the *alcabala*. While the abrogation of the last two imposts perhaps benefited the small busi-

Epilogue: When the Laurel Leaves Begin to Wither

nessman, the wealthy clearly emerged with the greatest advantage. Henceforth the large *hacendado* or rentier avoided paying taxes on his land, income, capital, and his estate. The decision not to retain these direct imposts, while perhaps understandable, ensured that the state would not have to redistribute income while allowing the affluent to escape its fair share of taxation. Consequently, the gap between the rich and the poor widened into a chasm which did not go unnoted in the *salitreras* or the *conventillos* of Old Chile. Not without reason did the Left gain some of its most enthusiastic supporters in the nitrate districts of the north and the urban slums of the south (See Table 45).

While insulating the wealthy, *salitre* also appears to have warped Chile's economic development. While many have described Chile as a bastion of free trade, Santiago, beginning in the late 1860s, passed laws protecting certain industries. Then, in the early and mid-1870s, the legislature approved an omnibus tariff law, which enveloped more industries in the protective mantle of the state. As we observed earlier, it was these factories that provided the nation with the industrial base that served the country so well during the War of the Pacific. Despite their ability to fabricate quality products at competitive prices, Santiago's national industries never developed to their full potential because Chileans continued to import enormous quantities of consumer goods. In part, this was because Chileans refused to invest in national industries, preferring to put their money in short term investments—such as purchasing shares in a nitrate corporation—or into areas of the economy where the risks were fewer and the returns greater. In addition to suffering from a lack of capital, however, national industries failed to win the loyalty of the Chilean consumer.

Prior to the War of the Pacific, Chileans, even in the upper class, had led a relatively spartan life. The wealth from the pampas, however, became addictive. Flush with the easy nitrate money, the new and the old rich, distressed if they did not "appear important and wealthy at all cost," became locked in a deadly race of conspicuous consumption. Baroque palaces appeared in the Chilean countryside as well as the streets of Santiago. Consumed by "the thirst for luxury"—what contemporaries excoriated as "snobismo" or "extranjerismo"—Chile became awash in a sea of French perfumes, British woolens, and German toys.[2] Thus the nitrate profit passed through the hands of the Chileans to enrich the foreign industrialist. By fueling this spiral of consumption and by siphoning off investments from more productive sectors of the economy, nitrates aborted the movement toward economic self-sufficiency and corrupted the nation. Without the money from the north, Chileans could not have engaged in this dance of the millions. It was not without reason that various critics described the *salitreras* as tumors which had metastasized throughout Chile, destroying old values and self-pride.[3]

Regrettably the government seemed as profligate with its share of the nitrate revenues as the private sector. Chile's southern provinces became procurers which appropriated the wealth of the *salitreras* to build highways, sanitation systems, communication networks, pave roads, expand the railroads, and construct some Belle Epoque government buildings for the benefit of the Central Valley. Some could argue that this transfer of assets was logical: after all, most of the nation resided in the south and thus the money flowed to satisfy legitimate needs. Unfortunately, however, the Moneda and later the legislature also used the nitrate revenues to expand the bureaucracy and to fund projects whose only purpose was to employ hack politicians, their families, and their minons.

Unfortunately, this abuse seemed to gain momentum. In 1891, the navy and sectors of the army raised to defend Chile from its enemies in the altiplano and the Argentine, turned on the Moneda. President José Manuel Balmaceda, who earlier tried to limit the Pinto's power, now strived to preserve the Moneda's prerogatives; arrayed against him were those who wished to weaken the executive branch of government. The champions of the Congressionalist supremacy fled to Iquique where they used nitrate revenues to raise and equip an army of disgruntled miners who defeated Balmaceda's legions. Once again *salitre*, and thus indirectly the War of the Pacific, altered the course of Chile's history.

The victorious politicians abolished the presidential form of government and substituted in its place a bastard form of parliamentary rule. Through a combination of bribery and vote buying, again financed by the levy on *salitre*, the political leadership managed to insulate itself from the public's rage. When nitrate revenues disappeared, thus drying up the wardheelers' and the city bosses' source of patronage, the political system collapsed, plunging the country into a crisis that lasted for over a decade.

Consequently, whatever benefits the War of the Pacific had conferred had started to disappear by the turn of the century. By 1900, Chile began suffering from a "crisis moral," a slow descent into political sterility and economic mismanagement in which the nation remained mired for decades. The country once respected for its political morality saw its destiny consigned to the hands of a self-serving oligarchy who, in league with venal politicians, managed to stymie reform. Chile, the nation known in the nineteenth century for its fiscal rectitude and honest government, foundered in a twentieth century morass of corruption.

Benjamin Franklin once argued that the absence of a horseshoe nail lost a war. In Chile's case, the presence of nitrates poisoned the nation.

Epilogue: When the Laurel Leaves Begin to Wither

Without the 1879 conflict, the country might have succeeded in diversifying its economy and creating a more equitable tax structure. Perhaps a less generous flow of taxes would not have allowed the ward politicians to perpetuate themselves in office. Perhaps the partisanship would have become less acute if the spoils of government had not been so attractive. Perhaps a more peaceful Chile would not have had to waste its revenues purchasing naval equipment and armaments which, like the men who directed them, succumbed either to the ravages of the elements or old age.

Ironically, although the gains of the the War of the Pacific have long since evaporated, the 1879 conflict nonetheless serves an important purpose. Precisely because the monocultural economy foundered and the political system failed to resolve the country's problems, the War of the Pacific stands out as a happy period, a Golden Age of civic virtue when all men presumably rushed to serve their country, a time of glory and victory. Indeed, one could argue that Chileans have deliberately chosen to accept the various myths about the conflict precisely because the fantasies provide the strength to sustain them in a real world characterized by corruption, incompetence, and immorality.

Few of the prizes won during the war remain. The once coveted north remains sparsely populated; the booming *salitreras*, like Wild West mining towns, lie deserted; and the nitrates remain spurned by a world which has turned to synthetic fertilizers. Even the palaces of the *salitreros* are giving way to the developer. Psychologically, however, the nation vividly savors its earlier triumphs. And thus on the days of glory—the anniversaries of Iquique, Tarapacá, and Concepción—Chileans collectively reaffirm their belief in their nation's worth. Each celebration of an epic battle evokes the happy memories when Chile was worth dying for; when the nation dominated the seas; when it reigned triumphant over its neighbors; when it had won the War of the Pacific.

Appendix: Tables

In order to compare imports and exports more effectively during this period, it was necessary to establish a baseline. Obviously, prewar Chile did not compare in area or population with post-1881 Chile. "Old Chile," the nation as of 1 January 1879, did not include the populated provinces of Antofagasta or Tarapacá, which were annexed; Tacna and Arica, which were occupied; or that portion of Peru which the Chileans remained until early 1884. "New Chile," at its zenith, extended from Punta Arenas to Peru. Thus, unless the import-export figures were adjusted to reflect this change, they would appear skewed.

To make the comparison more accurate two formulas were developed:

Imports = gross imports minus the material entering the nation through New Chile.

Exports = gross exports + the material entering New Chile via the coastal traffic.

Unfortunately, certain problems might arise using this method. Imports entering Iquique, for example, might have been transhipped to the Central Valley. Similarly, material might be exported from one southern port to Valparaíso and from Valparaíso to a foreign nation. In the first case, there would be double counting; in the second, a failure to include every export leaving the nation.

In order to minimize the double counting of exports, I tended to use only the figures for Valparaíso which, if one excluded exports of ore or *salitre*, dominated the export sector. Shipments from other ports were included if they originated from an area which was known to possess the capacity to fabricate the items. Coquimbo, for example, lacked an industrial base. It did, however, possess a brewery and hence its exports were considered to have been fabricated locally and were not dismissed as having been imported from Valparaíso and then shipped abroad.

Similarly, imports could have arrived in a port in New Chile and then have been shipped to the south. Statistics indicate that most of the material reaching Chile entered the nation through Valparaíso. Thus, the amount of material which filtered down from the new territories must have been neglible.

Table 1
Harvests According to Crops
1877 = 100 (in lit.)

Crop	1878	1879	1880	1881	1882	1883
Trigo blanco (wheat, white)	90.42	121.91	132.23	115.68	154.35	131.47
Trigo amarillo (wheat, yellow)	95.63	89.07	112.40	113.14	95.48	112.10
Cebada (barley)	192.91	130.10	124.03	127.39	176.10	151.90
Maíz (corn)	174.17	99.40	166.76	179.70	198.60	167.60
Frejoles (beans)	153.23	180.56	193.18	184.75	179.55	131.31
Garbanzos	128.86	125.31	181.10	265.47	237.37	172.18
Arvejas (green beans)	112.61	251.42	278.80	233.02	210.39	176.55
Papas (potatoes)	119.82	184.71	178.19	174.52	164.75	143.54

Source: *Estadística Agrícola*, 1876–1880; *Anuario Estadística*, 1876–1884.

Note: The figures for 1881 are incomplete. The provincial officials of Concepción failed to provide Santiago with the agricultural statistics for that year. The government therefore simply used the figures for the 1880 harvest for 1881. Obviously this action distorted the statistical run. From 1876 to 1882, the cultivation of major crops in Concepción constituted approximately 7% of all the land sown in Chile. Thus, even if Concepción had not produced any agricultural products in 1881, the amount of land down would still not be substantially lower than the preceding year. Conversely, it is more likely that Concepción produced at the same levels as the rest of Chile.

Appendix

Table 2
Annual Rainfall in Chile 1874-1883
(in millimeters)

	Serena	Valparaíso	Santiago	Talca	Concepción	Valdivia
1874	128	424	263.6	831.2		2285
1875	94	301	238.9	575.5		2228
1876	93	329	202.7	658.1		2694
1877	190.5	847	650.4	1064.5		2572
1878	70	510	401.1	667	1347.1	3054
1879	125.5	322	165.5	553.5	1102.5	3132
1880	366	915	652.7	1265.9	1715.3	
1881	235.5	398	441	714.5	1283.3	
1882	79	436	303.5	607.2	1240.9	
1883	194	581	365	566.1	1130.2	

Source: *Sinopsis Estadística de la República de Chile* (1919), p. 3.

Table 3
Percentage of Land Devoted to the Cultivation of Specific Crops

Crop	1876	1877	1878	1879	1880	1881	1882	1883
Trigo blanco (Wheat, white)	64.45	61.11	59.20	59.82	60.36	60.35	60.06	61.42
Trigo amarillo (Wheat, yellow)	8.90	7.65	9.11	11.50	10.89	8.48	10.17	7.45
Maíz (Corn)	6.62	11.41	7.99	4.12	7.17	10.40	10.85	11.22
Papas (Potatoes)	3.88	3.03	3.74	5.40	3.58	3.35	3.29	5.71
Arvejas (Green beans)	2.55	2.04	3.06	2.83	2.82	1.92	2.26	2.52
Garbanzos	3.70	2.94	3.00	2.43	4.03	3.55	2.17	2.66
Frejoles (Beans)	6.5	6.15	7.66	8.16	7.10	6.46	6.03	5.71
Cebada (Barley)	6.70	8.03	8.24	7.00	6.83	7.30	7.79	7.36

Source: *Anuario Estadístico,* 1876-1885; *Estadística Agrícola,* 1876-1880.

Table 4
Amount of Land Devoted to the Cultivation of Nontraditional Crops
1876 = 100

Crop	1877	1878	1879	1880	1881	1882	1883
Cáñamo en semilla (Hemp)	146.57	110.85	185.28	213.07	225.16	247.22	217.32
Centeno (Rye)	215.09	90.27	97.14	94.98	125.45	99.45	71.08
Linaza (Linseed)	151.93	174.92	213.84	237.51	515.13	463.99	319.71
			Livestock Produced				
Animal vacuno (Cattle)	232,125	307,138	267,310	244,050	255,941	288,440	297,857
Ovejuno y cabrío (Sheep, goats)	843,616	865,694	819,365	751,830	821,456	931,703	962,311

Source: *Anuario Estadístico*, 1876–1885; *Estadística Agrícola*, 1876–1880.

Table 5
Production of Spirits (in liters)

Spirit	1878	1879	1880	1881	1882	1883
Chicha	22,647,311	19,486,059	27,154,091	19,998,458	23,013,578	24,372,923
Vino/mosto (Wine/must)	24,701,685	21,796,483	19,454,716	20,509,994	28,659,515	38,780,905
Aguardiente (Spirits)	4,435,382	4,487,795	5,233,071	6,227,904	6,181,751	7,439,032

Source: *Anuario Estadístico*, 1878–1884.

Table 6
Exports of Alcoholic Beverages, 1878–1883

		1878	1879	1880	1881	1882	1883	
Aguardiente (Spirits/brandy)	D	57	66	896	30	32	213	NC
					5,819	8,306	213,545	
					5,849	8,338	13,758	
	L	131,887	34,850	47,825	45,212	14,107	12,836	NC
					820,867	706,376	816,715	
					876,049	720,483	829,557	
Cerveza (Beer)	D	2,346	1,326	3,004	2,798	2,932	1,315	NC
					17,134	40,070	32,966	
					19,932	43,002	34,281	
	L	463,719	160,563	31,050	94,258	146,188	95,290	NC
					1,870,153	2,187,651	2,077,795	
					1,964,411	2,333,839	2,173,085	
Chicha	D	14		16	36	100	50	NC
	L	279,775	16,640	36,767	36,590	19,748	26,860	
					627,946	703,521	1,011,774	
					664,536	723,269	1,038,634	
Vino (white)	D	306	152	101	221	278	114	NC
					3,258	7,893	4,735	
					3,479	8,171	4,849	
	L	5,933	5,285	4,360	18,144	896	11,201	NC
					39,000	330,430	92,941	
					57,144	330,326	104,142	
Vino (red)	D	2,198	942	1,486	1,821	991	1,693	NC
					7,143	56,797	9,734	
					8,964	57,788	11,427	
	L	350,485	95,759	526,788	256,506	155,485	148,234	NC
					1,541,747	1,960,932	2,305,117	
					1,798,253	2,116,417	2,453,351	

Source: *Estadística Comercial de la República de Chile*, 1878–1883.

D = dozens. L = liters.

Table 7
Imports of Alcoholic Beverages, 1878–1883

		1878	1879	1880	1881	1882	1883	
Aguardiente (Spirits/brandy)	D	27,637	19,897	15,129	27,293 (3,339) 23,954	31,283 (5,362) 25,921	31,504 (5,067) 26,437	NC
	L	23,136	14,809	25,009	75,760 (28,710) 47,050	52,346 (17,302) 35,044	45,127 (26,239) 18,888	NC
Cerveza	D	30,970	22,143	76,691	87,043 (35,532) 51,511	94,350 (38,030) 56,220	120,656 (61,600) 59,056	NC
	L	800	960	3,452	7,596 (944) 6,652	8,152 (2,317) 5,835	4,502 (1,565) 2,937	NC
Chicha								
Vino (white)	D	9,301	6,557	9,627	14,315 (1,813) 12,502	15,909 (2,004) 13,905	20,489 (4,151) 16,338	NC
	L	40,784	24,446	23,550	27,069 (12,345) 14,724	39,552 (2,144) 37,408	72,961 (13,757) 59,204	NC
Vino (red)	D	27,117	13,843	14,734	26,593 (3,468) 23,125	36,772 (4,465) 32,307	38,150 (10,933) 27,217	NC
	L	550,805	305,632	141,173	242,598 (41,221) 201,377	323,057 (48,194) 274,863	348,489 (126,260) 222,229	NC

Source: *Estadística Comercial de la República de Chile, 1878–1883.*

D = dozens. L = liters.

Appendix

Table 8
Land under Cultivation, 1876-1883

Year	Amount of land (in areas)	Percentage variation
1876	—	100.0
1877	61,480,685[a]	103.75
1878	61,388,318	104.4
1879	61,357,307	104.3
1880	65,202,457	111.8
1881	70,693,424[b]	120.2
1882	70,139,875	119.2
1883	69,374,947	117.3

Source: *Estadística Agrícola*, 1876-1880; *Anuario Estadístico*, 1876-1884.

[a]The figures for *centeno* seen extremely high for 1877. Although these figures may be inaccurate because of a mistake in printing, they have, nonetheless, been used.

[b]These figures reflect the duplication of the statistical error already explained in table 1. Henceforth, all tables will include the questionable data for 1881.

Table 9
Amount of Land Cultivated According to Crop
(1876 = 100)

Crop	1877	1878	1879	1880	1881	1882	1883
Trigo blanco (Wheat, white)	99.62	96.36	97.34	104.37	112.95	110.20	112.99
Trigo amarillo (Wheat, yellow)	90.29	107.33	135.44	136.33	115.04	135.11	99.27
Cebada (Barley)	123.41	128.99	109.25	113.64	131.64	137.60	130.24
Maíz (Corn)	176.84	126.63	65.25	120.60	181.94	189.73	200.93
Garbanzos	83.50	85.05	287.18	121.26	115.98	69.49	273.04
Arvejas (Green beans)	84.13	125.74	116.46	123.06	90.95	104.71	117.23
Papas (Potatoes)	82.13	101.30	146.00	103.00	104.54	100.30	93.14
Frejoles (Beans)	98.84	123.11	131.00	121.13	119.44	109.14	103.61
Lentejas (Lentils)	53.31	100.13	158.35	51.90	90.75	65.08	84.96

Source: *Estadística Agrícola*, 1876-1880; *Anuario Estadístico*, 1876-1885.

Table 10
Price of Copper on the London Market
(£ per ton)

	1879	1880	1881	1882	1883	1884
Jan	57^{10}-58	$66^{10\text{-}15}$	61^{15}-62	$70^{1/4\text{-}1/2}$	$65^{1/2}$	57^5
Feb	56-^{10}	72-^{10}	6^{15}-62	$65^{1/2\text{-}3/4}$	$64^{3/4}$65	56^5
March	54^{10}-55	68^{10}-69	$60^{10\text{-}15}$	$63^{1/2}$-4	65-1/2	55
April	57^{10}-58	$64^{5\text{-}10}$	$61^{\text{-}5}$	$64^{7\text{-}15}$	$64^{2\text{-}10}$	54^7
May	56	60^{10}	$58^{\text{-}15}$	$64^{1/4\text{-}1/2}$	$61^{3/4}$-$62^{1/4}$	57^{10}-58
June	$55^{5\text{-}10}$	$56^{\text{-}5}$	$59^{\text{-}10}$	$68^{10\text{-}175}$	$63^{3/4}$-64	
July	55-^{15}	60-^{10}	$58^{10\text{-}15}$	$67^{10\text{-}15}$	63^{7}-63^{10}	
Aug	53^{55}	$61^{10\text{-}15}$	59-	$67^{10\text{-}15}$	$63^{1/2}$-64	
Sept	55^{10}-56	60-61	$59^{5\text{-}15}$	68^5	$63^{3/4}$64	
Oct	$63^{\text{-}05}$	$60^{\text{-}5}$	$62^{\text{-}5}$	70^{15}-71^5	$62^{7/8}$-62	
Nov	66^{10}-66	$61^{10\text{-}15}$	63^{10}	68^{10}-69	$61^{1/4\text{-}1/2}$	
Dec	$65^{0\text{-}15}$	61^5	$67^{5\text{-}10}$	$66^{1/2}$	59^{10}	

Source: *The Economist* (London).

Price of Silver on the London Market
(in pence per ounce)

1878	52 9/16
1879	51 1/4
1880	52 1/4
1881	51 11/16
1882	51 5/8
1883	50 9/16
1884	50 5/8

Source: *Resumen de la Hacienda Pública desde 1833 hasta 1900*, pp. 33–35.

Table 11
Ore Produced in Chile

	GOLD		GOLD & COPPER	SILVER		SILVER & COPPER	SILVER & LEAD	COPPER		COAL
	Mined[2]	Minted[4]	Mined[2]	Mined[2]	Minted[3]	Mined[2]	Mined[2]	Mined[2]	Minted[2]	Mined[1]
1878	99,800			19,451,900	60,733,180	918,200	3,020,100	283,998,019	38,030,300	408,215,000
1879	209,800	139.46	158.400	18,984,400	56,491,841	1,118,900	5,900	280,383,800	53,917,775	515,939,000
1880	1,022,900	252	72,537	14,325,471	35,360,253	1,040,900	4,569,905	362,156,000	47,337,403	409,978,000
1881	416,701	850	14,416	15,712,804	33,688,492	177,479	GOLD & SILVER	206,661,357	29,046,148	432,488,000
1882	595,512	883	13,100	20,641,881	70,639,626	613,088	21,643	254,406,010	31,830,329	252,497,100*
1883	1,843,690	3,168	179,348	36,565,723	100,719,241	236,176		351,759,174*	588,931,000	
1884	2,170,639	4,904	1,626,593	37,053,963	112,821,718	504,306	16,415	260,173,717	32,042,440	565,299,000

Source: *Anuario Estadística*, 1877–1884.

[1]Metric quintals. [2]Kilos. [3]Grams. [4]Ounces.

*Has to be an error, does not jibe with book.

Note: Because this table incorporates the figures for mines utilizing more than one ore, totals for silver and copper may differ from those in tables 12–15. The metals produced from mixed mines were added to the metals extracted from mines utilizing only one ore. Sometimes the combination of ores produced higher totals than the silver or copper extracted from the mines specializing in only one metal.

Table 12
Copper Ore Produced, 1878-1883
(in kilos)

	1878	1879	1880	1881	1882	1883
Linares			31,000			
Talca		21,600	30,000	35,328	18,400	27,600
Curicó			5,000	30,000		
Santiago	5,225,141	5,299,106	36,265,500			
Valparaíso	2,913,940	4,187,557	1,816,000	12,021,701	4,757,840	1,102,900
Aconcaqua	66,561,664	69,477,759	19,916,564	5,941,024	7,218,654	12,098,712
Coquimbo	155,699,704	140,467,019	212,097,006	70,127,624	144,318,552	212,455,184
Atacama	53,639,520	60,930,683	92,994,943	118,441,980	98,092,563	126,061,438
Totals	284,040,019	280,383,724	362,156,013	206,597,657	254,406,009	351,745,834

Source: *Anuario Estadístico*, 1878-1883.

Note: Does not include mines producing more than one type of ore.

Table 13
Copper Mined: Net Production
(in kilos)

	1878	1879	1880	1881	1882	1883
Linares			2,410			
Talca		4,428	5,400	6,712	2,699	4,416
Curicó			600	3,000		
Santiago	1,112,168	562,587	4,512,659			
Valparaíso	285,815	432,053	159,889	891,340	472,843	92,748
Aconcaqua	8,605,545	8,321,535	2,723,135	855,441	843,893	1,432,795
Coquimbo	18,873,563	36,250,782	29,526,658	11,295,705	16,503,885	27,131,365
Atacama	6,696,909	8,346,390	10,406,642	15,944,755	13,907,636	17,170,495
Totals	35,574,000	53,917,775	47,337,393	28,996,953	31,730,956	45,831,819

Source: *Anuario Estadístico*, 1878-1883.

Appendix

Table 14
Silver Ore Mined
(in kilos)

	1878	1879	1880	1881	1882	1883
Linares						
Talca						
Curicó				1,500		
Santiago		786,068	70,656			
Valparaíso					18,000	
Aconcaqua			947,238	11,233	34,832	647,680
Coquimbo	389,261	847,407	192,760	302,430	183,765	1,142,690
Atacama	19,062,593	17,350,900	13,109,817	15,391,641	20,405,284	34,760,719
Totals	19,451,854	18,984,375	14,320,471	15,706,804	20,641,881	36,551,089

Source: *Anuario Estadístico*, 1878–1883.

Note: Does not include mines producing more than one type of ore.

Table 15
Silver Mined in Chile: Net Production
(in grams)

	1878 1879	1880	1881	1882	1883	
Linares						
Talca						
Curicó				1,800		
Santiago		1,125,502	156,621			
Valparaíso			1,049,164	495,500	79,496	
Aconcaqua						
Coquimbo	1,477,491	2,080,748	1,258,659	1,900,122	2,648,768	6,310,549
Atacama	56,986,636	49,660,002	23,852,545	30,349,703	67,025,866	91,018,022
Totals	58,464,127	52,866,252	26,316,989	32,747,125	69,754,130	97,328,571

Source: *Anuario Estadístico*, 1878–1883.

Table 16
Smelters in Chile, 1878-1883

	Number	Workers	Ore Smelted[1]	Gold[2]	Silver[3]	Copper: Barra[1]	Ejes
1878	61	3,048	472,531,077	365	18,807,181	103,169,813	27,955,560
1879	44	2,434	213,523,877	266.52	2,000,280	47,245,722	39,129,637
1880	51	2,464	203,706,387	135	7,752,669	23,088,789	13,628,229
1881	45	2,752	168,718,237	100	17,566,841	33,418,110	10,600,673
1882	41	2,592	121,249,676	178	7,258,331	25,923,454	4,169,222
1883	35	2,536	303,520,117	160	19,700.000	30,482,972	19,610,834

[1]Kilos. [2]Ounces. [3]Grams.

Source: *Anuario Estadístico*, 1878-1883.

Note: Does not include Atacama Province.

Appendix

Table 17
Imports Related to Metallurgical Industries, 1874-1883
(in kilos)

	1874	1875	1876	1877	1878	1879	1880	1881	1882	1883
Acero en barra						133,593	420,572	269,923	326,933	255,007
Acero surtido	249,097	195,941	354,533	316,186	107,641	16,022	40,128	17,811	58,212	30,780
Agua fuerte	38,617	69,079	63,812	55,853	65,884	36,833	55,748	94,638	120,093	143,716
Albayalde	22,777	28,833	37,041	16,900	5,259	13,220	8,769	12,203	23,211	12,560
Azogue	47,185	123,474	38,141	34,471	14,855	40,373	46,444	11,025	66,929	38,561
Azufre	80,616	30,092	91,878	116,905	302,599	276,423	226,210	538,887	1,392,333	955,181
Cobre en planchas	18,122	14,521	13,018	7,306	6,342	7,884	11,778	20,562	45,040	29,034
Hierro surtido	5,336,859	4,586,740	4,388,950	4,808,849	1,734,249	5,626,889	5,785,891			
Hierro en planchas	1,602,046	420,133	621,405	966,238	286,065	865,838	1,509,787	2,898,936	2,301,749	2,975,399
Hierro galvanizado	1,273,388	1,006,775	2,013,239	1,047,816	1,006,970	1,212,704	1,969,651	2,070,182	2,798,187	4,104,050
Hierro en barra					1,734,249	3,437,171	5,469,942	6,736,551	8,176,066	9,166,488
Zinc en planchas	248,865	287,843	368,982	278,450	125,992	114,719	811,600	170,753	200,954	270,865
Zinc en barra						1,020		262	1,857	7,482

Source: *Anuario Estadístico*, 1878-1883.

Acero en barra = steel ingots. Acero surtido = assorted steel. Agua fuerte = nitric acid. Albayalde = lead. Azogue = mercury. Azufre = sulphur. Cobre en planchas = copper plate. Hierro surtido = assorted iron. Hierro en planches = iron plate. Hierro galvanizado = galvanized iron. Hierro en barra = iron ingots. Zinc en planchas = zinc plate. Zinc en barra = zinc ingots.

Table 18
Commercial Institutions, 1875–1884

	1875	1876	1877	1878	1879	1880*	1881	1882	1883	1884
Caldererías i Cerrajerías (Boilermakers & forges)	33	31	32	43	33	39	40	49	48	53
Cigarrerías (Cigar shops)	252	256	245	224	190	169	191	215	205	219
Colchonerías (Matress makers)	16	18	17	11	9	11	11	8	10	12
Curtidurías o tenerías (Tanneries)	100	107	179	101	100	97	120	115	114	102
Doradores i galvanizadores (Gilders & galvanizers)	7	8	7	8	6	5	6	8	9	10
Dulcerías (Confectioners)	39	45	48	53	47	41	51	57	58	61
Herrerías (Blacksmiths/ironworks)	177	168	170	170	164	161	203	204	212	231
Hojalaterías (Tinsmiths)	66	55	62	55	47	37	58	81	58	82
Imprentas litográficas (Lithographers)	5	6	5	2	7	4	5	7	3	7
Imprentas tipográficas (Typographers)	61	64	58	78	77	69	77	78	81	93
Molinos (Mills)	534	596	575	553	585	597	625	621	642	656
Mueblerías (Furniture stores)	28	34	28	27	25	21	23	30	34	35
Mueblerías con taller (Furniture makers)		7	10	6	2	4	6	5	6	7
Sasterías (Tailors)	154	137	129	134	97	103	126	142	144	152
Sombrerías (Milliners)	23	19	23	23	18	19	24	23	21	48
Talleres de constructores de edificios (Constructors)		8	7	4	3	2	4		1	3
Talabarterías (Saddleries)	44	44	38	38	35	33	41	45	44	48
Tornerías (Machine shops)	3	3		7	2	13	2	6	5	4
Zapaterías (Shoemakers)	249	255	227	239	257	208	276	309	333	345

Source: *Anuario Estadístico*, 1878–1883.

*Does not include the *departmento* of Rancagua.

Table 19
Factories in Chile, 1875–1884

	1875	1876	1877	1878	1879	1880*	1881	1882	1883	1884
Aciete (Oil)	10	9	7	11	11	9	9	9	11	10
Almídon (Starch)	82	66	46	48	55	45	51	64	68	51
Aserrar por vapor con taller de carpintería (Lumbermills)	6	8	6	7	10	8	8	11	16	13
Cal (Lime)	3			4			5	6		
Calzado (Shoes)					1					
Carretas y Carretones (Carts)	30	29	38	30	23	20	26	31	36	38
Carruajes (Carriages)	16	17	16	15	19	14	12	13	16	16
Cerveza (Beer)	82	82	70	77	71	72	73	80	96	104
Chocolate	1	1		2	2	2	2	2	2	3
Destilacion de aguardiente	42	44	49	33	28	32	35	62	57	51
Fideos (Noodles)	10	11	10	10	10	8	9	10	9	9
Gas	2		1				2	8		3
Jabón (Soap)	1	4			2	4	1	14	18	17
Jarcía (Cordage)										
Ladrillos (Bricks)	2	6		1		1				
Limonada (Lemonade)			1	2	2	1			2	1
Papel (Paper)		1					1			
Pódvora (Powdermill)										
Sacos a máquina (Sacks)	2	4	4	3	3	3	2	3	2	1
Tejas i labrillos (Tiles)	397	343	270	302	275	456	302	299	314	310
Velas i jabon reunidas (Candles & soap)	39	34	38	38	37	37	41	41	39	42
Velas para buques (Ships' candles)	3	1	2	2	2	2	2	2	3	3
Valas (Candles)					2		3			
Alumbrado (Lighting oil)				1	3					1
Acido sulfurico (Sulfuric acid)										1
Pianos										1

Source: *Anuario Estadístico*, 1878–1883.

*Does not include the *departmento* of Rancagua.

Table 20
Imports of Raw Materials Related to Chilean Domestic Industries

		1874	1875	1876	1877	1878	1879	1880	1881	1882	1883
Cloth											
Alumbre	K	28,213	6,686	44,563	43,109	20,341	10,279	33,164	39,196	46,954	36,363
Añil de C. Am.	K				12	8,111	11,195	11,930	7,487	12,361	9,530
Añil de Prussia	K	199,637	144,447	141,733	129,605	111,908	83,730	201,730	141,490	158,053	287,446
Azufre	K	80,616	30,092	91,878	116,905	302,599	276,423	226,210	538,887	1,392,333	955,181
Cochinilla	K	3,173	2,253	2,857	1,519	1,244	981	2,144	2,181	3,082	1,984
Palos de tinte	K							15,065	24,800	25,031	19,725
Sulfato de cobre	K	100,052	106,500	201,680	79,417	130,971	91,613	204,016	364,995	110,012	157,045
Chocolate											
Cacao	K	112,515	133,897	97,699	94,014	56,425	80,419	98,555	74,270	96,443	61,394
Shoes											
Betún	D	92,143	79,796	95,113	63,677	25,712	11,864	106,469	118,912	101,738	104,853
	K						44,681				
Cueros									11,802	8,832	7,545
Suelas		339	11	58	8	10	15	168	60		
Paper											
Alumbre		see above									
Resina	K	268,541	448,740	463,844	158,879	302,644	480,059	529,754	617,990	495,665	883,804
Soda Cáustica	K	627,895	1,093,136	481,865	1,047,816	657,027	750,455	922,595	563,664	799,741	703,407

Appendix

Table 20 *(continued)*

		1874	1875	1876	1877	1878	1879	1880	1881	1882	1883
Sacks/Rigging											
Cáñamo	K	44,210	22,687	59,373			16,092	4,852	159,018	114,486	92,594
Hilo de Cor. de Cáñamo	K	62,056	38,544	39,691	35,009	38,340	57,926	44,052	66,972	89,078	84,797
Jarcia de Cáñamo	M	263,126	210,864	258,150	210,900	102,352	89,121	144,648	172,170	182,917	159,708
Jénero para Sacos	M					1,194,722	1,461,586	2,132,247	3,597,198	2,407,283	2,571,848
	K								3,069		321,997
Soap and Candles											
Cera	K	98	321	3,048	3,356						50
Esperma de pasta	K	468	313	620	499	207	828	140	818	528	521
Potasa para Jabon	K	104,817	8,959	17,627	908	700	1,835	1,565	20,908	83,012	
Pulpo de Coco	K		456,300	287,747	1,726,689	412,775	165,304	1,044,367	595,021	673,443	1,261,468
Sebo	K	2,665,300	3,076,639	1,837,055	1,320,268	2,898,877	1,138,842	222,569	1,273,969	2,213,438	2,082,204
Aqua fuerte	K	38,617	69,079	63,812	55,853	65,884	36,833	55,748	94,638	120,093	143,726

Source: *Anuario Estadístico*, 1878–1883.

K = kilos. D = docenas. M = meters.

Alumbre = alum. Añil de Cen. Am. = dye (central America). Añil de Prussia = dye (Prussia). Azufre = sulphur. Conchinilla = conchineal. Palos de tinte = dye. Sulfato de cobre = copper sulphate. Betún = shoe blacking. Cueros = hides. Suetas = soles. Resina = resin. Soda cáustica = caustic soda. Cáñamo = jute. Hilo de Cor. de Cáñamo = jute cord. Jarcia de Cáñamo = raw jute. Jénero para sacos = sacking. Cera = wax. Esperma de pasta = sperm paste. Potasa para Jabon = potash. Pulpo de Coco = copra. Sebo = tallow. Agua fuerte = nitric acid.

Table 21
Machinery Imported, 1875-1884

Industries		1875	1876	1877	1878	1879	1880	1881	1882	1883	1884
Textiles											
To make textiles	B	186		4	1				51	81	38
For "Tejidos de Lana de Tomé and Santiago"	B						24	25		28	
For Tomé textile mill	B						57			106	
Shoes											
To press soles			2	2	10		1				
To make shoes			3			3	1				
Metal											
To twist iron				11	2				4	3	9	20
To refine metals		315	3	2			7				
To grind metals		2	5	3	3	2	7	8	6	14	9
To cut iron		7	7				7	5	4	11	38
To extract minerals							1				
To bore iron		30	2	12	2		11	1	8	23	39
To shape iron		15					5				
To make screws		4	1								
Sugar											
To refine sugar	B	282	907	225	28		17		3		
Paper											
To rule paper			3		1		1			2	2
For paper factory	B	1	182	41				92	15	23	
Miscellaneous industries											
To make noodles					1	2		2			
To make matches		1									
To make moldings		4	2								
For distilling		6	1								
To make bread		1	12	1	1						
To make candles		2									
To make oil		2	2								
To make bricks		1	2								
To make hemp		2	1								
To make beer		2	4								
To make mineral water							1		1		

Source: *Estadística Comercial*, 1875-1884.

B = bultos.

Appendix

Table 22
Chile's Manufactured Exports

		1874	1875	1876	1877	1878	1879	1880	1881	1882	1883	
Aciete para lámparas (oil for lamps)	L	1,136,703	74,795	194,044	389,273	207,276	86,614	8,160	8,294	2,180	6,802	NC
									64,564	56,197	345,436	
									72,858	58,277	352,238	
Alquitrán (tar)	K		3,266	6,904	4,228	5,000	3,086	3,981	3,214	3,774	2,000	NC
									6,096	3,144	5,401	
									9,310	6,918	7,401	
Artículos navales (naval stores)	B		16	61	58	34	8		0	4	4,237	NC
									51	1	2	
									51	5	4,239	
Calzado surtido (assorted shoes)	D	1,120	1,039	1,238	1,154	907	360	153	225	167	1,803	NC
									14,561	19,231	19,846	
									14,786	19,398	21,649	
Canastos surtidos (assorted baskets)		36	26	148	19	73	12		22	400	20	NC
									3,316	8,178	4,864	
									3,338	8,578	4,884	
Carretas i carretones (carts)		29	46	59	3	27	13	3				
Chocolate	K		4,011	7,220	7,730	5,140	340	50	80	100	16,278	NC
								1,626	14,769	20,025	16,278	
								1,676	14,849	20,125		
Colchones (mattresses)		344	440	540	311	191	56		50		30	NC
									755	1,909	2,181	
									806	1,909	2,211	

Table 22 (continued)

		1874	1875	1876	1877	1878	1879	1880	1881	1882	1883	
Cuadros a pincel (canvas)		6	23	4	54	29	15	6	9 118 127	13 50 63	11 98 109	NC
Dulces (candies)	K	3,204	3,794	4,309	2,267	2,802	935	2,470	1,200 4,550 5,750	972 13,047 14,019	4,689 29,572 34,261	NC
Escobas (brooms)	D D	1,229	500	1,936	623	314	235	514	284 1,704 1,988	291 910 1,201	525 1,564 2,089	NC
Esteras chicas (hats)	D	20,889	6,098	3,169	1,666	586	5,878	6,579	4,043 3,579 7,622	3,452 3,452	1,991 1,911	NC
Fideos (noodles)	K	533,075	577,397	368,876	454,594	525,366	307,873	246,296	440,104 126,092 566,196	338,352 206,395 544,747	372,562 238,778 611,340	NC
Fósforos (matches)	G			103	312				58 46,648 46,706	15,410 15,410	26,540 26,540	NC
Frutas en conserva (brandied fruits)	D B			3	5	22		321	584 434 1,018	122 90 212	74 160[1] 234	NC
Hilos i cordeles de cáñamo (burlap cord and thread)	K	45,637	29,780	28,033	27,649	28,434	5,863	3,255	5,817 45,161 50,978	5,481 49,629 55,110	39,186 39,186	NC

Appendix 251

Table 22 *(continued)*

		1874	1875	1876	1877	1878	1879	1880	1881	1882	1883	
Jabon Comun (soap)	K	61,549	82,148	102,219	110,020	116,949	25,710	13,966	100,640	275,962	78,295	NC
										168,774	363,085	
									100,640	444,736	441,385	
Jabon de olor (perfumed soap)	D							50	6,711	2,638	1,471[2]	NC
									6,711	2,638		
Jarabes (syrups)	D	164	262	154	291	91	25	27	468	26	372	NC
	D								468	230		
										256		
Jarcia (rigging)	K	34,013	22,934	21,075	16,615	18,034	5,228	8,959	6,050	11,785	5,847[3]	NC
									8,506	11,785	19,526	
									14,556		25,373	
Ladrillos a fuego (fire bricks)		158,000	76,859	23,350	87,890	35,740	24,700	3,956	28,620	25,330	11,200	NC
									850,000	646,000	138,000	
									878,620	671,330	149,200	
Libros en blanco (note books)	B	5	29	6	10	18	3		10	1	6	NC
									101	133	80	
									111	134	86	
Libros impresos (books)	B	64	111	108	44	31	33	17	57	43	50	NC
									55	187	85	
									112	230	135	
Limonada (lemonade)	D	956	1,140	2,153	1,335	940	256	3	796	24	25	NC
									796	24	232	
											257	

Table 22 *(continued)*

		1874	1875	1876	1877	1878	1879	1880	1881	1882	1883	
Loza (china)	B	24	66	25	21	14			4 647 651	713 713	1,108 1,108	NC
Mantas (blankets)			49	66	56	171	28		1,377 1,377	1,161 2,967 4,128	81 7,583 7,664	NC
Muebles (furniture)	B	272	271	96	232	99	39	64	28 486 514	547 547	14 504 518	NC
Pellones (saddle blankets)		5,150	4,496	5,907	5,736	7,242	7,652	10,286	7,733 47 7,780	7,637 176 7,813	6,906 950 7,856	NC
Plumeros (feather dusters)	D	52	80	45	81	85	18		161 161	121 121	26 162 162	NC
Ropa hecha (clothing)	B	25	52	18	11	7	2	5	5 597 602	41 777 818	3,720 718 4,438	NC
Sacos vacios (sacks)			1,250	16,600	10,848	1,151		29,355	40,031 872,726 912,757	24,487 1,450,715 1,475,202	41,870 577,533 2,619,403	NC
Sillas de montar (riding saddles)		12	10	15	40	13	3	4	56 56	6 71 77	2 214 216	NC

Appendix

Table 22 *(continued)*

		1874	1875	1876	1877	1878	1879	1880	1881	1882	1883
Velas para buques (ships candles)		109	50	40	54	87	39	13	7	55	37 89 NC 126
Velas de sebo (tallow candles)	K	6,070	6,280	8,776	6,995	5,653	3,624		8,346 8,346	5,981 5,981	92 5,383 NC 5,475
Velas de esterina y composición (fine candles)									120,468	123,282	122,570

Source: *Estadística Comercial de la República de Chile*, 1878–1883.

¹Plus 45 cajones.   ²Expressed in kilos.   ³Plus 15,590 meters.

L = liters. K = kilos. B = bultos. G = gruesas. D = docenas. R = resmas. NC = New Chile.

Note: See appendix for explanation.

Table 23
Imports of Consumer Goods (Adjusted), 1874-1883

		1874	1875	1876	1877	1878	1879	1880	1881	1882	1883
Calzado	D	34,545	37,381	40,847	24,619	22,063	14,726	8,097	11,661	11,950	13,014
Chocolate	K	11,596	6,939	7,705	6,806	6,919	5,717	1,999	5,010	12,189	26,143
Dulces confitados	K	88,159	77,297	55,253	47,651	41,904	25,762	41,270	44,364	63,459	66,701
Dulces en almibar	K	9,317	9,128	24,114	23,385	14,058	30,678	77,704	90,864	122,208	96,641
Fosforos	B	5,763	5,340	6,114	5,192	3,561	2,394	4,184	5,646	5,489	4,984
Frutas en conserva	K	13,004	17,154	10,162	10,200	7,009	702	4,722	4,730	11,239	8,122
Hilos de cáñamo	K	62,056	38,544	39,691	35,009	38,340	57,926	40,436	66,977	89,078	84,797
Jabon de olor	K	20,075	23,084	30,875	12,092	11,116	21,279	32,326	36,670	44,593	35,924
Jabon de olor	D	15,960	15,295	11,878	12,132	10,815	1,473	1,594	1,110	367	
Jabon comun	K	107,000	61,595	51,066	44,936	13,944	19,066	47,085	79,379	213,359	281,834
Jarabes		2,915	2,669	2,561	2,125	585	185	145	403	74	116
Jarcia en cáñamo	K	263,126	210,864	258,150	210,900	102,352	89,121	127,620	172,170	182,917	159,708
Mantas		29,705	26,614	20,969	17,166	9,988	13,023	5,508	21,043	70,489	53,584
	K										21,247
Muebles	B	3,910	3,048	2,908	1,944	1,236	767	702	1,695	2,684	2,125
Papel de imprenta	K					327,719	415,943	824,327	819,541	718,457	615,106
Paños	M	127,759	104,404	111,092	75,697	39,659	62,174	85,571	119,610	142,292	101,498
Ropa hecha	B	2,602	2,187	2,004	1,899	1,334	1,179	1,378	1,756	2,057	1,668

Appendix

Table 23 *(continued)*

		1874	1875	1876	1877	1878	1879	1880	1881	1882	1883
Sacos		2,580,503	3,753,213	1,778,427	1,462,935	1,569,671	3,370,930	5,075,710	4,716,859	4,110,437	4,999,130
Sillas de montar		1,333	958	557	657	442	280	192	412	667	664
Sombreros											
de varias clases	D	59,293	50,962	54,241	55,253	59,856	32,905	66,068	92,334	53,535	55,957
de pelo y felpa		6,844	5,370	5,372	3,937	2,369	1,150	3,089	2,421	3,290	2,064
surtidas para mujeres	D	28,097	23,462	13,160	30,887	10,403	10,987	13,009	19,185	16,106	14,401
de petate	K					8,852	7,040	13,854	20,703	13,885	6,056
											2,786
de paja	D					23,902	8,876	23,345	31,995	36,454	17,850
	K										11,951
Velas de cera	K	38	35	89	61				375		
Velas de esperma	K	725,003	676,126	733,786	873,235	733,464	588,696	581,316	1,120,850	1,158,553	1,411,558

Source: *Estadística Comercial de la República de Chile*, 1875-1884.

Note: Imports take into account goods arriving in ports of New Chile.

D = docenas. K = kilos. B = bultos. M = metros.

Calzado = shoes. Chocolate = chocolate. Dulces confitados = candied sweets. Dulces en Almibar = sweets in syrup. Fósforos = matches. Frutas en conserva = preserved fruit. Hilos de cáñamo = jute cord. Jabon de olor = perfumed soap. Jabón comun = soap. Jarabes = syrups. Jarcia en cáñamo = rigging. Mantas = blankets. Muebles = furniture. Papel de imprenta = paper for printing. Panos = cloth. Ropa hecha = ready-made clothing. Sacos = sacks. Sillas de montar = saddles. Sombreros de varias clases = various types of hats. Sombreros de pelo y felpa = felt hats. Sombreros surtidas para mujeres = hats for women. Sombreros de petate = Panama hats. Sombreros de paja = straw hats. Velas de cera = wax candles. Velas de esperma = sperm candles.

Table 24
Surcharge on Paper Pesos

	Jan.	Feb.	Mar.	Apr.	May	June	July	Aug.	Sept.	Oct.	Nov.	Dec.
1880	4.10	4.10	5.55	10.43	18.75	17.83	21.28	31.03	43.39	46.15	31.03	32.62
1881	28.81	28.81	28.81	28.81	36.93	38.63	32.82	27.20	19.12	14.94	14.86	10.96
1882	7.04	5.97	7.31	8.18	8.18	10.04	9.65	7.92	8.28	7.29	5.80	4.32
1883	4.10	6.37	7.42	8.38	10.79	11.09	8.66	7.23	7.31	6.67	7.16	9.00
1884	35.41	11.67	14.24	18.75	24.74	19.06	20.24	20.54	21.33	20.71	24.75	28.04

Source: Santelices, *Los bancos chilenos* (Santiago: Imprenta Barcelona, 1893), p. 250.

Table 25
Corporations Founded in Chile, 1879–1883

	Trans.	Bank	Min. & Smelt.	Agri.	Comm.	Indus.	Insur.	Rec.	Other	Capital Invested ($)	Total Failed	Total Founded
1879											3	0
1880	1		3		1					1,422,000	0	5
1881		1	4	1		1				1,534,140	1	8
1882	2	1	10		2	2	2	1	1	6,209,850	1	22
1883		1	6			2				980,000	2	9

Source: *Diario Oficial*, 1879–1884

Table 26
Stock Market Prices, 1879–1883

	1/79	3	6	9	12	3/80	6	9	12	3/81	6	9	12	3/82	6	9	12	3/83	6	9	12
Banks																					
Nacional	60	50	46	85	91.50	125	133.50	170	S	175	194	179	187	182.50	194	185.75	187	169	181.50	172.50	165.50
Consolidado	60	50	46	100																	
Valparaíso	50	S	47	97	90.50	110	123	140	143.50	135	143	150	158	154	162.50	158.50	157	141	142	138.25	137.50
Agrícola	66	60	59	92	90.50	113	110	112	114	112.50	132	127	136	129	138.50	134.50	138	128.50	131	124	126
La Unión	50	S	43	70	S	S	72	70	S	S	75	S	73	67	70	S	S	65	70	S	S
Mobiliario	50	S	43	70	85	94	96	90	110	S	150	S	S	S	S	S	S	S	S	S	S
Railroads																					
Copiapó	59	S	S	65	70	85	86	80	85	S	S	100	85	S	83	84	87	85	90	S	95
Carrizal	44	S	S	57	75	85	S	90	98	106	107	105	103	100	102	101	104	108	S	S	S
Coquimbo	30	26	28	30	35	50	47	40	48	50	65	50	S	49	55	57	54	65	S		70
Cerro Blanco	30	S	36	57	78	85	86	90	96	105	120	105	100	S	104	101	104				
Tongoi	20	S	22	25	37	51	65	60	63	66	68	55	35	S	40	39	37	S	34	S	
Urbano de Sgto.	50	45	S	50	69	77	105	110	113	123	157	152	157	166	182	179	177	168	171	197.50	203
Urbano de Valparaíso	118	110	120	128	144	165	148	155	160	185	190	194	205	S	220	218	220	224	240	246	236
Miscellaneous																					
Madera y Buques	40	38	S	85	88		95		99	105	S	112	115	122	111	118	115	S	120	112.50	113.50
Sud Americana	82	S	S	95	108	124	130	148	145	146	194	165	176	166	151.25	136	122	109	119	118	117.50
Remolcadores	25	22	26	50	45	125	130	150	154	170	190	180	187	15	175	171	160	144	135	130	S
Diques	70	S	S	S	S	110	145	185	S	137	144	185	S	122	116	104	115	112	98	85	88
Chilena de Balleneros						200	250	350	320	340	300	S	S	S	S	S	S	S	S	S	S

Table 26 *(continued)*

	1/79	3	6	9	12	3/80	6	9	12	3/81	6	9	12	3/82	6	9	12	3/83	6	9	12
Miscellaneous																					
Madera y Carbon										85	89	97	96	95	141	145	S	S	S	123	S
Cia de Gas de Sgto.	100	S	104	S	S	110	125	130	134	141	171	158	130	111	115	133	127	122	124	126	132.50
Consumidores de Gas Valparaiso	160	S	S	200	165	185	190	200	250	258	250	260	225	155	150	151	155	160	163	150	155
Beneficiadora de metales	48	52	45	100	75	77	73	99	97	108	116	119	S	121	117.50	114	100	95.50	81	80.50	72
Minas y fundición Chañaral	25	S	25	40	29	43	37	55	50	49	50	35	46.50	26.50	14	14	10	8	3.75	4	4
Telegrafo Transandino	95	90	96	120	109	122	130	150	S	159	160	152	171	174	168	161.50	151	114	110	107	114.50
Insurance*																					
Cia Chilena	150	S	155	200	240	250	297	340	335	340	350	S	S	317	325	330	S	325	320	294	293
America	140	150	160	240	S	255	285	305	315	300	335	325	S	325	335	325	330	S	320	325	285
Unión Chilena	50	48	47	65	80	99	98	95	96	93	96	92	98	102	111	112	119	113	S	110	113

Source: *El Mercurio*, 1879–1883.

*Current pesos. S = same.

Note: Unless otherwise noted, prices are expressed as a percentage of paid in value.

Table 27A

Quotations of Chilean Government Bonds on London Market, 1879-1884

Loan of	%	1879					1880				1881				1882				1883				1884
		1/4	3/1	6/7	9/7	12/6	3/6	6/5	9/4	12/4	3/5	6/4	9/3	12/3	3/4	6/3	9/2	12/2	3/3	6/2	9/1	12/1	3/1
1858	5												81-4	80-3	S	82-5	81-4	80-3	81-4	79-82	83-6	86-9	84-6
1866	7	88-91	83-6	79-82	96-8	97-9	103-5	S	108-10	102-5	106-8	103-5	108-10	106-8	107-9	108-10	106-8	107-9	101-3	104-6	102-4	106-8	100-2
1867	6	79-82	73-6	69-72	68-70	87-9	83-5	85-7	87-9	93-5	97-9	104-6	97-100	101-3	98-100	104-06	102-4	S	101-3	104-6	102-4	106-8	100-2
1870	5	64-7	60-3	60-63	59-61	77-9	72-4	71-3	75-7	81-3	87-9	95-7	89-91	90-2	89-91	94-6	91-3	90-2	88-91	92-4	93-5	96-8	92-4
1873	5	65-8	61-4	57-9	57-9	70-2	68-70	74-6	77-9	86-8	91-3	88-90	S	S	87-90	92-4	90-2	88-91	91-3	S	S	94-6	92-4
1875	5	65-8	61-4	57-9	57-9	74-6	70-2	74-6	77-9	86-8	91-3	88-90	88-90	S	87-90	92-4	90-4	88-91	91-3	S	S	94-6	92-4

Source: *The Economist* (London), 1879–1884.

Table 27B
Price of Chilean Bonds, 1879–1883

	%	3/15	1879 6/8	9/7	1/4	3/12	1880 6/6	9/1	12/12	3/1	1881 6/12
Internal debt	3	25	24.50*	37*	34.50*	36.50*	38	50	49	48	S
1865 loan	8	76	67.50*	93.50*	S	101.50*	99	107	105	108	106
1877 loan	8	66	67.50*	91.50*			99.50	109	105	110	108.50
1882	8										
FF. CC. Sur	6	62	62.50*	81*	74	78	86	100.50	99	98	100
San Fernando-Curicó	6	52	52.50*	77.50*	71	77	79	100	99	98	100
LLaiLLai-San Felipe	6	47	52.50*	77.50*	71	77	81	98	99	97	100
Santiago-Quillota	6	63	62.50*	81*	74	78	86	100	99	98	100
Muncipalidad Santiago	8	66	69*	97*	93	94	97.50	106	103	107	107.50
Muncipalidad Valparaíso	7						95	102	S	103	106
Banco Mobilario	7						92	96	S	S	106
Garantizador de Valores	8	79	86.50	99.50*	98.50*	100.50*	104	103	105	102.50	105
Garantizador de Valores	8	76	79*	94.50*	95.50*	S					
Caja Hipotecaría	8	83	89.50*	100.50*	99.50*	101.50*	105	103	105	102.50	105
Caja Hipotecaría	7	76	79*	96.50*	95.50*	96	99.50	102	104	102.50	104
Caja Hipotecaría	5	60	59*	72.50*	74	80	82.25	93	92.50	92.25	89
Caja Hipotecaría	6										

Appendix

Table 27B (*continued*)

	%	1881		1882				1883			
		9/8	12/12	3/22	6/2	9/5	12/28	3/11	6/10	9/2	12/25
Internal debt	3	49	S	50	S	50.50	S	49	46	45	45.25
1865 loan	8	105	103	104	101.50	102.50	101.50	S			
1877 loan	8	103	104.50	104	S	S	S				
1882	8							100.50	95	91	91.50
FF. CC. Sur	6	S	101								
San Fernando-Curicó	6	99	98	100	103.25	101.75	100.25	97	S	92.75	93.25
LLaiLLai-San Felipe	6	97	98	99	102.50	100.75	102.25	100	96	92.25	S
Santiago-Quillota	6	97.50	98	99	102.50	101.25	102.75	100	96.50	91.50	92.25
Muncipalidad Santiago	8	108	105	110	110.50	111	108	S	105	106.50	105.50
Muncipalidad Valparaíso	7	S	S	S	103	104	108				
Banco Mobilario	7	S	S	100	S						
Garantizador de Valores	8	103	104.75	103.50	105	103	105	102	104	102.50	105.50
Garantizador de Valores	8										
Caja Hipotecaría	8	103	104.50	103	105	103	105	102	104	S	105.50
Caja Hipotecaría	7	103	100.50	102	102.50	S	103.75	101.50	103	94.75	95.25
Caja Hipotecaría	5	90	87.75	91.50	90.75	92.50	91.50	89.75	86.75	85	85
Caja Hipotecaría	6							100.25	98.50	96.50	95.25

Source: *El Mercurio*, 1879–1883.

Table 28
Chilean Population, 1875-1885

	1875	1885
New North		
Antofagasta		7,588
Iquique		15,391
Tacna		14,183
Taltal	134	4,761
Tocopilla		1,816
Central Zone		
Santiago	129,807	189,332
Valparaíso	97,737	104,952
Viña del Mar	1,318	4,859
The Old South		
Concepción	18,277	24,180
Coronel	5,658	2,292
Lota	5,337	3,956
Talcahuano	2,495	5,030
Tomé	3,529	5,530
New South		
Angol	3,845	6,331
Anjeles	3,960	4,570
Lebu	5,783	2,699
Mulchen	4,826	7,958
Temuco		7,958
Total of the nation	2,075,971	2,527,320

Source: *Sinopsis Estadística de 1918*, p. 7.

Table 29
Building Permits Issued in Santiago, 1878-1882

	Number of Permits Issued	Amount[1] Constructed	Value
1878	167		$300,752
1879	118	2,276	232,000
1880	235	5,496	515,000
1881	221	4,728	655,000
1882	246	4,883[2]	836,893

Sources: *El Ferrocarril; El Diario Oficial*, 1878-1882.

[1]In square meters.   [2]Frontage.

Table 30
Funds dedicated to Road Construction and Repair 1879-1884

1879-1880	$ 40,954
1880-1881	93,520.55
1881-1882	317,207.23
1882-1883	202,567.65
1883-1884	240,187

Source: *Memoria de Hacienda Pública*, 1880-1884.

Table 31
Revenues Generated by Nitrate Exports

	Duty	Surcharge	Total	Percent of Ordinary Revenue
1880	$1,170,235	166,646	1,336,881	5.15
1881	4,601,710	1,076,777	5,678,487	15.6
1882	7,588,899	558,310	8,147,209	20.3
1883	9,309,354	724,254	10,033,608	22.7
1884	8,954,341	1,744,327	10,698,668	26.8

Source: *Memoria de Hacienda Pública*, 1880-1885.

Table 32
Nitrate Exports, 1879-1883
(in kilos)

	1879[1]	1880[2]	1881[3]	1882[3]	1883[3]
Pisagua			23,822,706	112,759,585	215,967,531
Iquique		18,831,463	193,155,603	271,114,898	275,813,417
Antofagasta	43,431,379	55,403,604	70,552,933	53,479,189	54,686,036
Tocopilla		8,912,701	8,755,316	10,188,757	12,568,490
Taltal/Chañaral	9,747,346	40,335,295	61,819,315	41,804,122	25,762,959
Valparaíso	6,165,390				
Totals	59,314,115	123,483,063	358,105,873	489,346,551	584,798,433

Sources: [1]Diario Oficial, 4 July 1881, p. 988. [2]*Estadística Comercial de la República de Chile*, 1880, 1883. [3]*Memoria de Hacienda Pública*, 1883, p. LXXXVI.

Table 33
Sources of Chile's Ordinary Income, 1877–1884
(in pounds sterling)

	1877	1878	1879	1880	1881	1882	1883	1884
Customs	1,117,760	1,021,710	941,861	1,388,042	2,890,729	4,286,302	4,450,726	3,472,936
Monopoly income (Estanco)	267,787	292,960	251,527	339,195	79,650			
Land tax (Agrícola)	181,403	170,789	143,630	135,774	135,907	151,093	157,752	151,184
Excise (Alcabala)	73,846	56,801	57,166	82,475	91,499	117,217	103,364	95,335
License fees (Patente)	69,815	60,430	38,448	37,829	48,486	71,497	82,113	50,643
Stamped paper & stamps	27,155	35,396	36,657	46,558	52,734	70,651	76,951	61,994
Railroads	491,338	491,755	440,721	503,341	569,634	740,925	810,023	794,281
Income tax (Haberes)			27,075	80,981	102,869	121,859	162,644	91,570
Inheritance (Herencia)			2,291	6,414	9,665	23,611	23,227	27,901

Source: *Resumen de la Hacienda Pública de Chile desde 1833 hasta 1914*, pp. 27–28.

Table 34
Income from Taxes Levied on Imports into Chile, 1878–1884
(in Chilean pesos)

	Specific Taxes	4%	10%	15%	25%	35%	Partial Total	10% Surcharge	Differential	Total
1878	484,857		26,341	283,078	3,953,770	412,054	5,160,100	443,266		5,603,366
1879	619,103	49		239,552	2,829,533	1,849,533	5,537,828	305,749	48,031	5,891,608
1880	774,636	274		399,804	3,252,352	2,275,835	6,702,901	370,101	1,627,989	8,700,991
1881	1,084,056	602		545,279	4,371,588	3,162,056	9,163,581	501,063	2,223,175	11,887,819
1882	1,383,840	1,117		676,617	5,739,171	3,965,156	11,765,901	639,343	1,493,844[1]	13,899,088
1883	1,395,173	602		813,950	5,678,379	4,112,218	12,000,322	600,464	1,640,000[1]	14,240,787[2]
1884	1,417,001	399		705,334	5,114,287	4,650,372	11,887,393	555,227	3,855,110[1]	16,297,730

Source: *Estadística Comercial de la República de Chile*, 1878–1884.

[1] *Memoria de Hacienda Público*, 1883–1885. [2] Includes revenues collected from Arica in accord with Peruvian law.

Table 35
Money Supply in Chile
(in millions of pesos)

	Notes and coins in public hands	Bank deposits	Total
1876	15	39	54
1877	15	41	56
1878	16	37	53
1879	17	37	54
1880	22	66	88
1881	30	61	91
1882	22	51	73
1883	21	56	77
1884	21	62	83

Source: P. S. Conoboy, "Money and Politics in Chile, 1878-1925," unpublished doctoral dissertation, University of Southampton, 1977, p. 351.

Table 36
Bank Activity, 1878-1883
(in Chilean pesos)

	Specie	Loans	Bills	Deposits
Dec. 1878	2,911,528	46,634,882	9,198,052	35,782,550
June 1879	2,411,505	41,392,319	10,897,819	33,989,021
Dec. 1879	1,429,126	43,925,768	13,691,524	42,403,678
June 1880	596,146	45,937,279	11,159,954	50,101,477
Dec. 1880	666,494	55,645,946	12,396,828	65,887,952
June 1881	1,162,444	56,222,999	10,043,495	59,749,281
Dec. 1881	914,409	59,397,273	9,448,791	66,720,141
June 1882	1,463,469	61,126,067	9,144,355	57,825,967
Dec. 1882	1,563,397	61,516,447	9,539,096	57,168,468
June 1883	1,322,260	64,372,376	9,906,188	57,563,886
Dec. 1883	1,219,818	65,914,214	10,065,948	56,803,917

Source: Diario Oficial, 1878-1884.

Note: Banks included are: Agrícola, Concepción, Edwards, Matte, Consolidado, Melipilla, Mobilario, Nacional, Ossa, de la Unión, Valparaíso. After December, 1879, Banco Concepción ceased to exist. Three more banks were created after June 1882: Banco de Bunster, Banco Caupolicán, Banco de Curicó.

Appendix

Table 37
Food Prices in Valparaíso, 1878–1884

Commodity	Weight (W)	1/78	3	6	9	12	3/79	6	9	12	3/80	6	9
Cebada	71.3K	2.25	3.25	3	2.87	2.12	2.21*	1.812	3.07*	2.50	3	3.25*	3.43*
Charqui	46K	19	16.50								29*		
Frejoles													
Bayos Gr.	92K	9.50	S	6	S	5.50	6	4.50	S	5	4		
Bayos Chicos	92K	9	9	4.87*	4.75	4.87*	4.75*	S	3.75	4	3.50		
Bayos	92K										3.75	4.37*	S
Blancos	92K												
Grasa	46K										19	17.13*	22
Harina													
Flor de Sgto.	92K	10.60	13	11	10.75	7.88*	6.50*	F	10.62*	9.25	8.25*	7.93*	10.25*
del Sur	92K	10	12	10.25	9.38*	6.80*	6.10*	6.67*	10.25*	8.50	7.63*	S	9.88*
Candeal	46K						3.25*	S	5.25*	3.50	3	2.94*	3.37*
Maíz	73.60*												
Trigo													
En esta	71.3K	5.25	6		4.55	3.25	3.75	3.92*	5	4	3.90	3.95*	4.87*
Blanco	71.3K												
Candeal	73.60K										3.75*	4.50*	4.57*

Table 37 (continued)

Commodity	Weight (W)	12/80	3/81	6	9	12	3/82	6	9	12	3/83	6	9	12	3/84
Cebada	71.3K		3.50	3.56	3.38	3.06	2.75 F	2.81	2.75		2.63	S	2.32	2.38*	2.50
Charqui	46K	31*	22.50	23.50	20.50	31.50*	21.50*	30	34.50*	39*	34	33	31.50*	39.50*	32
Frejoles															
Bayos Gr.	92K														
Bayos Chicos	92K														
Bayos	92K	4*	3.75*	4.375*	4.25*	4.18*	3.88*	4.75*	4.88	4.45*	S	5.63*	5.38*	8.50	8
Blancos	92K		4*	4.25*	4*	S	3.88*	4.13*	4.50*	4.43*	4.70	6*	7.50*	9.50	7.75
Grasa	46K	26.34*	22.50*	23.50	20.50*	21.75	20.50*	21	19*						
Harina															
Flor de Sgto.	92K	9.13	9.38*	9.45*	9.13*	8.70*	7.70*	7.50*	S	7.40	7.67*	7.55*	7.70*	8.80*	7.75*
del Sur	92K	8.87*	8.63*	8.75*	8.50*	8.37*	7.35*	7.40*	S						
Candeal	46K	3.90*	3.50	4	S	S	3.60	3.13*	S	6.80*	3.13	S	S	3.25	3
Maiz	73.6K						4.50	2.88*	2.75 F	2.50	S	2.60	S	4	3
Trigo															
En esta	71.3K	4.40	4	4.30	S	3.90									
Blanco	71.3K					4									
Candeal	73.6K	4.58*	4	4.38*	4*	3.88*	S	3.75*	S	3.43*	3.88*	3.125	3.281	3.75*	4*

Source: *El Mercurio* (Valparaíso), 1878–1884.

*Averaged.   F = fanega.

Note: A *fanega* should equal 71.30K. Unfortunately, the fanega sometimes varied from one region to another. Hence, in this table a hectolitre is equal to 73.6K. A fanega is so designated and not converted to kilograms.

Cebada = barley. Charqui = charqui. Frejoles = beans. Bayos Gr. = bayos, large. Bayos Chico = bayos, small. Bayos = bayos. Blancos = white. Grasa = lard/fat. Harina = flour. Flor de Sgto = flor de Santiago. del Sur = del Sur. Candeal = candeal. Maíz = corn. Trigo = wheat. En esta = en

Appendix

Table 38
Food Prices in Santiago, 1878–1883

Commodity	Weight (W)	1/78	3	6	9	12	3/79	6	9	12	3/80	6	9
Cebada	72K	1.60	2.50	2.25	2.50	1.37	1.50	1.25	2.50	1.40	2.25	2.65	9
Charqui	46K	12	16	15.50	12	10	17	15	19	25	24	23	3.90
Frejoles													S
Bayos Ch.	100K	10	9	4.25	3	4.50	5	3.75	4	3	S	S	3.25
Bayos Gr. Cab.	100K	9.50	8	4	S	S	4	3.25	3.50	3	2.75	3.50	S
							5	4	4.25	4.50	3.75	4	S
Grasa	46K	16.50	14.50	13.50	12	S	11.50	11.25	18	15	16.50	S	19
Harina													
1st	46K	4.25	5	4	4.25	S	2.75	3	4.50	4.30	3.40	S	4.30
2nd	46K						2.25	2.50	4.50	3.50	3	2.90	3.80
3rd	46K						2.30	2.25	4	3	2.50	S	3.40
Maiz	80K	4.50	4	1.75	1.50	1.75	1.40	1.25	2	1.50	1.60	1.70	1.80
Trigo													
Blanco	72K	4.25	5.75	5	4.75	4	2.87	3.30	5	3.75	3.40	3.37	4.40
Candeal lgo	72K						2.62	2.75	4.50	3	3	2.85	3.50
Candeal Rdo.	72K						2.55	3	4	2.75	2.75	S	3.50
Animals Gordos													
Bueyes		56.50*	55*			57.50*	50	S	55	60	S	67.50	S
Novillos		39.50*	34.50*			34*	24	23	27	30	S	42.50	S
Vacas		28.50*	S			28*	S	33	40	S	32	33.50*	S
Corderos						2.50	2	2.50	2	S	2.67	S	S
Animales Flacos													
Bueyes		33*	32.50*			32.50*	30	26	S	35	40	42.50	S
Novillos		24.50*	22.50*			20*	16	14	18	20	28	29	S
Vacas		21.50*	20.50*			17.50*	20	18	21	26	33	24.50*	S
Corderos		2.50	2.40			2.40	1.50	S	2	S	S	1.675*	S

Table 38 *(continued)*

		12/80	3/81	6	9	12	3/82	6	9	12	3/83	6	9	12
Cebada	72K	2.40	2.34	3	2.80	2.50	2.20	S	2.10	1.50	2.10	1.95	1.85	1.60
Charqui	46K	28	25	24	19	25	29	28	34	S	27	30	29	37
Frejoles														
Bayos Ch.	100K	3.30	2.25	3.40	3	S	3.25	3.40	3.50	S	3.10	4.50	4.25	6.75
Bayos Gr.	100K	3.10	2.50	3.60	3.50	S	S	4.10	4.50	S	3.40	5.25	4.90	7.80
Cab.		3.30	2.75	3.40	3.50	3	2.25	3.50	S	S	3.80	5.50	7.50	9
Grasa	46K	24.50	19	23	21	S	20	21	19.50*	S	16	S	15.50	16.50
Harina														
1st	46K	3.90	4	S	4	3.62*	3.22*	S	3.15	S	3.30	3.25	S	3.60
2nd	46K	3.30	3.40	S	3.25	3.12*	2.62*	2.75	2.70	2.50	2.65	S	S	2.80
3rd	46K	2.50	3.125	2.60	2.50	2.62*	2.12	2.37	2.20	S	2.30	2.20	S	2.25
Maíz	80K	2	1.50	2.50	2	2.25	2.75	2.10	2	1.80	2.10	2.20	2	3.80
Trigo														
Blanco	72K	3.80	4.50	4.40	4.10	3.45*	3.27*	3.32*	3.27*	3.22	3.50	3.35	3.50	3.60
Candeal lgo.	72K	3.25	3.40	3.60	3.50	3.30*	2.95*	2.85*	2.75*	S	3.20	3.15	S	3.20
Candeal Rdo.	72K	3.10	3.40	3.60	3.20	3.05*	2.67*	2.65*	S	S	3.05	2.85	2.80	S
Animals Gordos														
Bueyes			72.50*	77.50*	82.50*	S	87.50*	S	82.50*	92.50*	77.50*	72.50*	77.50*	S
Novillos			47.50*	52.50*	S	S	57.50*	S	62.50*	67.50*	45.50*	49*	S	47*
Vacas			37	45	S	36*	43.50*	S	42.50*	50*	51.50*	43.50*	57.50*	S
Corderos			2.125*	S	3.25*	3	3.25*	S	S	S	S	S	S	S
Animales Flacos														
Bueyes			47.50*	54.50*	59*	67.50*	59.50*	S	57.50*	62.50*	57.50*	61.50*	S	59*
Novillos			37*	39*	44*	47.50*	44.50*	S	42.50*	52.50*	35*	S	S	36.50*
Vacas			25*	27.50*	31*	34.50*	34*	S	S	37.50*	48*	S	46.50*	42.50*
Corderos			1.75*	S	S	2	2.50	S	S	S	S	S	S	S

Source: *El Ferrocarril, El Independiente, El Estandarte Católico*, 1878–1883.

Cebada = barley. Charqui = charqui. Frejoles = beans. Bayos Ch. = bayos, small. Bayos, Gr. = Bayos, large. Cab. = caballeros. Grasa = lard/fat. Harina = flour. 1st = 1st. 2nd = 2nd. 3rd = 3rd. Maíz = corn. Trigo = wheat. Blanco = white. Candeal lgo = candeal,long. Candeal Rdo = candeal, round. Animals gordos = fattened animals. Bueyes = bulls. Novillos = steers. Vacas = cows. Corderos = sheep. Animales Flacos = unfed animals.

Appendix

Table 39
Food Prices in Concepción, 1879–1883

Commodity	Weight (W)	1/7/79	4/26	7/29	11/4	1/3/80	3/23	1/27/81	3/19	6/29	9/2
Arroz de la India	46K	7.75	S	8	9	7	6.50	7	7.40	8	S
Azucar Hamburguesa	A	4	S	4.75	5.75	5	4.80				
Café Brazil	46K			34			34	33	34.35	35	46K
Cebada	F	2	11.50	2.50	S	S	S		2.75	3.60	S
Charqui	46K		11.34*	9.767*	18.90*		17.64*	32.56*	43.52	41.97	40.41
Fideos	46K	9.50	S	S	S	S	9				
Frejoles											
Bayos	100K	5.26*	S	4.20*	5.61*	S		2.36*	S	2.15*	2.50
Cabelleros	F	6	S	3	4	S					
Harina flor	46K	2.75	S	4.25	5.25	4.50	3.60	3.65	S	3.70	4
Maíz	F	3.50	S	3	S	2.50		2.50*	2.23*		
Trigo	F	3.50	S	4.50	5	4.25	3.88	3.89*	4.03*		2.68

Period ending:

Table 39 *(continued)*

Commodity	Weight (W)	12/17/81	1/8/82	4/18	7/9	10/12	1/7/83	4/18	7/8	10/6
Arroz de la India	46K	7.50	S	6.75	S					
Azucar Hamburguesa	A			3.95	S					
Café Brazil	46K	S	31	S	30					
Cebada	F	S	3	3.50	S	S	2.50	3	2.50	S
Charqui	46K	43.52	S	46.63	49.74	S	52.85	54.40	56.29	S
Fideos	46K					9	S	S	S	S
Frejoles										
Bayos	100K	3.22	3.04	S	3.15	3.22	3.04	3.58		
Cabelleros	F									
Harina flor	46K	3.90	4	3.90	3.25	3.15	2.80	3.30	3.50	3.60
Maíz	F		2.68	2.68	3.13	2.68	2.23	2.68	2.68	3.35
Trigo	F	4.13*	3.64	S	3.41*	S	S	3.41*	S	

Source: *Revista del Sur* (Concepción).

F = fanega (71.3 kilos). A = arroba (35.552 liters).

*Adjusted.

Arroz de la India = rice from India. Azucar Hamburguesa = sugar. Café Brazil = coffee. Cebada = barley. Charqui = charqui. Fideos = noodles. Frejoles = beans. Bayos = bayos. Harina flor = flour. Maíz = corn. Trigo = wheat.

Appendix

Table 40
Cost of Living
(Wholesale Agricultural Price Index)
(1940 = 100)

	Index	Percentage Variation
1879	3.7	
1880	4.1	+10.81
1881	4.7	+34.33
1882	4.1	+10.81
1883	5.5	+42.65
1884	5.4	+45.95

Source: Adolfo Latoore Subercaseaux, "Relación entre el Circulante y Los Precios en Chile." *Memoria de Prueba.*

Table 41
Crime 1878-1884

	1878	1879	1880	1881	1882	1883
Crimes by public employees in the course of their work	64	53	35	62	41	65
Crimes against family order and public morality	185	144	142	169	175	195
Crimes against public order and the security by private individuals	462	481	377	526	384	399
Crimes against public faither, falsifications, false testimony and perjury	70	84	88	69	103	110
Crimes against property	3,295	3,038	2,657	1,888	2,316	2,530
Crimes against persons	1,343	1,422	1,191	998	1,046	1,342
Crimes against national security and the sovereignty of the state		1	104			
Crimes against internal security of the state	18	52	6	109	23	31
Crimes of the military	77	16	9	19	45	9
Crimes which affect the constitution	42	21	12	12	50	15
Diverse crimes	296	227	545	442	1,578	825
	5,852	5,539	5,166	4,294	5,761	5,521

Source: *Anuario Estadístico*, 1878-1883

Table 42
Military Expenditures as a Percent of Chile's Budget

Year	Total Expenditures	Percentage Spent for the Army	Navy
1875	$ 22,052,187	8.82	7.69
1885	40,882,484	13.01	7.50
1886	54,623,271	8.53	5.49
1887	58,633,930	7.88	4.51
1888	46,092,535	10.31	7.95
1889	59,390,144	12.98	11.20
1890	75,063,376	9.32	9.10
1891	Civil War against Balamceda		
1892	73,764,481	10.87	8.19
1893	63,074,248	11.71	17.81
1894	72,703,243	10.44	13.78
1895	92,878,454	25.15	8.75
1896	115,401,115	15.27	26.90
1897	84,614,284	13.59	13.56
1898	114,110,099	29.90	13.57
1899	108,482,591	14.22	9.31
1900	112,708,570	10.57	7.89

Source: *Resumen de la Hacienda Publíca* (1901).

Table 43
Comparison of Taxes Paid on Imports and Exports
(in pesos of gold worth 18 pence)

Year	Import Taxes	Export Taxes
1870	$14.758,695	$ 1,341,760
1875	18,405,523	583,301
1880	14,924,616	3,093,330
1885	18,756,931	14,907,034
1890	23,364,033	35,048,293
1895	20,803,753	41,084,777
1900	28,489,711	50,142,830
1905	33,414,134	57,300,592
1910	48,764,571	80,421,329

Source: *Sinopsís Estadística de la República de Chile*, p. 67.

Table 44
Percentage of Ordinary Income Generated by the Nitrate Export Tax
(in pesos of 18 pence)

Year	Total ordinary Income	Nitrate tax	Percent
1885	$ 50,784,759	14,386,810	28.21
1890	72,784,042	35,048,749	48.15
1895	78,331,456	43,059,959	56.12
1900	102,532,272	50,138,281	48.90
1905	119,475,631	57,336,350	47.99
1910	156,654,314	80,394,939	51.32

Source: Ministerio de Hacienda, *Seccíon Salitre. Antecedentes Sobre la Industria Salitrera*, p.21.

Table 45
Comparison of Sources of Ordinary Government Revenues

Tax	1875	1880	1883	1885	1890	1895	1900
Aduana	48.95	37.98	68.48	65.96	74.92	78.89	76.65
Estanco	10.83	9.28	0	0	0	0	0
Agrícola	6.55	3.71	2.43	3.17	2.17	0.014	.00007
Patente	2.7	1.04	1.26	1.13	0	0	0
Papel Sellado	0.99	1.27	1.18	1.31	0.82	0.58	0.53
Haberes		2.22	2.50	0.96	0.85	0	0
Herencia		.18	.36	.41	0.20	0	0

Source: *Resumen de la Hacienda Pública* (1914).

Appendix

Figure 1
Crimes Against Property and Persons, 1879-1883

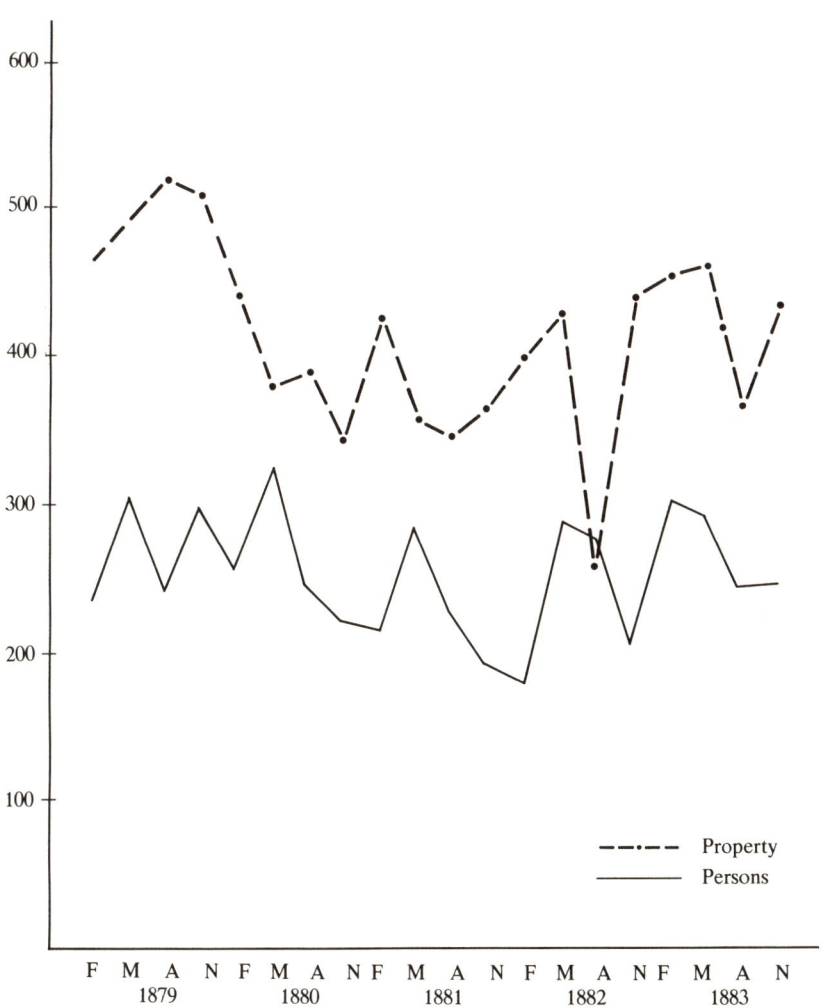

F = Period ending in February. M = Period ending in May. A = Period ending in August. N = Period ending in November.

Solid line traces crimes against persons; dotted line traces crimes against propery. These figures do not reflect those crimes which were not reported as occurring within these time periods.

Notes

Abbreviations

ARCHIVES

ABVM	Archivo de Benjamín Vicuña Mackenna, Archivo Nacional, Santiago, Chile
AJE	Archivo Jaime Eyzaguirre, Archivo Nacional, Santiago, Chile
AJFV	Archivo de José Francisco Vergara, Biblioteca del Congreso, Santiago, Chile
AMH	Archivo de Ministerio de Hacienda, Archivo Nacional, Santiago, Chile
AMI	Archivo de Ministerio del Interior, Archivo Nacional, Santiago, Chile
AMM	Archivo de Ministerio de Marina, Archivo Nacional, Santiago, Chile
FV	Fondos Varios, Archvio Nacional, Santiago Chile

GOVERNMENT DOCUMENTS

BGP	*Bolétin de la Guerra del Pacífico*
BPS	*British Parliamentary Sessions*
CDSE	*Cámara de Diputados, sesiones estraordinarias*
CDSO	*Cámara de Diputados, sesiones ordinarias*
CDSS	*Cámara de Diputados, sesiones secretas*
CSSE	*Cámara de Senado, sesiones estraordinarias*
CSSO	*Cámara de Senado, sesiones ordinarias*
CSSS	*Cámara de Senado, sesiones secretas*
DO	*El Diario Oficial*
MMG	*Memoria de Ministerio de Guerra*
MMHAC	*Memoria de Ministerio de Hacienda*
MMINT	*Memoria de Ministerio del Interior*

JOURNALS

BSNA	*Bolétin de la Sociedad Nacional de Agricultura*
EHIPS	*Estudios de Historia de Instituciones,*
HAHR	*Hispanic American Historical Review*
JLS	*Journal of Latin American Studies*
RC	*Revista Chilena*
RCHG	*Revista Chilena de Historia y Geografía*
RMIN	*Revista de Mineria*

NEWSPAPERS

ARO	*El Araucano* (Lebu), 1879-1882
ARA	*La Araucania* (Mulchén), 1879-1883
AUR	*La Aurora* (Curicó), 1878-1879
BAQ	*El Baquedanista* (Cauquenes) 1881
BB	*El Bío Bío* (Anjeles), 1879-1884
CACH	*El Cachapoal* (Rancagua), 1879
CAU	*El Caupolicán* (Rengo), 1879-1882
CEN	*El Censor* (San Felipe), 1879-1880
CENT	*El Centinela* (San Carlos), 1879
CHT	*The Chilian Times* (Valparaíso), 1876-1884
CHIL	*El Chilote* (Ancud), 1879-1884
COMC	*El Comercio* (Coquimbo), 1879
COM	*El Comercio* (San Felipe), 1879-1884
CONS	*El Constituyente* (Copiapó), 1876-1884
COR	*El Correo* (Osorno), 1880-1882
CQ	*El Correo de Quillota* (Quillota), 1879-1884
CLS	*El Correo de La Serena* (Serena), 1879
COV	*El Corvo* (Santiago), 1881
CUR	*El Curicano* (Curicó), 1879-1884
DA	*El Diario de Avisos* (Santiago), 1879
DG	*El Diario de Guerra* (Santiago), 1879
DIQ	*El Dique* (Talcahuano), 1881
DIS	*La Discusion* (Chillán), 1876-1884
ES	*El Eco del Sur* (Angol), 1883-1884
ET	*El Eco de Taltal* (Taltal), 1881
EPSC	*La Epoca* (San Carlos), 1881-1882
EPS	*La Epoca* (Santiago), 1881-1883
ESMER	*La Esmeralda* (Coronel), 1879-1883
ESP	*La Esperanza* (Cauquenes), 1879
ECAT	*El Estandarte Católico* (Santiago), 1876-1884
FEN	*El Fénix* (Rancagua), 1880-1884
FERR	*El Ferrocarril* (Santiago), 1876-1884
FERS	*El Ferrocarril del Sur* (Curicó), 1883
FERRO	*El Ferrocarrilito* (Santiago), 1880
HER	*El Heraldo* (Santiago), 1880-1881
INDEP	*El Independiente* (Santiago), 1876-1884
INDUS	*El Industrial* (Antofagasta), 1881-1884

JUV	*La Juventud* (San Fernando), 1879-1882
LAU	*El Lautaro* (Rancagua), 1879
LIBT	*La Libertad* (Talca), 1880-1883
LIBV	*La Libertad* (Valdivia), 1876-1884
LIBL	*El Liberal* (Vallenar), 1879
LIBLU	*El Liberal* (Lebu), 1881-1882
LON	*El Lontué* (Molina), 1881
LOTA	*El Lota* (Lota), 1878-1884
LUZ	*La Luz* (Vichuquén), 1881-1882
MAI	*El Maipo* (San Bernardo), 1879-1882
MER	*El Mercurio* (Valparaíso), 1879-1884
LN	*Las Noticias* (Talca), 1879
NOV	*Las Novedades* (Santiago), 1879-1880
ÑUB	*El Ñuble* (Chillán), 1880
OB	*El Obrero* (Chillán), 1879
OP	*La Opinion* (Talca), 1879
PC	*El Padre Cobos* (Santiago), 1881-1882
PAR	*El Parralino* (Parral), 1880-1884
LAP	*La Patria* (Valparaíso), 1876-1884
POR	*El Porvenir* (Tomé), 1881-1883
PORPM	*El Porvenir* (Puerto Montt), 1881-1883
PORL	*El Porvenir* (Ligua), 1882
PORC	*El Porvenir* (Curepto), 1883-1884
PRE	*El Precursor* (Santiago), 1882
PROM	*El Progreso* (Meilipilla), 1879-1883
PROS	*El Progreso* (Serena), 1879-1884
PCH	*El Pueblo Chileno* (Antofagasta), 1879-1881
REP	*El Republicano* (Yumbel), 1878-1884
RVS	*La Revista del Sur* (Concepción), 1876-1884
SEM	*La Semena* (Parral), 1879
SUF	*El Sufragio* (Curicó), 1879
TAL	*El Taller* (Santiago), 1879
TEL	*El Telégrafo* (Chillán), 1880-1881
LOT	*Los Tiempos* (Santiago), 1876-1882
UN	*La Unión* (Parral), 1879
VER	*El Vergara* (Constitución), 1882
VM	*El Veintiuno de Mayo* (Iquique), 1880-1884
VC	*La Voz Chilena* (Iquique), 1880
VI	*La Voz de Itata* (Quirihue), 1879-1884

CHAPTER ONE

1. John Mayo, "La Compañía de Salitres de Antofagasta y la Guerra del Pacífico," *Historia* 14 (1979):73; Robert N. Burr, *By Reason or Force* (Berkeley: University of California Press, 1965), pp. 118-23, 128-31

2. Richard Snyder Phillips, Jr., "Bolivia in the War of the Pacific, 1879-1884" (Ph.D. diss., University of Virginia, 1973), pp. 66-70; Daza to unknown correspondent, in Pascual Ahumada Moreno, ed., *La Guerra del Pacífico, Recopilación Completa.* 8 vols. (Valparaíso: Imprenta El Progreso, 1884-1892), 1:93-94; Alberto Gutierrez's *La Guerra del Pacífico* (3rd ed.; Buenos Aires: Francisco de Aguirre, 1975), p. 185, denies the authenticity of the letter. Various Bolivians were mystified by Daza's actions and a congressional committee subsequently took the former dictator to task, claiming that it was his "imprudent policy ... with respect to the question sustained by the Compañía de Salitre ... which caused ... the disasterous War of the Pacific." See *Proceso político contra el ex presidente general Hilarión Daza, sus ministros de estado y otros ciudadanos particulares organizado por la legislatura de 1893* (La Paz: Imprenta y Lit. de El Nacional, 1894), quoted in Phillips.

3. Pinto, 16 October 1878, "Apuntes," RC 13 (1921):345; Burr, pp. 132-34.

4. DIS, 25 October 1878; Pinto, Deciembre de 1878, "Apuntes," pp. 352-53, 355-59; Burr, p. 135.

5. *Al pueblo de Santiago* (Santiago: Imprenta de El Independiente, 1879); AUR, 12 August 1878; INDEP, 1 January 1879; LOT, 29 January 1879; MER, 17 January 1879.

6. DIS, 19 December 1878; FERR, 30 November 1878, 31 January 1879; LIBV, 28 December 1878; NOV, 13 January 1879; ECAT, 14 January 1879; INDEP, 1, 12, 25, 31 January 1879; LAP, 9, 15, 23, 27 January 1879; MER, 17 January 1879.

7. RVS, 19 December 1878.

8. CSSS, 12 December 1878, p. 56; Pinto, "Apuntes," pp. 356-58.

9. Ahumada Moreno, 1:93; H. Daza to Severino Zapata, 6 February 1879 in Benjamín Vicuña Mackenna, *Historia de la campaña de Tarapacá* (Santiago: Imprenta de P. Cadot, 1880), 1:394-95; P. N. Videla to Minister of Foreign Relations, 14 February 1879, J. L. Quinones to Minister of Foreign Relations, 5 February 1879 in Ahumada Moreno, 1:39, 116.

10. Pinto, "Apuntes," p. 347; Abdón Cifuentes, *Memorias*, 2 vols. (Santiago: Nascimento, 1936), 2:153; Ramón Subercaseaux, *Memorias de Ochenta Años*, 2 vols. (Santiago: Nascimento, 1936), 1:369; José Manuel Balmaceda, *Discurso de S. E. el Presidente de la República en la apertura del Congreso Constituyente de 1891* (Santiago: Imprenta Nacional, 1891), pp. 7-8; LAP, 31 January 1879.

11. FERR, 20, 25 January 1877, 21 January, 11 February 1879; CONS, 27 November 1876, 26 January, 3 February, 16 April 1877; MER, 15, 25 February 1879; LOT, 16 February 1879; INDEP, 14, 18 February 1879; CHT, 22 February 1879; ECAT, 10, 17 February 1879; DA, 14 January 1879; DIS, 8 January 1879; LAU, 15 February 1879; NOV, 3, 22, 25 January, 10 February 1879; LAP, 21 January, 10, 11 February 1879; SUF, 8 February 1879; CDSE, 27 March 1879, p. 711.

12. TAL, 10, 12 February 1879; ECAT, 24 January 1879; LAP, 10 February 1879.

13. FERR, 13, 14, 18 February 1879; LAP, 12, 13 February 1879.

14. Nov, 17 February 1879.

15. CDSE, 25, 27 March 1879, pp. 711, 717; NOV, 1 March 1879; CHT, 23 March 1879; DA, 29 March 1879; FERR, 3 March, 1 April 1879; INDEP, 5, 20

March 1879; LAU, 12 March 1879; LAP, 18, 21 February, 2, 18 March 1879; RVS, 22 February 1879.

16. Gibbs to Evarts, 19 February 1879 in Dispatches from U.S. Ministers to Peru; E. Altamirano to Minister of Interior, 5 March 1879; AMI, vol. 903; Blest Gana to Intendent of Valparaíso, 6 March. AMI, vol. 891. José Antonio de Lavalle, *Mi misión en Chile* (Lima: Instituto de Estudios Historica Marítimos del Perú, 1979), pp. 14-15, 36, 39-41.

17. Lavalle, pp. 62-63.

18. Ibid., pp. 71, 76, 88-89, 93-99; D. Santa María to Aníbal Pinto, 16 February, 1 March 1879, FV, vol. 416.

19. Lavalle, p. 100; Ignacio Santa María, *La Guerra del Pacifíco*, 2 vols. (Santiago: Imprenta Universitaria, 1919), 1:263-65.

20. T. Bader, "A Willingness to War" (Ph.D. diss., UCLA, 1967).

21. Francisco A. Machuca, *Las cuatros campañas de la Guerra del Pacífico*, 4 vols. (Valparaíso: Imprenta Victoria, 1926), 1:63-65; CHT, 22 March 1879; Pinto, "Apuntes," pp. 344-45; ECAT, 20, 27 February 1879; NOV, 16 February 1879; C. Saavedra to A. Pinto, 13, 17 March 1879, FV, vol. 412. This statement is based on a study of volumes 890-893 and 901-904 in the Archives of the Ministry of Interior; CDSE, 27 March 1879, p. 710; Mariano Paz Soldán, *Narración histórica de la guerra de Chile contra el Perú y Bolivia* (Buenos Aires: Imprenta de Mayo, 1884), pp. 87-89; F. A. Armayo, *Chilian Chicane* (New York: n.p., 1882), pp. 7-11; *14th memoria de la Compañía de Salitres y Ferrocarril de Antofagasta* (Valparaíso: Imprenta Mercurio, 1879); Document No. 16, in Luis Ortega, "Change and Crisis in Chile's Economy and Society, 1865-1879" (Ph.D. diss., University of London, 1979).

22. W. Gibbs and Co. to A. Gibbs and Sons, 7, 14, 26 March 1878, Gibbs MS, 11470. The best works to appear on the role of the Compañía de Salitres are John Mayo, "A Company War? The Antofagasta Company and the Outbreak of the War of the Pacific," *Boletín de Estudios Latinoamericanos y del Caribe* 28 (1980):3-11 and the excellent article by Thomas F. O'Brien, "The Antofagasta Company: A Case Study of Peripheral Capitalism," HAHR 60, no. 1 (1980):1-32. Another more recent article is the excellent study of Luis Orteaga, "Nitrates, Chilean Entrepreneurs and the Origins of the War of the Pacific," JLAS 16, no. 2 (1984):337-380.

23. W. Gibbs to A. Gibbs & Sons, Valparaíso, 14, 27 January 1879, Gibbs MSS, vol. 11, 470.

24. William Gibbs & Co. to A. Gibbs & Sons, 7 February 1879, ibid. The author wishes to thank Professor O'Brien for kindly sharing his information on this topic. This statement on the interest of the press on the Bolivian issue is based on a study of the following newspapers: *El Estandarte Católico* (Santiago); *Las Novedades* (Santiago); *El Mercurio* (Valparaíso); *La Patria* (Valparaíso); *El Ferrocarril* (Santiago); *El Independiente* (Santiago); *Los Tiempos* (Santiago).

25. LOT, 9 January 1879, stated that it did not care about the nitrate company; Bolivia's violation of Chile's sovereign rights was the primary issue. INDEP, 8-12 October 1879; LAP, 8 March 1879; CDSE, 27 March 1879, pp. 711, 714; CSSS, 5 April 1879, p. 22; FERR, 2 April 1879; TAL, 8 March 1879; INDEP, 19, 22 April; NOV, 8 November 1879.

26. CHT, 1 February 1879; NOV, 5, 22 March 1879; Mayo, "A Company War?" p. 8. Concha i Toro had ample reason to fear such a fate. The value of "Huanchaca de Bolivia" declined on the Santiago Bourse from $900, in January 1879, to $775 in

February. After 5 March, the stock was no longer quoted (INDEP, 2 January, 21 February, 5 March 1879; Compañía Huanchaca de Bolivia, *Tercera Memoria del directorio e informe de la administración jeneral de Huanchaca* [Valparaíso: Imprenta del Universo, 1878]).

27. INDEP, 15 January 1879; TAL, 19 March 1879; L. Claro to A. Pinto, 26 December 1879, in FV, vol. 838. This was also mentioned in the Gibbs Correspondence, See letter of 14 February 1879 in Gibbs MSS, vol. 11, 470. Puelma warned that there were many influential people, such as Concha i Toro and Jeronimo Urmeneta—who opposed Chile's involvement in defense of the Compañía. See Miller to Gibbs, 14 January 1879, Gibbs MSS, 11:470. Concha i Toro, for example, tried to speak with Prats. We do not know, however, if he managed to have an appointment and, if so, what was the topic of discussion. Telegram of M. Concha i Toro to B. Prats, 2 February 1879 in AMI, vol. 902.

28. W. Gibbs to A. Gibbs, 15, 24 February 1879, ibid.; Mayo, "Compañía," 97; "Protestas de la Compañía de Salitre y Ferrocarril de Antofagasta," 8 November 1879, 31 December 1880, 29 August 1881, 2 August 1882, FV, vol. 419; Von Gulich to Minister von Bulow, Santiago, 23 November 1879, in *Informes inéditos de diplomáticos extranjeros durante la guerra del Pacífico*, ed. H. Aranguiz and R. Couyoumdjian (Santiago: Editorial Andrés Bello, 1979), p. 32. La Compañía was anything but grateful to Chile. During the war, it refused to allow Santiago to use its telegraph lines, fearful that to do so would upset the Peruvian government. A. Gibbs to W. Gibbs, 17 April 1879, Gibbs, MSS, 11, 471. Hicks to Browne, 11 February 1879 in Manuel Ravest M., *La Compañía Salitrera y la ocupación de Antofagasta, 1878-1879* (Santiago: Editorial Andrés Bello, 1983), pp. 117-18.

29. FERR, 5, 23, 25 March, 1 April 1879; INDEP, 25 March 1879; LAP, 3, 8, 17, 24 March 1879; NOV, 20 February, 4, 8, 21, 24 March 1879; CDSE, 27, 29 March 1879, pp. 712-13, 720-22, 730-31.

30. FERR, 18, 20 February, 25 March, 6 April 1879; INDEP, 25 March 1879; LAP, 12, 13, 15 February, 3, 5, 7, 8, 21, 24 March 1879; William F. Dennis, *Tacna and Arica* (2nd ed.; n.p.: Archon, 1967), p. 72.

31. CHT, 15 February, 29 March 1879; FERR, 5 March 1879; Subercaseaux, I:369; Osborn to Evarts, 20 February 1879, Dispatches from U.S. Ministers to Chile; Lavalle, pp. 58-59, 62-63; I. Santa María, 1:198-99, 263-65; Baron D'Avril to Minister of Foreign Relations, Santiago, 28 March 1879 in *Informes*, p. 258

33. CDSE, 27 March 1879, p. 712; TAL, 21 March 1879.

34. José J. Larraín Zañartu and Nicolás Peña Vicuña, *La guerra ilustrada de Chile, Perú, i Bolivia* (Valparaíso: Imprenta del Mercurio, 1879), pp. 51-53; A. Varas to A. Pinto, quoted in Mario Barros, *Historia diplomática de Chile* (Barcelona: Editorial Ariel, 1970), p. 332; B. Prats to C. Saavedra, in Gonzalo Bulnes, *La Guerra del Pacífico*, 3 vols. (Valparaíso: Imprenta Universo, 1911), 1:122.

CHAPTER TWO

1. William F. Sater, *The Heroic Image in Chile* (Berkeley: University of California Press, 1973), pp. 37-39 and "Chile during the First Months of the War of the Pacific," JLS 5, no. 1 (1973):136. In order to complete this chapter, the author has also read the works noted in the "Sources Consulted but Not Cited" in addition to the materials which are specifically cited.

2. CLS, 20 March 1879; COM, 26 April 1879; CONS, 3 March, 29 April 1879; CUR, 1 November 1879; LAP, 26 March 1879; LAU, 12 May 1879; RVS, 4 March,

14 June 1879; TEL, 2 May 1879; ARA, 15 April 1879; BB, 1 April 1879; COMC, 21 March 1879; DA, 19 March 1879; INDEP, 9 April 1879; FERR, 6, 12 April 1879; NOV, 9 April 1879.

3. J. Arteaga to A. Pinto, 9, 16 May, *Correspondencia de Pinto*, vol. I, FV, vol. 415.

4. Diego Dublé Almeida, "Diario de campaña," in *La Guerra del Pacífico*, ed. F. Ruz T. (Santiago: Editorial Andrés Bello, 1979), pp. 111-12; Sater, "Chile," pp. 151-152; D. Santa María to A. Pinto, 26 July 1879, FV, vol. 416.

5. Juan Williams Rebolledo, *Operaciones de la escuadra chilena miéntras estuvo a las órdenes del contra-almirante Juan Williams Rebolledo* (Valparaíso: Imprenta del Progreso, 1882), pp. 20-21; Sater, "Chile," p. 144.

6. LAP, 9, 16 April, 9 May 1879; FERR, 6, 12 April 1879; CHT, 19 April 1879; DG, 16 May 1879; Williams, pp. 45-70; OPIN, 15 May 1879.

7. R. Sotomayor to A. Pinto, 5 May, 4 June 1879 in "Correspondencia de don Rafael Sotomayor con don Aníbal Pinto sobre la Guerra del Pacífico," RC 6, no. 58 (1922), 286-89, 292-93 (hereafter cited as CRS 2); R. Sotomayor to Pinto, Junio de 1879, 16 June 1879 in "Correspondencia de don Rafael Sotomayor con el General don Justo Arteaga y don Aníbal Pinto sobre la Guerra del Pacífico," RC, 7, no. 69 (1924):415-16, 420 (hereafter cited as CRS 3); Santa María to A. Varas, 27 June 1879; E. Altamirano to A. Varas, 27, 29 May, 2, 7 June 1879, in *Correspondencia de don Antonio Varas sobre la Guerra del Pacífico* (Santiago: Imprenta Universitaria, 1919), pp. 107-8, 118, 121, 136, 155; R. Sotomayor to C. Saavedra, 27 May 1879, FV, vol. 559; FERR, 24, 28 May 1879; LAP, 30 May 1879; MER, 24, 30 May 1879; LOT, 25, 27, 29 May 1879; DG, 30 May 1879; CENT, 5, 12 June 1879; CD SE (Secret Sessions), 19 June 1879, pp. 131-32.

8. Sater, "Chile," 148-50.

9. Varas, *Cartas*, pp. 152-54; Sater, *Image*, pp. 41-42; A. Pinto to G. Matta, 7 August 1879, in "La captura del transporte Rimac en 1879," RC 4, no. 34 (1920): 395-96.

10. A. Varas to Santa María, 29 July 1879 in Varas, pp. 208, 210; Williams Rebolleo, pp. 113-14.

11. Sater, "Chile," p. 175.

12. R. Sotomayor to A. Pinto, 11 August 1879, CRS 3, 425-26.

13. Santa María to G. Matta, 26, 27, 28 August 1879, G. Matta to Secretario, 29 August 1879 in Intendencia de Atacama, vol. 529; R. Sotomayor to D. Santa María, 2 October 1879; A. Alfonso to Minister of Interior, 4 October 1879; unknown writer to Minister of the Interior, 5 October 1879; J. Walton to Intendent, 5 October 1879 in Archivo del Ministerio del Interior, vol. 910 (hereafter cited as AMI).

14. Bulnes, *La Guerra del Pacífico*, 1:508-11, 514-17, 522-23; D. Santa María to José V. Lastarria, 5 November 1879 in "Cartas de don Domingo Santa María a don José V. Lastarria," RC 2, no. 19 (1918):66; José Francisco Vergara, "Memorias de José Francisco Vergara," in *Guerra del Pacífico*, ed. Ruz, pp. 35-36; Ignacio Santa Maria, "La Guerra del Pacífico," RCHG 55 (1927):34-39, 43-47

15. Bulnes, 1:531, 544-46, 549-57, 568, 587-88. See also Holger Birkedal, "The Late War in South America," *Overland Monthly* 2nd ser., 3 (1881):188-89 and his *Peru-Bolivia-Chile. Krigen i sudamerika* (Chicago: Scandinavens Boghandel, 1884), pp. 68-69; R. Sotomayor to Pinto, 17 November 1879 in Bulnes, 1:567; Pinto, 3 January 1880 in "Apuntes," RC 6, no. 52 (1922):119.

16. *Guerra con Chile. La Campaña del Sur* (Lima: Carlos Milla Batres, 1967),

pp. 32, 57; R. Phillips, "Bolivia in the War of the Pacific, 1879-1884" (Ph.D. diss., University of Virginia, 1973), pp. 148-50; Carlos Dellepiane, *Historia militar del Perú*, 2 vols. (Buenos Aires: Círculo Militar, 1941), 2:122-23; *Apuntes para la historia de la Guerra del Pacífico* (La Paz: Imprenta de la Unión Americana, 1883), p. 9.

17. *Guerra del Pacífico*, pp. 42, 60; Andrés Cáceres, *La guerra del 79: Sus campañas* (Lima: Milla Batres, 1973), pp. 26, 28; Dellepiane, 2:134-40; Vergara, p. 56.

18. DO, 17 November 1879; E. de la Barra to A. Matte, 14 November 1879, FV, vol. 826; Pio Puelma to M. Guerrero Bascuñán, 5 November 1879, FV, vol. 826; J. Alfonso to A. Pinto, 12 November 1879, FV, vol. 414; M. Baquedano to A. Pinto, 6 December 1879, FV, vol. 415.

19. Wilhelm Ekdahl, *Historia militar de la Guerra del Pacífico entre Chile, Perú, i Bolivia*, 3 vols. (Santiago: Imprenta Universo, 1917), 1:577, 587, 590-92, 635.

20. Dellepiane, 2:160-65; Bulnes, 1:650, 655-65, 671-93; Ekdahl, 1:653-55, 693-701; Santa María, "Guerra del Pacifico," RCHG 55, no. 59 (1927):100-104; M. Baquedano to A. Pinto, 22 December 1879, FV, vol. 415.

21. R. Sotomayor to Minister of War, 30 November, 5, 11 December 1879, in DO, 3, 6, 11 December 1879; telegrams, DO, 4, 5 December 1879; N. Zenteno to Minister of Interior, 2 December 1879 in DO, 3 December 1879; E. Escala to Minister of War, 4, 5 December 1879 in DO, 5, 16 December 1879; NFERR, 8, 11, 22 December 1879; CEN, 11, 18 December 1879; LOT, 23 December 1879; 13 February, 1 March 1880; RVS, 13 December 1879; ESMER, 21 December 1879; MER, 27 December 1879, 28 February 1880; CEN, 18 December 1879; PAR, 6 December 1879; FERR, 12, 15, 19, 20 December 1879; ARO, 20 December 1879; ECAT, 23 December 1879; E. Escala to A. Pinto, 15 January 1880, in Archivo Jaime Ezyaguirre, vol. 1 (hereafter cited as AJE 1); A. Pinto to R. Sotomayor, 6 December 1879 quoted in Bulnes, 1:703-4.

22. Rafael Pizarro Barahona, *Los abastecimientos militares en la Guerra del Pacífico* (Santiago: Editorial del Pacífico, 1967), pp. 30-31, 34; Fernando Ruz Trujillo, *Rafael Sotomayor Baeza, el organizador de la victoria* (Santiago: Andrés Bello, 1980), pp. 116, 207-8; R. Sotomayor to A. Pinto, 2, 11 January 1880 in Archivo Jaime Eyzaguirre, vol. 2 (hereafter cited as AJE 2); DO, 15 January 1880; COM, 28 January, 24 February 1880; PAR, 1 January 1880; RVS, 15 January 1880.

23. Bulnes, 2:47-51; R. Sotomayor to A. Matte, 13 January 1880, FV, vol. 826; R. Sotomayor to A. Pinto, 2 January 1880, AJE 2.

24. ESP, 4 January 1880; ECAT, 19 February 1880; ARO, 16 January 1880; CONS, 26 January 1880; CEN, 13 March 1880; ESMER, 1 February 1880; MER, 19 January 1880; FERR, 15, 28 February 1880; NFERR, 29 January 1880; LOT, 2 January 1880; PROM, 1 March 1880.

25. FERR, 28 February 1880; MER, 9, 20, 24 February 1880; LOT, 19, 25, 27 January 1880; LAP, 9 February 25, 27 January 1880; CQ, 7 March 1880; CEN 14 March 1880; MER, 20, 24 February, 15, 29 March 1880; LAP, 29 March 1880; INDEP, 24 January 1880; PROS, 30 January 1880.

26. Bulnes, 2:14-15, 17.

27. Ibid., 20, 29, 65-70, 72-73; R. Sotomayor to A. Pinto, 17 March 1880, AJE 2; LOT, 19, 21 January 1880.

28. Bulnes, 2:78-81, 84, 87-88; R. Sotomayor to A. Pinto, 11 January, 7, 11 February AJE 2, FV, vol. 412.

29. Vergara, p. 34; R. Sotomayor to A. Pinto, 13, 27 January 1880, AJE 2.

30. R. Sotomayor to A. Pinto, 11 January, 7, 11, 17 February 1880, AJE 2.
31. Bulnes, 2:72-73, 120-128; E. de la Barra to A. Matte, 14 November 1879, FV, vol. 826; D. Santa María to A. Pinto, 21 January, 2, 6, 12, 14 February 1880, FV, vol. 416; J. Alfonso to A. Pinto, 12 November 1879, FV, vol. 414; E. Sotomayor to E. Altamirano, 11 August 1879 in Varas, p. 235; INDEP, 4 March 1880; RVS, 6 March 1880; R. Sotomayor to A. Pinto, 28 February 1880, FV, vol. 412.
32. RVS, 20 March 1880; Luis Novoa de la Fuente, *Historia naval de Chile* (3rd. ed.; Valparaíso: Escuela Naval "Arturo Prat," 1958), pp. 209-14; Carlos López U., *Historia de la marina de Chile* (Santiago: Andrés Bello, 1969), pp. 287-92; Luis Uribe Orrego, *Los combates navales en la Guerra del Pacífico* (Valparaíso: Imprenta de la Patria, 1886), pp. 101-18; A. García Castelblanco, *Estudio critico de la operaciones navales de Chile* (Santiago: Imprenta de la Armada, 1929), pp. 244-49; LAP, 20 March 1880; FERR, 6 April 1880; MER, 5 March 1880; LOT, 3, 21 March 1880; Ahumada Moreno, 3:21, 97-109; DO, 5 May 1880; Bulnes, 2: 144-154; R. Sotomayor to A. Pinto, 4, 12 March 1880, FV, vol. 412; LOT, 31 March, 8 April 1880.
33. Bulnes, 2:170-77.
34. Bulnes, 2:183-191, 195, 197-202; R. Sotomayor to A. Pinto, 19, 28 March 1880, FV, vol. 412; P. Lagos to A. Pinto, 17 March 1880, AJE 1.
35. J. Vergara to A. Pinto, 10 March 1880; D. Santa María to R. Sotomayor, 25 March 1880; A. Gandarillas to R. Sotomayor, 26 March 1880 in Bulnes, 2:209-12.
36. Bulnes, 2:221-234; Dellepiane, 2:212-232.
37. DO, 5 July 1880; M. Lira to A. Pinto, 22 May 1880 AJE 1; Dellepiane, 2:245-257, 276, 288-299; Cáceres, pp. 53-60; Bulnes, 2:329-345, 357-90.
38. LAP, 3 March 1880; MER, 16, 20, 25 March 1880; NFERR, 1, 4 March 1880; INDEP, 16 May, 1880; LOTA, 25 April 1880; PCH, 10 April 1880, LOT, 4 May 1880.
39. Pinto, 1 April 1880 in "Apuntes," p. 120.
40. LOT, 6 March 1880.
41. NFERR, 5, 12 April, 6 May 1880.
42. MER, 25 March 1880; INDEP, 29 April, 16 May, 1880; LAP, 2, 5 April 1880.
43. RVS, 9 March 1880; NFERR, 11 March 1880; MER, 20 March 1880; LOT, 28, 30 March 1880.
44. MER, 18 May 1880.
45. MER, 24 February, 30 March, 18 May 1880; LOT, 6 March 1880; 1NDEP, 16 May 1880.
46. NFERR, 7 June 1880; NOV, 4 June 1880.
47. D. Santa María to A. Pinto, 2 June 1880, FV, vol. 416.
48. LOT, 3, 4 June 1880; LAP, 3 June 1880; Ekdahl, 2:371-72; INDEP, 4 June 1880; MER, 14-17 June 1880; M. Baquedano to A. Pinto, 30 June 1880, FV, vol. 415.
49. FERR, 10 April, 12 June, 14, 17 July 1880; NOV, 11, 12, 25, 26 June 1880; MER, 10, 14 May 1880.
50. FERR, 3 May 1880.
51. Novoa, pp. 216-19; López, pp. 298-99.
52. MER, 10, 12, 19 July 1880; LAP, 10 July, 11 August 1880; D1S, 13 July 1880.
53. ECAT, 21 September 1880; INDEP, 18, 23 September, 1880; LAP, 24 September 1880; DO, 29 September, 22 October 1880; López, pp. 299-300.
54. Novoa, pp. 220-21; LIBT, 21 October 1880; FERR, 9 October 1880; CUR, 10 July 1880; INDEP, 11 July 1880.
55. MER, 23 July 1880; LIBT, 31 October 1880.

56. MER, 18 November 1880; INDEP, 3 June 1880; RVS, 14 October 1880; LOT, 6, 10 November 1880; NFERR, 28 October, 8 November 1880.

57. LAP, 8 October 1880; CHIL, 26 February 1880; ESPER. 2 October 1880; FERRO, 11 November 1880; HER, 25 November 1880; CSSE, 11 December 1880, p. 32.

58. A. Pinto to E. Altamirano, 24 July 1880 in Luis Jofré A., "Don Eulojio Altamirano," RCHG, 65 (1930):74; Pinto, "Apuntes," p. 125; FERRO, 11 November 1880.

59. Bulnes, 2:611-613; FERR, 30 November 1880; HER, 2 December 1880; MER, 30 November 1880; INDEP, 1 December 1880; LOT, 1 December 1880.

60. E. Altamirano to A. Pinto, 10 November, 23, 29 December 1880 in "Cartas a don Aníbal Pinto," RCH 5, no. 48 (1921):246-47, 251-55.

61. J. Vergara to A. Pinto, 24 December 1880 in Bulnes, 2:625.

62. Ekdahl, 3:122-126; Bulnes, 2:637-81; Dellepiane, 2:339-66; Alberto del Solar, *Diario de campaña* (3rd ed.; Buenos Aires: Francisco de Aguirre, 1967), pp. 221-28.

63. Vicente Holguín, "La toma de Lima," RC, 10 (1926):28-31; Dellepiane, 2:388-400; Bulnes, 2:682-98.

CHAPTER THREE

1. Diego Dublé Almeida, "Diario de Campaña," in *Diario de la Guerra del Pacífico*, ed. F. Ruz (Santiago: Editorial Andrés Bello, 1979), pp. 51, 92-93, 103-4.

2. Jorge Carmona Y., *Baquedano* (Santiago: Estado Mayor General del Ejército, 1946), pp. 46-47; D. Santa María, 23 March 1880 in "Las dificultades de la Guerra del Pacífico," RC, 1, no. 5(1917):514, 516.

3. J. Arteaga C. to A. Pinto, 6, 16 June, 2, 4, 6, 16 July 1879, Correspondencia de Pinto, vol. 1, Fondos Varios.

4. D. Santa María to J. V. Lastarria, "Cartas de don Domingo Santa María a don José Victorino Lastarria," RC, 2, no. 18 (1918):255-56; José Alfonso to A. Pinto, 6 June 1879, FV, vol. 414; Pinto, "Apuntes," RC, 5, no. 49 (1922):363; D. Santa María to A. Pinto, 25 June 1879, FV, vol. 416; Ignacio Santa María, *La Guerra del Pacífico*, 2 vols. (Santiago: Imprenta Universitaria, 1920), 2:131-35.

5. D. Arteaga Alemparte to José Francisco Vergara, 16 May 1879, in Archivo José Francisco Vergara, a collection of letters in the Biblioteca del Congreso.

6. J. Alfonso to D. Santa María, 25 May 1879, in I. Santa María, 2:163, 261, 282; J. Alfonso to A. Pinto, 27 May 1879, FV, vol. 414.

7. José Francisco Vergara, "Memorias de José Francisco Vergara" in *Guerra del Pacífico. Memorias de José F. Vergara y Diario de Campaña de Diego Dublé Almeida*, ed. F. Ruz T. (Santiago: Editorial Andrés Bello, 1979), p. 27; I. Santa María, 2:155.

8. Vergara, "Memorias," p. 29.

9. Pinto, "Apuntes," RC 5, no. 4, p.49 (1922):363; J. Arteaga to A. Pinto, 9, 16 May, 16 June 1879, Correspondencia de Pinto, vol. 1.

10. Vergara, "Memoria," pp. 31-33; I. Santa María, 2:294-300, 302-4, 362; D. Santa María to A. Pinto, 19 July 1879. FV, vol. 416.

11. Roberto Souper to C. Saavedra, 3, 15 July 1879, FV, vol. 559; LOT, 11, 23, 24 July, 28 August 1879; FERR, 11 August 1879.

12. LAP, 21 July 1879; FERR, 12 August 1879.

13. LOT, 24 July 1879.
14. R. Sotomayor to C. Saavedra, 7, 19 April 1879, FV, vol. 559; R. Sotomayor to A. Pinto, 7 April 1879 in "Correspondencia de don Rafael Sotomayor con don Aníbal Pinto sobre la Guerra del Pacífico," RC 6, no. 57 (1922):178-179 (hereafter cited as CRS 1); E. Sotomayor to A. Pinto, 4 April 1879, AJE I; R. Sotomayor to C. Saavedra, 19 April 1879, FV, vol. 559.
15. R. Sotomayor to A. Pinto, 5,12 May 1879, "Correspondencia de don Rafael Sotomayor a don Aníbal Pinto durante la Guerra del Pacífico," RC 6, no.58 (1922):287-88 (hereafter cited as CRS 2); Juan Williams Rebolledo, *Operaciones de la escuadra chilena miéntras estuvo a las órdenes del contra almirante Juan Williams Rebolledo* (Valparaíso: Imprenta del Progreso, 1882), pp. 20-22, 25, 28, 33; entry of 16 April 1879 in Ejército del Perú. "Apuntes para la historia. Diario de la Campaña," vol. 2, FV, vol. 220.
16. J. Alfonso to A. Pinto, 27 May 1879, FV, vol. 414; R. Souper to C. Saavedra, 29 May 1879, FV, vol. 559; R. Sotomayor to A. Pinto, junio de 1879, "Correspondencia de don Rafael Sotomayor con el General Justo Arteaga y don Aníbal Pinto sobre la Guerra del Pacífico," RC 7, no. 69-70(1924):415 (hereafter cited as CRS 3). D. Santa María to A. Varas, 27 June 1879 in Antonio Varas, *Correspondencia de Antonio Varas sobre la Guerra del Pacifíco* (Santiago: Imprenta Universitaria, 1918), pp. 155-56.
17. R. Sotomayor to A. Pinto, junio de 1879, CRS 3, 415-16; J. Alfonso to A. Pinto, 23, 27 May 1879, 13 June 1879, FV, vol. 414.
18. INDEP, 17 June 1879; MER, 30 May, 5 June 1879, 7 July 1879.
19. J. Alfonso to A. Pinto, 27 May, 13 June 1879, FV, vol. 414; D. Santa María to A. Varas, 27 June 1879, E. Altamirano to A. Varas, 27, 29 May, 2, 7 June 1879 in Varas, pp. 107-8, 118, 136, 155.
20. J. Alfonso to A. Pinto, 27 May 1879, FV, vol. 414; CDSO, 19 July 1879, pp. 131-132; INDEP, 17, 22 June, 3 July 1879; R. Sotomayor to A. Pinto, junio de 1879, CRS 3, 415-16; CONS, 2, 5 July 1879.
21. J. Alfonso to A. Pinto, 1 August 1879, FV, vol. 414; R.Sotomayor to A. Pinto, junio de 1879, 5, 16 June 1879, CRS 3, 414, 416-17, 420; R. Souper to C. Saavedra, 29 May, 4 June, 15 July 1879, FV, vol. 559; R. Sotomayor to A. Varas, 5, 16 June 1879 in Varas, pp. 128-129, 147-148; R. Sotomayor to A. Pinto, 5 May 1879, 4 June 1879, CRS 2,287, 292-293; Pinto, 11 July 1879, "Apuntes," RC 5, no.49 (1921):363; R. Sotomayor to C. Saavedra, 19 April 1879, FV, vol. 559; D. Santa María to A. Pinto, 26 July 1879, FV, vol. 416; A. Varas to D. Santa María, 29 July 1879, in Varas, p. 208; D. Santa María to J. V. Lastarria, 6 October 1879 in "Cartas," RC 2, no. 19 (1918):255-256; R. Souper to C. Saavedra, 29 July 1879, FV, vol. 559; D. Santa María to A. Pinto, 25 June 1879, FV, vol. 415.
22. R. Sotomayor to A. Varas, 5 June 1879 in Varas, p. 128; R. Sotomayor to A. Pinto, 4 June 1879, CRS 2, 292; J. Alfonso to A. Pinto, 1 August 1879, FV, vol. 414; NOV, 14, 28 June 1879; DIS, 18 June 1879; LN, 22 July 1879; SUF, 19 June 1879; CQ, 24 July 1879; CHT, 21 June 1879.
23. R. Sotomayor to A. Pinto, 4 June 1879, CRS 2, 292; D. Santa María to J. V. Lastarria, 6 October 1879 in "Cartas," 255-56; Ejercito del Peru, "Diario," 26 May 1879, FV, vol. 220.
24. Sessions of the Council of State, 4, 5 August 1879, in Varas, pp. 350-51. See also LOT, 9, 10, 11, 20 July 1879.
25. LOT, 16, 17 August 1879; NFERR, 18 August, 1 September 1879.
26. CLS, 19, 21 August 1879; NFERR, 18 August 1879.

27. E. Altamirano to A. Varas, 4, 5 August 1879 in Varas, pp. 227, 231-232.
28. Bulnes, 1:370-72.
29. Rafael Pizarro B., *Los abastecimientos militares en la Guerra del Pacífico* (Santiago: Estado Mayor del Ejército, 1967), pp. 465-67; Rafael Poblete, "El Servicio Sanitario en el Ejército Chileno durante la Guerra del Pacífico," RCHG 33, no. 37 (1920):25-26.
30. Bulnes, 2:108-15.
31. Ruz, pp. 179-180, 190; R. Sotomayor to A. Pinto, 27 January 1880, AJE 2; Bulnes, 1:368-69.
32. CEN, 2 August 1879; CONS, 1 August 1879; CLS, 28 August, 2 September 1879; DIS, 25 June 1879; ESPER, 22 August 1879; LOT, 1 August 1879; INDEP, 21 December 1879; NFERR, 22, 29 December 1879. See LAP, 19 December 1879.
33. INDEP, 22 December 1879, 4, 31 March, 19, 28 April 1880; COM, 20 April 1880; NFERR, 22 March, 19, 22 April 1880; MER, 9, 20 February 1880; LAP, 5 April 1880.
34. D. Santa María to A. Pinto, 16, 19 January 26, 14 February, 29 July 1880, FV, vol. 416; R. Sotomayor to A. Pinto, 2 January 1880, AJE 2.
35. R. Sotomayor to A. Pinto, 3 October 1879 in I. Santa María "La Guerra del Pacífico," RCHG 56 (1928):227 (hereafer cited as ISM, 3); R. Sotomayor to A. Pinto, 12, 19, 28 March 1880, AJE 2; LAP, 29 March 1880.
36. R. Sotomayor to A. Pinto, 2, 27 January 4, 7, 15 February 1880, AJE 2; R. Sotomayor to C. Saavedra, 5 April 1880, FV, vol. 559; Francisco Puelma to A. Pinto, 20 January 1880 in ISM, 3, 265; Sotomayor described Zubiria as a man of little military value whose sole skill consisted of fomenting discord. Letter of 27 January 1880; S. Amengual to A. Pinto, 19 March 1880, FV, vol. 416.
37. R. Sotomayor-A. Pinto, 19 March 1880, FV, vol. 559; 27 January 1880, AJE 2; D. Santa María to A. Pinto, 16, 28 January, 2 February 1880, FV, vol. 416; ISM, 3, 263-73, 306; P. Lynch to A. Pinto, 18 February1880 in ISM, 3, 263.
38. R. Sotomayor to A. Pinto, 15 February 1880, AJE 2.
39. D. Santa María to J. F. Vergara, 3 February, 25 March 1880 in "Cartas políticas de Domingo Santa María a José Francisco Vergara," EHIPS 1 (1966): 341-42, 345.
40. INDEP, 16 March 1880; ECAT, 21, 23-25 February, 9 March, 1, 2 April 1880; LAP, 23 February 1880; NOV, 21 February 1880; see also MER, 9 February 1880; CEN, 1 April 1880; PCH, 1, 7, 9 April 1880.
41. R. Sotomayor to A. Pinto, 7 February, 19, 28 March 1880, AJE 2; R. Pacheco to B. Vicuña Mackenna, 18, 28 March 1880, ABVM, vol. 383; E. Altamirano to A. Matte, 3 April 1880, FV, vol. 828, ISM, 3, 297-98; R. Sotomayor to D. Santa María, 11 February 1880, ISM, 3, 299. See also pages 300-301.
42. R. Sotomayor to A. Pinto, 28 March 1880, AJE 2; Bulnes, 2:186; R. Pacheco to B. Vicuña Mackenna, 28 March 1880, ABVM, vol. 383; Ekdahl, 2:198.
43. R. Sotomayor to A. Pinto, 28 March 1880, AJE 2; Bulnes, 2:188-193, 188-193; Pinto, "Apuntes," 120-21.
44. CHT, 17 April 1880; INDEP, 20 April 1880; FERR, 4 May 1880; NFERR, 15 April 1880.
45. INDEP, 15, 20, 28, 30 April 1880; ECAT, 2 April 1880; CHT, 17 April 1880; LIBT, 1 May 1880; CUR, 1 May 1880; LOTA, 25 April 1880; INDEP, 15 April 1880; CHT, 24 April 1880; ESMER, 7 April 1880; PROS, 9, 16 April 1880; CQ, 4 April 1880; EAT, 20, 29 April 1880.

46. PC, 7, 14 April 1880; LIBT, 2 May 1880; CEN, 1 April 1880; RVS, 20 April 1880; LIBT, 2 May 1880.
47. ECAT, 21 April 1880; MER, 15 April 1880; EPS, 21 August 1883; INDEP, 23, 24 August 1883, 4, 6 March 1884.
48. D. Santa María to A. Pinto, 3, 29 January 1880, in Ignacio Santa María "Guerra del Pacifíco," RCHG 56 (1928):271.
49. E. Altamirano to A. Matte, 3 April 1880, FV, vol. 826.
50. Bulnes, 2:194; R. Sotomayor to A. Pinto, 13 April 1880, FV, vol. 412.
51. ECAT, 27 May 1880; INDEP, 25, 26 May 1880. For an opposing attitude see FERR, 23 May 1880 which called Sotomayor "the most beautiful and noble personification of the civic virtues of the patriot in this heroic conflict." MER 24 May 1880.
52. Vergara, "Memorias," pp. 34, 37.
53. Ibid., pp. 57, 60–62; Bulnes, 2:97-9; D. Santa María to A. Pinto, 27 March 1880, FV, vol.416.
54. Vergara, "Memorias," p. 60; R. Sotomayor to A. Pinto, 2 January, 16, 28 March 1880, AJE 2; E. Altamirano to A. Matte, 3 April 1880, FV, vol. 828.
55. R. Sotomayor to A. Pinto, 13, 20 April, 7 May 1880, AJE 2; Bulnes, 2:240.
56. Bulnes, 2:257, 293–94; FERRO, 6 May 1880.
57. Bulnes, 2:310–11, 314, 351-56, 411-12; D. Santa María to A. Pinto, 6, 12 February, 2 June 1880, FV, vol. 416; MER, 19 July 1880; RVS, 20 July 1880; LAP, 17 July 1880; CHT, 24 July 1880; *La Patria* (Caracoles), 29 July 1880, quoted in PC, 31 July 1880; PROS, 30 July 1880.
58. M. Lira to A. Pinto, 23 July 1880, AJE 1; Bulnes, 2:412; A. Pinto to V. Dávila, 3 August 1880 in Bulnes, 2:414-15.
59. NFERR, 16, 30 September 1880; FERRO, 6 June 1880; LOT, 19 July 1880.
60. Bulnes, 2:570, 588, 637–38.
61. NFERR, 30 September 1880. This charge was subsequently denied in INDEP, 1 October 1880.
62. Vergara, "Memorias," p. 64; E. Altamirano to A. Pinto, 6 December 1880 in "Cartas a don Aníbal Pinto," RC 13, no.48 (1921):250; M. Baquedano to A. Pinto, 8 December 1880, FV, vol. 415; M. Lira to A. Pinto, 23 July 1880, AJE 1.
63. E. Altamirano to A. Pinto, 3, 10 November 1880, in "Cartas a don Aníbal Pinto," pp. 243–44, 247.
64. Ibid., 25 January, 19 February 1881 in "Cartas a don Aníbal Pinto," RC 5. no. 59 (1922):401, 409–10; R. Sotomayor to A. Pinto, 28 March 1880, AJE 2; INDEP, 14 March 1881; HER, 21 March 1881; Bulnes, 2:637.
65. Bulnes, 2:714.
66. Isidoro Errázuriz, *Hombres y Cosas* (Valparaíso: Imprenta La Patria, 1882), pp. 16–17.
67. M. Baquedano to A. Pinto, 20 January 1881, FV, vol. 415.
68. LAP, 14 May 1881; RVS, 13 April 1881.
69. LOT, 30 April 1881; INDEP, 12 April, 1 June 1881.
70. E. Altamirano to A. Pinto, 31 January 1881 in "Cartas a don Aníbal Pinto," RC 5, no.59 (1920):405.
71. HER, 17 April, 5 May 1881; MER, 11 April, 22 March 1881; ÑUB, 7 May 1881; LAP, 29 April, 31 May 1881; RVS, 23, 24 February, 10 March 1881; COM, 24 April, 30 May 1881; ÑUB, 16 March, 6 April 1881.
72. ARA, 3 April 1881; ÑUB, 23 February, 13 April 7 May 1881; COM, 27

March 1881; HER, 7 May 1881; LAP, 31 May 1881; RVS, 20 April 1881. The general, of course, had his admirers. One journalist praised him as the guarantor "of domestic order, of integrity in the management of wealth and of respect for all the rights"—an apolitical leader not the zealot of one party. (*El Baquedanista* [Cauquenes], 13 May 1881.

73. ARO, 14 May 1881; COM, 16 April 1881; CQ, 29 May 1881; ÑUB, 6 April 1881; LAP, 25, 31 May, 3 June 1881; RVS, 31 March 1881.

74. COR, 5 March 1881; LAP, 6, 7, 22 June 1881.

75. ARO, 23 July 1881; COR, 9 February, 1881; MER, 11 April 1881; ÑUB, 7 May 1881; RVS, 20, 21 April 1881; TEL, 26, 29 April 1881.

76. MER, 22, 29 March, 11 April 1881; RVS, 23 February, 23 April 1881; ARA, 24 April, 1881; ÑUB, 23 February, 7 May 1881.

77. COM, 24 April 1881; MER, 11 April 1881; ÑUB, 7, 11, 18 May 1881; LAP, 31 May 1881.

78. LAP, 31 May 1881; RVS, 24 February, 13 June 1881; PC, 21 May 1881.

79. CQ, 29 May 1881; HER, 5 May 1881; RVS, 20 April, 10 May 1881. Vicuña Makenna claimed that the Lynch expedition, which he blamed on the government not the admiral, delayed the prosecution of the war by seventy days (10 December 1880, CSSE, p. 21; ÑUB, 7, 14 May 1881; PC, 26 April 1881; LAP, 31 May 1881).

80. ARA, 24 April 1881; COM, 27 March, 9 April 1881; CQ, 29 May 1881; LAP 23. 31 May 1881; RVS, 28 March, 5 April 1881; VI, 17 April 1881.

81. ARA, 24 April 1881; CQ, 2 April 1881; COM, 2 April 1881; COR, 26, 30 March, 25 May 1881; ÑUB, 11 May 1881.

82. COR, 30 March, 9 April, 21 May 1881.

83. TEL, 26 May 1881; COR, 6 Apr, 7 May 1881.

84. RVS, 13 June 1881; HER, 5 May 1881.

85. CDSO, 2 June 1881, pp. 2, 5-6.

86. Ibid., 2, 7, 23 June, 21, 28 July, 1881, pp. 7-10, 13, 24-26, 28-29, 66-67, 259-63; CSSO, 29 July 1881, pp. 248-51.

87. *Memoria de Guerra* (Santiago: Imprenta de la Epoca, 1881), pp. 18-20, 36-38, 42-46, 52-61, 74.

88. CHT, 1 July 1882.

89. INDEP, 13 July 1882.

90. CONS, 5 July 1882; LIBT, 2 July 1882.

91. José Francisco Vergara to I. Errázuriz, 5 July 1882 in Errázuriz, *Hombres*, pp. 4-10.

92. Máximo Lira, *Para la historia. Observaciones a la memoria de ex-ministro de la guerra don José Francisco Vergara* (Santiago: Imprenta de El Independiente, 1882), pp. 42, 62, 66-67, 77-79, 91-94, 108-9.

93. Pinto, "Apuntes," RC 6 (1922):273-274; M. Baquedano to A. Pinto, 12, 25 June 1882, 29 July, 22 September, 6 October, 8 December 1880, FV, vol. 415; Errázuriz, *Hombres*, pp. 24, 36, 88-89. 152, 159.

94. Galvarino Riveros, *En la escuadra* (Santiago: Imprenta de El Independiente, 1882), pp. 10, 13-25, 52-60. MER, 5 July 1882 claimed that the work was ghost written by Rafael Egaña.

95. A. Varas, "Reminiscencias históricas y diplomáticas," RCHG 78 (1935):6; G. Riveros, *Angamos* (Santiago: Imprenta de la República de J. Núñez), pp. 21, 23-25.

96. B. Vicuña Mackenna, *Historia de la Campaña de Tarapacá*, 2 vols. (Santiago: Rafael Javier, 1880), 2:387.

97. Riveros, *Angamos*, pp. 34-35, 40-44, 50-51, 60-66..
98. ESMER, 9 February 1881. Riveros apparently also worked to stop the government from appointing Montt to command the *Huáscar*. C. Condell to M. Lemus Valdivieso, 21 February 1880, in Sergio Fernández Larraín "Cartas," RCHG 147 (1979):158; LAP, 13 August 1881.
99. CQ, 22 November 1881.
100. R. Sotomayor to A. Pinto, 15 February 1880, AJE 2; D. Santa María to A. Pinto, 2, 6, 14 February 1880, FV, vol. 416; R. Sotomayor to A. Pinto, 28 February 1880, AJE 2; Errázuriz, *Hombres*, pp. 188-193; A. Varas, "Reminiscencias historicas," 67-69; Carlos Condell to M. Lemus V., 21 February 1880 in Sergio Fernández Larraín "Cartas," p. 158.
101. Pinto, "Apuntes," RC 14 (1922), 115-17; This correspondence can be found in the archive of the Intendencia of the Province of Atacama, vol. 513. See also R. Sotomayor to D. Santa María, 2 October 1879 and R. Sotomayor to Minister of War, 3 October 1879, AMI, vol. 910; R. Sotomayor to A. Gandarillas, 4, 5 October 1879, AMI, vol. 910; R. Sotomayor to Minister of War, 5 P.M. and 5:40 P.M., 7 October 1879, AMI, vol. 910; R. Sotomayor to D. Santa María, 7 October 1879, AMI, vol. 910. Sotomayor wrote that he had told Latorre to take on coal and that he presumed Latorre would inform him if the *Blanco* arrived (R. Sotomayor to D. Santa María, 7 October 1879, AMI, vol. 910; R. Sotomayor to Minister of War, 5:40 P.M., 7 October 1879 AMI, vol. 910; R. Sotomayor to J. Latorre, 7 October 1879 and J. Latorre to R. Sotomayor, 7 October 1879, in AMM, vol. 395; telegrams from Latorre to Sotomayor and from Sotomayor to Latorre, 7 October 1879 in Ahumada Moreno, 1:577-88; I. Santa María, "Guerra del Pacifico," RCHG 54, no. 58 (1927):48-51; R. Sotomayor to D. Santa María, 7 October 1879, AMI, vol. 910); *El Chileno* (Santiago), 8 October 1897 included the statement of Lillo in which he agreed that Latorre not Riveros had made the crucial suggestion.
102. EPS, 29 October 1882; FERR, 21 October 1882.
103. Ambrosio Montt, *Dictámenes del Fiscal de la Corte Suprema de Justicia de Chile*, 2 vols. (Santiago: Imprenta Nacional), 2:29-30.
104. O. Espinosa Moraga, *Latorre y la vocación marítima de Chile* (2nd ed.; Santiago: Eire, 1980), pp. 28-29; Errázuriz, *Hombres*, p. 183.
105. These articles appeared in various newspapers including *El Mercurio*. Unless otherwise noted, these citations were taken from Williams, *Operaciones*, pp. 21-22, 32-34, 36, 39, 85-88, 102-4, 108-11, 116, 121-24, 127-29. See also MER, 25, 26 September 1882.
106. FERR, 4 October 1882.
107. EPSC, 15 July 1882.
108. RVS, 9, 18 July 1882; MER, 5, 10 July, 3 August 1882.
109. EPS, 6 February 1882.
110. LAP, 31 July 1882.

CHAPTER FOUR

1. NFERR, 12 January 1880.
2. DIS, 18 November 1880; RVS, 21 August 1879; CQ, 7 September 1879; LN, 12 June 1879; CHT, 2 August 1879; ARO, 8 February 1880; DIS 18 November 1880.
3. CQ, 5, 12 August, 2 September, 24 October, 4, 11, 18, 21, 28 November 1880.

4. CEN, 29 August, 7 September, 4 November 1880; COM, 17 August, 18 September, 29 November 1880.
5. DIS, 23, 29 March 1881.
6. CHT, 24 March 1880, 11 March 1882; LN, 23 April, 11 June 1879; DG, 9 June 1879; DIS, 18 November 1882; MAI, 23 April, 28 May 1882; PC, 18 February 1882; CEN, 16 December 1880; INDEP, 23 March 1880; ÑUB, 9 April 1881; CEN, 16 December 1880; LIBT, 7 July 1882.
7. RVS, 9 April 1882.
8. CHT, 11 March 1882; MAI, 28 May 1880, 26 March 1882; DIS, 4 August 1880.
9. LAP, 7 February, 10 August, 17 September 1880; MER, 2 August 1880; J. A. Gandarillas to Jeneral en Jefe de Ejército del Norte, 17 February 1880; 11 March, 30 April 1880 in D. Rispatron, *Legislacion militar de Chile*, 3 vols. (Santiago: Imprenta Gutenberg, 1882), 3:143–44. Apparently this problem persisted well into the war. See D. Santa María to P. Lynch. 14 December 1883, FV, vol. 414.
10. Ricardo Anguita, *Leyes promulgadas en Chile*. 5 vols. (Santiago: Barcelona, 1912), 2:254.
11. Eugenio Orrego Vicuña, *Vicuña Mackenna, Vida y trabajos* (3rd ed.; Santiago: Zig Zag, 1951), pp. 331–332; C. A. Logan to Secretary of State, 6, 25 March 1876, in *Dispatches from US Ministers in Chile*. The author wishes to thank Professor Simon Collier for referring him to the Orrego Vicuña citation.
12. FERR, 11 June, 27 February 1876.
13. DIS, 27 January 1876; ARA, 13 March, 5 April 1879; CONS, 10 July 1879; Estanislao del Canto, *Memorias del Estanislao del Canto* (Santiago: Imprenta La Tracción, 1927), pp. 36–37. FERR, 27 February 1876; LAP, 28 January 1878.
14. Luis de la Cuadra, *Album del Ejército Chileno* (Valparaíso: Imprenta del Mercurio, 1877), p. 68; Carmona, *Baquedano*, p. 47; Del Canto, *Memorias*, p. 46; Victor Larenas Q., *Patricio Lynch* (Santiago: Editorial Universitaria, 1981), pp. 27, 29.
15. CDSE, 7 January 1881, pp. 74–75.
16. LOT, 9, 11 January 1881; DIS, 8 January 1881; LAP, 9, 11 January 1881; INDEP, 8 January 1881.
17. CDSO, 9 January 1881, pp. 97–104.
18. NFERR, 1 January, 1 April 1880; MER, 17 February 1880
19. NFERR, 1, 12, 22 January, 26 February 1880; LOT, 5 February 1880; FERR, 2 February, 17 July 1880; MER, 19 July 1880; PCH, 25 February 1880.
20. LOT, 5, 11, 22 July 1880; NFERR, 5 January 1880; PC, 13 June, 19 August 14 September 1880; ECAT, 18 February 1880; MER, 1 April 1880; LAP, 11 May 1880.
21. CSSS, 9, 10, 16 July 1880, pp. 55–61, 69–70; CSSO, 20 August 1880, p. 254.
22. CSSE, 14 July 1880, pp. 60–61; CSSO, 5, 19, 21 July 1880, pp. 35–36, 69, 81; CDSO, 15, 20 July 1880, pp. 207-8, 222–26, 4 June 1881, pp. 17-18. See also CDSO, 12 June, 9 August 1880, pp. 20–21, 396–97; LAP, 9 May 1881.
23. R. Sotomayor to C. Saavedra, 13 April 1879, FV, vol. 559; Pinto, 4 July 1879, "Apuntes," RC 6, no. 52 (1922):113.
24. ECAT, 8 March 1880.
25. CQ, 12 September 1880; MER, 10 September 1880.
26. MER, 8, 9, 13 September 1880; M. Baquedano to A. Pinto, 30 August 1880, FV, vol. 415.

27. INDEP, 8 September 1880; LOT, 13 September 1880; See also NOV, 9-10 September 1880.
28. NOV, 10 September 1880; LAP, 9 September 1880; A. Edwards to J. Vergara, telegram, 8 September 1880, in possession of the author.
29. LIBT, 11 September 1880; LAP, 9 September 1880; CUR, 11 September 1880; NOV, 9, 10 September 1880.
30. LAP, 22 March 1880. A letter from Roberto Venegas Díaz demanded that Escala allow reporters into the war zone (CQ, 11 April 1880). Williams also apparently acted in the same fashion (CHT, 5 July 1879; CQ, 12 September 1880).
31. INDEP, 10 September 1880; NFERR, 17, 21 June 1880; LAP, 10 September 1880; Edwards to Vergara, 8 September 1880.
32. INDUS, 23 February 1883; VM, 23, 24 February 1883.
33. Luis Barros Borgoño, *El Vice Almirante don Patricio Lynch* (Santiago: Imprenta de la Union, 1886), pp. 19, 27-29; Victor Larenas, *Patricio Lynch* (Santiago, Edotrial Universitaria, 1981), p. 27; J. A. Rodríguez, *Patricio Lynch, vicealmirante y general en jefe* (Santiago: Nascimento, 1967), pp. 11-37; Bulnes, 2:167-68.
34. D. Santa María to P. Lynch, 7 August 1883, FV, vol. 414; José Goñi to A. Pinto, 16, 19 August 1879, AJE 1; LAP, 13 August, 13, 18, 21, 25, 28 October, 25, 26, 28 November, 14, 17 December 1881, 28 January, 21 August, 8 November 1882; BB, 1, 8, 15, 29 October, 5 November 1882; LOT, 20 July 1881; PC, 22 July 1882.
35. MMG, 1879 and 1880 (Santiago: Imprenta Nacional, 1879, 1880); A. Letelier to Minister of Interior, 8, 22 March 1879, AMI, vol. 903.
36. P. Lynch to A. Pinto, 21 May 1881, AJE 1; "Espedición Letelier; Sentencia del Consejo de Guerra," in Ahumada Moreno, 6:214-24; P. Lynch to Minister of War, 22 July 1881, in Ahumada Moreno, 6:36-37; "Investigación sumaria sobre la espedición Letelier," in Ahumada Moreno, 6:214-215; "Espedición Letelier: sentencia del consejo de guerra de oficiales jenerales sobre el proceso seguido en Lima contra Letelier i demas jefes de esta espedición," Ahumada Moreno, 6:392-96; "Aprobacion de la sentencia cuartel jeneral," Ahumada Moreno, 6:396.
37. R. Murillo, *Defensa del Teniente Coronel de ejército don Ambrosio Letelier* (Santiago: Imprenta de la Liberería Americana, 1882).
38. "Dictámen Fiscal de la Corte Suprema," 17 May 1882, in Ahumada Moreno, 6:396; "Nota de la Escma. a Corte Suprema al Honorable Consejo de Estado," 27 September 1882, Ahumada Moreno, 7:335-36; P. Lynch to Presidente de la Corte Suprema, 23 August 1882, Ahumada Moreno, 7:328; P. Lynch, Nota al Consejo del Estado Entablando competencia, 23 August 1882, in Ahumada Moreno, 6:328-33; "Proceso Letelier," in Ahumada Moreno, 7:326.
39. PC, 5 January, 18, 25 April 1882; FERR, 22 June 1882; LAP, 5, 26 September, 9, 14 October 1882; CQ, 12 October 1882; See also LIBT, 18 October 1882; EPS, 19 October 1882.
40. "Sentencia del Consejo del Estado," 22 May 1883, DO, 26 May 1883; "Sentencia de la Corte Suprema," 24 October 1883, Ahumada Moreno, 8:267-69.
41. LAP, 21, 28 October 1881; BB, 1 April 1879; ARA, 2, 13 March 1879; A. Letelier to Minister of Interior, 8, 22 March 1879; P. Lagos to Minister of Interior, 20, 28 March 1879, AMI vol. 903; INDEP, 10 November 1883.
42. FERR, 9, 10 April 1880; CEN, 8 April 1880; BB, 29 July 1880; PCH, 1 April 1880; CQ, 11 April 1880; CUR, 3 April 1880; INDEP, 6 February 1880; LAP, 12

April 1880; MER, 2 August 1880; LAP, 7 February, 10 August, 17 September 1880; NOV, 9 April 1880. See also J. A. Gandarillas to General in Chief, 17 February, 22 March, 30 April 1880, in Riospatrón, 3:113-14; CONS, 24 February 1880; MER, 24, 28 February 1880; NFERR, 12 February 1880; LAP, 26 May 1880, 28 February 1881.

43. LOT, 13 January 1880; LAP, 3 January 1881; CQ, 18 January 1880.

44. INDEP, 11 December 1879; ECAT, 17 May 1880, 8 January 1881; FERR, 4 September 1880, 2 February, 22 March, 20 June, 8 October 1881; NFERR, 22 January, 17 June 1880; LOT, 31 January 1880; LAP, 6 October 1880; 4, 24 March, 28 June 1881; COM, 17 June 1881; CUR, 29 January 1881; HER, 18 February 1881; LIBT, 20 March 1881; EPS, 15 July 1882.

CHAPTER FIVE

1. FERR, 11 October 1876.

2. CONS, 30 August, 7 September, 11 October 1876; see also 10 January, 13 July, 10 November 1877; DIS, 8, 10 August 1876, 29 May 1877; RVS, 11, 15 November 1877.

3. CONS, 14 July 1879; DIS, 7 May, 30 August 1879; RVS, 22 May 1879; INDEP, 29 August 1880.

4. RVS, 19 April, 22 May, 14 August 1879; CLS, 1 March 1879; CQ, 12 June 1879; LN, 27 July 1879; DIS, 15 April 1879; CONS, 20 May 1879; CHT, 14 June 1879; TEL, 26 December 1879; CUR, 28 June 1879; COM, 10 May, 7 July 1879; CLS 20 March, 17, 22, 24 May 1879; ESPER, 24 June, 9 November 1879; ESMER, 23 July 1879; LOTA, 30 March 1879; FERR, 10 June 1879; C. Saavedra to Intendent of Aconcagua, 14 May 1879, AMI, vol. 905.

5. David Werlich, *Peru, a Short History* (Carbdondale: Southern Illinois Press, 1978), p. 113; Robert B. Burr, *By Reason or Force* (Berkeley: University of California Press, 1965), p. 143; Clements R. Markham, *The War between Peru and Chile* (London: Sampson Low, 1883), pp. 79-80; John Lloyd Mecham, *A Survey of United States Latin American Relations* (Boston: Houghton Mifflin, 1965), p. 413; Herbert S. Klein, *Bolivia* (New York: Oxford University Press, 1982), pp. 145-147; Atropos, "El inquilino en Chile. Un siglo sin variaciones," *Revista Mapocho* 5 (1966):199-201 (this article originally appeared in a 1861 edition of *Revista del Pacífico*); LN, 19 July 1879; CONS, 23 May 1879; TEL, 13 June, 19 August, 21 October 1879.

6. CQ, 19 June 1879; ESP, 5 August 1879; ESMER, 21 December 1879; COM, 7 July 1879; J. Salinas to Minister of Hacienda, 3 March 1879; N. Guerrero to Minister of War, 3 March 1879, AMI, vol. 903.

7. "Un chileno" claimed that it was cheaper to put criminals in the army than to maintain them in jail. BB, 20 April, 15 May 1879; TEL, 27 June 1879; CQ, 19 June, 20 July 1879; ESMER, 23 July 1879; LOTA, 30 March 1879.

8. M. Aldunate to E. Gomez, 14 June 1879, AMI, vol. 906.

9. BB, 15 May, 31 August 1879; COM, 7, 14 July 1879; ESMER, 31 December 1879; LN, 23 April 1879; ESPER, 24 June 1879; TEL, 20 April 1879; OPIN, 7 May, 21 June, 2, 3 July 1879; LN, 29 April, 1, 3, 9, 19 July 1879.

10. UN, 10 May 1879; SEM, 10 May 1879; TEL, 26 August 1879; OPIN, 16 May, 8 June 1879; VI, 11 October, 29 November 1879.

11. CDSO, 1 July 1880, pp. 109-10.

12. Ibid., pp. 111-13; CSSO, 7, 15, 20 July 1880, pp. 61-64, 198-200, 202-4, 220-33.
13. ESPER, 23 October, 11 December 1880; LIBT, 20 October 1880; CQ, 29 August 1880; TEL, 16 March 1880; FEN, 26 October 1880.
14. ESPER, 10 July 1880.
15. LIB, 30 October 1880.
16. ESMER, 24 November 1880; CQ, 9 December 1880.
17. LOT, 13 December 1880.
18. NFERR, 11 November 1880; TEL, 11 November 1880; LOT, 25 March, 25 July, 5 November 1880; V, 3 October 1880; CDSE, 8 January 1881, p. 89; ESMER, 11, 15, 25 August, 24 November 1880.
19. ESMER, 18 January, 21 July 1880; CQ, 9 December 1880; COM, 19 July, 23 April 1880; VI, 5 November 1881.
20. ESMER, 18 January, 21 July, 11 August 1880; LIBT, 5, 30 October, 10, 15 December 1880; ESPER, 3 July 1880; TEL, 11 November 1880.
21. PROM, 21 November 1880; LIBT, 10, 14 December 1880.
22. LIBT, 25 March, 14 October 1880; CQ, 29 August 1880; ÑUB, 13 November 1880; ESMER, 11 August 1880; ESPER, 13 November 1880; PC, 2 August 1880; FEN, 19 October 1880; CAU, 3 March 1880; CONS, 23 April, 13 August 1880.
23. TEL, 11 November 1880.
24. CQ, 29 August 1880; VI, 10 January 1880; LOT, 10 March 1880.
25. LIBT, 10 August 1880.
26. LIBT, 15 September 1880; CDSE, 8 January 1881, p. 92; ARA, 21 November 1880.
27. CDSO, 8 January 1881, pp. 90-91.
28. CHT, 1 April 1882; LIBT, 30 June, 12 July, 27 September 1881; INDEP, 26 June 1881; MER, 6 October 1881; DIS, 29 December 1881; ÑUB, 29 March, 3 May 1882; PC, 30 January, 13 March 1883; CONS, 28 April 1883; RVS, 31 May 1883; ECAT, 11 December 1882, 21 July 1883; DIS, 10 April 1882, 10 April 1883; ES, 5, 8 April 1883; CSSE, 1 September 1882, p. 123; LOTA, 2 October 1881; COR, 20 June 1881; ESPER, 12 March 1883; INDEP, 10 January 1883; CDSO, 12 January 1881, pp. 185, 191; CSSE, 1 September 1882, p. 123.
29. PC, 30 January 1883.
30. Alberto del Solar, *Diario de Campaña* (3rd ed.: Buenos Aires: Francisco de Aguirre, 1967), pp. 69-71; Hipólito Gutiérrez, "Crónica de un Soldado," in *Dos Soldados en la Guerra del Pacífico* (Buenos Aires: Francisco de Aguirre, 1976), pp. 166-67, 186; Diego Dublé Almeida, "Diario," p. 104; Arturo Benavides Santos, *Seis años de vacaciones* (3rd ed.: Buenos Aires: Francisco de Aguirre, 1967), pp. 34, 35, 61; LN, 26 April, 17, 19 June 1879; CLS, 23 August 1879; CONS, 22 July 1879; ECAT, 22 March, 12 May 1879; MER, 23 January 1880; LOT, 21 January 1880; CQ, 23 December 1879; FERRO. 16 May 1880; LIBT, 29 November 1880; DIS, 16 March 1880; LAP, 13 January 1881; LIBT, 22, 30 March 1881; David Tagle to B. Vicuña Mackenna, 27 November 1883 ABVM, vol. 383; CQ, 7 September 1879; NFERR, 14 July 1879; Poblete, "El servicio sanitario," RCHG 35, no. 39 (1920):465-70; 39, no. 38 (1920):484-487; 41, no. 45 (1922):457, 459. For the failures of the Chilean army's supply system see Arturo Sepúlveda Rojas, *Así vivieron y vencieron (1879-1884)* (Santiago: Imprenta Esparza, 1980), pp. 9, 13.
31. BGP, 14, 22, 26 April, 2, 12 May, 24 June 1879, pp. 23, 43, 64, 78-79, 208-9; DO, 26 April 1879; 8, 10, 15, 20, 23, 26, 30, 31 May, 21 June 1879, pp. 713, 725, 749,

769, 777, 788, 818, 826, 1017; José Tocornal to Intendent Jeneral del Ejército i Armada, 13 May 1879 in BGP, 21 May 1879, p. 97; FERR, 18 January, 1 April 1880; LIBT, 14 August 1880; CDSE, 17 January 1881, p. 178; Report of the Comité Central de Donativos, CDSO, 12 November 1881, pp. 127-29; Rafael B. Pizarro, *Los Abastecimientos militares en La guerra del Pacífico* (Santiago: Ministerio de Defensa Nacional, 1967), pp. 25-28; MAI, 3 August 1879; MER, 20 December 1879; LAP, 20 January 1880; CONS, 11 November 1880; Francisco Echaurren to General E. Escala, 10 August 1879 in Ahumada Moreno, 2:43-44.

32. V. Dávila Larraín to Minister of War, 9 January 1880, Ahumada Moreno, 2:321-22; Pizarro, *Abastecimientos*, p. 35; PAR, 9 January 1880; Sepúlveda, *Vivieron*, pp. 21, 37, 39..

33. LAP, 20 January 1880; Pizarro, *Abastecimientos*, p. 34; "Diario de la campaña a Lima, agregardo al Regimiento de Infantería, 'Esmeralda' " in Ahumada Moreno, 8:37; Gutiérrez, "Crónica," pp. 197-98; CQ, 18 July 1880; LAP, 20 January 1880; E. Sotomayor to A. Pinto, 25 April 1879, AJE 1; PAR, 9 January, 1 August 1880; Daniel Riquelme, *La Expedicion a Lima* (Santiago: Editorial Paci fico, 1967), pp. 46, 86, 105.

34. Poblete, " Servicio," RCHG 33, no.37 (1920):465-66, 468-69.

35. Ibid., 470, 475-78; 39, no. 38 (1920):469-72, 477-84; MER, 22 December 1879; LAP, 20 November 1879; INDEP, 4 November 1879. Apparently these problems did not stop either. (see LAP, 17 July 1880. CDSO, 1 July 1880, pp. 109, 117-18; LAP, 13 September 1880; MER, 21 August 1880; CONS, 21 October 1880; LIBT, 13 October 1881; CDSE, 17 January 1881, pp. 177-79; Jose Gandarillas to General en Jefe del Ejército del Norte, 19 November 1879, Ahumada Moreno, 2:253; FERR, 7 December 1880). The statement of Gandarillas only mentioned those men "wounded in the campaign." This policy certainly seems consistent with the treatment accorded to the families of the men who died of battle connected injuries and those who succumbed to natural diseases. ECAT, 26 November 1880; FERR, 11 July 1880; NFERR, 15 November 1880; LAP, 18 March, 15 June 1880; PCH, 24 March 1880.

36. LAP, 30 June 1880.

37. LOT, 27, 28 January 1880; INDEP, 8 February 1881.

38. ECAT, 1 February 1881; INDEP, 30 January 1881; ÑUB, 16 February 1881; CQ, 17 March 1881; LIBT, 27 January 1881.

39. RVS, 11 February 1881; DIS, 24 February 1881; LAP, 25 January 1881.

40. ÑUB, 16 February 1881; COM, 7, 16 February 1881; CQ, 13 February 1881; CUR, 26 February 1881; DIS, 22 February 1881.

41. FERR, 3 March 1879; G. Matte to Minister of Hacienda, 10, 27 December 1879, 6 March 1880, 5 February, 6 March, 8 April 1880; 16 January 1882, Intendency of Atacama, vol. 528 (hereafter cited as IA); G. Matte to Minister of Hacienda, 26 April, 21 July 1879; 16 January 1880, AMH, vols. 1017, 1053; A. Errázuriz to Minister of Hacienda, telegram, 23 November 1880, AMH, vol. 1113; A. Martínez to Minister of Hacienda, 10 January 1882, AMH, vol. 1173 (note: the Archivo Nacional has since renumbered the volumes dealing with the Intendency of Atacama. These citations refer to the old system, not the latest version). Pinto, 29 November 1879 in Ahumada Moreno, 2:254; LAP, 17, 22 September 1880; Abraham Quiroz, "Epistolario inédito de su campaña como soldado raso durante toda la Guerra del Pacifíco, 1879-1884," in *Dos Soldados*, pp. 64, 72, 75-77, 82-83, 89, 92, 94-95, 102, 104, 107, 125. Officers also had to pay for a variety of services,

including "bad food," FERR, 3 March 1879. A report by Benjamín Vicuña Mackenna concluded that after paying the expenses demanded by the army, a soldier had but $2.25 of his $11.00 salary left for his family. The same study also claimed that a junior officer had to spend $10.00 more than his salary in order to live. CSSO, 28 June 1882, p. 128; M. Le León, *Recuerdos de una misión en el Ejército Chileno* (Buenos Aires: Francisco de Aguirre, 1969), p. 183; LAP, 13, 24 September 1880; MER, 26 August 1880.

42. Anguita, 2:5-8; CDSE, 16 January 1879, p. 9; D. Santa María to C. Castellón, Santiago, 20 March 1880, in Rispatrón, *Legislación*, 3:589; LAP, 17, 22 September 1880; ESMER, 21 December 1879; VI, 27 December 1879; LAP, 11 December 1879.

43. CDSE, 16 December 1879, pp. 2-3, 7 -12; CSSE, 22 December 1879, pp. 6, 13-15.

44. CQ, 15 July 1880; LOT, 10 January 1880; DIS, 5 June 1880; LIBT, 18 January 1880; LAP, 20 January 1880; ESPER, 13 November 1880; CONS, 15 January 1881; ARO, 21 January 1881.

45. FERR, 3 February 1880; LAP, 4 February, 18 March, 9 December1880; CQ, 4 November 1880; CDSO, 28 July 1881, p. 269.

46. CDSO, 12, 25 June, 10, 20, 27, 30 August, 4 September 1880, pp. 26, 94, 400-01, 492, 575, 611, 652-53.

47. CDSE, 17 January 1881, p. 179.

48. VI, 9 January 1881; PC, 6 May 1881.

49. CDSO, 2, 14, 21 June, 16 July 1881, pp. 11, 53-54, 194-99.

50. PC, 2 August 1881.

51. CDSO, 1 September 1881, pp. 377, 380-85.

52. CDSE, 18, 22, 25 October 1881, pp. 8-9, 12-13, 25, 36-38.

53. Ibid., 3, 24 November 1881, pp. 77, 226, 228-34; CSSE, 13, 16 December 1881, pp. 175-76, 198; LAP, 6 December 1881.

54. FERR, 29 March 1882; ÑUB, 28 June 1882; VM, 20 January, 29 December 1882; ESMER, 14 January, 11 November 1883; INDEP, 11 March 1883; "Memoria del Inspector Jeneral del Ejército," in *Memoria de Guerra de 1882* (Santiago: La Epoca,1882), p. 20; DIS, 21 December 1882; PRE, 7 September 1882.

55. DIS, 21 December 1882.

56. PRE, 7, 26, 31 August, 2 September 1882; CDSO, 13 June, 8 August 1882, pp. 63-64, 450, 7 June, 21, 24 July, 7 August, 30 September 1883, pp. 37, 271, 278-79, 336-37; Anguita, 2:562, 613.

57. DO, 29 March 1881, pp. 422-23; CONS, 8 April 1881; LIBT, 30 March, 7 April 1881.

58. CQ, 17 March 1881; ÑUB, 23 February, 16 March 1881; INDEP, 23 March 1881; DIS, 15 March 1881.

59. DIS, 15 March 1881.

60. LAP, 1, 2 April, 4 August, 13 September 1881; DIS, 7, 9 July 1881; LIBT, 13, 27 August 1881; PC, 5 July 1881; FERR, 29 March 1882; CAU, 3 December 1882; ESMER, 14 January, 11 November 1883; INDEP, 11 March 1883; CONS, 8 February, 14 April 1881; COV, 12 March 1881.

61. LAP, 20 November 1879, 2, 9-11, 19, 23, 25 February 1881.

62. Ibid., 11 February, 22 July 1881; LOT, 29 July 1881; INDEP, 23, 26 July, 25 August 1881; FERR, 30 January, 24 June 1881.

63. PC, 17 September 1881; FERR, 11 March 1881.

64. Ibid., COR, 5 February 1881; CDSO, 12 June 1880, pp. 19-20, 9 August 1881, pp. 309-10. See also RVS, 9 November 1883; ARO, 18 March 1883; ES, 9 April 1883, 3 April 1884.

65. CDSO, 2, 22, 21, 25 June, 10 July, 9 August 1881, pp. 5-6, 53-54, 78, 90, 173, 179, 308-09; CDSE, 3, 26, 30 November 1881, pp. 72-76, 252-53, 260; LAP, 5 September 1881.

66. CDSO, 3, 8, 10 July, 6, pp. 291-92, 16 August 1881, pp. 123, 151, 179, pp. 291-92, 441-42.

67. Ibid., 8 June, 3 July 1880, pp. 12-13, 123; 28 July 1883, p. 302; 21 June 1884, p. 80; FERR, 16 January 1881; ECAT, 20 July 1881 opposed it, calling them "prisoners in a golden palace"; CDSO, 27 June 1882, p. 53; CDSE, 18 January 1881, pp. 187-89; FERR, 3, 11, February 1881; CDSO, 6 August 1881, pp. 291-92, 7 June 1883, pp. 37-38; CDSE, 12 November 1881, pp. 124-26.

68. CDSO, 30, 31 July, 2, 19 August 1880, pp. 320-31, 335-36, 347-53; CDSE, 12 January 1882, pp. 620, 623-25; Anguita, 2:5-6, 519; 4:126-27. The United States was much more generous with its troops. See William F. Glasson, *History of Pension Legislation in the United State* (New York: Columbia University Press, 1900).

69. PC, 13 January 1883.

70. ESPER, 13 November 1880, NOV, 16 June 1880; CUR, 28 March 1879; LN, 19 July 1879; CHT, 24 May 1879; MER, 7 January 1882; CDSE, 12 November 1881, p. 126.

71. LAP, 22 September 1880.

CHAPTER SIX

1. Ramón Domínguez, "Nuestro sistema de inquilinaje en 1867," *Revista Mapocho* 5 (1966):296, 313 (this article appeared originally in 1867). Atropos, "El inquilino en Chile. Su vida. Un siglo sin variaciónes," *Revista Mapocho*, 5 (1966), 197-215 (originally published in 1861); Horacio Aránguiz Donoso, "La situatión de los trabajadores agrícolas en el siglo XIX," EHIPS 2 (1967):6-30.

2. M. G. [Marcial González], *Condición de los trabajadores rurales en Chile* (Santiago: Imprenta de la República de Jacinto Núñez, 1876), pp. 12-13; CHT, 15 February 1879.

3. W. F. Sater, "Chile and the World Depression of the 1870s," JLS 11 (1979):71-79; LAP, 10 January 1879.

4. *La Unión* (San Fernando), 12 January 1879 in FERR, 14 January 1879; PAR, 26 January 1879; VI, 9 January 1879; ARA, 20 February 1879; DIS, 16 February 1879; FERR, 28 January 1879.

5. RVS, 15 February 1879; BSNA, 20 December 1879; ECAT, 10, 19 February, 25, 29 March 1879; ÑUB, 4 January 1879; DIS, 22 January 1879; BB, 9 February 1879; PAR, 26 January 1879; LOTA, 2 March 1879; INDEP, 13 January 1879.

6. LAP, 13 January 1879.

7. *The Economist*, 8 March, 20, 30 August, 11 October, 15 November 1879, 13 March 1880. Julio Menadier warned the Chileans not to speculate, FERR, 6 September 1879.

8. ARO, 27 March. 3 April 1880; BB, 8 January 1880; ESMER, 7 April 1880; LIBV, 3 April 1880; RVS, 8, 17 January 1880.

9. *The Economist*, 25 June, 22 July, 30 August 1881, 18 February, 22 April 1882.

10. ESMER, 11 May, 22 August 1880; VI, 17 July, 22 August 1880; CAU 20, 27 June, 1 August 1880; LIBT, 12 August 1880; PAR, 1 August 1880; RVS, 22 July, 7 August, 9 October 1880; MER, 10, 24 July, 27 August 1880; *Sinopsis Estadística de la República de Chile* (Santiago: Imprenta Universo, 1919), p. 3; *El Tamaya* (Ovalle), 15 July 1880 in MER, 24 July 1880; VI, 31 July 1880.

11. FERR, 18 November, 18 December 1880; CUR, 4 December 1880; LIBV, 31 July, 18 December 1880; LOT, 3 September 1880; ESMER, 28 July 1880; RVS, 11 December 1880; VI, 2 January, 12 March 1881; ÑUB, 8 October 1881; BB, 20 June, 5, 15 July, 1 August 1880.

12. INDEP, 18 October 1881; DIS, 4 February 1882. See also *Los Principios* (Parral), 3 January, 1 February 1882; *El Condor* (Linares), 4 March 1882 in ECAT, 7 March 1882; RVS, 22, 26 January, 28 February 1882; EPSC, 28 February 1882; ESMER, 5 March 1882; BB, 16 February 1882; VI, 11 February 1882; VER, 19 August 1882; LIBT, 19 January 1882; LUZ, 22 April 1882; PORL, 28 October 1882.

13. CHIL, 16 March 1882; LIBLU, 8 April 1882; ESMER, 16 April 1882; INDEP, 14 April 1882; COR, 21 January, 4 February 1882.

14. DIS, 20 April 1883; INDEP, 16 February, 2 April 1882; VI, 26 March 1882; FERR, 15 February 1882.

15. *The Economist*, 16 September 1882; 24 February 1883.

16. PORL, 28 October 1882; BB, 1, 4, 8 March 1883; DIS, 3, 29 March 4, 20 November 1882, 27 February 1883; ARA, 24 February 1883; ESMER, 14 January, 25 February 1883; RVS, 21 February 1883; INDEP, 23 February 1883; JUV, 22 October 1882; ARO, 6 January 1883; BB, 14 January 1883.

17. ECAT, 6, 22 November, 7 December 1878. The size of the Chilean army varied but by December, 1880, there were 41,981 men serving in the Army of the North, in units occupying parts of Peru, Bolivia, and doing garrison duty in Chile. These figures do not include those in the navy or the National Guard. (Ahumada Moreno, 7:411).

18. SUF, 2 January 1879; DIS, 12 January 1879; *El Tamaya*, 15 January 1879 in LAP, 20 January 1879; ARO, 3 August 1879; 8 May 1880; ESMER, 26 October 1879; ECAT, 7 December 1880; FERR, 2 November 1880; LAP, 3 September 1880; FEN, 19 October 1880; ESPER, 6 November 1880; CHIL, 29 July 1880; LAP, 3 September 1880; DIS, 13 January 1880.

19. ESPER, 4 January, 21 December 1880; TEL, 16 November, 21 December 1880.

20. ECAT, 10 January, 14 February 1881; REPUB, 16 January 1881; LIBT, 9 January 1881; LUZ, 29 March 1881; RVS, 25 January 1881.

21. ECAT, 22 November 1881; CUR, 19 February 1881.

22. ESPER, 22 July 1882; MAI, 26 March 1882; ECAT, 11, 20 January, 16 February, 11 March 1882; CUR, 8 January 1882; LUZ, 24 February 1882; DIS, 10 January, 28 February 1882; RVS, 9 February, 5 April 1882; LAP, 2 January 1882; ÑUB, 11, 25 March 1882; LIBLU, 11, 18 March 1882.

23. MER, 14 April, 20 August 1883; MAI, 18 June 1882; ES, 21 October 1883. In Quillota, they began to recruit men for the National Guard unit. The mere rumour that it might be sent north sent people fleeing out of the area and thereby damaging the local economy. CQ, 22 November 1883; FERR, 24 January 1883;

LIBLU, 1 April 1883; *El Constitución* (Maule), 10 January 1884 in MER, 17 January 1884; DIS, 9 January 1884; LIBT, 12 February 1884.

24. CQ, 5 February, 7 December 1882; CHT, 11 March 1882; CUR, 8 January 1882; LAP, 19 January 1882; TEL, 13 February 1884; DIQ, 28 January 1881.

25. CUR, 19 February 1881; COR, 1 January 1881; CQ, 2 June 1881; DIS, 8 November 1881, 7 April, 24 November, 4 December 1883; BSNA, 5 December 1883; EPS, 24 November 1882.

26. FERR, 22 August 1881; COM, 20 February 1882; ARA, 14 December 1879; JUV, 26 November 1882; LOTA, 20 August 1882; FEN, 23 January 1883; CUR, 20 February 1882; ARA, 14 December 1879.

27. RVS, 9 February 1882; ES, 25 January 1883; INDEP, 3, 4 March 1882; CHT, 11 March 1882, 3 February 1883; MER, 14 April 1883; ÑUB, 4 February 1882.

28. CUR, 24 January 1880, 26 February 1881; ÑUB, 8 March 1882; LIBT, 7 December 1883; ARA, 29 January 1884; ES, 10 January 1884; RVS, 23 February 1883; BB, 4 March 1883; ARA, 29 January 1884; *El Eco del Sur*, 6 December 1883 reported that Collipulli had twenty steam driven *trillas*; VER, 11 March 1882; DO, 8 June 1880; BB, 17 February 1884. During the period 1878-1884, farmers imported the following; 506 machines for cleaning wheat; 305 for reaping; 296 threshers. (*Estadística Comercial de la República de Chile* [1878-1884]). These figures do not include agricultural machinery produced by Chilean foundaries.

29. CONS, 25 August, 11 November 1879; CQ, 6 September 1883; LOT, 8 January 1880; RVS, 25 January 1881; LUZ, 23 December 1882 noted that "workers of all ages and sexes are seen working in the fields, indeed, women are better reapers than men."

30. BSNA, 5 January 1880, p. 101; 5 August 1881, pp. 390-395.

31. Ibid., 5 August 1881, pp. 394-395; 5 September 1882, p. 440; 5 December 1883, pp. 97-98; CEN, 20 June 1880; EPS, 3-5 January 1883.

32. EPS, 9 March 1882; BSNA, 20 November 1879, p. 49, 5 February 1880, pp. 153-55, 20 August 1881, pp. 401-6, 5 January 1882, pp. 106-9; DO, 22 March 1880, pp. 411-12.

33. ECAT, 7 April 1879; BSNA, 20 November 1879, pp. 81-84. The government continued to control the entry of foodstuffs into Peruvian ports, as well as Arica. This prohibition was eventually extended to include coal as well (DO, 3 November, 3 December 1880; OPIN, 30 July 1879).

34. INDEP, 4 January 1882. The National Society of Agriculture stressed the importance of Tarapacá as a future market for Chilean goods (BSNA, 20 May, 20 June, 5 July 1880, pp. 291-93, 331-34, 357-61, 5 November pp. 21-26). See also DO, 25, 27 October 1879, 6 April 1880; RVS, 29 January 1881; LAP, 9 September 1880, 22 July 1881; INDEP, 7 January, 16 December; MER, 8 November 1883.

35. CDSO, 20, 27, 28, 29 August, 1, 2, 6 September 1879, pp. 406-9, 462-77, 484, 487-91, 509-13, 619-20, 536-37. See also CSSO, 5 July, 17, 19 August 1880, pp. 37, 223-38, 241-49, 256-62; CSSE, 2 December 1881, pp. 127-28. Statistics indicate that the amount of tobacco imported dropped from 1,004,703 kilos in 1877 to 96,113 in 1884. Imports of tobacco also declined from 1,975,726 sheaves to 0 in the same period of time. Cigarette paper imports rose from 84,083 kilos in 1877 to 178,530 kilos in 1884.

36. LIBT, 22 January 1880; MER, 26 December 1879. for example, noted that the government's use of the railroad's rolling stock prevented farmers from shipping their goods to market (LAP, 22 July 1882). The mobilization of Batallón Numero Uno absorbed so many stevadores that the price of labor increased

substantially. The replacements not only demanded twice as much, plus lunch, they apparently also stole more.

37. Sater, "Depression," 68-72; *The Economist*, 10 March 1879, 13 March 1880; CONS, 7 January, 11 February 1879; FERR, 19 June 1879; COMC, 17 March 1879.

38. *El continjente de la provincia Atacama en la Guerra del Pacifíco* (Copiapó: Libreria "El Atacama," n.d.); DO, 28 May 1880.

39. DO, 17 November 1879; *The Economist*, 13 March 1880; BPS 74 (1880), 1523-527. In 1878 Chile imported approximately 142,000 kilos of silver ore and 7.4 million kilos of copper ore from Bolivia and Peru. By 1882, Santiago's imports from these two nations had declined to but 6,000 kilos of silver and 1,118 kilos of copper core.

40. MER, 17 January 1880.

41. CONS, 12 March, 6, 9 July, 13 August, 15 November, 6, 12 December 1880; BPS, 91 (1881):1451; 74 (1880):1508, 1511.

42. CONS, 1 May 1880; BPS, 75 (1880):1508, 91 (1881):1451.

43. CHT, 24 July 1880; CONS, 3 August 1880; A. Larrunaga, "Memoria de Mineria," 19 August 1880, AMH, vol. 1088; G. Blest Gana to Minister of Interior, AMI, vol. 875; BPS, 78 (1883):1174.

44. R. Núñez to Minister of Hacienda, 10 May 1881, AMH, vol. 1112; BPS, 78 (1883):1171; LAP, 23 September 1881; RVS, 27 September, 6 October 1881; ESMER, 25 September, 5 October 1881.

45. A. Martínez to Minister of Interior, 12 March 1883, AMH, vol. 1034; J. Guzmán to Intendent of Atacma, 14 March 1880, AMH, vol. 1088; CONS, 7 Jan, 12 April, 14 September, 15, 28 November 1881.

46. Ibid., 21 January 1882; *The Economist*, 24 February 1883; EPS, 15 September 1882; INDUS, 19 October 1882; CONS, 12-17 June 1882, 11 April 1883; RMIN, 1 January, 1 February 1884; MMHAC, 1882, pp. cxxiv-cxxviii.

47. RMIN, 1 January 1884.

48. CONS, 8 March, 11, 26 April, 9 August, 21 September 1883; VM, 6, 20 March 1881; CONS, 11 April 1883.

49. R. Núñez to Minister of Hacienda, 10 May 1881, AMH, vol. 1112. Francisco Arancena, *Apuntes de viaje. La industria del cobre en las provincias de Atacama i Coquimbo i los grandes i valiosos depósitos carboníferos de Lota i Coronel en la provincia de Concepción* (Valparaíso: Imprenta del Nuevo Mercurio, 1884), pp. 118-19, described *pirquineros* as a "Strange and ruinous plague" and argued that each time an owner retrieved a mine from one of them, he had to spend large sums on restoration of the work site. Leland R. Pederson, *The Mining Industry of the Norte Chico, Chile* (Evanston: Northwestern University Press, 1966), studies the etymology of the term. The author describes the "pirquinero" as an individual wJune 1879.

50. CONS, 9 January, 1 November 1883; DO, 24 July 1883; "Memoria del Superintendente de Aduanas," MMHAC, 1883, p. 168; INDEP, 1 November 1883; RMIN, 15 December 1883.

51. *The Economist*, 24 February 1883, 23 February 1884; MMHAC, 1883, p. cxiii; BPS, 74 (1880):1509; 63 (1883):1870; BB, 21 August 1880.

52. ESMER, 22 June, 5 October, 21 December 1879, 11 Auviaje. La industria del cobre en las provincias de Atacama i Coquimbo i los grandes i valiosos depósitos carboníferos de Lota gust 1880.

53. RVS, 24 January 1880; ESMER, 11 August, 17, 24 November 1880, 16 January, 6 November 1881.

54. ESMER, 28 November 1880; LIBV, 22 May 1880; RVS, 20 February 1883.
55. BPS, 78 (1883):1171; Aracena, pp. 290-335; *Lota*, ed by Octavio Astorquiza (Valparaíso: Imprenta Universo, 1942), pp. 34-40.
56. Benjamín Vicuña Mackenna, *El libro del cobre i del carbón de piedra en Chile* (Santiago: Editorial del Pacífico, 1966), Cuadro 3, pp. 10-11; CHT, 28 February 1880; RMIN, 1 January, 1 February 1884; Aracena, pp. 142-44, 213-15, 223-24.
57. CONS, 7 April, 23 October 1880, 17 June 1882.
58. CDSO, 15 July 1882, p. 249-50; CSSE, 28, 30 December 1882, pp. 303-04, 315-22; CDSO, 14, 17 June 1884, pp. 53-54, 63.
59. CONS, 12 June 1882, 9 January 1883 calculated that a miner employing ten people paid more in taxes than an *hacendado* who owned 1,000 cuadras of land farmed by 300 *inquilinos*. C. J. Huidobro to Minister of Hacienda, 2 October 1879, AMH, vol. 1088; Arancena, pp. 29, 35, 118; *El Liberal*, 23 July 1882 printed a cartoon showing agriculture as a cow being milked dry by the state.
60. Francisco A. Encina, *Historia de Chile*, 20 vols. (Santiago: Nascimento, 1946-1952), 17:418-19.
61. Sater, "Economic Nationalism and Tax Reform in Late Nineteenth Century Chile," *The Americas* 33 (1976):311-27.
62. MER, 12 February, 11, 13 October 1880; LOT, 20 January, 23 February, 8 August 1880.
63. CACH, 15 May 1879; "Memoria del Director Jeneral del Parque i Maestranza de Santiago," in MMG, 1882, pp. 133-47; "Memoria presentada por el Coronel don Tomás Walton al senor Ministro de Estado el departamento de guerra," MMG, 1882, pp. 149-158; LAP, 2 February 1882.
64. RVS, 24 June, 27 July, 3 August 1882; TAL, 22 February 1879; LOT, 3 January 1880; FERR, 12 July 1880; NFERR, 29 January 1880; CHT, 17 December 1881.
65. INDEP, 4 April 1884; PC, 10 December 1881, 11 February 1882.
66. RVS, 16 October 1881, 11 February 1882, 10 June 1883; DIS, 8 March 1881; LAP, 25 October 1881; LAU, 8 February 1880; FERR, 25 July 1882; Anguita, 2:521; PORC, 15 December 1883.
67. ESMER, 13 August 1879, 17 March 1880; HER, 8 July 1881; RVS, 31 January 1882, 22 July 1883; NFERR, 4 March 1880; LAP, 11 October 1881; INDEP, 3 December 1881; FERR, 21 January 1882; LIBV, 27 August 1881; TAL, 7 February 1879.
68. CONS, 24 March 1880; ESMER, 13 August 1879; TAL, 7 February 1879.
69. FERR, 30 January, 18 July 1881; MER, 8 July 1881; EPS, 8 April 1883; LAP, 30 January, 1 August 1882.
70. LIBV, 29 October 1881; FERR, 5 May 1881, 1 August 1882; LAP, 11 October 1881. On 7 July 1882, *La Patria*, for example, complained that the lack of ships from Europe paralyzed local commerce.
71. LAP, 1 August 1882; FERR, 1 August 1882; Pedro N. Urzúa, *Don Zorobabel Rodríguez o las exajeraciones del libre cambio* (Santiago: Imprenta Cervantes, 1884); PC, 3 August 1882, 28 November 1883; FERR, 1 August 1882; LIBV, 26 October 1881; LAP, 3 August 1882, 28 November 1883.
72. PC, 18 February 1882; LAP, 29 October 1881, 1, 4 August 1882; FERR, 16 July, 20 October 1881, 12 September 1883; NFERR, 29 January 1880; LIBV, 26 October 1881, 13 February 1883; RVS, 7, 21, 22 July 1883; EPS, 29 January, 5 August 1882.

73. FERR, 5 August 1881.
74. PC, 4 August 1881; ESMER, 25 January 1880; LIBV, 29 October 1881; LAP, 11 October 1881, 15 November 1882; FERR, 5 August 1880, 1 August, 10 September 1883, 28 January, 11 February 1884; RVS, 22 July 1883; LAP, 15 November 1882.
75. BPS, 78 (1885):1016.
76. ÑUB, 21 December 1881; FERR, 1 June 1881. *El Ferrocarril*, on 1 August 1882, called for a policy of "Prudent and rational protectionism" which would not increase the cost of consumer goods. LAP, 15 November 1882; ESMER, 13 August 1879; MER, 24 April 1883; DIS, 19 June 1883; FERR, 9 May 1880; INDEP, 26 August 1883; RVS, 2 March, 2 May 1883; FERR, 30 January 1881, 26 January 1884.
77. CSSE, 18 October, 29 December 1881, pp. 6-7, 491-95; PC, 1 September 1881 was furious that the state purchased these cars from abroad.
78. DO, 26 February, 9 May, 9, 21 July 1883.
79. RVS, 30 June 1883.
80. R. Espech, "La industria fabril en Chile," *Boletín de la Sociedad de Fomento Fabril* 1 (1884):8.
81. *Sinopsis Estadíistica de la República de Chile* (Santiago: Imprenta Universo, 1919), pp. 4-7; FERR, 1 January 1880; Memorias del Intendente de Santiago, DO, 21 June 1881, 10 June 1882, 4 August 1883; CQ, 9 January 1881. Apparently this building craze was not confined solely to Santiago. In Talca, more than twenty five building permits, as well as an additional seventeen permits for repairs, worth a total of $140,000, were approved in 1882 (DO, 10 September 1883; ECS, 14 October, 6 December 1883; PORC, 29 December 1883).
82. See the various intendents' reports: DO, 2, 4, 7, 9, 14, 16 May, 11, 14, 22 June 1881, 13 May, 10, 13 June, 14, 21, 27 July 1882, 2, 4, 17 August, 5 September 1883.
83. DO, 18, 24, 28 June, 1 July, 9, 14, 18, 20 August 11, 21 September, 5, 6, 27, 29 October 1880. 30 April, 4, 5, 13 May 1881; MMINT of 1881, in DO, 26 September 1881; 11 September, 16 October, 11 December 1880, 7 May, 18 June AMI, vols. 875, 985, 986. Manuel Recabarren to Intendentes de provincia, 7 April 1881, in DO, 7 April 1881, noted that they should start to repair the roads now that the harvest had been completed. See also DO, 10 February, 11 August 1881.
84. Oscar Bermúdez, *Historia del salitre* (Santiago: Universidad de Chile, 1963), pp. 287-88, 295, 302, as well as his "El salitre de Tarapacá y Antofagasta durante la occupación militar chilena," *Anales de la Universidad del Norte* 5 (1966), 161, 163, 165-67.
85. CONS, 11 May 1880, 7 May, 11 September, 28 November 19, 21 December 1881; ET, 5 September, 10 November 1881.
86. CDSO, 18, 30 June, 29 August 1881, pp. 39-41, 82-83, 370-73; CDSE, 18 October, 12, 14, 26, 28 December 1881, 9, 10, 11, 13 January 1882, pp. 5, 249-52, 326-28, 330-34, 353, 469, 609-12, 615-16, 622; CSSE, 26, 28 December 1881, 13 January 1882, 248-50, 251-52, 330-32; Anguita, 3:514-515; CDSO, 23 August 1882, p. 510; CSSO, 14 August, 24 September 1882, pp. 212, 360-61; VM, 26 January 1883.
87. Bermúdez, *Historia*, pp. 226, 230-38.
88. INDUS, 27 September, 22 October, 2 November 1881, 28 March 1882, 31 March 1883; LAP, 4 October 1883; Dr. Semper and Dr. Michels, *La industria del salitre en Chile*, trans. by Javier Gandarillas y Orlando Ghigliotto (Santiago: Imprenta Barcelona, 1908), pp. 136-37.

89. Robert G. Greenhill and Rory M. Miller, "The Peruvian Government and the Nitrate Trade, 1873 to 1879," JLS 5, no.1 (1973):113-18.

90. Thomas F. O'Brien Jr., "British Investors and the Decline of the Chilean Nitrate Entrepreneurs, 1870 to 1889" (Ph. D. diss., University of Connecticut, 1976), pp. 109 to 113. Semper and Michels estimated that cost at £4,194,264. Nationalization of the southern nitrate lands would have cost an additional £225,000. p. 137).

91. "Informe de la Comisión Consultiva de Salitre," DO, 22 June 1880.

92. FERR, 10 July 1880; INDEP, 20 January, 22 April 1880; DO, 13 April, 4 May, 15 June 1881.

93. FERR, 29 June 1881, 4 April, 11 August 1882; LAP, 13, 14 September 1881.

94. O'Brien, pp. 114-15. Harold Blakemore noted that by returning the nitrate lands to private ownership "the Chilean government satisfied ... the Peruvian certificate holders, and escaped the diplomatic pressure from claimants on Peru's general debt as heir to the mortgaged territory. Pressure for this course of action, therefore, came from Chile's needs and from the laissez-faire lobby." "The Politics of Nitrate in Chile. Pressure Groups and Policies, 1870-1896. Some Unanswered Questions." *Revue Française d'Histoire d'Outre-Mer* 66 (1979): 244-45. Markos Mamalakis noted, moreover, that Chile did not posses the financial means—which he described as requiring "astronomical resources"—to obtain legal title to the nitrate mines. Although he believed that the nation could have accumulated these funds, albeit it at some sacrifice, he doubted that foreign nations would have permitted Chile to take the nitrate lands. "Nitrate," he noted, "was too important to be left to the Chileans." "The Role of Government in the Resource Transfer and Resource Allocation Process: The Chilean Nitrate Sector, 1880-1930," in Gustavo Ranis, *Government and Economic Development* (New Haven: Yale University Press, 1971), pp. 197-98.

95. Semper and Michels, pp. 137, 140; VM, 6, 8, 20 March 1881, 7 March 1883; FERR, 12 September 1881; LAP, 9 February 1883; INDEP, 11 May 1883. The best discussion of this topic can be found in O'Brien's work.

CHAPTER SEVEN

1. LAP, 16, 20,28 January 1879; UN, 18, 25 October 1879; FERR, 26 January 1879; NOV, 4 February 1879. The economic situation during the war proved extremely precarious. Chile's envoy to Europe, Alberto Blest Gana, wished to purchase equipment from Germany. Krupp, however, would not turn over the artillery until payment was received. The envoy also lacked the funds to pay for the insurance. Alberto Blest Gana to A. Pinto, 10 October 1879, FV, vol. 413, Alberto Blest Gana to A. Matte, 31 December l879, FV, vol. 826.

2. Sater, "Economic Nationalism," pp. 324-26; CSSE, 4, 7 April 1879, pp. 22-23, 26-27; CDSE, 10 May 1879, pp. 740-45.

3. NOV, 16, 18 May 1879; FERR, 17 June 1879; CQ, 18 July 1880; ESMER, 22 June, 2 July 1879.

4. OPIN, 11 May 1879; UN, 25 October 1879; NOV, 21 June 1879; CHT, 14 August 1880.

5. RVS, 4 August 1882; FERR, 6 October 1881; VM, 6 January, 4 February 1883; MMHAC, 1880 in DO, 12 September 1880; MMAHC, 1881, pp. lxxiii, 2, 6-9; MMHAC, 1882, pp. lxxxiii-v, "Memoria del comisario de la contribución

mobiliaría en Santiago," MMAHC, 1882, pp. 2, 19-20, 22; CDSE, 29 December 1882, p. 394; CSSE, 3 January 1883, pp. 325-26; CDSO, 9 June 1883, pp. 41-43.
  6. Sater, "Economic nationalism," p. 321.
  7. CDSO, 19 July 1879, 13, 21 August 1879, pp. 394-95, 400-401, 417-20, 423, 432.
  8. Ibid., 13, 28 August, 3 September 1879, pp. 398-99, 401, 481-82, 528; CSSO, 6, 9 September 1879, pp. 225-26, 235-39, 243-49.
  9. CDSO, 25 June, 1 July 1879, pp. 120, 156-62.
  10. ECAT, 15 July 1879. See also MER, 10 July 1879; LOT, 12 August 1879; INDEP, 8 July, 26 August 1879; RVS, 31 July 1879; CDSO, 1 July 1879, pp. 159-60.
  11. CDSO, 1, 3, 5, 9 July 1879, pp. 156-61, 180-85, 191-95, 216, 224.
  12. NFERR, 14 July 1879; LOT, 14, 15, 19 August 1879; NOV, 15 July 1879.
  13. ECAT, 15 July 1879; INDEP, 22, 26 August 1879.
  14. CSSO, 18, 20, 25, 27, 28, 29, 30 August, 5 September 1879, pp. 133-34, 148, 157-58, 160, 166, 168-71, 182, 190, 194, 197-98, 201-3, 218-20; CDSO, 4 September 1879, p. 532.
  15. CSSO, 27, 28, 29 August 1879, p. 168, 182, 190; NOV, 24 July 1879; ECT, 5 September 1879, claimed that interests tried to favor the salitreros of Antofagasta over those of Old Chile.
  16. CSSE, 8 January 1880, pp. 109-10; MER, 13, 17, 22 January, 19, 20 February, 18, 19, 22 March, 23 April 1880; FERR, 21 February 1880.
  17. CHT, 28 February 1880.
  18. LOT, 22 April, 8, 10 May 1880.
  19. LOT, 11, 13, 20, 28 May, 27 June 1880; PCH, 21 January, 9 February, 7, 12 May 1880.
  20. "Informe de la comisión consultiva de salitre," DO, 22 June 1880.
  21. Ibid.
  22. FERR, 10 July 1880; INDEP, 22 January, 22 April 1880.
  23. CDSO, 6 July, 5, 6, 16, 17, 19, 20, 21 August 1880, pp. 136-37, 377, 454-55, 459-63, 487-89, 492-93, 506-7; CHT, 8 May, 21 August 1880; MER, 28 June 1880; FERR, 30 June, 11, 13, 16 July 1880; LOT, 11, 13, 20, 28 May, 19, 27, 28 June, 8 August 1880; LAP, 15, 17 July, 18, 24, 25 August 1880; PCH, 17, 20, 22 April, 4, 7, 11 May 1880; CHT, 21 August 1880; MER, 30 June, 17 July, 12, 26 August 1880.
  24. INDEP, 31 July, 3, 7 August 1880; CDSO, 3 August 1880, p. 366; NFERR, 17 May 1880; CDSO, 22 August 1880, pp. 526-28.
  25. CDSO, 21 August 1880., p. 527.
  26. INDEP, 9 July 1880.
  27. NFERR, 10, 13 May 1880.
  28. INDEP, 11 May 1880; NFERR, 10, 13 May 1880.
  29. CDSO, 23, 30, 31 August, 16, 28 September 1880, pp. 531, 625, 693-94, 757-59; CSSO, 9, 14 September 1880, pp. 274-76, 318-21.
  30. NFERR, 23 August 1880; CHT, 28 August 1880.
  31. LAP, 24 August 1880.
  32. Sater, "Economic Depression," pp. 79-84.
  33. *Los Tiempos*, cited in CONS, 5 August 1878.
  34. MMHAC, 1879, pp. xlviii-l; NOV, 3, 4 February 1879.
  35. DO, 9 May 1879.
  36. NOV, 19, 23, 24 April 1879.
  37. LAP, 10 May 1879; FERR, 2, 6 May 1879.
  38. INDEP, 4, 7 May 1879.

39. CDSO, 21, 23 August 1879, pp. 414-15, 427-35; CSSO, 20, 25 August 1879, pp. 142, 146, 152-53.
40. LOT, 3, 8 January 1880; INDEP, 3, 4 January 1880.
41. CDSE, 26, 27, 30 December 1879, pp. 53-54, 69-73. 82-83.
42. NFERR, 2, 12 February, 1 April, 1 July 1880
43. CDSE, 30 December 1879, pp. 82-83.
44. CSSE, 26, 31 December 1879, pp. 24-27, 40-42; CDSE, 3 January 1880, pp. 92-98.
45. CDSO, 25 June, 1 July 1880, pp. 91, 120.
46. INDEP, 15, 23 July 1880; NFERR, 26 August 1880; FERR, 29 July 1880.
47. LOT, 20 July 1880.
48. Ibid., NFERR, 15 July, 26 August, 4 November 1880; FERR, 29 July 1880.
49. LOT, 13 July 1880; FERR, 29 July 1880; NFERR, 12 July 1880; CDSO, 3, 6, 8, 25 July 1880, pp. 125-36, 137-40, 159-64, 166-68, 270-73.
50. FERR, 29 July 1880.
51. CDSO, 6, 24, 25 July 1880, pp. 140, 255-57, 276-77.
52. Ibid. 3, 6, 8, 22, 24, 25, 27 July 1880, pp. 124, 140, 145-48, 153-58, 244-46, 263-69, 289-93.
53. Ibid., 25 June, 1, 27 July 1880, pp. 91, 120, 298.
54. Ibid., 27 July, 10, 11 August 1880, pp. 302-4, 401, 410-17; CSSO, 30 July 1880, 114-16; CSSS 4, 6 August 1880, pp. 62-63, 65.
55. CDSO, 9, 10 August 1880, pp. 386-87, 402.
56. Ibid., 11 August 1880, pp. 414-16.
57. PROS, 6 August 1880.
58. CHT, 14 August 1880. See also MER, 29 July, 13, 16, 31 August 1880; CONS, 21 October 1880.
59. NFERR, 18 November 1880.
60. FERR, 16, 24, 28, 29 October 1880.
61. LOT, 1 December 1880; FERR, 25, 28 November, 3, 4, 18, 19 December 1880.
62. CDSE, 23 December 1880, pp. 26-27.
63. Ibid., p. 28; CSSE, 28 December 1880, pp. 126-28.
64. CDSO, 2 June, 29 August 1881, pp. 4-5, 358-59.
65. Ibid., 28 July 1881, pp. 265-67; CDSE, 5, 8 January 1882, pp. 573-76, 599-604; CDSO, 25, 27 July 1882, pp. 310-16, 334-35.
66. CSSE, 28, 30 December 1881, pp. 261-62, 266-73.
67. BB, 5 August 1880.
68. NOV, 3, 4 February. 19 April 1879; CEN, 8 August 1880.
69. FERR, 25 January 1879; CONS, 21 October 1880.
70. CDSO, 28 August 1879, p. 478; OPIN, 4 February 1879; BB, 5 January 1879.
71. ECAT, 17 June 1879; NFERR, 2 February 1880.
72. CDSO, 4, 13 August 1881, pp. 277-78, 334-35; 11, 21 August 1882, pp. 468, 497; CSSO, 5 July, 17 August 1881, pp. 183, 335, 339, 14 July 1882, p. 213; Anguita, 2:519, 600.
73. CHT, 14 August 1880; CQ, 14 April 1881; DIS, 10 April 1883.
74. LIBT, 10 February, 10 August 1880; PC, 5 July 1881.
75. LAP, 16 January 1879; PC, 2 July 1881; CQ, 16 July, 31 August 1882.
76. RVS, 12 June 1883; CONS, 23 February, 10 May 1883.
77. Anguita, 2:485; CDSE, 20 December 1879, pp. 33-35; CDSO, 19 June 1883, p. 83; CSSO, 16, 30 June 1880, pp. 22, 80.
78. CDSO, 15 July 1882, pp. 249-51; CSSE, 28, 30 December 1882, pp. 303-4.

CHAPTER EIGHT

1. COM, 5 September 1881; R. Nelson Boyd, *Chili: Sketches of Chili and the Chilians during the War of the Pacific* (London: Wm. Allen, 1881), pp. 121-22.
2. INDEP, 5 August 1880; FERR, 9 September 1881.
3. LAP, 25 June, 26 August 1880, 27 February, 19 April, 4 Sept. 1, 20 June 1881, 20 April 1882; NFERR, 10 May 1880; FERR, 18 March 1882; PORPM, 15 October 1880; JUV, 28 December 1879; CUR, 31 January, 14 August, 1880; COM, 23 July 1881; ESMER, 27 April 1881, 16 June 1880; LIBT, 7 May, 1880; LIBV, 24 January 1880; LOTA, 29 February 1880; INDEP, 30 July, 1880; DIS, 1 April 1880, 5 July 1881, 28 February 1882; FERR, 17 May 1882; VI, 22 August 1880.
4. CUR, 31 December 1880; 5 September 1881; LAP, 12 June 1880; 12 January, 19, 27 July 1881, 31 January, 10 March 1882; LIBT, 7 May 1880; CHT, 17 April 1880; COM, 29 November 1880; DIS, 19 February 1880 FERR, 23 February 1881; LOTA, 2 August 1880; INDEP, 30 July 1880; LIBT, 14 August 1880; NFERR, 6 May 1880; DIS, 12 October 1882; FERR, 9 March 1882, 16, 20 February, 5 April 1883.
5. CUR, 24, 31 December 1880; LIBT, 7 May 1880, 30 July 1881; NFERR, 10 May, 26 December 1880; INDEP, 7 February, 18 March, 7 April, 12 June, 28, 30 July 1880; ESPER, 5 June 1880; DIS, 17 January, 11 March 1880; FERR, 17 May 1880, 5, 6 May 1881; LIBT, 21, 29 August 1880; LAP, 7 June 1882; MAI, 2 May 1880.
6. LAP, 5 April 1880, 9 April 1881; LOTA, 15 October 1882; DIS, 12 February, 1880; ESMER, 12 September 1880, LIBV, 24 April, 14 August 1880; CQ, 9 March 1882; LOTA, 21 March, 4 April, 3 September 1880; RVS, 13 August 1880; INDEP, 23, 25 January 1880.
7. JUV, 1 February 1880; INDEP, 11 January 1880, 4 April, 15 August 1883; FERR, 19 March 1882.
8. LIBV, 28 February 1880; LOTA, 25 May 1879; DIS, 20 January 1881; JUV, 28 December 1879.
9. CONS, 28 May 1880, 26 June 1882; COM, 18 December 1880, 7 February 1881; ARO, 24 July 1880; VI, 3 October 1880; CQ, 13 November 1881; LIBT, 27 April 1880; CUR 17 July 1881; LAP, 26 May 1882; COR, 22 January 1881.
10. MMINT, 1879, pp. xi, xvi, xxx; MMINT, 1880, in DO, 30 August 1880, p. 1427; MMINT, 1881, in DO, 24, 26 September 1881, pp. 1568, 1577; MMINT, 1882, in DO, 10 November 1882, p. 1829. See also the reports of the various provincial intendents, DO, 25 April 1881, p. 576.
11. ARO, 9 August 1880; ESPER, 18 April, 15 July 1880; LAP, 1 October 1880; OP, 25 May, 4 June 1879; ARA, 10 August 1879; G. Blest Gana to Minister of Hacienda, 28 August 1879, ANH, vol. 975; Gmo. Davison Minister of Hacienda, n.d., AMH, vol. 982; M. Marrarosoba to Gob. de Melipilla, 15 November 1879, AMH, vol. 987; Gmo. Matte to Minister of Hacienda, 21 July 1879, AMH, vol. 1017; E. Altamirano to Minister of Hacienda 5 August 1879, AMH, vol. 1019; N. Guerrero to Minister of Hacienda, 20 November 1880; AMH, vol. 9876; C. Castellón to Minister of Hacienda, 16 May 1881, AMH, vol. 1114; DIS, 15 January, 30 September 1880; LAP, 3 September 1880.
12. OPIN, 3 July 1879; CHIL, 17 October 1879; Felipe Anguita to Minister of Hacienda, 6 December 1879, AMH, vol. 985; TEL, 26 August 1879; BB, 21 August 1879; LAP, 6 June 1879.
13. TEL, 22 August 1879; CLS, 12 June, 28 August 1879; ESMER, 16, 23 July, 10, 24 August 1879; ARA, 2 November 1879.
14. LAP, 10 September 1879; ARO, 6 December 1879; JUV, 7 September 1879;

VI, 16 August, 6 September 1879; PAR, 14 September 1879.

15. LIBL, 6 September, 4 October 1879; COMC, 27 January 1879; TEL, 26 August 1879; PAR, 14 September 1879; LIBL, 6 September, 4 October 1879; D. Sanhueza to Minister of Hacienda, 21 April 1883, AMH, vol. 1287; CONS, 8 January 1880; Z. Freire to Minister of Hacienda, Santiago, 19 August 1879, AMH, vol. 977.

16. Carlos Fuchsloger to Intendent of Illanquihue, 25 May 1881. AMH, vol. 1115; DO, 6 September 1879, p. 1557; MMHAC, 1879, pp. xxxviii-ix, CDSO 5, 10 June 1879, pp. 21-22, 49-56; CSSO, 6, 9, 11 June, 25 August 1879, 22-23, 26-30, 152-53, CSSO, 21 July 1880, p. 82; Anguita, 2; 474, 486.

17. VI, 12 March 1881; UN, 31 January 1880; RVS, 17 October 1882; CONS, 8 January 1880; Z. Freire to Min. Hac, 16 August 1879, AMH, vol. 977; TEL, 22 August 1879; A. Solar to Minister of Hacienda, 2 October 1879, AMI, vol. 910; COR,, 8 May 1880, 26 March, 9 April 1881; A. Muñoz to Minister of Hacienda, 26 August 1882; C. Castellón to Minister of Hacienda, 16 May, 30 July 1881, AMH, vol. 114; COR, 26 March 1881; RVS, 14 October 1882.

18. ESMER, 24 September, 26 October 1879; ECAT, 11 September 1879; ESPER, 26 October 1879; JUV, 10 August 1879; OPIN, 12 July 1879

19. ESMER, 24 September 1879, 13 November 1880; JUV, 17 August 1879; CAU, 3 March 1880; ESPER, 17 July 1880.

20. ESMER, 23 July 1879, 19 June 1881; ESPER, 17 July 1880; LOTA, 1 June 1879.

21. LAP, 2 June 1881.

22. CONS, 10 July 1880; BB, 28 October 1880; LOTA, 1 August 1880; CHT, 13 March 1880; *Estadística comercial de la República de Chile de 1880*, pp. xii-xiii.

23. CQ, 3 October 1880, 13, 17 January 1881, 15 February 1883; CONS, 10 June, 16 July 1880; LOTA, 25 April 1880; VER, 5 August 1882; LIBV, 24 June, 4 October 1882; LAP, 2 June 1881; VI, 15 November 1879, 11 March 1882; ESPER, 22 October 1881; BB, 28 October 1879.

24. CUR, 14 August 1879, 14 August 1880, 19 February 1881; TEL, 7 October 1879; RVS, 5 August 1880, 21 October 1881; 27 April, 8 July 1882; ESP, 27 May 1882; CQ, 15 February 1883; VI, 3 October 1880; 6 October 1883; ESMER, 4 November 1883; CONS, 6 August, 27 September 1880; LOTA, 8 August 1880, 16 April, 26 November 1882; HER, 28 August 1880; ECAT, 11 September 1879; FERR, 22 December 1880; CEN, 29 February, 23 May 1880; LAP, 4, 21 June, 11, 20 July, 27 August 1881; VM, 12 March 1882.

25. LAP, 6 May 1881; FERR, 5 May 1881; MER, 3 December 1884; Adolfo Latorre Subercaseaux, "Relación entre el circulante y los precios en Chile," Memoria de Prueba, Catholic University, Santiago, 1958.

26. LOT, 5 April, 1880; LAP, 10 February 1882; BB, 13 January 1879; INDEP, 9 January 1880; CUR, 31 January, 21 February 1880; LAP, 24 January 1880; JUV, 1 February 1880; FERR, 12 January 1881, 8 January 1882; ÑUB, 8 January 1881; CHT, 12 August 1882; CUR., 28 January 1882.

27. TEL, 4 February 1880; CUR, 21 February 1880; INDEP, 7 February 1880; FERR, 7 January 1882, 4 February 1883; MAI, 25 January 1880; LAP, 24 January, 18 March 1880; CUR, 31 January 1880; ESMER, 14 March 1880.

28. LAP, 23 March 1880, 13, 18 April 1881, 10 December 1881, 26 March 1883; FERR, 28 March 1880, 14, 17-19 October 1881; COR, 7, 28 August 1880; DIS, 3 April 1880; NFERR, 25, 29 March 1880.

29. NFERR, 25 March 1880; LAP, 18 April 1881; INDEP, 28 March 1880; FERR, 28 March 1880.

30. HER, 4 November 1880; FERR, 27 January, 1880, 12 January, 20 February, 14 July, 4 November 1881, 29 October, 2 November 1882. In 1883, the public could enter Cerro Santa Lucia free on feast days. FERR, 30 August 1883; INDEP, 27 January 1880; COR, 23 October 1880; VI, 30 September 1880; LAP, 14 December 1882.

31. MAI, 27 February 1881; COM, 18 September 1880; INDEP, 17, 29 July, 30 September 1881; CHT, 18 March 1882.

32. FEN, 1 February 1882; DIS, 6 January 1880, 21 June 1881; CUR, 21 February 1880; COM, 27 January 1881; LIBV, 17 April, 19 June 1880; MAI, 25 January 1880; PORPM, 3 June 1882.

33. DIS, 5 March, 13 April 1880; LIBV, 1 May 1880.

34. LOTA, 17 April 1883; CHT, 15 October 1881, 7 October 1882; RVS, 25, 28 November 1882; ESMER, 9 March 1881.

35. ESMER, 9 March 1881; RVS, 1 June 1881, 28 January 1883.

36. CUR, 8 February, 29 July 1882; ECAT, 23 September 1879; Adolfo Murillo, "Jeografía Médica. Breves apuntes para servir a la estadística médica i o la nosología chilenas": in *Estudios jeograficos sobre Chile* (Santiago: Imprenta Nacional, 1875), p. 26.

37. LOTA, 20 August 1882; ARO, 9 August 1879; ARA, 14 December 1879; COM, 14 February 1880; POR, 23 September 1880; BB, 29 May 1879; ECAT, 17 June 1881; RVS, 30 August 1882, 18 January 1883; CONS, 19 October 1880; CEN, 18 March 1880; ESMER, 12 January 1881; FERR, 30 August 1883.

38. LAP, 22 February 1881; COM, 14 February 1880.

39. LAP, 27 December 1880; CUR, 28 December 1881; ESMER, 29 December 1880; PORPM, 4 February 1881.

40. MAI, 8 February 1880; JUV, 28 September 1879; BB, 23 September 1880; CHIL, 16 September 1880; CUR, 25 September 1880; LIBT, 17 September 1881; COM. 22 September 1881; LOT, 13 June 1880; FERR, 30 May, 1 June 1880.

41. INDEP, 23 July 1880.

42. LAP, 15, 22 January 1881; PROM, 23 January 1881; MAI, 6 February 1881; FERR, 21, 22, 24 January 1881; CUR, 29 January 1881; LIBT, 25 January 1881; DIS, 27 January 1881.

43. LAP, 7 March 1881; FERR, 11 January 1880, 26 February, 10, 14 March 1881; DIS, 19 March 1881. See, for example, *Reseña de las fiestas cívicas con que el pueblo de Copiapó recibío al Rejimiento Atacama* (Copiapó: Imprenta de El Atacama, 1881).

44. CUR, 24 December 1880; ESMER, 29 December 1880.

45. COM, 20 March 1880.

46. CUR, 8 January 1881.

47. LAP, 27 December 1880.

48. INDEP, 29 September 1880, 30 August 1881; COM, 5 September 1881.

49. NFERR, 17 Jun. 1880; PROM, 26 September 1880; CUR, 3 July 1880; FERR, 28, 29 January 1880; LOT, 29 January 1880; DO, 16 June 1880, p. 755.

50. ARO, 3, 24 April 1880; DIS, 13 March, 1 April, 1 May 1880.

51. RVS, 18 January 1883; LAP, 28 April, 27 July 1880; COM, 14 February 1880, 28 July 1881; LOT, 31 March, 8 April, 9 May 1880; FERR, 25 March, 17 April 1880, 24 February 1882; LOT, 23 April, 7, 19 May 1880; LAP, 28 May 1880; MER, 26 May 1880; LOTA, 21, 28 March 1880; CONS, 10 June 1880; LIBT, 20 April 1880; BB, 9 October 1879; ARA, 30 November 1879.

52. LOT, 5, 13 March 1880; DIS, 23 July 1881 FERR, 13, 21 July, 4, 19 August 1881, 21 March, 19 August 1882; DIQ, 2 April 1881; CHT, 13 April 1881; DIS, 7

March, 25 April, 31 October 1882, 25 January 1883; ESMER, 6 April 1881, 5 February 1882; LAP, 6 May, 13 June, 8 September 1881; RVS, 10 November 1882; ÑUB, 18 February, 8 September 1882; PC, 7 October 1882; MAI, 17 April 1881.

53. MAI, 29 February, 7 March 1880. See also LOT, 5 March 1880; CHT, 7 February, 7 August 1880; PROM. 28 March 1880; LOTA, 7 March 1880; LIBT, 10 February 1881; ESMER, 24 July 1881; ECAT, 19 March, 12 April 1879.

54. CHT, 7 February 1880; DO, 14, 21 June 1880, pp. 743-44, 787; LAP, 1 March 1880; MER, 31 January 1880; DO, 26 May, 16 June 1880, pp. 652-53, 755.

55. DO, 6, 7 May 1880, pp. 615, 623.

56. LIBT, 30 June 1881; ÑUB, 13 July 1881; DIS, 9 July 1881; LIBT, 19 February 1882.

57. DIS, 20 August, 13 October 1881; INDEP, 4 September, 27 October 1881, 31 July 1883; FERR, 24 November 1881; ES, 14 January 1883; REP, 17 July 1881.

58. ET, 2 August 1881; DIS, 7, 9, 14 February, 15 July 1882; ECAT, 14 June 1881; MAI, 11 June 1882; POR, 4 October 1882; FERR, 19 May, 28 October 1882; LAP, 15 February, 28 December 1881; 5 September 1883; CONS, 15 March 1882.

59. ÑUB, 8 March 1882; LOTA, 2 July 1882; DIS, 25, 27 April 1882; LIBLU, 8 April 1882; CHT, 13 April 1881.

60. FEN, 13 December 1881; CQ, 2 January 1881; RVS, 12 January 1881; HER, 6 January 1881; INDEP, 6 March, 7 December 1881; LIBT, 23 December 1881; DIS, 18 January 1881; ECAT, 13 January 1881.

61. INDEP, 8, 9 December 1881; ÑUB, 4 February 1882; CONS, 7 January 1881.

62. BSNA, 12 (1881):391-92, 394-95; 14 (1883):171.

63. CHT, 30 April, 16 July, 11 June 1881; HER, 26 May 1882.

64. INDEP, 14, 22, 28 April 1882; PC, 3, 10 November, 7 December 1881, 22 April 1882.

65. INDEP. 28 April 1882; BSNA, 11 (1880):357-62; ECAT, 25 April 1882.

66. FEN, 17 October 1883; INDEP, 26 September 1883; DIS, 27 February 1883; ARO, 16, 26 June 1880; RVS, 29 July 1881; CHT, 5, 11 June 1881; FERR, 3 March 1883.

67. CUR, 19 February 1881; CQ, 5, 24 September 1882; LAP, 24 September 1881.

68. CHT, 4 June 1881.

69. NFERR, 13 May 1880; CQ 28 April 1881; LAP, 3, 5 December 1879; 12 July, 4 November, 1, 5 December 1881, 22 February 1882; DIS, 9 January 1879, 31 March 1881; 22 April, 14 September 1882; RVS, 28 October 1881; EPS, 21 January 1882; Murillo, pp. 21-25; LOTA, 31 January 1883; CQ 28 April 1881; RVS, 28 October 1881; INDEP, 11 May 1880; MMHAC, in DO, 8 June 1880, p. 702; ARO, 30 July 1881.

70. Wenceslao Díaz, "Enfermedades reinantes en Chile," in *Estudios jeográficos sobre Chile* (Santiago: Imprenta Nacional, 1875), pp. 143-44, 149, 155-56; CHT, 3 December 1881; FERR, 9, 22 January 1880; CONS, 19 January, 23 February 1880; COM, 29 April 1880; CUR, 3 April, 1 May 1880; DIS, 17, 28 February 1880; ESMER, 7 January, 21 March 1880; FEN, 10 April 1880; LOTA, 11 July 1880; PAR, 6 April 1880; RVS, 8 January, 5 February, 30 March 1880.

71. FERR, 3, 7 February, 25 March, 2 April, 16 May 1880; LAP, 19 July 1881; CUR, 5 September 1881; COM, 29 March, 5 April, 17 August 1880; DIS, 1, 11 May, 1880; LIBV, 11 September, 11 December 1880; LIBT, 29 January 1880; ESMER, 26 September, 1880; ESPER, 10 April 1880; DIS, 11 May 1880; LOT, 11 May 1880; INDEP, 5 May 1880; CHIL, 9 November 1882; MAI, 2 May 1880.

Notes 313

72. ESMER, 26 September, 13, 26 October 1880; 28 August 1881; DIS, 22 April, 1 July 1882; VI, 26 February 1881; CUR, 31 December 1880; FERR, 15 June, 17 October 1880.
73. MAI, 25 April 1880; COM, 4 June 1883; LOTA, 10 January 1884; ARO, 17 February 1881.
74. CUR, 31 December 1880; PROM, 1 February 1880; DIS, 12 January 1882; INDEP, 10 June 1880; LAP, 30 March, 25 April 1883.
75. INDEP, 29 February 1880; LOT, 26 January, 7 March 1880; CHT, 31 January 1880; NFERR, 8, 25 March 1880.
76. CHT, 7 February 1880; COM, 17 August 1880; ESP, 10 April 1880; FERR, 19 October 1880.
77. ARA, 19 August 1882; CQ, 13 April 1880; RVS, 22 June 1880; ESMER, 11 January 1880; CQ, 18 April 1880; LIBT, 10 April 1880; FERR, 1 May 1880.
78. DIS, 3, 24 April 1880; VI, 26 February 1881; ESMER, 1 February, 26 October 1880; RVS, 15 April 1880; LIBT, 27 May 1880.
79. LOTA, 11 July 1880; UN, 4 October 1879; CQ, 9 September, 7 October 1880, 6 August 1882; CUR, 17 July 1881; ESMER, 12 March 1882; LIBV, 25 March 1882; DIS, 26 May, 24 July 1883; INDEP, 13 July 1881; RVS, 4 March 1880; PROM, 8 August 1880; ARO, 30 July 1881; CAU, 25 July 1880; INDEP, 4 September 1881; DIS, 16 June 1883.
80. FERR, 18 February, 29 March 1880, 14 May, 20 July 1882; CUR, 1 May 1880; DO, 14 June 1880, p. 1742; FERR, 21 May 1880; COM, 29 March, 5 April 1880; DIS, 10 April 1880; LOTA, 29 August 1880; FERR, 6 May 1880; CONS, 15 May 1880; CQ, 9 May 1880; MAI, 25 April 1880; COM, 16, 26 February 1881; DIS, 17 November 1881; FERR, 6 May 1880, 27 April 1883; CONS, 15 May 1880; CQ, 9 May 1880; MAI, 25 April 1880; COM, 16, 26 February 1881; DIS, 17 November 1881, 2 June 1883; PROM, 4 January, 28 March 1880; LIBT, 27 May 1880; INDEP, 2 April 1880.
81. DO, 14 June 1880, p. 742; FERR 16 May 1880; CUR, 3 April 1881; RVS, 5 February 1880; FERR, 6 February 1881; CHT, 27 August 1881; CUR, 24 July 1880; MER, 25 April 1880; LAP, 23 June 1882.
82. FERR, 30 March 1880; RVS, 10 April 1880; CQ, 6 June 1880; DIS, 28 February 1880; ESPER, 10 April 1880; PROM. 2 May 1880; FERR, 4, 7 April, 21 May 1880; RVS, 8 January 1880; CQ, 6 June 1880; FEN, 10 April 1880.
83. FERR, 17 April 1880; MAI, 28 April 1880; DO, 12 April, 7 July 1880, pp. 483, 918; MAI, 2 May 1880; LAP, 2 February 1882.
84. DO, 29 April 1882, pp. 661-62; FERR, 22 May 1882; RVS, 23, 31 August, 8 September 1882; CHT, 3 December 1881; RVS, 28 October 1881; FERR, 22 May 1882; PROM, 2 June 1882.
85. FERR, 23 April 1880; COM, 29 March 1880; PAR, 6 April 1880; PROM, 2 May 1880; MMINT, in DO, 1 September 1880, p. 1452; RVS, 8 June 1880; INDEP, 5 June 1880.
86. INDEP, 16 June 1882; FERR, 23 June 1882; ECAT, 19, 28 June 1882; RVS, 12, 10 July 1882; VM, 19 May 1882; LAP, 2 February 1882; PROM, 2 June 1882; PROS, 14 June 1882; PC, 8 July 1882.
87. ECAT, 14 July 1882; DIS, 18 March 1882; CSSO, 23, 26 June 1882, pp. 111-13, 181.
88. CDSO, 3, 8, 13, 18 July 1882, pp. 197-202, 205-06, 212-15, 222-24, 243-56, 271-74, 277.
89. INDEP, 22 May, 17 July 1880; RVS, 3 June 1882; PC, 18 August 1881;

INDEP, 28 May 1882; RVS, 1 May, 1880; NFERR, 5 May 1880; LAP, 12 November, 1880; COM, 23 April 1882; LOTA, 2 July 1881.
90. INDEP, 31 May 1879; CONS, 25 July 1882; FERR, 10 August 1883; FERR, 3, 10 August, 7 November 1883; LIBT, 2 May, 30 August, 25 November 1882; CUR, 8 February 1882; RVS, 2 April 1884.
91. EPS, 3, 4, 5 January 1883; DIS, 27 February 1883.
92. EPS, 10, 21 December 1881; ARA 18 March 1883.
93. EPS, 25 Jan 1882; 20 December 1881.
94. HER, 23 August, 9, 12, 14 September, 2, 5, 7 October 1880; FERR, 7 February 1880, 12 May 1881; ECAT, 12 May 1881; RVS, 4 March 1881; ESPER, 15 October 1881.
95. LAP, 13 April 1883; LIBT, 2 May, 30 August 1882, 25 November 1883; EPS, 21 December 1881; 2, 11 August 1883; INDEP, 7 August 1883.
96. NFERR, 22 March 1881; REP, 20 March 1881; CONS, 3 September 1880; FERR, 3 April 1881; VM, 29 March 1880; MER, 10 August 1880; PCH, 29 January, 3 February 1880; DIS, 18 October 1883.
97. LAP, 11 June 1882; PRE, 20, 27 May 1882; DIS, 30 March, 22 April 1882; RVS, 25 March 1882; POR, 13 October 1883; INDEP, 7 December 1880.
98. MER, 8 January 1880; VM, 29 March 1881; *El Salitrero* (Taltal), 14 December 1881.
99. CHT, 29 July 1882; CONS, 18 January 1882; VM, 9 March, 20 July 1882; LOTA, 24 January 1884; INDEP, 4 April 1884; ÑUB, 31 January 1880; INDEP, 12 September 1884.

CHAPTER NINE

1. FERR, 1 February 1879; LAP, 28, 29, 31 January 1879; RVS, 20 March 1879; TAL, 3 February, 24 March 1879.
2. DIS, 12 September 1878; RVS, 10 September 1878; Cristián Zegers, "Historia política del gobierno de Aníbal Pinto," *Historia* 6 (1967):34–41.
3. DA, 17 January 1879; NOV, 16 January 1879; ECAT, 14 February 1879; TAL, 27, 28 March 1879.
4. B. Prats to G. Blest Gana, n.d. AMI, vol. 890; B. Prats to F. Velasco, 27 March 1879, AMI, vol. 892.
5. F. Pinto to M. Concha i Toro, 1 April 1879, AMI, vol. 904; M. Concha i Toro to F. Pinto, n.d. AMI, vol. 892.
6. Luis Jordan to D. Urrutia Flores, 2 April 1879, AMI, vol. 893; ARA, 2, 13, 19 March 1879; BB, 1 April 1879; CHIL, 15 March, 5 April 1879; COMSF, 8 March 1879; FERR, 1 February 1879; Horacio Pinto A. to Minister of Interior, 1 April 1879, AMI, vol. 904; Juan Prats to B. Prats, 1 April 1879, AMI, vol. 904; Abdón Cifuentes to L. Mamita, n.d., AMI, vol. 893.
7. ARA, 5 April 1879; BB, 1 April 1879; COMC, 21, 26 March 1879; COM, 16 February, 12 March 1879; CLS, 20 March, 8 April 1879; OPIN, 30 March 1879; BB, 6 April 1879; COM, 12 March 1879; ECAT, 13 February 1879; INDEP, 25, 30 March 1879.
8. LAP, 29 January, 29 March 1879; JUV, 23 March 1879.
9. FERR, 5 March 1879; INDEP, 16 March 1879; CDSE, 27, 29 March, 9 April, 1878, pp. 708, 733; CDSS, 9 April 1879, pp. 123–25; Pinto, April, "Apuntes," RC 13

(1921): 362-63; Osborn to Evarts, 23 April 1879, *Dispatches from U.S. Ministers to Chile*.
    10. Pinto, 15 April 1879, "Apuntes," RC 13 (1921):361-62.
    11. Ibid., 4 July 1879, "Apuntes, RC 14, no. 54 (1922):113; I. Santa María, "Apuntes sobre la Guerra del Pacifíco," RC 6, no. 54 (1922):407-19; Zegers, 68-69; CDSO, 7, 21, 24 June 1879, pp. 38-42, 95-98, 109-10; CDSS, 19 June 1879, pp. 131-32.
    12. R. Sotomayor to A. Pinto, 24 April 1879 in "Correspondencia de don Rafael Sotomayor con don Aníbal Pinto sobre la Guerra del Pacífico," RC 6, no. 57 (1922):187-88; R. Sotomayor to C. Saavedra, 19, 24 April 1879, FV, vol. 559; José Alfonso to A. Pinto, 6 June 1879, FV, vol. 414.
    13. INDEP, 16 March 1879; NOV, 20 February 1879; COMC, 16 April 1879; CDSO, 3, 5, 7, 10, 14, 17, 21, 24, 26, 28 June, 1, 2, 10, 12, 15-17, 24 July, 7 August 1879, pp. 5-9, 23-32, 42-47, 59-62, 65-76, 78-91, 92-107, 111-16, 133-40, 144-49, 152-53, 167-78, 226-28, 233-35, 240-57, 260-67, 269-76, 286-93, 309-14, 356-65, 368-71; INDEP, 27 March, 19 July, 8 August 1879; NOV, 9, 14 April 1879; OPIN, 18, 20 May, 11 June 1879; NFERR, 15 September 1879; X, *La patria está en peligro* (n.p.: 1879); Pinto, 4 July 1879, "Apuntes," RC 6, no.52 (1922):113.
    14. LOT, 31 July, 1, 2 August 1879; R. Errázuriz to Minister of Interior, 1 August 1879, AMI, vol. 908; R. Vial to Minister of Interior, 30 July 1879; J. J. Anguita to Minister of Interior, 31 July 1879, AMI, vol. 907.
    15. Pinto, 24, 27 July 1879, "Apuntes," RC, 13 (1921):364, 367-68; NFERR, 4 August 1879; OP, 30, 31 July 1879; DIS, 7 August 1879; TEL, 1, 5 August 1879; ESMER, 10 August 1879; LOT, 31 July 1879.
    16. Pinto, 25 July, "Apuntes," RC 5, no. 59 (1921):365-66; D. Santa María to J. V. Lastarria, 20 May, 2, 17 June 1879, Santiago in "Cartas de don Domingo Santa María a don José Victorino Lastarria," RC 2, No.18 (1918):251-53, 255; CSSS, 23, 30, 31 July, 1, 2 August 1879, pp. 28-52; Pinto, 15, 16, 26 August 1879, "Apuntes," RC 5, No. 49 (1921):368-72. See also Ignacio Santa María, "La caída del ministerio Varas—Santa María en agosto de 1879," RC 3, no. 21 (1919):21-29; R. Sotomayor to C. Saavedra, 27 August 1879.
    17. CDSO, 26 July, 5, 12 August 1879, pp. 321-24, 344-47, 378; CDSS, 14, 16, 19 August 1879, pp. 133-44.
    18. ARO, 16, 30 August 1879; CONS, 1 August 1879; FERR, 17, 19, 20, 23 August 1879; LIBV, 30 August 1879; DIS, 7, 9 August 1879; INDEP, 8 August 1879; NFERR, 25 August, 15 September 1879.
    19. TEL, 1, 23 August 1879; DIS, 21 August 1879; INDEP, 26 August 1879.
    20. CDSO, 21 August 1879, pp. 412-14, 416-17.
    21. CDSO, 29 July, 5 August 1879, pp. 330-32, 344-46; CDSS, 16 August 1879, pp. 141-42; CSSS, 23 July, 1 August 1879, pp. 28, 43-44; R. Sotomayor to A. Pinto, 19 March 1880, FV vol. 559 and 27 January 1880, AJE 2; D. Santa María to A. Pinto, 16, 28 January, 2 February 1880, FV vol. 416; CDSO, 23 September 1880., p. 729.
    22. CDSO, 8 June 1880, pp. 13-17; A. Pinto, "La renuncia del ministerio Santa María y la formación del ministerio Recabarren en 1880," RC 6, no.51 (1922): 62-66.
    23. FERRO, 17 May 1880; INDEP, 27 May 1880; CHT, 29 May 1880; MER, 25, 27 May 1880.
    24. D. Santa María to J. V. Lastarria, Santiago,19 June 1880, "Cartas de don Domingo Santa María a don José Victorino Lastarria," RC 3, no. 24 (1919):

541-42; A. Pinto to J. V. Lastarria, 19 June 1880, "El hundimiento del transporte Loa en 1880," RC 1, no.8 (1917):247; Pinto, "Renuncia," pp. 67-68; CDSO, 17 July 1880, pp. 216-17; Bulnes, 2:412-13; CDSS, 17, 18 July 1880, pp. 280-81.

25. CONS, 6 August 1880; CHT, 19 June 1880; CEN, 20 June 1880; MER, 22 June 1880; NFERR, 14 June 1880; CAU, 20 June 1880.

26. CDSO, 10, 13, 15 July 1880, pp. 174-75, 185-90, 193-95, 206; FERR, 18 July 1880.

27. CDSO, 14, 16, 2 September 1880, pp. 684-87, 688-89, 699-702, 715-16.

28. Ibid., 23 September 1880, pp. 723-24, 727-28, 731-34.

29. FERR, 16 September 1880; HER, 15, 16 September 1880.

30. MER, 17 September 1880.

31. CDSO, 23, 25 September 1880, pp. 736, 747-48, 751-57; HER, 17, 22, 23 September 1880; INDEP, 17 September 1880; MER, 16 September 1880; VM, 25, 30 September 1880.

32. CSSE, 6, 10, 11, 12 December 1880, pp. 15-20, 21-30, 32-40, 46-49; FERR, 23 December 1880; HER, 7, 10 December 1880; INDEP, 18 December 1880; MER, 8 December 1880; LAP, 8 December 1880; LOT, 10, 17 December 1880.

33. *Sesiones de la Comisión Conservadora*, 28 April, 3 May 1881. pp. 1-13; CSSO, 3, 4, 5, 6, 7, 8, 9, 13, 14, 15, 18, 20 June 1881, pp. 12-14, 18-20, 26-30, 38-42, 45-53, 56-62, 65-75, 78-87, 89-98, 99-109, 113-23, 127-38, 139-44; CDSO, 2, 4, 21, 30 June, 1, acta de lo occurido en la noche del 1 de Julio de 1881; 3, 4, 5 July 1881, pp. 5-13, 19-28, 56, 85-93, 99-112, 112-13, 115-17, 137-44, 144-53, 157-68.

34. FERR, 4, 5 July 1881; HER, 3 July 1881; LIBT, 3 July 1881; ÑUB, 9 July 1881; CHT, 9 July 1881; LOT, 2, 3, 5, 7, 9 July 1881; INDEP, 7, 8, 10 July 1881.

35. Carlos Walker Martínez, *Historia de la administración Santa María*, 2 vols. (Santiago: Imprenta Progreso, 1889) and his *Las elecciones de 1881* (Santiago: Imprenta de "El Independiente," 1881); Encina, 17:443-525; Cifuentes, 2:157-64; Luis Urzúa, *Discurso pronunciado en el teatro de variedades* (Santiago: Imprenta de El Independiente, 1881), pp. 8-10, 20-22, 39, 45-47; *Los estafadores sin máscara* (Santiago: Imprenta Victoria de H. Izquierdo, 1882); Ramón Rozas, *Cárta del diputado por La Laja a sus electores* (Santiago: Imprenta de la República de J. Núñez, 1881).

36. CDSO, 25 July 1882, pp. 318-20; CSSO, 2, 26, 28 June 1882, pp. 15-16, 119-20, 130-31. Also CSSO, 8 June 1883, in DO, 11 June 1883. "Un Chileno," apparently Ramón Ricardo Rozas, claimed that Santa María used the clerical issue to divert the nation from the stalemated war (*Carta a S. E. El Presidente de la República por un Chileno* [n.p.: Imprenta Victoria, 1883?]).

37. CDSO, 15 September 1882, pp. 651-54; CDSE, 9, 11, 14, 16, 18, 21, 23, 25, 28, 30 November 1882, pp. 16-24, 29, 40-45, 48-57, 62-75, 79-89, 98-107, 121-25, 128-34, 136-42, 255-62, 267-74.

38. CSSE, 10 January 1883, pp. 401, 403.

39. CDSO, 12 July 1884, pp. 194, 196; CSSE, 13 January 1884, pp. 561, 567; CDSE, 12 January 1884, p. 438.

40. PRE, 25 March, 1 April, 6 May, 29 July 1882.

41. DIS, 30 March 1882; EPS, 24 January, 8, 30 June, 14 July, 10 December 1882; CQ, 19 February 1882; LAP, 18 July 1882.

42. RVS, 29 May 1883.

43. INDEP, 18 December 1883; RVS, 29 May 1883; EPS, 24 January, 6 June 1883; DIS, 26 August 1882.

44. PC, 28 March 1882; EPS, 18, 19 April 1882; INDEP, 16 November 1883; RVS, 12 July 1883.

CHAPTER TEN

1. CONS, 14, 23 February 1881; LAP, 3 February 1881; VI, 23 January 1881.
2. FERR, 10 December 1879.
3. MER, 17 December 1879.
4. FERR, 12, 16 December 1879.
5. Ibid., 17 December 1879.
6. NFERR, 22 December 1879; MER, 18 December 1879; LAP, 12 December 1879.
7. TEL, 23 December 1879; RVS, 18 December 1879.
8. LAP, 20 December 1879.
9. Ibid., 13 December 1879; RVS, 11, 18 December 1879.
10. CDSE, 3, 8 January 1880, pp. 89-92, 102-108.
11. FERR, 3, 5, 9, 16 January 1880; LIBL, 31 January 1879; INDEP, 15 January, 14 February 1880; LAP, 13, 15 January 1880; LOT, 5, 9 January 1880; LIBV, 31 January 1880.
12. INDEP, 13, 15 January 1880; LOT, 4 January, 31 May 1880; RVS, 9 January, 12 February 1880.
13. LOT, 1 April 1880.
14. Herbert Millington, *American Diplomacy during the War of the Pacific* (New York: Columbia University Press, 1948), pp. 54-58, 66-73: Pinto, "Apuntes de Aníbal Pinto en el año de 1880 y 1882," RC 6, no. 53 (1922):260, 261, 269.
15. LAP, 19, 26 October 1880; PRO, 20 October 1880; RVS, 16 October 1880; INDEP, 8, 20, October 1880; LIBT, 16 October 1880; FERRO, 11, 22 October 1880; MER, 13, 23 October 1880; LOT, 26 October 1880; NFERR, 30 August, 13 September, 18 October 1880; ECAT, 9 October 1880; HER, 10, 11, 14, 18, 24 October 1880.
16. MER, 27 October 1880.
17. FERRO, 17 September 1880; PRO, 18 October 1880.
18. CEN, 3 June 1880; CHT, 16 September 1880; LAP, 14, 15 September 1880; INDEP, 13 June, 8 October 1880; CUR, 16 October 1880; LOTA, 5 September 1880; LAP, 14 September 1880; MER, 3 September, 19 October 1880; ECAT, 23 October 1880; INDEP, 11 September 1880; LOT, 12 October 1880.
19. CONS, 21 October 1880; ESMER, 17 October 1880; LAP, 14, 15 September, 1 October 1880; MER, 9, 19 October 1880; CHT, 16 September 1880.
20. ECAT, 23 October 1880; INDEP, 11 September 1880; MER, 19 October 1880; LOT, 12 October 1880.
21. DIS, 14 October 1880; HER, 15 October 1880; LOT, 5 September 1880; LAP, 15 September 1880; MER, 9 October 1880; ESMER, 17, 23 October 1880; FERR, 15 October 1880.
22. ARO, 21 November 1880; CUR, 16 October 1880; HER, 8 December 1880; FERRO, 10 October 1880; NFERR, 23 October 1880; INDEP, 12 October 1880.
23. ECAT, 29 October, 16 November 1880; LOT, 16 October 1880; INDEP, 12 September, 14 October 1880.
24. INDEP, 10, 11, September, 12, 26 October 1880; LOT, 1, 11 September, 10, 14, 16 October 1880; MER, 11 October 1880.
25. INDEP, 12 September, 12 October, 24 November 1880; FERR, 11 November 1880; FERRO, 10 October 1880; MER, 26 June, 11, 22 October 1880; LAP, 1 September 1880; CUR, 16 October 1880.
26. FERR, 11 November 1880.
27. CUR, 16 October 1880; LAP, 15 September 1880; INDEP, 23 October 1880; LOT, 16 October 1880.

28. INDEP, 23 October 1880.
29. CDSO, 14 September 1880, pp. 683-88, 690.
30. Ibid., 14, 21 September 1880, pp. 685, 710-11, 715-16.
31. Ibid., 23, 25 September 1880, pp. 731-32, 742.
32. Ibid., 25 September 1880, p. 748, 751-53.
33. Pinto, "Apuntes . . . 1882," RC 6, (1922):266-70; J. Godoy to A. Pinto, 2 November 1880, AJE 2; CDSE, 5 October 1880, pp. 790-92, 794-97; INDEP, 5, 9, 10 October 1880.
34. Millington, pp. 73-75. See also the remarks of *The Chilian Times*, 23 October 1880.
35. FER, 28 October, 19, 28 November, 16 December 1880; HER, 29, 30 October 1880; INDEP, 17 November 1880; LAP, 28 October 1880; RVS, 4 November 1880; Millington, pp. 77-78.
36. E. Altamirano to A. Matte, 4 November 1880, FV, vol. 826; E. Altamirano-A. Pinto, 22, 25, 29 October 1880, "Cartas a don Aníbal Pinto," RC 5, no. 48 (1921):238-41; FERRO, 28 October 1880; HER, 16 November 1880; MER, 29, 30 October 1880; INDEP, 24, 25 November 1880.
37. LIBT, 29 October 1880; MER, 29 October 1880.
38. CQ, 30 January 1881; LAP, 28 January, 4, 8, 10 February 1881; RVS, 29 January 1881; LOT, 23 January 1881; COM, 16 February 1881; FERR, 31 January, 4, 11, 25 February 1881; HER, 2, 5, 15 February 1881; FEN, 22 April 1881; LOT, 26 January, 5 February 1881.
39. LOT, 12, 31 January 1881; Jorge Basadre, *Historia de la República del Perú*, 11 vols. (Lima: Ediciones Historia, 1962), 6:2542-554: Bulnes, 3:8-9.
40. D. Santa María to A. Pinto, 10 February [1881], FV, vol. 416; FERR, 28, 31 January 1881; INDEP, 28 January 1881; ESMER, 9 February 1881; LAP, 19 February 1881; CUR, 6, 26 February 1881; FERR, 13 March 1881; ÑUB, 19 February 1881.
41. CONS, 22 February 1881.
42. HER, 28 January, 5 February, 25 April 1881; LAP, 29 January, 1, 11 February, 4 April 1881; ESMER, 13 February 1881.
43. ECAT, 29 January 1881; HER, 23 January 1881; INDEP, 28 January, 3 February 1881: ÑUB, 2 February 1881; NFERR, 30 January 1881; RVS, 14, 16, 19 February 1881.
44. RVS, 19 February 1881.
45. ECAT, 18 May 1881; CUR, 6 February 1881; HER, 31 January 1881; CHT, 12, 19 February 1881; CONS, 14 February 1881; ESMER, 13 February 1881.
46. RVS, 9, 14 February 1881; INDEP, 6, 25 1881.
47. NFERR, 3 February 1881; CHT, 5 February 1881.
48. J. M. Balmaceda to C. Saavedra, 31 January 1881 in "Carta de don José Manuel Balmaceda a don Cornelio Saavedra, el 31 de enero de 1881," RCHG 8, no. 12 (1912):134; telegram of A. Lastarria to A. Pinto, 17 February 1881, FV, vol. 412; E. Altamirano to A. Pinto, 26 January 1881, in "Cartas," RC 5, no. 49 (1922):402.
49. Basadre, 6:2543-554.
50. M. Valderrama to J. F. Vergara, 26 February 1881, AJFV; E. Altamirano to A. Pinto, 3, 4, 6, 25 February 1881 in "Cartas," RC 5, no. 49 (1922):405-408, 412-14; D. Santa María to A. Pinto, 10 February [1881], FV, vol. 416.
51. Basadre, 6:2546-47, 2550-51.
52. Bulnes, 3:47-50.

Notes 319

53. Ibid., 58–61; CHT, 9 April 1881.
54. Bulnes, 3:26–28, 30, 35, 38.
55. CDSO, 6 August 1881, p. 299.
56. ECAT, 6, 11, 18 May 1881.
57. Ibid., 29 June, 12, 16 July 1881; CDSO, 6 August 1881, p. 297, 301–2; LAP, 9 August 1881.
58. CDSO, 6, 9 August 1881, pp. 297, 304–6, 313–14; LAP, 16, 17, 26 August 1881.
59. ECAT, 21, 22 April 1881; LAP, 26 August 1881; CHT, 23 April 1881; PC, 23 July, 27 September 1881; ÑUB, 23 November 1881; CQ, 30 January 1881; CHT, 12 November 1881; CDSO, 11 August 1881, p. 330.
60. Millington, pp. 42, 82–93.
61. INDEP, 8, 14 October 1881; RVS, 11 October 1881; FERR, 10 October 1881: LIBT, 11 October 1881; PC, 8, 13 October 1881; DIS, 13 October 1881; PRO, 12 October 1881.
62. Millington, pp. 87, 97–114; Basadre, 6:2557.
63. Bulnes, 3:127–29, 135–36, 157; Basadre, 6:2557–63.
64. E. Altamirano to A. Pinto, 4, 6 February 1881, in "Cartas," RC 5, no. 49 (1922):407–9; Bulnes, 3:182–87; D. Santa María to J. Novoa, 9 December 1881; J. Novoa to J. M. Balmaceda, 14 December 1881; J. Novoa to D. Santa María, 19 December 1881 in Bulnes,3:184–87.
65. DIS, 15 November 1881.
66. ET, 3 November 1881; LAP, 23, 24 November, 13 December 1881.
67. CHT, 27 May 1882; Millington, pp. 91–96.
68. Ibid., pp. 96, 121–24; Bulnes, 3:212.
69. ECAT, 10, 30 January, 1 February 1882; INDEP, 12, 17 January 1882; FERR, 9 January, 12 May, 30 June 1882; CHT, 7, 21, 28 January 1882; RVS, 4 December 1881; LAP, 27, 30 January, 6 February 1882; CQ, 29 January 1882.
70. Millington, pp. 124–125; LAP, 20, 21, 23 January, 28 February 1882; CQ, 2, 18 February 1882.
71. Baron D'Avril to M. B. St. Hilaire, 20 November 1881, in *Informes inéditos de diplomáticos extranjeros durante la Guerra del Pacifico* (Santiago: Ed. Andrés Bello, 1980), pp. 319–20; Bulnes, 3:171–73, 177.
72. Bulnes, 3:167–70, 261–62, 262–71, 271–308; Del Canto, pp. 159–248; INDEP, 28 July 1882.
73. LIBT, 20 July 1882.
74. CUR, 29 July 1882; *El Comercio* (San Felipe) for example, virtually ignored the war in 1882; CHT, 3 June 1882; INDEP, 30 April 1882; LIBT, 10 February, 14, 16, 24 March 1882.
75. INDEP, 22, 30 July, 10 August, 14 September 1882; MER, 19 July 1882; DIS, 12 August 1882; FERR, 18 July 1882; ÑUB, 5 August, 6 September 1882; LAP, 1, 4, 17 August 1882.
76. FERR, 9, 16, 18 August, 9 September 1882; RVS, 26 July, 20 August 1882: LIBT, 20 July 1882.
77. CHT, 11 Feb, 2 September 1882; EPS, 13 April 1882; FERR, 10, 29, 30 July 1882.
78. ECAT, 13 July, 8, 16 August 1882.
79. INDEP, 30 April, 10 August 1882; CONS, 27 September 1882; MER, 21, 26 July 1882; LOT, 15 October 1882.
80. Bulnes, 3:318; D. Santa María to E. Altamirano, 12, 20 August 1882, in

Bulnes, 3:319; CDSE, 28 November, 9 December 1882, pp. 138, 259-61; FERR, 17, 18, 20 August 1882.
 81. Bulnes, 3:251-52; D. Santa María to J. Novoa, 21 March 1882 in Bulnes, 3:255-57; Millington, pp. 128-29.
 82. ESMER, 10 October 1882; RVS, 23 September 1882; CQ, 28 September, 5 October 1882.
 83. LAP, 4 October 1882; RVS, 6, 31 October 1882; INDEP, 22, 27 September 1882; CONS, 27 September 1882; Millington, pp. 130-32.
 84. Basadre, 6:2609-13; Bulnes, 3:361; J. Novoa to D. Santa María, 1 November 1882 in Bulnes, 3:364.
 85. D. Santa María to J. Novoa, 27 January 1883 in Bulnes, 3:366-67.
 86. D. Santa María to P. Lynch, 9 February 1883, in Bulnes 3:391.
 87. Bulnes, 3:392-424.
 88. CONS, 27 September 1882; CQ, 28 September 1882; DIS, 1 February 1882; COM, 19 February 1882; RVS, 6 April 1883; INDEP, 3 May 1883
 89. DIS, 10 April 1883; RVS, 6 April 1883; INDEP, 3 May 1883; FERR, 26 March 1883; LAP, 15 January 1883.
 90. CONS, 27 September 1882.
 91. DIS, 27 February 1883; FERR, 26 March, 7 May 1883; LAP, 9 October 1883; ECAT, 18 October 1883.
 92. INDEP, 6 October 1882; 24 October 1883.
 93. ECAT, 13 October 1883; INDEP, 23 February 1883.
 94. INDEP, 18 May 1883.
 95. INDEP, 17 May, 23, 24, 25 October 1883; LAP, 23 February, 27 April 1883; ECAT, 13 November 1883; LIBT, 5 May 1883.
 96. Bulnes, 3:431; Basadre, 6:2620-22.
 97. DIS, 1 February 1883; INDEP, 27 May 1883; ECAT, 3 November 1883; EPS, 9 October 1883; RVS, 28 February 1883.
 98. Bulnes, 3:434-87, 498-510; Alejandro Binimelis, "Datos sobre la batalla de Huamachuco," in N. Molinare, *Historia de la Batalla de Huamachuco* (Santiago: Imprenta Antigua Iglesia, 1913), pp. 283-305. See also N. N., *La Batalla de Huamachuco ante la historia* (Lima: Carlos Prince, 1886); Cáceres, pp. 231, 244; Basadre, 6:2647; D. Santa María to J. Novoa, 7 August, 15 September 1883, FV, vol. 414; D. Santa María to P. Lynch, 18 July, 15 September, 23 November 1883, FV, vol. 414; D. Santa María to L. Aldunate, 19 October 1883, FV, vol. 413; D. Santa María to A. Soffia, 12 October 1883, FV, vol. 416.
 100. ESMER, 5 December 1880; ECAT, 3 June 1880; FERR, 20 April, 10 May 1880; LAP, 17 January, 20 December 1880; LOT, 13 November 1880; MER, 7 July 1880; LIBV, 14 February 1880.
 101. LAP, 21 December 1880; FERR, 26 February 1881, 16 Mar, 24 July 1882, 17 July, 10 October 1883; ECAT, 16 July 1881; DIS, 1 February 1882.
 102. FERR, 13 May 1881, 22 March, 14 May, 5, 19 August 1882; LAP, 20 December 1880, 12 April, 19 May 1881, 15 April, 19 June 1882; INDEP, 9 February 1881, 3 November 1883; RVS, 7 December 1882.
 103. Phillips, pp. 235-43, 245-52, 264-67; *Informe del Ministro de la Guerra a la Convención Nacional de 1881* (La Paz: Imprenta de la Unión Americana, n.d.), pp. 6-8, 23, 29-31; Millington, pp. 122, 126-27; Barros, pp. 420-22.
 104. ECAT, 18 January, 21 March 1882; LIBV, 21 January 1882; CUR, 25 March 1883; CONS, 23 January 1882; LAP, 18 January, 13 February 1882, 4 January, 18 April 1883; RVS, 7 December 1882; EPS, 18 December 1883; FERR, 1 November

1883; INDEP, 25 November 1883; Phillips, pp. 296-315; CHT, 1 December 1883; CQ, 18 November 1883; RVS, 1 November 1883; Burr, pp. 164-65; Barros, pp. 433-36. D. Santa Maria-Luis Aldunate, 19 October 1883, FV, vol. 413; D. Santa María to A. Soffia, 12 October 1883, FV, vol. 416; D. Santa María to P. Lynch, 15 September, 30 October 1883, FV, vol. 414; D. Santa María to F. Valdes, 6 November 1883, FV, vol. 416; CHT, 13 October 1883; LAP, 5 October 1883; D. Santa María to A. Gorostiaga, 26 October 1883, FV, vol. 415.

EPILOGUE

1. Markos Mamalakis, *The Growth and Structure of the Chilean Economy* (New Haven: Yale University Press, 1976), pp. 54-55.
2. Julio Zegers, *Estudios economicos* (Santiago: n.p., 1907), p. 8.
3. Gonzalo Vial, *Historia de Chile*, 2 vols. (Santiago: Editorial Santillana del Pacífico, 1981), 2:642-44; F. A. Encina, *Nuestra inferioridad economica. Sus causas, sus consecuencias* (Santiago: Imprenta Universitaria, 1912), pp. 178, 182-84, 225-33.

Bibliography

PRIMARY SOURCES
Unpublished Materials and Archival Materials

Archivo Nacional, Santiago, Chile
  Archivo de Benjamín Vicuña Mackenna
    Correspondencia de Victor Bianchi to B. Vicuña Mackenna, 1879–1881, Vol. 357.
    Correspondencia de Ramón Pachecho to B. Vicuña Mackenna, 1880, Vol. 383.
  Archivo de la Intendencia de Atacama, Vols. 513, 514, 520, 524, 528, 529, 530, 536, Minute Book.
  Archivo Jaime Eyzaguirre.
    Correspondencia de Joaquín Godoy to Aníbal Pinto, 1879–1880. Vol. 1.
    Correspondencia de Pedro Lagos to Aníbal Pinto, 1880–1881, Vol. 1.
    Correspondencia de Máximo Lira to Aníbal Pinto, 1880, Vol. 1.
    Correspondencia de Patricio Lynch to Aníbal Pinto, 1880–1881, Vol. 1.
    Correspondencia de Emilio Sotomayor to Aníbal Pinto, 1879, Vol. 1.
    Correspondencia de Rafael Sotomayor to Aníbal Pinto, 1880, Vol. 2.
  Archivo Fondos Varios
    Correspondencia de José Alfonso to Aníbal Pinto, 1879, Vol. 414.
    Correspondencia de Eulojio Altamirano to Eduardo Matte, Vol. 826.
    Correspondencia de Santiago Amengual to Aníbal Pinto, 1880, Vol. 416.
    Correspondencia de Justo Arteaga to Aníbal Pinto, 1879, 1881, Vol. 412.
    Correspondencia de Justo Arteaga Cuevas to Aníbal Pinto, 1879, Vol. 415.
    Correspondencia de Manuel Baquedano to Aníbal Pinto, 1879–1881, Vols. 415, 515, 826.
    Correspondencia de Eduardo de la Barra to A. Matte, 1879–1880, Vol. 826.
    Correspondencia de Alberto Blest Gana to A. Matte, 1879, Vol. 826.

Correspondencia de Alberto Blest Gana to A. Pinto, 1879, Vol. 413.
Correspondencia de Lorenzo Claro to Aníbal Pinto, 1879, Vol. 838.
Correspondencia de Erasmo Escala to Aníbal Pinto, 1880, Vol. 416.
Correspondencia de Aníbal Pinto.
Correspondencia de Pío Puelma to Mariano Guerrerro, 1879, Vol. 826.
Correspondencia de Cornelio Saavedra to Aníbal Pinto, 1879-1881, Vols. 412, 414.
Correspondencia de Cornelio Saavedra to Eulojio Altamirano, 1879, Vol. 559.
Correspondencia de Domingo Santa María to Luis Aldunate, 1883, Vol. 413.
Correspondencia de Domingo Santa María to A. Gorostiaga, 1883, Vol. 826.
Correspondencia de Domingo Santa María to Patricio Lynch, 1883, Vol. 414.
Correspondencia de Domingo Santa María to Augusto Matte, 1880, Vol. 826.
Correspondencia de Domingo Santa María to Jovino Novoa, 1883-1884, Vols. 414, 416.
Correspondencia de Domingo Santa María to Aníbal Pinto, 1879-1881, Vol. 416.
Correspondencia de Domingo Santa María to A. Soffia, 1883-1884, Vol. 413.
Correspondencia de Domingo Santa María to Francisco Valdés, 1883, Vol. 413.
Correspondencia de Rafael Sotomayor to A. Matte, 1879-1880, Vol. 826,
Correspondencia de Rafael Sotomayor to Cornelio Saavedra, 1879-1880, Vol. 559.
Correspondencia de Rafael Sotomayor to Antonio Varas, 1879, Vol. 838.
Correspondencia de Roberto Souper to Cornelio Saavedra, 1879, Vol. 559.
Correspondencia de Domingo de Toro to Aníbal Pinto, 1880, Vol. 416.
Correspondencia de Juan Williams Rebolledo to Aníbal Pinto, 1879,
Correspondencia de Juan Williams Rebolledo to Antonio Varas, 1879, Vol. 838.
Ejército del Perú. Apuntes para la historia. Diario de la campaña. Vol. 220.
Archivo de Ministerio de Hacienda Vols. 975, 978-988, 991, 1011, 1017, 1020-1022, 1027, 1035, 1045, 1053, 1054, 1056, 1058, 1060, 106l, 1071, 1088, 1111-1117, 1122, 1173-1178, 1180-1193, 1277, 1278, 1274, 1276, 1282, 1287, 1323, 1340. 1472.
Archivo de Ministerio de Marina Vols. 366, 395.
Archivo de Ministerio del Interior Vols. 868-884, 889-899, 901-911, 913, 947-950, 999-1002.

Biblioteca del Congreso
Archivo de José Francisco Vergara (A collection of uncatalogued letters to José Francisco Vergara in the Library of Congress annex.)
Correspondencia de Domingo Arteaga Alemparte to J. F. Vergara, 1879.
Correspondencia de Vicente Dávila Larráin to J. F. Vergara, 1880.
Correspondencia de M. Valderrama to J. F. Vergara, 1880-1881.

Great Britain
Foreign Office. General Correspondence, Chile (F.O. 16), 1879-1884.
———. General Correspondence, Peru (F.O. 6l), 1879, 1881.
Gibbs Papers. General Archive, vols. 11, 470.

Bibliography

United States of America
    Department of State. Dispatches from U. S. Ministers to Chile, 1876-1884.
    ———. Dispatches from U.S. Ministers to Peru, 1878-1879.

PUBLISHED SOURCES
Journals

Boletín de la Sociedad Nacional de Agricultura, 1879-1884.
Boletín de la Sociedad de Fomento Fabril, 1884.
The Economist (London), 1879-1884.
Revista Minera, 1883-1884.

Newspapers

La Araucania (Mulchén), 1879-1883.
El Araucano (Lebu), 1879-1882.
La Aurora (Curicó), 1879.
El Baquedanista (Cauquenes) 1881.
El Bío Bío (Anjeles), 1879-1884.
El Caupolicán (Rengo), 1879-1882.
El Censor (San Felipe), 1879-1880.
El Centinela (San Carlos), 1879.
The Chilian Times (Valparaíso), 1876-1884.
El Chilote (Ancud), 1879-1884.
El Comercio (Coquimbo), 1879.
El Comercio (San Felipe), 1879-1884.
El Constituyente (Copiapó), 1876-1884.
El Correo (Osorno), 1880-1882.
El Correo de Quillota (Quillota), 1879-1884.
El Correo de la Serena (Serena), 1879.
El Corvo (Santiago), 1881.
El Curicano (Curicó), 1879-1884.
El Diario de Avisos (Santiago), 1879.
El Diario de Guerra (Santiago), 1879.
El Dique (Talcahuano), 1881.
La Discusión (Chillán), 1876-1884.
El Eco del Sur (Angol), 1883-1884.
El Eco de Taltal (Taltal), 1881.
La Epoca (San Carlos), 1881-1882.
La Epoca (Santiago), 1881-1883.
La Esmeralda (Coronel), 1879-1883.
La Esperanza (Cauquenes), 1879.
El Estandarte Católico (Santiago), 1876-1884.
El Fénix (Rancagua), 1880-1884.
El Ferrocarril (Santiago), 1876-1884.
El Ferrocarril del Sur (Curicó), 1883.
El Ferrocarrilito (Santiago), 1880.
El Heraldo (Santiago), 1880-1881.
El Independiente (Santiago), 1876-1884.

El Industrial (Antofagasta), 1881-1884.
La Juventud (San Fernando), 1879-1882.
El Lautaro (Rancagua), 1879.
El Liberal (Lebu), 1881-1882.
El Liberal (Vallenar), 1879.
La Libertad (Talca), 1880-1883.
La Libertad (Valdivia), 1876-1884.
El Lontué (Molina), 1881.
El Lota (Lota), 1878-1884.
La Luz (Vichuquén), 1881-1882.
El Maipo (San Bernardo), 1879-1882.
El Mercurio (Valparaíso), 1879-1884.
Las Noticias (Talca), 1879.
Las Novedades (Santiago), 1879-1880.
El Ñuble (Chillán), 1880.
El Nuevo Ferrocarril (Santiago), 1879-1880.
El Obrero (Chillán), 1879.
La Opinión (Talca), 1879.
El Padre Cobos (Santiago), 1881-1882.
El Parralino (Parral), 1880-1884.
La Patria (Valparaíso), 1876-1884.
El Porvenir (Curepto), 1883-1884.
El Porvenir (Ligua), 1882.
El Porvenir (Puerto Montt), 1881-1883.
El Porvenir (Tomé), 1881-1883.
El Precursor (Santiago), 1882.
El Progreso (Meilipilla), 1879-1883.
El Progreso (Serena), 1879-1884.
El Pueblo Chileno (Antofagasta), 1879-1881.
El Republicano (Yumbel), 1878-1884.
La Revista del Sur (Concepción), 1876-1884.
La Semana (Parral), 1879.
El Sufragio (Curicó), 1879.
El Taller (Santiago), 1879.
El Telegrafo (Chillán), 1880-1881.
Los Tiempos (Santiago), 1876-1882.
La Union (Parral), 1879.
El Veintiuno de Mayo (Iquique), 1880-1884.
El Vergara (Constitución), 1882.
La Voz Chilena (Iquique), 1880.
La Voz de Itata (Quirihue), 1879-1884.

GOVERNMENT DOCUMENTS

Bolivia. Ministerio de Guerra. *Informe de la Guerra a la Convención Nacional de 1881*. La Paz: Imprenta de la Unión Americana, n.d.
Chile. *El Boletín de la Guerra del Pacífico*. 1879-1881.
———. Oficina Central de Estadística. *Anuario Estadístico de la República de Chile correspondiente a los años 1877-1878*. Santiago: Imprenta Nacional, 1879.

Bibliography

―――. ―――. *Anuario... 1878-1879, 1879-1880, 1881-1883, 1883-1885*, Santiago: Imprenta Nacional, 1879, 1881, 1882, 1884, 1886.

―――. ―――. *Estadística agrícola de la República de Chile correspondiente a los años de 1877 i 1878, 1879 i 1880.* Santiago: Imprenta Nacional, 1879, 1881.

―――. ―――. *Estadística comercial de la República de Chile correspondiente al año de 1874.* Valparaíso: Imprenta del Mercurio, 1875.

―――. ―――. *Estadística comercial... 1875-1884.* Valparaíso: Imprenta del Universo, 1876-1885.

―――. ―――. *Sinopsis Estadística de la República de Chile.* Santiago: Imprenta Universo, 1919.

―――. *Cámara de Diputados. Sesiones ordinarias de 1879-1884.* Santiago: Imprenta Nacional, 1879-1884.

―――. ―――. *Sesiones estraordinarias de 1879-1883.* Santiago: Imprenta Nacional, 1879-1884.

―――. *Cámara de Senado. Sesiones ordinarias de 1879-1884.* Santiago: Imprenta Nacional, 1879-1883.

―――. ―――. *Sesiones estraordinarias de 1879-1883.* Santiago: Imprenta Nacional, 1879-1884.

―――. ―――. *Sesiones secretas de la Cámara de Senadores celebradas durante la Guerra del Pacífico.* Santiago: Imprenta Nacional, 1881.

―――. *El Diario Oficial* (Santiago), 1879-1884.

―――. Ministerio de Guerra. *Memoria del Ministerio de guerra correspondiente al año de 1879.* Santiago: Imprenta de J. Núñez, 1879.

―――. ―――. *Memoria del Ministerio de Guerra i Marina... 1880.* Santiago: Imprenta de J. Núñez, 1880.

―――. ―――. *Memoria del Ministerio de Guerra... 1881, 1882.* Santiago: Imprenta de la Epoca, 1881, 1882.

―――. Ministerio de Hacienda. *Memoria de Ministerio de Hacienda correspondiente a los años de 1879 y 1880.* Santiago: Imprenta Nacional, 1879-1880.

―――. ―――. *Memoria de Ministerio de Hacienda correspondiente a los años de 1881.* Santiago: Imprenta de P. Cadot, 1881.

―――. ―――. *Memoria... 1882-1883.* Santiago: Imprenta de J. Núñez, 1882-1883.

―――. Ministerio del Interior. *Memoria de Ministerio del Interior correspondiente al años de 1878-1884.* Santiago: Imprenta Nacional, 1878-1884.

―――. ―――. *Anexo a la Memoria del Ministerio del Interior en 1883 y 1884.* Santiago: Imprenta Nacional, 1883-1884.

Great Britain, Parliament. *British Sessional Papers.* 1880, Vol. 74; 1881, Vol. 91; 1882, Vol. 70; 1883, Vols. 72, 73; 1885, Vol. 78.

Books

Acland, William. *Six Weeks with the Chilean Army.* Norfolk Island: Melanesian Mission, n.d.

Ahumada Moreno, Pascual, ed. *La Guerra del Pacífico.* 8 vols. Valparaíso: Imprenta El Progreso, 1884-1892.

Al pueblo de Santiago. Santiago: Imprenta de El Independiente, 1879.

Anguita, Ricardo. *Leyes promulgadas en Chile.* 5 vols. Santiago: Barcelona, 1912. Vols. 2 and 3.

Apuntes para la historia de la Guerra del Pacífico. La Paz: Imprenta de la Unión Americana, 1883.

Aracena, F. M. *Apuntes de viaje. La industria del cobre en las provincias de Atacama i Coquimbo i los grandes i valiosos depósitos carboníferos de Lota i Coronel en la provincia de Concepción.* Santiago: Imprenta del Nuevo Mercurio, 1884.

[Aramayo, F. A.] *Chilian Chicane.* New York: n. p. 1882.

Aránguiz, Horacio and Ricardo Couyoumdjian. *Informes inéditos de diplomaticos extranjeros durante la Guerra del Pacífico.* Santiago: Editorial Andrés Bello, 1980.

[Balmaceda, José Manuel]. *Discurso de S.E. el Presidente de la República en la apertura del Congreso Constituyente de 1891.* Santiago: Imprenta Nacional, 1891.

Benavides Santos, Arturo. *Seis años de vacaciones.* 3rd. ed. Buenos Aires: Francisco de Aguirre, 1967.

Birkedal, Holger. *Peru-Bolivia-Chile. Krigen i Sudamerika.* Chicago: Standinavens Boghandel, 1884.

Boyd, R. Nelson. *Chili: Sketches of Chili and the Chilians during the War of the Pacific.* London: Wm. Allen, 1881.

Buendía, Juan. *Guerra con Chile.* Lima: Carlos Milla Batres, 1967.

Cáceres, Andrés. *La Guerra del 79: Sus campañas.* Lima: Milla Batres, 1973.

Canto, Estanislao del. *Memorias de Estanislao del Canto.* Santiago: Imprenta La Tracción, 1927.

[Caviedes, E.] *La batalla de Tacna descrita por El Corresponsal del Mercurio.* Santiago: n.p., 1880.

Cifuentes, Abdón. *Memorias.* 2 vols. Santiago: Nascimento, 1936. Vol. 1.

Compañía Huanchaca de Bolivia. *Tercera Memoria del directorio e informe de la administración jeneral de Huanchaca.* Valparaíso: Imprenta del Universo, 1878.

Compañía de Salitres y Ferrocarril. *14th memoria de la Compañía de Salitres y Ferrocarril de Antofagasta.* Valparaíso: Imprenta Mercurio, 1879.

Encina, Francisco. *Nuestra inferioridad económica. Sus causas, sus consecuencias.* Santiago: Imprenta Universitaria, 1912.

Errázuriz, Isidoro. *Hombres y cosas durante la guerra.* Valparaíso: La Patria, 1882.

Los estafadores sin máscara. Santigo: Imprenta Victoria de H. Izquierdo, 1882.

M. G. [Marcial González]. *Condición de los trabajadores rurales en Chile.* Santiago: República de Jacinto Pérez, 1876.

Larraín Zañartu, José Joaquín and Nicolás Peña Vicuña. *La Guerra ilustrada de Chile, Perú, i Bolivia.* Valparaíso: Imprenta del Mercurio, 1879.

Lavalle, José Antonio de. *Mi misión en Chile en 1879.* Lima: Instituto de Estudios Historico-Marítimos del Peru, 1979.

León, M. le. *Recuerdos de una mision en el ejercito chileno. Batallas de Chorillos y Miraflores.* Buenos Aires: Francisco de Aguirre, 1969.

Lira, Máximo. *Observaciones a la memoria del ex ministro de la guerra don José Francisco Vergara escritas por encargo i publicadas con autorización del Jeneral don Manuel Baquedano.* Santiago: Imprenta de El Independiente, 1882.

Montt, Ambrosio. *Dictámenes del Fiscal de la Corte Suprema de Justicia de Chile.* 2 vols. Santiago: Imprenta Nacional, 1894–1895. Vol. 2.

Murillo, Ruperto. *Defensa del Teniente Coronel de Ejército don Ambrosio Letelier.* Santiago: Imprenta de la Librería Americana, 1882.
N. N. *La Batalla de Huamachuco ante la historia.* Lima: Carlos Prince, 1886.
Ravest Mora, Manuel. *La Compañía Salitrera y la Ocupacíon de Antofagasta, 1878-1879.* Santiago: Andrés Bello, 1983.
Reseña de las fiestas cívicas con que el pueblo de Copiapó recibió al Rejimiento Atacama. Copiapó: Imprenta de El Atacama, 1881.
Resúmen de la hacienda pública de Chile desde 1833 hasta 1914. London: Spottiswoode & Co., Ltd., n.d.
Riquelme, Daniel. *La expedición a Lima.* Santiago: Editorial del Pacífico, 1967.
Risopatron, Dario. *Legislación militar de Chile.* 3 vols. Santiago: Imprenta Gutenberg, 1882. Vol. 3.
Riveros, Galvarino. *Angamos.* Santiago: Imprenta de Jacinto Núñez, 1882.
———. *En la escuadra.* Santiago: Imprenta de El Independiente, 1882.
[Rozas, Ramón Ricardo]. *Carta a S.E. El Presidente de la República por un Chileno.* n.p.: Imprenta Victoria, 1883?.
———. *Carta del diputado por La Laja a sus electores.* Santiago: Imprenta de la República de J. Núñez, 1881.
Solar, Alberto del. *Diario de campaña.* 3rd ed. Buenos Aires: Francisco de Aguirre, 1967.
Subercaseaux, Ramón. *Memorias de ochenta años.* 2nd ed. 2 vols. Santiago: Nascimento, 1936. Vol. I.
Urzúa, Luis. *Discurso pronunciado en el teatro de variedades.* Santiago: Imprenta de El Independiente, 1881.
Urzúa, Pedro N. *Don Zorobabel Rodríguez o las exajeraciones del libre cambio.* Santiago: Imprenta Cervantes, 1884.
Varas, Antonio. *Correspondencia de don Antonio Varas sobre la Guerra del Pacífico.* Santiago: Imprenta Universitaria, 1918.
[Walker Martínez, Carlos]. *Las elecciones de 1881.* Santiago: Imprenta del Independiente, 1881.
———. *Historia de la administración Santa María.* 2 vols. Santiago: Imprenta Progreso, 1889. Vol. 1.
Williams Rebolledo, Juan. *Operaciones de la escuadra chilena miéntras estuvo a las órdenes del contra-almirante Juan Williams Rebolledo.* Valparaíso: Imprenta Progreso, 1882.
X. *La patria está en peligro.* N.p., 1879.
Zegers, Julio. *Estudios Economicos.* Santiago: N.p., 1907.

Articles

Altamirano, Eulogio. "Cartas a don Aníbal Pinto." *Revista Chilena* 13 (1921): 225-55; *Revista Chilena* 13 (1922):398-419.
Aránguiz, Horacio. "Cartas políticas de don Domingo Santa María a don José Francisco Vergara (1879-1882)." *Estudios de Historia de Instituciones Políticos y Sociales* 1 (1966):313-371.
Atropos. "El inquilino en Chile. Su vida. Un siglo sin variaciones." *Revista Mapocho* 5 (1966):195-216.
Balmaceda, José Manuel. "Carta a don Cornelio Saavedra." *Revista Chilena de Historia Chilena* 8:12 (1913):132-36.
Binimelis, Alejandro. "Datos sobre la batalla de Huamachuco." In Nicanor

Molinare, *Historia de la Batalla de Huamachuco*. Santiago: Imprenta Antigua Iglesia, 1918, pp. 283–305.
Birkdahl, Holger. "The Late War in South America." *The Overland Monthly* 2d. ser. 3 (1884):188–98.
Díaz, Wenceslao. "Enfermedades reinantes en Chile." *Estudios jeográficos sobre Chile*. Santiago: Imprenta Nacional, 1875, pp. 115–67.
Domínguez, Ramón. "Nuestro sistema de inquilinaje en 1867." *Revista Mapocho* 5 (1966):296–313.
Dublé Almeida, Diego. "Diario de campaña de Diego Dublé Almeida." In *La Guerra del Pacífico*, edited by Fernando Ruz T. Santiago: Editorial Andrés Bello, pp. 77–135.
Fernández Larraín, Sergio. "Cartas de fé y patriotismo de Condell a su esposa." *Revista Chilena de Historia Chilena* 147 (1979):125–84.
Gutiérrez, Hipolito, "Crónica de un Soldado de la Guerra del Pacífico." In *Dos Soldados en la Guerra del Pacífico*. Buenos Aires: Francisco de Aguirre, 1976, pp. 143–231.
Holguín, Vicente. "La toma de Lima," *Revista Chilena* 10 (1926):1–33.
Huneeus, Antonio. "Libro reservado de actas de las sesiones del Consejo de Ministros referentes a la guerra con el Perú i Bolivia desde el 19 de abril de 1879." *Revista Chilena* 7, no. 20 (1919):153–164.
Murillo, Adolfo. "Jeografía médica. Breves apuntes para servir a la estadística médica i a la nosolojía chilenas." In *Estudios jeográficos sobre Chile*. Santiago: Imprenta Nacional, 1875, pp. 15–45.
Pinto, Aníbal. "Apuntes." *Revista Chilena* 13 (1921):337–73; 14 (1922):112–26.
———. "Apuntes de don Aníbal Pinto en el año de 1880 y 1882." *Revista Chilena* 6 (1922):259–80.
———. "La captura del transporte Rimac en 1879." *Revista Chilena* 4, no. 34 (1920):395–96.
———. "Desde la captura del Huáscar hasta la batalla de Tarapacá." *Revista Chilena* 1, no. 5 (1918):518–22.
———. "El hundimiento del tranporte Loa en 1880." *Revista Chilena* 2, no. 8 (1917):247–49.
———. "La renuncia del ministerio Santa María y la formación del Ministerio Recabarren en 1880." *Revista Chilena* 14 (1922):62–68.
Quiroz, Abraham, "Epistolario inédito de su campaña como soldado raso durante toda la Guerra del Pacífico, 1879-1884." In *Dos Soldados en la Guerra del Pacífico*. Buenos Aires: Francisco de Aguirre, 1976, pp. 49–143.
Santa María, Domingo. "Cartas de don Domingo Santa María a don Guillermo Matta." *Revista Chilena de Historia Chilena* 34, no. 18 (1920):324–41.
———. "Cartas de Domingo Santa María a don José Victorino Lastarria." *Revista Chilena* 2, no. 18 (1918):249–60; 2, no. 19 (1918):64–76; 3, no. 24 (1919):362–66.
———. "Cartas políticas de don Domingo Santa María a don José Francisco Vergara." *Estudios del Historia de Instituciones Políticos y Sociales* 1 (1966):313–71.
———. "Las dificultades de la Guerra del Pacífico." *Revista Chilena* 1, no. 5 (1917):514–16.
Sotomayor, Rafael. "El combate de Iquique el 21 de mayo de 1879 y la escursión de la escuadra al Callao." *Revista Chilena* 6, no. 51 (1922):30–39.
———. "Correspondencia de don Rafael Sotomayor con don Aníbal Pinto sobre

la Guerra del Pacífico." *Revista Chilena* 6, no. 57 (1922):178-94; 6, no. 58 (1922):285-94.
———. "Correspondencia de don Rafael Sotomayor con el General don Justo Arteaga Cuevas y don Aníbal Pinto sobre la Guerra del Pacífico." *Revista Chilena* 7, no. 69/70 (1924):410-30.
Sotomayor, Ramon. "La toma de Lima." *Revista Chilena* 10, no. 81/82 (1926): 1-33.
Varas, Antonio. "Reminiscencias historicas y diplomáticas." *Revista Chilena de Historia Chilena* 86 (1935):62-79.
Vergara, José Francisco, "Memorias de José Francisco Vergara." In *Guerra del Pacífico. Memorias de José F. Vergara y Diario de Campaña de Diego Dublé Almeida*. Edited by Fernando Ruz T. Santiago: Andres Bello, 1979, pp. 11-77.

SECONDARY SOURCES
Books

Astorquiza, Octavio, ed. *Lota*. Valparaíso: Imprenta del Universo, 1942.
Barros, Mario. *Historia diplomática de Chile*. Barcelona: Editorial Ariel, 1970.
Barros Borgoño, Luis. *El Vice Almirante don Patricio Lynch*. Santiago: Imprenta de la Unión, 1886.
Basadre, Jorge. *Historia de la república del Perú*. 5th ed. 17 vols. Lima: Ediciones Historia, 1962. Vol. 6.
Bermúdez, Oscar. *Historia del salitre*. Santiago: Universidad de Chile, 1963.
Bulnes, Gonzalo. *La Guerra del Pacífico*. 3 vols. Valparaíso: Imprenta Universo, 1911-1919.
Burr, Robert N. *By Reason or Force*. Berkeley: University of California, 1965.
Carmona, Jorge. *Baquedano*. Santiago: Estado Mayor del Ejército, 1946.
El continjente de la provincia Atacama en la Guerra del Pacífico. Copiapó: Imprenta de "El Atacama," 1880.
Cuadra, Luis de la. *Album del ejército chileno*. Valparaíso: Imprenta del Mercurio, 1877.
Cuevas, Arturo. *Estudios estratéjico sobre la campaña marítima de la guerra del Pacífico*. Valparaíso: Talleres de la armada, 1901.
Dellepiane, Carlos. *Historia militar del Perú*. 2 vols. Buenos Aires: Círculo Militar, 1941. Vol. 2.
Dennis, William J. *Tacna and Arica*. 2nd. ed. N.P.: Archon, 1967.
Ekdahl, Wilhelm. *Historia militar de la Guerra del Pacífico entre Chile, Peru, i Bolivia*. 3 vols. Santiago. Imprenta Universo and Imprenta del Ministerio de Guerra, 1917-1919.
Encina, Franciso. *Historia de Chile*. 20 vols. Santiago: Nascimento, 1946-1952. Vol. 17.
Escala Escobar, Manuel. *El General Erasmo Escala*. Santiago: Ed. Jerónimo de Vivar, 1971.
Espinosa Moraga, Oscar. *Latorre y la vocacíon marítima de Chile*. 2d ed. Santiago: Editorial Eire, 1980.
Fetter, Frank W. *Monetary Inflation in Chile*. Princeton: Princeton University Press, 1931.

García Castelblanco, Alejandro. *Estudio crítico de las operaciones navales de Chile*. Santiago: Imprenta de la Armada, 1929.
González Salinas, Edmundo. *La política contra la estrategia en La Guerra del Pacífica*. Santiago: Imprenta Esparza, 1981.
Glasson, William G. *History of Military Pension Legislation in the United States*. New York: Columbia University Press, 1900.
Kirsch, Henry. *Industrial Development in a Traditional Society*. Gainesville: University of Florida Press, 1977.
Klein, Herbert. *Bolivia*. New York: Oxford University Press, 1982.
Larenas Q., Victor. *Patricio Lynch*. Santiago: Editorial Universitaria, 1981.
López U., Carlos. *La historia de la marina de Chile*. Santiago: Editorial Andrés Bello, 1969.
Machuca, Francisco. *Los cuatros campañas de la Guerra del Pacífico*. 4 vols. Valparaíso: Imprenta Victoria, 1926–1930.
Meacham, J. Lloyd. *A Survey of United States Latin American Relations*. Boston: Houghton Mifflin, 1965.
Millington, Herbert. *American Diplomacy during the War of the Pacific*. New York: Columbia University Press, 1948.
Novoa de la Fuente, Luis. *Historia naval de Chile*. 3d ed. Valparaíso: Escuela Naval "Arturo Prat," 1958.
Orrego Vicuña, E. *Vicuña Mackenna, Vida y trabajos*. 3d ed. Santiago: Zig-Zag, 1961.
Paz Soldan, Mariano Felipe. *Narración histórica de la guerra de Chile contra el Perú y Bolivia*. Buenos Aires: Imprenta de Mayo, 1884.
Pederson, Leland R. *The Mining Industry of the Norte Chico, Chile*. Evanston: Northwestern University Press, 1966.
Pérez, José Antonio. *Apuntes biográficos sobre el mui ilustre jeneral de brigada don Pedro Lagos*. Santiago: Imprenta Cervantes, 1884.
Pizarro Barahona, Rafael. *Los abastecimientos militares en la Guerra del Pacífico (1879–1884)*. Santiago: Editorial del Pacífico, 1967.
Rodríguez, Juan Agustin. *Patricio Lynch, vicealmirante y general en jefe. Sintesis de la Guerra del Pacífico*. Santiago: Nascimento, 1967.
Ruz Trujillo, Fernando. *Rafael Sotomayor Baeza, el organizador de la victoria*. Santiago: Andres Bello, 1980.
Salinas, Florentino. *Los representantes de la provincia de Aconcagua en la Guerra del Pacífico*. Santiago: Imprenta Albión, 1893.
Santa María, Ignacio. *La Guerra del Pacífico*. 2 vols. Santiago: Imprenta Universitaria, 1919–1920.
Santelices, Ramón. *Los bancos chilenos*. Santiago: Imprenta Barcelona, 1893.
Sater, William. *The Heroic Image in Chile*. Berkeley: University of California Press, 1973.
Semper and Michels. *La industria del salitre en Chile*. Translated by Javier Gandarillas and Orlando Ghigliotto Salas. Santiago: Imprenta Barcelona, 1908.
Sepulveda Rojas, Arturo. *Así vivieron y vencieron, 1879–1884*. Santiago: Imprenta Esparza, 1980.
Subercaseaux, Guillermo. *Monetary and Banking Policy in Chile*. Oxford: Oxford University Press, 1922.
Vial, Gonzalo. *Historia de Chile*. 4 vols. Santiago: Editorial Santillana del Pacífico, 1981. Vol. 2.

Vicuña Mackenna, Benjamín. *Historia de la campaña de Lima*. 2 vols. Santiago: Rafael Jouer, 1881.
———. *El libro del cobre i del carbón de piedra en Chile*. Santiago: Editorial del Pacífico, 1966.
Werlich, David. *Peru, A Short History*. Carbondale: Southern Illinois University Press, 1978.

Books Consulted But Not Cited

Barros Arana, Diego. *Obras completas. Historia de la Guerra del Pacífico*. Santiago: Imprenta Barcelona, 1914. Vol. 16.
Caviano, Tomas. *Historia de la Guerra de America entre Chile, Perú, y Bolivia*. N.p: Libreria Italiana, 1904.
Civati Bernasconi, Edmundo. *Guerra del Pacífico*. 2 vols. Buenos Aires: Círculo Militar, 1946.
Estado Mayor del Ejército. *Historia Militar de Chile*. 3 vols. Santiago: Estado Mayor General del Ejército, 1969.
Estado Mayor General del Ejército. *Historia del Ejército de Chile*. 7 vols. Santiago: Estado Mayor General del Ejército. 1981-1982. Vols. 5-7.
Fuenzalida Bade, Rodrigo. *La Armada de Chile desde la Alborada al Sesquicentenario*. 4 vols. N.p., n.d. Vol. 3.
Gonzalez Salinas, Edmundo. *La política contra la estrategia en la Guerra del Pacífico, 1879-1883*. Santiago: Impresos Espara, 1981.
Gutiérrez, Arturo. *La Guerra del Pacífico*. Buenos Aires: Francisco de Aguirre, 1975.
Körner, Emilio, and J. Boonen Rivera. *Estudio sobre historia militar*. 2 vols. Santiago: Imprenta Cervantes, 1887. Vol. 1.
Langlois, Luis. *Influencia del poder naval en la historia de Chile desde 1810 a 1910*. Valparaíso: Imprenta de la Armada, 1911.
Markham, Clements R. *The War between Peru and Chile*. London: Sampson, Low, 1883.
Paz Soldán, Maríano Felipe. *Narración histórica de la guerra de Chile contra el Perú y Bolivia*. Buenos Aires: Imprenta de Mayo, 1884.
Pinochet Ugarte, Augusto. *La Guerra del Pacífico*. 4th ed. Santiago: Editorial Andrés Bello, 1980.
Poblete M., Rafael. *Monografía de los generales que actuaron como comandantes superiores del Ejército y como jefes de Estado Mayor en la campaña de 1879-1883*. 2d ed. Santiago: Empresa Gabriela Mistral, n.d.
Querejazu Calvo, Roberto. *Guano, Salitre, Sangre*. La Paz: Editorial Los Amigos del Libro, 1979.
Téllez, Indalicio. *Historia militar de Chile, 1541-1888*. 2d ed. Santiago: Editorial Universitaria, 1917.
Uribe Orrego, Luis. *Los combates navales en la Guerra del Pacífico*. Valparaíso: Imprenta de la Patria, 1886.
Vicuña Mackenna, Benjamín. *Historia de la campaña de Tarapacá*. 2 vols. Santiago: Imprenta de P. Cadot and Imprenta de Rafael Jover, 1880.

Articles

Aránguiz Donoso, Horacio. "La situación de los trabajadores agrícolas en el siglo

XIX." *Estudios de Historia de Instituciones Políticos y Sociales* 2 (1967): 5-31.
Bermúdez, Oscar. "El salitre de Tarapacá y Antofagasta durante la ocupación militar chilena." *Anales de la Universidad del Norte* 5 (1966):129-83.
Blakemore, Harold. "The Politics of Nitrate in Chile Pressure Groups and Policies, 1870-1896," *Revue Franciese d'Historie d'Outre Mer* 61 (1979):285-98.
González Osben, Julio. "Logística naval en la Guerra del Pacífico. 3. Campana de Tacna-Arica," *Revista de Marina* no. 2 (1981):191-208.
Greenhill, Robert G. and Rory M. Miller. "The Peruvian Government and the Nitrate Trade, 1873-1879." *Journal of Latin American Studies* 5, no. 1 (1973): 107-31.
Jarpa Gerhard, Sergio. "Campaña marítima de 1879." *Revista de Marina* no. 5 (1981):553-62.
Jofré Alvarez, Luis. "Don Eulogio Altamirano." *Revista Chilena de Historia Chilena* 65, no. 63 (1930):63-84.
Mahuzier Manriquez, Marcelo. "Logística naval en la Guerra del Pacífico. 2. Campana de Tarapacá." *Revista de Marina* no. 1 (1981):26-66.
Mamalakis, Markos. "The Role of Government in the Resource Transfer and Resource Allocation Processes: The Chilean Nitrate Sector, 1880-1930." In Gustavo Ranis, *Government and Economic Development*. New Haven: Yale University Press, 1971, pp. 181-215.
Mayo, John. "A Company War? The Antofagasta Company and the Outbreak of the War of the Pacific." *Boletín de Estudios Latinoamericanas y del Caribe* 28 (1980):3-11.
———. "La compañía de Salitres de Antofagasta y la Guerra del Pacífico." *Historia* 14 (1979):71-103.
O'Brien, Thomas F. "The Antofagasta Company: A Case Study of Peripheral Capitalism." *Hispanic American Historical Review* 60, no. 1 (1980):1-32.
Orteaga, Luis. "Nitrates, Chilean Entrepreneurs and the Origins of the War of the Pacific," *Journal of Latin American Studies* 16, no. 2 (1984):381-402.
Poblete M., Rafael. "El servicio sanitario en el Ejército de Chile durante la Guerra del Pacífico." *Revista Chilena de Historia Chilena* 33, no.37 (1920):465-79; 34, no. 38 (1920):469-99; 35, no. 39 (1920):463-89; 37, no.39 (1921):474-83; 39, no.43 (1921):474-97; 41, no.45 (1922):456-82.
Reyno Gutiérrez, Manuel. "El mando militar y la injerencia del gobierno en la guerra de 1879." *Revista Chilena de Historia Chilena* 147 (1979):53-58.
Santa María, Ignacio. "Apuntes sobre la Guerra del Pacífico." *Revista Chilena* 6, no. 54 (1922):407-27.
———. "La caída del ministerio Varas-Santa María." *Revista Chilena* 3, no. 8 (1919):21-29.
———. "La Guerra del Pacífico." *Revista Chilena de Historia Chilena* 54, no. 58 (1927):5-61; 55, no.59 (1927):18-114; 56, no. 60 (1928):195-310.
Sater, William F., "Chile during the First Months of the War of the Pacific." *Journal of Latin American Studies* 5, no. 1 (1973):133-58.
———. "Chile and the World Depression of the 1870s." *Journal of Latin American Studies* 11, no.1 (1979):67-99.
———. "Economic Nationalism and Tax Reform in Late Nineteenth Century Chile." *The Americas* 33, no.2 (1976):311-35.
Wilson Browne, Arturo. "Logística naval en la Guerra del Pacífico, 4. Operaciones navales marzo-noviembre 1880." *Revista de Marina* 3 (1981):313-52.

Zegers, Cristian. "Historia política del gobierno de Aníbal Pinto," *Historia* 6 (1967):7-127.

Unpublished Material

Bader, Thomas M. "A Willingness to War." Ph.D. dissertation, University of California, Los Angeles, 1967.
Brown, Stephen D. "The Power of Influence in United States-Chilean Relations," Ph.D. dissertation, University of Wisconsin, 1983.
Conoboy, P. S. "Money and Politics in Chile, 1878-1925." Ph.D. dissertation, University of Southampton, 1977.
Latorre Subercaseaux, Adolfo. "Relación entre el circulante y los precios en Chile." Memoria de Prueba, Catholic University, Santiago, 1958.
Mayo, John. "British Influence in Chile, and Their Influence, 1851-1886." Ph.D. dissertation, Oxford University, 1977.
O'Brien, Thomas F. "British Investors and the Decline of the Chilean Nitrate Entrepreneuers, 1870-1890." Ph.D. dissertation, University of Connecticut, 1976.
Orteaga, Luis. "Change and Crisis in Chile's Economy and Society, 1865-1879." Ph.D. dissertation, University of London, 1979.
Phillips, Richard S. "Bolivia in the War of the Pacific, 1879-1884." Ph.D. dissertation, University of Virginia, 1973.

Index

Adams, Charles, 222
Aderman, Gustvao, 116
Aldea, Juan de Dios, 177
Aldunate, Luis, 125, 146, 151, 192
Alfonso, José, 7, 37, 145, 146, 147, 149, 152, 184, 187, 191
Allendes, Eulojio, 88, 92, 95
Altamirano, Eulojio, 47, 175, 203, 204, 206, 211; and Baquedano, 49-51; and Riveros, 50; attitudes of, 42, 47
Amunátegui, Miguel Luis, 186
Ancón, Treaty of, 115, 154, 220, 224
Andwanter, Carlos, 158
Arce, Ancieto, 221
Argentina, 13; conflict with Chile, 7-9, 92, 195; involvement in Bolivia, 221; rise of, 224-225
Arica Conference, 49, 149, 200-204, 207
Arteaga, Colonel Luis, 23
Arteaga Alemparte, Benjamín, 37
Arteaga Alemparte, Domingo, 37, 145; activities of, 37-38
Arteaga Alemparte, Justo, 37, 138, 199; activities of, 37-38
Arteaga Cuevas, General Justo, 18, 44, 84, 186; and Echaurren, 83; career of, 37, 39, 65; controversy about, 37-38; military campaign of, 38; resignation of, 39

Arthur, Chester Alan, 212-213, 216-217

Balmaceda, José Manuel, 53, 144, 188-189, 192, 194, 202, 206, 211, 224
Baptista, Mariano, 220
Baquedano, General Manuel, 60, 69, 189, 192, 204; and E. Caviedez, 68-69; and I. Errazuríz, 56 and Pinto, 3-5; and R. Sotomayor, 27, 55; and J. F. Vergara, 55; and General Villagrán, 33, 66; career of, 27, 47, 50, 65-66; compared to: Lagos, 68; Sotomayor, 48-51, 53; Vergara, 53; compensation of, 54; conduct of the Tacna Campaign by, 26-29; criticism of, 28, 29, 33, 51-53; defense of, 53-54; description of, 48; judgment of, 22; political career of, 51-54; resignation of, 54-55
Barboza, Colonel Orozimbo, 67
Barceló, Colonel Francisco, 45-46; and Escala, 44
de la Barra, Eduardo, 22
Barros Arana, Diego, 7
Barros Luco, Ramón, 92, 93, 114, 136, 147, 169
Barros Morán, Miguel, 81
Beoto, Belisario, 222
Bilbao, Manuel, 7

Blaine, James G., 210; foreign policy of, 209, 212
Blaine, Walker, 212-213
Boletín de la Sociedad Nacional de Agricultura (BSNA), 106, 168
Bolivia, 4, 9, 119, 141, 198, 224; alliance of with Peru, 9, 11; Chilean hostility toward, 9-10; Chilean image of, 5; compared to Chile, 78, 194; military preparedness of, 17-18; peace policy of, 221-222; political life in, 179-180; postwar development of, 224; precipitating war by, 6-7, 9; prewar diplomatic policies of, 4-7, 25; resistance of, 196; search for peace with, 194
Buendía, General Juan, 21, 23
Bulnes, Manuel, 51-52

Cáceres, General Andrés, 207, 209, 212; resistance of, 211-212, 218-220
Campero, General Narciso, 179, 221-222
del Canto, Estanislao, 65
Carrasco Albano, Adolfo, 50
Carvallo, Manuel, 93
Castellón, Carlos, 192, 194
Castro, Colonel Ricardo, 67
Caviedes, Eloi; and Baquedano, 55, 68-69
El Censor Incident, 68
Chile: antipathy toward the war effort in, 31-32, 214-216, 219; congressional elections in 1879, 180-182; in 1882, 192; cost of living in, 159-161; crime in, 164-167; criticism of, 95; cultural life in, 162-165; currency, lack of in, 158-159; decline of after War of the Pacific, 225-228; health conditions in, 170-175; labor, lack of in, 167-169; motivations of for declaring war, 12-16; occupation policies of, 205-206; peace demands of, 208, 212-213; prewar diplomatic problems of, 9, 10; prewar political problems of, 9; prewar tax system of, 131-132; religious life in, 161; selfperceptions of, 204; social life in, 155-165; social problems of during, 175-178; urban life in, 156-157
Christiancy, Issac, 200, 204, 212
Cifuentes, Abdón, 89, 182, 191, 192, 195
Claro, Lorenzo, 14, 132, 135, 146, 150, 198-200; peace plans of, 198-200
Cochet, Alexander, 210
Compañía de Salitres y Ferrocarril, 5, 9, 11-15, 126, 135-136
Concha i Toro, Melchor, 90, 134, 182; economic interests of, 14
Condell, Captain Carlos, 40, 49
Conservative Party, 15, 41, 43, 47, 147, 153, 180-187, 191, 191-193; support of for Baquedano, 51-52, 54; support of for Escala, 45; support of for Williams, 41. See also: Politics
Credit Industriel, 210
Cuadra, Pedro, 143, 152, 193
de la Cruz, General José María, 51
"Cucalon", 41, 47-48, 55; definition of, 36
Cucalon, Antonio, 36

Davila Larrain, Vicente, 83
Daza, Hilarión, 13, 14, 21, 179; diplomatic policies of, 9-10; tax policies of, 6-7
del Vento, Colonel, 218

Echenique, Juan Martin, 204
Echeverría, Felix, 87-88, 95, 133
Echaurren, Francisco, 83, 180
Economy: impact of the War of the Pacific on: agriculture, 98-107; industry, 115-124; mining, 108-115; prewar condition of, 18

Index

Edwards, Agustín, 68–69, 95–96, 135, 147
Egaña, Rafael, 56
Elizondo, Diego, 92–93, 95
Encina, Francisco, 115
Encina, José Manuel, 185
Errázuriz, President Federico, 65, 141, 180
Errázuriz, Isidoro, 12, 13, 38, 59, 183; and Arteaga Cuevas, 32
Errázuriz, Máximo, 65
Escala, General Erasmo, 43, 45, 65, 186; and Conservative Party, 45; and Lagos, 24, 46; and Santa María, 44; and Sotomayor, 44–45, 48; and press, 69; and Vergara, 45; career of, 44, 46, 65; criticism of, 24, 29, 45–46, 84; description of, 48; fall from power by, 27; opposition to Tacna Campaign, 25; participation of in Tarapacá campaign, 22, 24; religious zeal of, 18
Evarts, William, 210

Fabres, Clemente, 78, 81, 89, 147, 192
Ferrari, Captain Pablo, 31, 201
Fierro Sarrata Treaty, 8–9, 15
Freire, General Ramón, 53
Frelinghuysen, Frederick, 212–213

Gandarillas, Francisco, 114
Gandarillas, José Antonio, 186, 187
García Calderón, Francisco, 208–209, 212, 217; fall of, 210; foreign policy of, 209–210; government of, 206–208
García de la Huerta, Manuel, 78, 88, 187, 188
Garfield, James, 208
Gibbs, Guillermo, 13
Gubbs, House of, 127, 134
Godoy, Joaquin, 203
Goni, Admiral Luis, 41, 42
González, Marcial, 133, 136
González Julio, Nicolas, 89, 98

Grau, Admiral Miguel, 19, 20, 41
Guardia Nacional, 181; recruiting for, 76–77; status of, 76
Guzmán, Dr. Mariano, 171

Hall, Diego, 117
Huneeus, Jorge, 184, 185
Hurlburt, Steven, 209–210, 212
Hurtado, Manuel, 89

Iglesias, Miguel, 217–218, 220
Industria incident of, 69–70

de la Jara, José Miguel, 81
Jordan, Luis, 93–94, 175, 188
Kilpatrick, Judson, 209, 212
Klein, Carlos, 116
Klein, Otto, 116

Lagos, Anacleto, 73
Lagos, Colonel Pedro, 26–27, 29, 45, 52, 65, 67, 71, 212; and Escala, 24, 27; and Letelier, 73
Landreau, Jean C., 210
Las Casas, Aníbal, 186
Lastarria, Valentín, 67
Latorre, Adolfo, 161
Latorre, Captain Juan, 20; at Angamos, 57–58
Lavalle, José Antonio, 11, 12, 15, 201, 218
Letelier, Ambrosio, 71–73
Letelier, Rocardo, 66, 144, 146, 148, 149, 175, 180, 191, 192
Letelier, Valentin, 81
Liberal Party, 15, 144, 182–183, 186, 190, 192; factions in, 180, 183; hostility of toward Baquedano, 51; See also: Politics
Liberal Democratic Party, 15, 181; See also: Politics
Liberales Echaurrenistas, 51, 186; See also: Politics
Lima: Chilean campaign for, 32–34; demands for capture of, 31–32

Lindsay-Corral Treaty, 6
Lillo, Eusebio, 187, 221
Lira, Máximo, 49-50, 55, 60
Logan, Dr. Cornelius, 216, 219
López, Teodoro, 158
López, Vitalicio, 137
Lynch, General Patricio, 33, 65, 193, 203, 211, 213, 218, 219; and Letelier, 71-73; and John T. North, 70; and Riveros, 70; career of, 70; hostility toward, 73; occupation policies of, 70

MacIver, Enrique, 67, 94, 144, 1898, 193, 199, 202
Mackenna, Juan, 93
Maney, George, 216
Mangano, Juan Anselmo, 159
Martínez, Juan, 66
Matte, Augusto, 89, 132-133, 134, 145, 146, 184, 186-187, 193, 194
Maturana, General Marcos, 52, 54, 116
Melgarejo, Mariano, 6
Military of Chile: civilian involvement in, 36, 39; civilian support of, 82-86; compensation of, 92-95; conditions in, 82-87; conduct of, 63-64; criticisms of, 36, 74; deficiencies of, 42, 76, 82; evaluation of, 61-63; image of, 62; myths about, 35-36, 64-65; pension system of, 86-90; political divisions within, 36; preparation of, 18, 36, 42-43, 60-61, 75; promotion process of, 66-67; recruiting policies of, 76-82; relations with: civilian population, 63-65; court system, 70-73; Pinto, 36, press, 67-70; welcome accorded to, 90-92
Ministries of: Recabarren, 187-192; Santa Maria, 186-187; Varas, 183-186; Vergara, 192-193
Monetary system: paper money, debts on, 143-152; prewar condition of, 140-142

Montero, Admiral Lizardo, 25-26, 204-205, 211, 217-218
Montt, Ambrosio, 54, 78
Montt, Manuel, 181, 183
Montt Varista Party, 13, 153, 180-181
Murillo, Dr. Adolfo, 163, 174-175
Murillo, Roberto, 72

National Party (Montt Varista), 13-15, 93, 136, 143-144, 151, 153, 181, 182, 186; See also: Politics
National Society of Agriculture, 102, 105-106
Navy: campaigns of, 19-20, 26; failures of, 30-31; preparation of, 18; public's anger toward, 19, 30-31, 41
Nitrates (*Salitre*): and war, 124-129; decline of, 225-226; impact of on Chile, 226-228; taxation of, 135-140
Nolasco Donoso, Pedro, 37
Novoa, Jovino, 93, 144, 146, 149, 150, 211-212, 216

O'Higgins, Bernardo, 53, 176
Orrego Luco, Dr. Augusto, 174, 175
Ortiz, Colonel José L., 67
Ortiz, José, 162
Osborne, Thomas, 200

Pardo, Mariano, 126
Partridge, James, 216
Peace, search for: Arica Conference, 200-201; Chilean popular vision of, 204-206; Claro proposal, 198-200; Peruvian vision of, 206-213
Peña, Captain Juan, 30-31, 201
Peru, 119, 141, 198; Chilean image of, 5; compared to Chile, 77, 179, 195, 204; entry into war by, 10-12; hostility of toward Chile, 11; pacification of: campaign of, 213-214; hostility toward program of, 214-216, 218-219; naval campaign of, 19-20; nitrate policy of, 126-127, 138; political life in,

Index

179-180; postwar problems with, 224; preparation of, 17-18; resistance of, 197-198

Peruvian Company, 209

Pierola, Nicolás, 33-34, 179, 200, 201, 203, 207, 218; as seen by Chileans, 205, 211; government of, 205, 209; political career of, 179; relations with other Peruvian figures, 206

Pinto, Aníbal, 13, 14, 27, 29, 35, 42, 49, 50, 53, 66, 82, 142, 144, 145, 152, 179, 182, 183, 184, 185, 186, 187, 189, 190, 203-205: *aduana* policy of, 133-134; and Arteaga Cuevas, 37; and Baquedano, 50; and Escala, 24; and Pena, 31; and the press, 68; and Riveros, 53, 60; and Sotomayor, 42; and Vergara, 47; and Villagrán, 47; Bolivian policy of, 25; career of, 65; compensation proposal of, 94; criticism of, 188; declaration of war by, 12; finance measures of, 143-148; foreign policy of, 207-208; peace efforts of, 200-203; pension proposal of, 87; Peruvian policy of, 11-12; political problems of, 180-181, 189-192; prewar diplomatic policies of, 8-12, 15-16; prewar economic policies of, 18; public hostility toward: his foreign policy, 10; peace initiative of, 202; involvement in war of, 35-36; nitrate policy of, 127, 136, 139; strategy of, 20-21, 25-26, 32, 34; tax policy of, 132-134

Politics: parties, description of, 180-181; complications caused by, 188-194; congressional elections in, 180-181; political system, public hostility of toward, 194-196; political instability of, 9, 184-185; presidential elections in, 51-53

Prado, Manuel, 11, 179, 206

Prat, Captain Arturo, 40, 53, 93, 164, 177

Prats, Belisario, 16, 182-186, 190

Puelma, Francisco, 13, 152, 194

Quiroz, Abraham, 86

Radical Party, 180-181, 182; See also: Parties

Ramírez, Colonel Eluterio, 23, 90, 93

Ramírez, Isais Francisco, 177

Ramırez, Manuel Jesus, 166

Recabarren, Manuel, 81; ministry of, 187-193, 203

Recabarren, E. Fosten, 176

Reyes, Alejandro, 67

Riveros, Admiral Galvarino, 50, 53, 60; and Baquedano, 56; and I. Errazuríz, 59; and Latorre, 57-58; and Jorge Montt, 56-58; and Pena, 58; and Sotomayor, 57; and Thompson, 58; and Vergara, 56; and Vicuña Mackenna, 57-58; criticism of, 31, 58; defense of, 56-58; demands of, 58-59; rise of, 20, 42; strategy of, 20

Rodríguez, Manuel, 177

Rodríguez, Zorobabel, 55, 133, 134, 142, 169, 174-175, 183, 184, 191-193, 202

Romero, Basilio, 73

Ross, Jorge, 162

Saavedra, Cornelio, 65, 182

Salinas, Belisario, 222

Santa Cruz, Colonel Ricardo, 90

Santa María, Domingo, 11, 12, 27, 46, 49, 60-61, 92, 180, 184-186, 188-189; and Arteaga Cuevas, 37-38, 48; and Baquedano, 30; and Escala, 44-45; and Williams, 20; criticism of land and naval campaigns by, 26, 30, 36; description of, 192-193; foreign policy of, 206-207, 211-212, 221-222; hostility toward, 43; involvement in military by, 46; ministry of, 186-187; political intervention of, 192-193; presi-

dency of, 192-195; prosecution of war by, 213-220; search for peace by, 211-213, 216-218, 220
Sarratea, Mariano, 8
Shipherd, Jacob, 209
Simpson, Captain Enrique, 21-22, 41, 186
del Solar, Pedro, 205
Sotomayor, Colonel Emilio, 22, 33, 48
Sotomayor, Rafael, 18, 20, 52, 60, 185-186: and Arteaga, 37-38; and Baquedano, 27; and Conservatives, 47; and Escala, 25, 27, 43-46; and Lagos, 46; and Pinto, 43; and Villagran, 47; and Williams, 40-41; career of, 42, 185; death of, 24; family of, 90, 93; hostility toward, 29, 43-44; participation in the war by, 21, 24, 26, 28, 42-43; rise of, 38-39; role of, 34
Sotomayor, Virgina, 43
Souper, Roberto, 38
Suárez, Clemente, 68

Tacna: campaign of, 24, 31; Chilean perceptions of, 24-25, 27, 29-30
Tagle Arrate, Jose, 134, 144, 146, 148, 184
Tarapacá: campaign of, 20-23; Chilean perception of, 23-25
Tax system, 131-132; imposition of taxes on income, 132-133; nitrates, 135-140; wartime changes in, 133-135, 153-154
Thompson, Captain Manuel, 26, 59
Tocornal, Enrique, 94, 132, 135
de la Torre, Colonel, 213
Trescott, William, 212-213

United States of America: Chilean hostility toward, 209, 211; peace attempts of, 200-204, 209-210, 212-213
Uribe, Captain Luis, 164
Urriola, Martiano, 47

Urrutia, General Basilio, 45, 48, 65, 184, 185
Urrutia, Lt. Colonel Gregorio, 46
Urzúa, Luis, 79, 89, 94, 134, 143, 145, 146-147, 191

Valderrama, Melquiades, 187, 202-203
Varas, Antonio, 16, 181, 186, 187, 194; and Williams, 40-41; criticism of, 43; ministry of, 183-86
Velasquez, General José, 27, 48-49, 67
Vergara, Francisco, 153
Vergara, José Eugenio, 192
Vergara, José Francisco, 30, 52, 56, 60, 186, 187, 191, 202; and Arteaga Cuevas, 37-38, 47; and Baquedano, 32-33, 48-50; and Escala, 25, 45, 47-48; and Pinto, 48, 50; and Riveros, 50, 56; and Velasquez, 49-50; attitude of, 27; career of, 47-49; criticism of, 49, 55-56; involvement in war, 21, 23, 32, 34; *Memoria* of, 54-55, 60; ministry of, 182-185; on industrial policy, 121; policies of, 50; praised, 51, 60; relations with: army, 49; navy, 49-50
Vergara Donoso, Francisco, 134, 146
Vial, Juan de Dios, 147, 150
Vicuña, Angel, 53
Vicuña Mackenna, Benjamín, 8, 23, 30, 90, 134, 137, 164, 174, 181, 185, 189, 190, 193, 216
Villagrán, General José, 45, 49; and Baquedano, 33, 66; career of, 47; description of, 48; in war, 32, 33; support of, 46
Vivanco, Fr. Pedro, 63
Vuletich, Mariano, 117

Walker Martínez, Carlos, 94, 132, 135, 186-187, 189, 195; and Williams, 40-42, 78, 94, 126
War of the Pacific: aftermath of,

Index

223–225; conclusion of, 197–222
Williams Rebolledo, Admiral Juan: and Arteaga C., 40, 184; and Conservative Party, 41, 184; and Pinto, 59; and Sotomayor, 40–41, 59–60; career of, 39; criticism of, 39–41; claims of, 59–60; government hostility toward, 40–41; naval strategy of, 19, 39–41; personality of, 20; political aspirations of, 40; resignation of, 20

Zegers, Julio, 132, 142
Zubiría, Colonel, 44, 48